Angelic Wisdom Concerning the Divine Providence
by Emanuel Swedenborg

Address:
HardPress
8345 NW 66TH ST #2561
MIAMI FL 33166-2626
USA
Email: info@hardpress.net

PRESENTED

To the Massachusetts
Historical Society,

by THE AMERICAN SWEDENBORG PRINTING AND
PUBLISHING SOCIETY, of the City of New York, incorporated A. D. 1850, for the Printing, Publishing
and Circulating of the Theological Works of Emanuel
Swedenborg, for Charitable and Missionary purposes.

Given to the
Massachusetts Historical Society
BY
the Amer. Swed. Pr. & Pub. Soc.
July 9, 1874.

TRANSFERRED
TO
HARVARD COLLEGE
LIBRARY

THE DIVINE PROVIDENCE.

Published by THE AMERICAN SWEDENBORG PRINTING AND PUBLISHING SOCIETY, *organized for the purpose of Stereotyping, Printing, and Publishing Uniform Editions of the Theological Writings of* EMANUEL SWEDENBORG, *and incorporated in the State of New York* A. D. 1850.

STEREOTYPED BY
RICHARD C. VALENTINE,
NEW YORK.

ANGELIC WISDOM

CONCERNING

THE DIVINE PROVIDENCE.

Translated from the Latin of
EMANUEL SWEDENBORG,
Servant of the Lord Jesus Christ.

ORIGINALLY PUBLISHED AT AMSTERDAM, MDCCLXIV.

FROM THE LAST LONDON EDITION.

NEW YORK:
AMERICAN SWEDENBORG PRINTING AND PUBLISHING SOCIETY.

1873.

. 13

ADVERTISEMENT.

In this new Edition of Emanuel Swedenborg's invaluable Treatise on the Divine Providence, an attempt has been made to render the Translation a little more smooth, without making it less faithful to the original, or even less literal ; but there are still some peculiarities of style, which it has been thought advisable to retain, rather than to incur the risk of weakening in any degree the force of the Author's sentiments.

The frequent occurrence of adjectives used as substantives (*internal*, *interior*, &c., for instance) may be objected to by many persons ; but, when practicable, this mode of rendering the Latin neuter adjectives was generally thought preferable to that of adding the substantive *thing*, or *principle*, &c., because there is a danger of such words conveying an idea not strictly in agreement with the Author's meaning.

The retention of the Latin word where no corresponding one could be found in English, occurs but very rarely ; and it may be fairly presumed, that in this work the reader will be as little troubled with technicalities of language as in the generality of works on abstract philosophy.

CONTENTS.

ANGELIC WISDOM

CONCERNING

THE DIVINE PROVIDENCE.

THAT THE DIVINE PROVIDENCE IS THE GOVERNMENT OF THE DIVINE LOVE AND THE DIVINE WISDOM OF THE LORD.

1. In order that it may be understood what the Divine Providence is, and that it may be seen to be the government of the Divine Love and the Divine Wisdom of the Lord, it will be useful that the propositions which have been advanced and illustrated respecting the Divine Love and the Divine Wisdom, in the treatise on that subject, should be known. They are as follows : That in the Lord the Divine Love is of the Divine Wisdom, and the Divine Wisdom is of the Divine Love, n. 34—39. That the Divine Love and the Divine Wisdom cannot but be and exist in other things created from Itself, n. 47—51. That all things in the universe were created from the Divine Love and the Divine Wisdom, n. 52, 53, 151—156. That all things in the universe are recipients of the Divine Love and the Divine Wisdom, n. 54—60. That the Lord appears before the angels as a sun, and that the heat thence proceeding is love, and the light thence proceeding is wisdom, n. 83—88, 89—92, 93—98, 296—301. That the Divine Love and the Divine Wisdom, which proceed from the Lord, form a one, n. 99—102. That the Lord from eternity, who is Jehovah, created the universe and all things therein from Himself, and not from nothing, n. 282—284, 290—295. These propositions are illustrated in the treatise, entitled ANGELIC WISDOM CONCERNING THE DIVINE LOVE AND THE DIVINE WISDOM.

2. From these propositions, compared with the views given in the same work respecting creation, it may indeed appear, that what is called the Divine Providence is the government of the Divine Love and the Divine Wisdom of the Lord : but as creation was there treated of, and not the preservation of the state of things after creation, which last is the government of

the Lord, therefore we shall now treat on this subject; considering, in this first article, the preservation of the union of the Divine Love and the Divine Wisdom, or the Divine Good and the Divine Truth, in the things which are created; of which we shall speak in this order: I. That the universe, with all and every thing therein, was created from the Divine Love by the Divine Wisdom. II. That the Divine Love and the Divine Wisdom proceed from the Lord as a one. III. That this one, in a certain image, is in every created thing. IV. That it is of the Divine Providence, that every created thing, both in the whole and in part, should be such a one; and if it is not, that it should be made so. V. That the good of love is not good, except so far as it is united to the truth of wisdom; and that the truth of wisdom is not truth, except so far as it is united to the good of love. VI. That the good of love not united to the truth of wisdom is not good in itself, but only *apparent good;* and that the truth of wisdom not united to the good of love is not truth in itself, but only *apparent truth.* VII. That the Lord does not suffer any thing to be divided; therefore it must either be in good and at the same time in truth, or it must be in evil and at the same time in falsity. VIII. That that which is in good and at the same time in truth, is something; and that that which is in evil and at the same time in falsity, is not any thing. IX. That the Divine Providence of the Lord causes evil and its attendant falsity to serve for equilibrium, relation, and purification, and thereby for the conjunction of good and truth in others.

3. I. *That the universe, with all and every thing therein, was created from the Divine Love by the Divine Wisdom.* That the Lord from eternity, who is Jehovah, is, as to his essence, Divine Love and Divine Wisdom; and that from Himself he created the universe and all things therein; was shown in the treatise concerning THE DIVINE LOVE AND THE DIVINE WISDOM: whence it follows, that the universe, with all and every thing therein, was created from the Divine Love by the Divine Wisdom. In the same treatise it was also shown, that love without wisdom cannot do any thing, nor wisdom without love: for love without wisdom, or the will without the understanding, cannot think of any thing, nor can it see, be sensible of, or speak of any thing; therefore neither can it do any thing. In like manner, wisdom without love, or the understanding without the will, cannot think of any thing, neither can it see, or be sensible of, or speak of any thing; nor, therefore, can it do any thing: for if love be taken away, there is no longer any volition, and consequently no action. And as this is the case with man when he does any thing, much more was it the case with God, who is love itself and wisdom itself, when he created and made the universe and all things therein. That the universe,

2

with all and every thing appertaining to it, was created from the Divine Love by the Divine Wisdom, is a proposition which may be confirmed from all things which are the objects of sight in the world : take for this purpose any object in particular, and if you examine it with some degree of wisdom, you will be confirmed. Take a tree, or its seed, its fruit, its flower, or its leaf, and, collecting all your wisdom, view it with a good microscope, and you will see in it wonderful things ; whilst the interiors, which you do not see, are still more wonderful. Observe the order in which the parts succeed each other during the growth of a tree from the seed till it produces new seed ; and consider whether there be not in every successive stage a continual endeavor to propagate itself further ; for the ultimate to which it tends is seed, in which its prolific principle exists anew. If then you reflect upon it spiritually, (and this you can do if you choose,) will you not see wisdom displayed ? This you will do especially if you so far think spiritually as to perceive that the prolific principle is not from the seed, nor from the sun of this world, which is pure fire, but that it is in the seed from God the Creator, who possesses infinite wisdom ; and that it is in it not only when created, but also continually afterwards : since, as support is perpetual creation, subsistence is perpetual existence : for, as the work ceases if you take away will from action, or as speech ceases if you deprive it of thought, or as motion ceases when the producing effort is withdrawn ; so in like manner, if you take away the cause from the effect, the effect perishes, and so on. Every created substance indeed is endued with power ; but power does not operate from itself, but from him who bestowed it. Examine also any other subject on earth, as a silk-worm, a bee, or any other insect ; view it first naturally, afterwards rationally, and lastly spiritually : then if you can think elevatedly, you will be astonished at every thing ; and if you permit wisdom to speak in you, you will say in astonishment, Who does not see a divine principle in these things ?—they are all effects of the Divine Wisdom. This will be the case still more, if you regard the uses of all things which are created, perceiving how they proceed in regular order even unto man, and from man to the Creator from whom they are ; and that upon the conjunction of the Creator with man the connection of all things depends, and, if you will acknowledge it, the preservation of all things. That the Divine Love created all things, but nothing without the Divine Wisdom, will be seen in what follows.

4. II. *That the Divine Love and the Divine Wisdom proceed from the Lord as a one.* This also is evident from what was shown in the treatise concerning THE DIVINE LOVE AND THE DIVINE WISDOM, especially from the following articles therein : That ESSE and EXISTERE [TO BE and TO EXIST] in the Lord are

3   B

distinctly one, n. 14—17. That in the Lord infinite things are distinctly one, n. 17—22. That the Divine Love is of the Divine Wisdom, and the Divine Wisdom of the Divine Love, n. 34—39. That love without a marriage with wisdom cannot do any thing, n. 401—403. That love does nothing but in conjunction with wisdom, n. 409, 410. That spiritual heat and spiritual light, in proceeding from the Lord as a sun, form a one, as the divine love and the divine wisdom in the Lord are a one, n. 99 —132. Although from what is shown in treating of these articles, the truth of this proposition is evident, yet, as it is not known how two things distinct from each other can act as a one, I will here show that a one does not exist without a form, but that the form itself makes a one ; and next, that the form makes a one, so much the more perfectly in proportion as the things which enter into it are distinct from each other, and nevertheless united. *That a one does not exist without a form, but that the form itself makes a one.* Every one who thinks intently on the subject may see clearly, that a one without a form does not exist, and if it does exist that it is a form : for whatsoever exists derives from its form that which is understood by quality, predicate, change of state, relation, and the like ; wherefore that which is not in a form has no quality, and that which has no quality has not any thing ; the form itself giving all these. And forasmuch as all things which are in a form, if the form is perfect, have mutually respect to each other, as one link in a chain has to another ; therefore it follows, that the form itself makes them a one, and, consequently, a subject, of which may be predicated quality, state, affection, and therefore something, according to the perfection of the form. Such a one is every thing which is an object of sight in the world, and such a one also is every thing which is not an object of sight, whether it be in interior nature or in the spiritual world ; such a one is man, and such a one is a human society ; such a one is the church, also the universal angelic heaven before the Lord ; in a word, such a one is the created universe, not only in general, but in every particular. Now, in order that all and every thing may be forms, it is necessary that he who created all things should be form itself, and that from form itself all things which are created should exist in forms : this, therefore, is what is shown in the treatise concerning THE DIVINE LOVE AND THE DIVINE WISDOM, under the following heads : viz. That the Divine Love and the Divine Wisdom are a substance and a form, n. 40—43. That the Divine Love and the Divine Wisdom are substance and form in themselves, consequently, the self-subsisting and the one only subsisting essence or principle, n. 44—46. That the Divine Love and the Divine Wisdom in the Lord are a one, n. 14—17, n. 18—22. And that they proceed as a one from the Lord, n. 99—102, and in other places

That the form makes a one so much the more perfectly in propor tion as the things which enter into it are distinct from each other, and nevertheless united. This is comprehended with difficulty unless the understanding be elevated, because there is an appearance that form cannot make a one except when there is a similarity in the things which constitute it. On this subject I have frequently conversed with the angels; who said that this is an arcanum, which the wise among them perceive clearly, but the less wise obscurely: that nevertheless it is a truth, that a form is so much the more perfect in proportion as the things which constitute it are distinct from each other, but still united in a particular manner. They confirmed this by reference to the societies in the heavens, which, taken together, constitute the form of heaven; and to the angels of each society, of which it may be affirmed, that the more every individual has a distinct identity of character, in which he freely acts, and thus loves his associates from himself or from his own affection, the more perfect is the form of the society. They also illustrated it by the marriage of goodness and truth, which, the more distinctly they are two, can more perfectly form a one; and, in like manner, by love and wisdom; showing that what is indistinct is confused, whence results all imperfection of form. But how things perfectly distinct are united, and thus make a one, they confirmed by many instances; especially by the nature or constitution of man, in which innumerable things are quite distinct, and yet united,—distinct by their coats, but united by ligaments. They also stated, that it is the same with love and all things appertaining to it, and with wisdom and all things appertaining to it, which are not perceived otherwise than as a one. More on this subject may be seen in the treatise concerning THE DIVINE LOVE AND THE DIVINE WISDOM, n. 14—22, and in the work concerning HEAVEN AND HELL, n. 56 and 489. This is adduced because it is an arcanum of angelic wisdom.

5. III. *That this one, in a certain image, is in every created thing.* That the Divine Love and the Divine Wisdom, which in the Lord are a one, and which proceed as a one from him are in a certain image in every created thing, may appear from what is proved throughout the treatise concerning THE DIVINE LOVE AND THE DIVINE WISDOM, but especially in n. 47—51, 54—60, 282—284, 290—295, 316—318, 319—326, 349—357; in which places it is shown, that the divine principle is in every created thing, because God the Creator, who is the Lord from eternity, from himself produced the sun of the spiritual world, and by that sun all things in the universe; consequently, that that sun, which is from the Lord, and in which is the Lord, is not only the first, but the one only substance, from which all things are; and forasmuch as it is the one only substance, it follows that it is in every created thing, but with infinite variety

5

according to different uses. Now, as in the Lord there is Divine Love and Divine Wisdom, and in the sun from him divine fire and divine effulgence, and from the sun spiritual heat and spiritual light, and these two form a one, it follows, that this one is in a certain image in every created thing. Hence it is, that all things in the universe have relation to good and truth, and, indeed, to the conjunction of them ; or, what is the same, that all things in the universe have relation to love and wisdom, and to their conjunction ; for good is of love, and truth is of wisdom, inasmuch as love calls all which appertains to it good, and wisdom calls all which appertains to it truth. That there is a conjunction of these in every created thing, will be seen in what follows.

6. It is acknowledged by many, that there is one only substance, which is also the first, from which all things are ; but what that substance is, it is not known. It is thought to be so simple that nothing can be simpler, and that it may be compared to a point which has no dimensions, and that from an infinite number of such points, the forms of dimension exist. This, however, is a fallacy originating from the idea of space : for from this idea there appears to be such a smallest particle ; when, nevertheless, it is a truth, that in proportion as a thing is more simple and more pure, it is more full and complete. It is on this account, that the more interiorly any object is inspected, the more wonderful, perfect, and beautiful are the things seen in it ; and consequently, that in the first substance are the most wonderful, perfect, and beautiful things of all. The reason of this is, that the first substance is from the spiritual sun, which, as before stated, is from the Lord, and in which is the Lord ; therefore, that very sun is the one only substance, which, forasmuch as it is not in space, is all in all, and in the greatest and least things in the created universe. As that sun is the first and one only substance, from which all things are, it follows that there are in it infinitely more things than can appear in the substances thence derived, which are called substantiate, and lastly material. The reason why the former cannot appear in the latter, is, because they descend from that sun by degrees of two kinds, according to which all perfections decrease. Hence it is that, as was said above, the more interiorly any object is viewed, the more wonderful, perfect, and beautiful are the things seen in it. These observations are made in order to confirm the truth, that in a certain image the Divine is in every created thing, but that it appears less and less in descending by degrees, and still less when, the inferior degree being separated from the superior degree by the closing of the latter, it is choked up with earthy matter. Such truths, however, cannot but seem obscure, unless what is said in the treatise on THE DIVINE LOVE AND THE DIVINE WISDOM,

concerning the spiritual sun, n. 53—172; concerning degrees, n. 173—281; and concerning the creation of the universe, n. 282—357, has been first read and understood.

7. IV. *That it is of the Divine Providence, that every created thing, both in the whole and in part, should be such a one, and if it is not, that it should be made so;* that is, that in every created thing there should be something from the Divine Love, and at the same time from the Divine Wisdom; or, what is the same, that in every created thing there should be good and truth, or a conjunction of good and truth : for as good is of love, and truth is of wisdom, as was said above, n. 5, so in what follows, instead of love and wisdom, the words good and truth will be used, and instead of the union of love and wisdom, the marriage of good and truth.

8. From the preceding article it is evident that the Divine Love and the Divine Wisdom, which in the Lord are one, and from the Lord proceed as one, exist in a certain image in every thing created by him; and it may now be expedient to speak particularly of that oneness or union, which is called the marriage of good and truth. That marriage is, I. in the Lord himself; for, as before said, the Divine Love and the Divine Wisdom in him are one. II. It is from the Lord, for in every thing which proceeds from him love and wisdom are perfectly united; and these two proceed from the Lord as a sun,—the Divine Love as heat, and the Divine Wisdom as light. III. They are received by the angels indeed as two, but are united in them by the Lord : and it is the same with the men of the church. IV. It is from the influx of love and wisdom from the Lord as one into the angels of heaven and men of the church, and from the reception thereof by angels and men, that the Lord in the Word is called the Bridegroom and the Husband, and heaven and the church the bride and the wife. V. As far therefore as heaven and the church in general, and an angel of heaven and a man of the church in particular, are in that union, or in the marriage of good and truth, so far are they an image and likeness of the Lord; because these two in the Lord are one, and indeed they are the Lord. VI. Love and wisdom in heaven and in the church in general, and in an angel of heaven and in a man of the church, are one, when the will and the understanding, and when therefore good and truth, make one; or, what is the same, when charity and faith make one; or, what is still the same, when doctrine from the Word and a life according to it make one. VII. But in what manner these two make one in man, and in all things appertaining to him, is shown in the treatise concerning THE DIVINE LOVE AND THE DIVINE WISDOM, PART V., where the creation of man, and particularly the correspondence of the will and the understanding with the heart and the lungs, are treated of, from n. 385 to 432.

7

9. But how these make one in the things which are below or without man, as well in the things of the animal kingdom as in those of the vegetable kingdom, will be shown in many places in what follows; previous to which these three things are to be premised: *First*, That in the universe, and in all and every thing therein, which was created by the Lord, there was a marriage of good and truth. *Secondly*, That this marriage after the creation was separated in man. *Thirdly*, That it is of the Divine Providence that what is separated should be made one, and thus, that the marriage of good and truth should be restored. These three particulars are abundantly confirmed in the treatise on THE DIVINE LOVE AND THE DIVINE WISDOM, and therefore need no further confirmation. Every one also may see from reason, that since a marriage of good and truth existed by creation in every created thing, and since this was afterwards separated, the Lord must operate continually, that it may be restored; consequently, that its restoration, and the conjunction thereby of the created universe with the Lord through man, is of the Divine Providence.

10. V. *That the good of love is not good, except so far as it is united to the truth of wisdom, and that the truth of wisdom is not truth, except so far as it is united to the good of love.* Good and truth derive this from their origin. Good in its origin is in the Lord, and so is truth; because the Lord is good itself and truth itself, and these two in him are one. Hence it is, that good in the angels of heaven and in men on the earth is not good in itself, except so far as it is united to truth, and that truth is not truth in itself, except so far as it is united to good. That all good and all truth is from the Lord, is well known; hence, as good makes one with truth, and truth with good, it follows that, in order to good being good in itself, and truth being truth in itself, they must make one in the recipient, which is an angel of heaven and a man on the earth.

11. It is known indeed that all things in the universe have relation to good and truth; because by good is understood that which universally comprehends and involves all things of love, and by truth is understood that which universally comprehends and involves all things of wisdom: but it is not yet known that good is not any thing unless united to truth, and that truth is not any thing unless united to good. It appears indeed as if good were something without truth, and as if truth were something without good; but still they are not: for love, all things appertaining to which are called good things, is the *esse* of a thing, and wisdom, all things appertaining to which are called truths, is the *existere* of a thing from that esse, as is shown in the treatise on THE DIVINE LOVE AND THE DIVINE WISDOM, n. 14—16; wherefore, as an *esse* without *existere* is not any thing, nor *existere* without an *esse*, so good without truth is not

8

any thing, nor truth without good. In like manner, what is good without relation to something?—can it be called good? for it is of no affection and of no perception. This, together with the good which affects, and which causes itself to be perceived and felt, has relation to truth, because it has relation to that which is in the understanding. Say barely to any one, good, and not this or that is good, and is good any thing? But by virtue of this or that which is perceived as a one with good, it is something. This is not united to good anywhere but in the understanding, and every thing of the understanding has relation to truth. It is the same with volition; to will without knowing, perceiving, and thinking what a man wills, is nothing, but together with these it becomes something. All volition is of love, and has relation to good; and all knowledge, perception, and thought are of the understanding, and have relation to truth. Hence it is evident, that merely to will is nothing, but to will this or that, is something. It is the same with all use, because use is good. Use, unless it be determined to something with which it may be a one, is not use; therefore it is not any thing. Use derives its being something from the understanding, and that which is thence conjoined or adjoined to use has relation to truth: from this use derives its quality. From these few hints it may appear that good without truth is not any thing; therefore, that neither is truth without good any thing. It is said that good with truth, and truth with good, are something; hence it follows, that evil with false, and false with evil, are not any thing: for the latter are opposite to the former, and opposition destroys; in the present case, it destroys that which is something. But more of this in what follows.

12. But there exists a marriage of good and truth in the cause, and there exists a marriage of good and truth from the cause in the effect. The marriage of good and truth in the cause, is the marriage of the will and the understanding, or of love and wisdom: in all that a man wills and thinks, and which he thence concludes and intends, there is this marriage. This marriage enters the effect and produces it; but in carrying into effect, these two appear distinct: because then what is simultaneous constitutes what is successive; as when a man wills and thinks to be nourished, to be clothed, to have a dwelling, to do any business or work, or to converse, he first wills and thinks at the same time, or concludes upon and intends, and when he has determined them to effect, then one thing succeeds after another; but still they continually make one in the will and in the thought. The uses in these effects belong to love or good, and the means for obtaining the uses belong to the understanding or truth. These general views any one may confirm by particulars, if he but distinctly perceive what has relation to

9

the good of love and what to the truth of wisdom, and also distinctly perceive how it is referable to the cause and how to the effect.

13. It has occasionally been said, that love makes the life of man; but love separate from wisdom, or good separate from truth in the cause, is not meant; because love separate, or good separate, is not any thing: wherefore the love which makes the inmost life of man, which is from the Lord, is love and wisdom together. Neither also is the love, which makes the life of man so far as he is a recipient, separated in the cause, but in the effect; for love cannot be understood without its quality, and its quality is wisdom. Quality or wisdom cannot exist except from its *esse*, which is love; hence it is that they are one; and it is the same with good and truth. Now since truth is from good, as wisdom is from love, therefore both taken together are called love or good; for love in its form is wisdom, and good in its form is truth: from its form and from no other source is all its quality. Hereby then it may appear that good is not in the least good, any further than as it is united to its truth, and that truth is not in the least truth, any further than as it is united to its good.

14. VI. *That the good of love not united to the truth of wisdom is not good in itself, but only apparent good; and that the truth of wisdom not united to the good of love is not truth in itself, but only apparent truth.* The truth is, that there does not exist any good which is good in itself, unless it be united to its truth, nor any truth which is true in itself unless it be united to its good; nevertheless, there does exist good separate from truth, and truth separate from good: this is in hypocrites and flatterers, in all the wicked whatsoever, and in those who are in natural good and not in spiritual good. These can do good to the church, to their country, to society, to their fellow-citizens, to the needy, the poor, and to widows and orphans; and they can also understand truths, from the understanding think them, and from thought speak and teach them. But still, not being from interior principles of good and truth, neither these good deeds nor truths are really such in the persons just mentioned, but are only such outwardly, and therefore merely in appearance; because they are only for the sake of self and the world, and not for the sake of good itself and truth itself, consequently not grounded in good and truth. Hence they are only of the mouth and of the body, and not of the heart; and may be compared to gold and silver enclosing dross, or rotten wood or dung; and truths thus uttered may be compared to respired air which is dispersed, or to an ignis-fatuus which vanishes. Still they outwardly appear as genuine; and though they are only apparent with those who speak them, they may seem otherwise to those who hear and receive them, and to whom this is

unknown; for what is external affects every one according to his internal, because truth enters, from whatever mouth it be uttered, into the hearing of another, and is received by the mind according to its state and quality.. With those who are hereditarily in natural good, and in no spiritual good, the case is nearly similar; for the internal of all good and of all truth is spiritual, and this shakes off falsities and evils; but the natural principle alone favors them, and to favor evils and falsities and to do good do not accord.

15. The ground and reason why good can be separated from truth, and truth from good, and when separated still appear as good and truth, is, because man has a faculty of acting, which is called liberty, and a faculty of understanding, which is called rationality; from the abuse of which faculties man can appear different in externals from what he is in internals; therefore a wicked man can do good and speak truth, or the devil can imitate an angel of light. But on this subject see the following propositions in the treatise on THE DIVINE LOVE AND THE DIVINE WISDOM. That the origin of evil is from the abuse of the faculties which are proper to man, and are called rationality and liberty, n. 264—270. That these two faculties exist as well in the wicked as in the good, n. 425. That love without a marriage with wisdom, or good without a marriage with truth, cannot do any thing, n. 401. That love does nothing but in conjunction with wisdom or the understanding, n. 409. That love joins itself to wisdom or the understanding, and causes wisdom or the understanding to be reciprocally joined to it, n 410, 411, 412. That wisdom or the understanding, by means of the power given it by love, can be elevated, and perceive the things which are of the light from heaven, and receive them, n. 413. That love can in like manner be elevated, and receive the things which are of the heat from heaven, if it loves its consort wisdom in that degree, n. 414, 415. That otherwise love draws down wisdom or the understanding from its elevation, that it may act as one with it, n. 416—418. That love is purified in the understanding, if they are elevated together, n. 419 —421. That love purified by wisdom in the understanding becomes spiritual and celestial; but that love defiled in the understanding becomes sensual and corporeal, n. 422—424. That it is the same with charity and faith and their conjunction, as it is with love and wisdom and their conjunction, n. 427—430. What charity is in heaven, n. 431.

16. VII. *That the Lord does not suffer any thing to be divided ; therefore it must either be in good and at the same time in truth, or it must be in evil and at the same time in falsity.* The divine providence of the Lord has especially for its end, and operates, that man may be in good and at the same time in truth, since thereby he is his own good and his own love, and

11

also his own truth and his own wisdom; for by this man is man being in such case an image of the Lord. But because man, while he lives in the world, can be in good and at the same time in falsity, likewise in evil and at the same time in truth, yea, can be in evil and at the same time in good, and thus as it were a double man; and since this division destroys that image, and consequently the man; therefore the divine providence of the Lord, in all and singular its operations, is directed against the existence of such division. Because, also, it is less hurtful to man to be in evil and at the same time in falsity, than to be in good and at the same time in evil, therefore the Lord permits the former, not as willing it, but as not able to resist it consistently with the end in view, which is salvation. The reason why man can be in evil and at the same time in truth, and why the Lord cannot resist it, on account of the end, which is salvation, is, because the understanding of man can be elevated into the light of wisdom, and see truths, or acknowledge them when he hears them, his love at the same time remaining below. Thus he can be with his understanding in heaven, but with his love in hell; and to be so, cannot be denied him, because the two faculties of rationality and liberty, by which he is man, and is distinguished from beasts, and by which alone he can be regenerated, and consequently saved, cannot be taken away from him. For by them man can act according to wisdom, and also according to the love not of wisdom, and from the wisdom above can see the love beneath; thus he can see his own thoughts, intentions, affections, and therefore the evils and falsities, as well as the goods and truths of his life and doctrine, without a knowledge and acknowledgment of which in himself he cannot be reformed. Of these two faculties something has already been said, and more will be said in what follows. This is the reason why man can be in good and at the same time in truth, also in evil and at the same time in falsity, and likewise in both alternately.

17. Man can with difficulty in this world come into either the one or the other conjunction or union, that is, of good and truth, or of evil and falsity; for so long as he lives here, he is kept in a state of reformation or regeneration. But after death every man comes into the one or the other, because he is then no longer in a state to be reformed and regenerated: he then remains such as his life has been in the world, that is, such as his ruling love has been. Therefore, if his life has been a life of the love of evil, every truth which he has acquired in this world from masters, preaching, or the Word, is taken away from him; and, being taken away, he imbibes the falsity which accords with his evil as a sponge does water. On the other hand, if his life has been a life of love and good, every falsity which he has imbibed by hearing or by reading in the

world, and which he has not confirmed in himself, is removed, and in its place is given truth which accords with his good. This is meant by these words of the Lord, " Take the talent from him, and give it unto him which hath ten talents ; for unto every one that hath shall be given, and he shall have abundance ; but from him that hath not shall be taken away, even that which he hath" (Matt. xxv. 28, 29 ; xiii. 12 ; Mark iv. 25 ; Luke viii. 18 ; xix. 24—26).

18. The reason why every one after death must either be in good and at the same time in truth, or in evil and at the same time in falsity, is, because good and evil cannot be joined, neither good and at the same time the falsity of evil, nor evil and at the same time the truth of good, for they are opposites, and opposites combat each other, until one destroys the other They who are in evil and at the same time in good, are understood by these words of the Lord to the church of Laodicea in the Apocalypse : " I know thy works, that thou art neither cold nor hot ; I would thou wert either cold or hot ; but because thou art lukewarm, and neither cold nor hot, I will spew thee out of my mouth" (iii. 15, 16). Also by these words of the Lord : " No man can serve two masters ; for either he will hate the one and love the other, or else he will hold to the one and despise the other" (Matt. vi. 24).

19. VIII. *That that which is in good and at the same time in truth, is something ; and that that which is in evil and at the same time in falsity, is not any thing.* That that which is in good and at the same time in truth, is something, may be seen above, n. 11 ; thence it follows, that what is evil and at the same time false is not any thing. By not being any thing, is meant that it has no power, and nothing of spiritual life. They who are in evil and at the same time in falsity, all of whom are in hell, have indeed power among themselves ; for a wicked spirit can do evil, and also does do evil a thousand ways. Nevertheless he can only from a principle of evil do evil to the wicked, but cannot in the least do evil to the good ; or if he does evil to the good, which sometimes is the case, it is by conjunction with their evil ; thence come temptations, which are infestations arising from evil spirits about a man, and consequent combats, whereby the good may be delivered from their evils. As the wicked have no power, the universal hell before the Lord is not only as nothing, but it is really nothing as to power : that it is so, I have seen confirmed by much experience. It is wonderful, however, that all the wicked think themselves powerful, and all the good think themselves not powerful. The reason of which is, that the wicked attribute every thing to self-derived prudence,—therefore to cunning and malice, and nothing to the Lord ; while the good attribute

13

nothing to self-derived prudence, but every thing to the **Lord**, who is omnipotent. Another reason why evil and its attendant falsity are not any thing, is, because they have no spiritual life; and this is the reason why the life of the infernals is not called life, but death : wherefore since every something appertains to life, there cannot be any thing appertaining to death.

20. They who are in evil and at the same time in truths, may be compared to eagles which soar aloft, but, when their wings are taken away, fall down. For men do the same after death, when they become spirits. They who understood truths, spake them, and taught them, and yet had no regard to God in their life, elevate themselves on high by their intellectual powers, and sometimes enter heaven, and feign themselves angels of light ; but when truths are taken away from them, and they are sent forth, they fall down into hell. Eagles also signify men of rapine, who have intellectual sight, and wings signify spiritual truths. It was said, that they are such who had no respect to God in their life : by having respect to God in their life, is meant nothing else but to think this or that evil a sin against God, and therefore not to do it.

21. IX. *That the Divine Providence of the Lord causes evil and its attendant falsity to serve for equilibrium, relation, and purification, and thereby for the conjunction of good and truth in others.* From the foregoing considerations it may appear, that the Divine Providence of the Lord continually operates, that in man truth may be united to good and good to truth, because this union is the church and is heaven ; for this union is in the Lord, and is in every thing that proceeds from the Lord. From this union it is, that heaven is called a marriage, and also the church, and hence the kingdom of God in the Word is likened to a marriage. From this union it is, that the sabbath in the Israelitish church was the most holy worship, for it signified this union. Hence also it is, that in the Word, and in all and every thing therein, there is a marriage of good and truth ; on which subject see THE DOCTRINE OF THE NEW JERUSALEM CONCERNING THE SACRED SCRIPTURE, n. 80—90. The marriage of good and truth is from the marriage of the Lord with the church, and the latter from the marriage of love and wisdom in the Lord : for good is of love, and truth is of wisdom. Hence it may be seen, that it is the perpetual object of the Divine Providence to unite in man good to truth and truth to good ; for so man is united to the Lord.

22. But as many have broken and do break this marriage, especially by the separation of faith from charity,—for faith is of truth, and truth is of faith, and charity is of good, and good is of charity,—and thereby conjoin in themselves evil and falsity, and thus have become, and do become, opposite, it is **pro**-

14

vided of the Lord that these nevertheless may serve for the conjunction of good and truth in others, by equilibrium, by relation, and by purification.

23. The conjunction of good and truth in others is provided for of the Lord by *equilibrium* between heaven and hell; for from hell continually exhale ·evil and its concomitant false, but from heaven continually exhale good and its concomitant truth; and every man is kept in this equilibrium as long as he lives in the world, and is thus in the liberty of thinking, willing, speaking, and acting, in which he may be reformed. Concerning this spiritual equilibrium, from which is derived the liberty of man, see the work on HEAVEN AND HELL, n. 589—596, and n. 597—603.

24. The conjunction of good and truth is provided for ot the Lord by *relation;* for good is not known as to its quality, but by relation to what is less good, and by opposition to evil. All the perceptive and sensitive principles are thence derived, because their quality is thence; for thus all delight is perceived and felt from what is less delightful, and by what is disagreeable; all beauty from what is less beautiful, and by what is ugly; in like manner, all good which is of love from what is less good, and by evil; and all truth which is of wisdom from what is less true, and by what is false. There must be variety in every thing, from its greatest to its least; and when ·there is variety also in its opposite, from its least to its greatest, and equilibrium intercedes, then according to the degrees on both sides relation is established, and the perception or sensation of the thing either increases or is diminished. But it is to be noted, that what is opposite may take away, and also may exalt perceptions and sensations; it takes them away when it mixes itself, and exalts them when it does not mix itself: on which account the Lord exquisitely separates good and evil, lest they should be mixed, in man, as he separates heaven and hell.

25. The conjunction of good and truth in others is provided for of the Lord by *purification,* which is effected in two ways,—in one by temptations, and in the other by fermentations. *Spiritual temptations* are no other than combats against evils and falsities, which are exhaled from hell and affect; by them man is purified from evils and falsities, and in him good is joined to truth, and truth to good. *Spiritual fermentations* are effected many ways, as well in the heavens as in the earths; but in the world it is not known what they are, and how they are effected: for they are evils and corresponding falsities, which, being let in upon societies, act like ferments put into meal and fermentable liquors, by which heterogeneous things are separated, and homogeneous things are conjoined and become pure and clear. This is what is understood by these words of the

15

Lord, "The kingdom of heaven is like unto leaven, which a woman took and hid in three measures of meal, till the whole was leavened" (Matt. xiii. 33; Luke xiii. 21).

26. These uses are provided by the Lord from the conjunction of evil and falsity, which is in those who are in hell; for the kingdom of the Lord, which is not only over heaven, but also over hell, is a kingdom of uses; and the Providence of the Lord is, that there should not be any ʼʼon or any thing, from and by which use is not performed.

THAT THE DIVINE PROVIDENCE OF THE LORD HAS FOR ITS END A HEAVEN OUT OF THE HUMAN RACE.

27. THAT heaven is not from any angels created such from the beginning, and that hell is not from any devil who was created an angel of light and cast out of heaven, but that heaven and hell are from the human race,—heaven from those who are in the love of good and thence in the understanding of truth, and hell from those who are in the love of evil and thence in the understanding of falsity,—has been made known and proved to me by a long intercourse with angels and spirits; concerning which see also what is shown in the work on HEAVEN AND HELL, n. 311—316; as well as in the tract on THE LAST JUDGMENT, n. 14—27; and in .the CONTINUATION CONCERNING THE LAST JUDGMENT AND THE SPIRITUAL WORLD, from beginning to end. Now, since heaven is from the human race, and heaven is a dwelling with the Lord to eternity, it follows that that was the end of creation intended by the Lord; and as it was the end of creation, it is the end of his divine providence. The Lord did not create the universe for his own sake, but for the sake of those with whom he will dwell in heaven; for spiritual love is such, that it wishes to give what it has to another, and in proportion as it can do this, it is in its *esse*, in its peace, and in its blessedness. This property spiritual love derives from the divine ve of the Lord, which possesses it in an infinite degree. Li: it follows, that the divine love, and consequently the divine providence, has for its end a heaven, which may consist of men made angels, and who are making such, to whom the Lord can give all the beatitudes and felicities which belong to love and wisdom, and give them out of himself in them. Nor can he do otherwise; because his image and likeness from creation is in them. His image in them is wisdom, and his likeness in them is love; and the Lord in them is love united to wisdom and wisdom united to love, or what is the

16

same, he is good united to truth, and truth united to good; which union was treated of in the preceding article. But as it is not known what heaven is in general or in many, and what heaven is in particular or in one; or what heaven is in the spiritual world, and what heaven is in the natural world, and yet it is important to know this, because it is the end of the Divine Providence, therefore I am desirous to place this subject in some degree of light, in the following order. I. That heaven is conjunction with the Lord. II. That a man by creation is such, that he can be more and more nearly conjoined to the Lord. III. That a man becomes wiser in proportion as he is more nearly conjoined to the Lord. IV. That a man becomes happier in proportion as he is more nearly conjoined to the Lord. V. That a man, in proportion as he is more nearly conjoined to the Lord, appears to himself more distinctly to be at his own disposal, and yet perceives more evidently that he is the Lord's.

28. I. *That heaven is conjunction with the Lord.* Heaven is not heaven from the angels, but from the Lord; for the love and wisdom, in which the angels are, and which constitute heaven, are not from them, but from the Lord, and are really the Lord in them. And since love and wisdom, which are of the Lord, and are the Lord in heaven, constitute the life of the angels, it is evident that their life is of the Lord, and indeed that it is the Lord. That they live from the Lord, the angels themselves confess. Hence it may appear that heaven is conjunction with the Lord. But as the conjunction with the Lord is various, and consequently one has not the same heaven as another, it also follows, that heaven is according to conjunction with the Lord. That there is a conjunction nearer and nearer, and also one more and more remote, will be seen in the following article. At present we shall state how that conjunction is effected, and what it is. There is a conjunction of the Lord with the angels, and of the angels with the Lord, and thus a reciprocal conjunction. The Lord flows into the life's love of the angels, and the angels receive the Lord in wisdom, and by this in their turn conjoin themselves to the Lord. But it is to be well observed, that it appears to the angels as if they conjoined themselves to the Lord by wisdom, when nevertheless the Lord conjoins them by wisdom to himself; for their wisdom is also from the Lord. It is the same if it is said, that the Lord conjoins himself to the angels by good, and that the angels in their turn conjoin themselves to the Lord by truth; for all good is of love, and all truth is of wisdom. But as this reciprocal conjunction is an arcanum, which few can understand unless it be explained, I will unfold it, so far as it can be done, by such things as may be comprehended. In the treatise concerning THE DIVINE LOVE AND THE DIVINE WISDOM, n. **404,**

17

405, it is shown in what manner love conjoins itself to wisdom, viz., by the affection of knowing, whence is derived the affection of truth; by the affection of understanding, from which is derived the perception of truth; and by the affection of seeing that which is known and understood, from which is derived thought. The Lord flows into all these affections, which are derivations from the life's love of every one; and the angels receive that influx in the perception of truth, and in thought; for in these the influx appears to them, but not in the affections. Now as perceptions and thoughts appear to the angels as if they were their own, although they are from affections, which are from the Lord, therefore there is still an appearance that the angels reciprocally conjoin themselves to the Lord, when nevertheless the Lord conjoins them to himself; for affection itself produces such perceptions and thoughts, affection, which is of love, being the soul of them; for no one can perceive and think any thing without affection, and every one perceives and thinks according to affection; from which it is evident, that the reciprocal conjunction of the angels with the Lord is not from them, but only seems to be from them. Such a conjunction also the Lord has with the church, and the church with the Lord, and it is called the celestial and spiritual marriage.

29. All conjunction in the spiritual world is effected by inspection. When any one there thinks of another from the affection of speaking with him, the other immediately becomes present, and one sees the other face to face. The same thing happens when any one thinks of another from the affection of love; but by this affection conjunction is produced, and by the other presence only. This is peculiar to the spiritual world; the reason of which is, that all there are spiritual. It is not so in the natural world, in which all are material. In the natural world, the same takes place with men in the affections and thoughts of their spirit; but as in the natural world there are spaces, while in the spiritual world spaces are only appearances, therefore in the latter that which has place in the thought of any spirit is actually effected. These things are stated, in order that it may be known in what manner is effected the conjunction of the Lord with the angels, and also the apparent reciprocal conjunction of the angels with the Lord; for all the angels turn their faces to the Lord, and the Lord looks at them in the forehead, and the angels direct their eyes towards the Lord. The reason is, because the forehead corresponds to love and its affections, and the eyes correspond to wisdom and its perceptions. Yet the angels from themselves do not turn their faces to the Lord, but the Lord turns them to himself; he turns them by influx into their life's love, and by it enters into their perceptions and thoughts, and so converts them. Such a circulation of the love to the thoughts, and from the thoughts to the love

18

from love, has place in all the human mind; which circulation or circle may be called the circle of life. On this subject see some particulars also in the treatise on THE DIVINE LOVE AND THE DIVINE WISDOM; as, That the angels constantly turn their faces to the Lord as the sun, n. 129—134. That all the interiors both of the minds and of the bodies of angels are in like manner turned to the Lord as a sun, n. 135—139. That every spirit, of whatsoever quality, in like manner turns himself to his ruling love, n. 140—145. That love conjoins itself to wisdom, and causes wisdom to be reciprocally conjoined to it, n. 410—412. That the angels are in the Lord, and the Lord in them; and, forasmuch as the angels are recipients, that the Lord alone is heaven, n. 113—118.

30. The Lord's heaven in the natural world is called the church, and an angel of this heaven is a man of the church who is conjoined to the Lord, and who also, after his departure out of the world, becomes an angel of the spiritual heaven: from which it is evident, that what is said of the angelic heaven, is to be understood of the human heaven, which is called the church. This reciprocal conjunction with the Lord, which constitutes heaven in man, is revealed by the Lord in these words in John: "Abide in me, and I in you." "He that abideth in me, and I in him, the same bringeth forth much fruit: for without me ye can do nothing" (xv. 4, 5, 7).

31. Hence it may appear, that the Lord is heaven, not only in common to all, but also in particular to each individual there; for every angel is a heaven in its least form: and from as many heavens as there are angels, heaven in common exists. That this is the case may be seen in the work on HEAVEN AND HELL, n. 51—58. Let not then any one cherish this error, which enters into the first thoughts of many, that the Lord is in heaven among the angels, or that he is with them as a king is in his kingdom: as to appearance in the sun there, he is above them; but as to their life of love and wisdom, he is in them.

32. II. *That a man by creation is such, that he can be more and more nearly conjoined to the Lord,* may appear from what is shown concerning degrees, in the treatise on THE DIVINE LOVE AND THE DIVINE WISDOM, Part III.; particularly from the following articles: That there are three discrete degrees or degrees of altitude in a man by creation, n. 230—235. That these three degrees are in every man by birth; and that as they are opened, a man is in the Lord and the Lord in him, n. 236—241. And that all perfections increase and ascend with degrees, and according to them, n. 199—204. From which it is evident, that a man by creation is such, that by degrees he can be more and more nearly conjoined to the Lord. But it should be well understood what degrees are; that they are of two kinds—discrete degrees

19   c

or degrees of altitude, and continuous degrees or degrees of latitude; and what is the difference between them : also, that every man by creation, and thence by birth, has three discrete degrees or degrees of altitude; that he comes into the first degree, which is called the natural degree, when he is born; and that he can increase this degree in himself by continuity, till he becomes rational; that he comes into the second, which is called the spiritual degree, if he live according to the spiritual laws of order, which are principles of divine truth; and that he may also come into the third or celestial degree, if he live according to the celestial laws of order, which are principles of divine good. These degrees are actually opened in a man by the Lord according to his life in the world, but not perceptibly and sensibly till after his departure out of the world; and as they are opened and afterwards perfected, so a man is more and more nearly conjoined to the Lord. This conjunction by nearer approach may be increased to eternity, and indeed is increased in the angels to eternity; but still an angel cannot arrive at the first degree of the Lord's love and wisdom, or attain it, because the Lord is infinite, and an angel is finite, and there is no proportion between infinite and finite. Since no one can understand the state of a man, and the state of his elevation and approximation to the Lord, except he knows these degrees, therefore they are particularly treated of in the treatise on THE DIVINE LOVE AND THE DIVINE WISDOM, n. 173—281; which see.

33. We shall briefly show how a man can be more nearly conjoined to the Lord, and then how that conjunction appears nearer and nearer. *How a man is more and more nearly conjoined to the Lord:* This is done, not by science alone, or by intelligence alone, or even by wisdom alone, but by a life conjoined to them. The life of a man is his love, and love is manifold. In general there is a love of evil and a love of good. The love of evil is the love of adultery, revenge, fraud, blasphemy, and the depriving others of their goods. The love of evil, in thinking and in doing these, feels pleasure and delight. The derivations, which are affections of this love, are as many as there are evils to which it has determined itself; and the perceptions and thoughts of this love, are as many as there are falsities which favor those evils and confirm them. These falsities make one with the evils, as the understanding makes one with the will; and they are not separated from each other, because one is of the other. Now, as the Lord flows into the life's love of every one, and by his affections into his perceptions and thoughts, and not *vice versa*, as was said above, it follows that he cannot conjoin himself more nearly than is permitted by the removal of the love of evil with its affections, which are lusts; and as these reside in the natural man, and whatsoever a man does from the

natural man, he feels as if he acted from himself, therefore he ought, as from himself, to remove the evils of his love, and then, in proportion as he removes them, the Lord approaches nearer, and joins himself to him. Any one may see from reason that lusts, with their delights, obstruct and shut the door against the Lord, and that they cannot be cast out by the Lord so long as a man himself keeps the door shut, and presses from without and prevents it from being opened. That a man himself ought to open it, is evident from the Lord's words in the Revelation : " Behold, I stand at the door, and knock ; if any man hear my voice and open the door, I will come into him, and will sup with him, and he with me" (iii. 20). Hence it is evident, that in proportion as any one shuns evils as diabolical, and as obstacles to the Lord's entrance, he is more and more nearly conjoined to the Lord, and he the most nearly, who abominates them as so many black and fiery devils ; for evil and the devil are one, and the falsity of evil and Satan are one ; because as the influx of the Lord is into the love of good and its affections, and by these into the perceptions and thoughts, all which derive from the good in which a man is principled that which constitutes them truths—so the influx of the devil, that is, of hell, is into the love of evil and its affections, which are lusts, and by these into the perceptions and thoughts, all which derive from the evil in which a man is principled that which makes them falsities. *How that conjunction appears nearer and nearer :* In proportion as evils are removed in the natural man by shunning and turning away from them, in such proportion a man is more nearly conjoined to the Lord. And as love and wisdom, which are the Lord himself, are not in space,—for affection which is of love, and thought which is of wisdom, have nothing in common with space,—therefore the Lord according to conjunction by love and wisdom appears nearer ; and, on the contrary, according to the rejection of love and wisdom, more remote. Space does not exist in the spiritual world, but in that world degrees of distance and presence are appearances according to similitudes and dissimilitudes of affections ; for as before said, affections which are of love, and thoughts which are of wisdom and in themselves spiritual, are not in space ; on which subject see what is stated in the treatise on THE DIVINE LOVE AND THE DIVINE WISDOM, n. 6—10, n. 69—72, and elsewhere. The conjunction of the Lord with a man, in whom evils are removed, is understood by these words of the Lord ; " The pure in heart shall see God" (Matt. v. 8) : and by these ; " He that hath my commandments, and keepeth them, I will make my abode with him." To have his commandments is to know them, and to keep his commandments is to love them; for it is also said there, " he who keepeth my commandments, he it is who loveth me."

34. III. *That a man becomes wiser in proportion as he is more*

nearly conjoined to the Lord. As there are three degrees of life in a man by creation, and thence by birth, as noticed above, n. 32, there are in him especially three degrees of wisdom. These are the degrees which are opened in a man according to conjunction; they are opened according to love, for love is conjunction itself. But the ascent of love according to degrees is not perceived except obscurely by a man, whereas the ascent of wisdom is clearly perceived in those who know and see what wisdom is. The reason why the degrees of wisdom are perceived, is, that love enters by the affections into the perceptions and thoughts, and these show themselves in the internal sight of the mind, which corresponds to the external sight of the body : hence it is that wisdom appears, and not so the affection of love which produces it. The case is the same with all things which are actually done by a man. It is perceived how the body effects them, but not how the soul does : so also it is perceived how a man meditates, perceives, and thinks, but not how the soul of his meditations, perceptions, and thoughts, which is the affection of good and truth, produces them. There are three degrees of wisdom—the natural, spiritual, and celestial. A man is in the natural degree of wisdom while he lives in the world. This degree then can be perfected in him to its height, and yet he cannot enter into the spiritual degree ; because this degree is not continued from the natural degree by continuity, but is joined to it by correspondences. He is in the spiritual degree of wisdom after death ; and this degree also is such, that it can be perfected to its height, but yet cannot enter the celestial degree of wisdom, because this degree also is not continued from the spiritual by continuity, but is joined to it by correspondences. Hence it may appear, that wisdom can be elevated in a triplicate ratio, and that in each degree it can be perfected in a simple ratio to its height. He who comprehends the elevations and perfections of these - degrees, can in some measure perceive what is said of angelic wisdom,—that it is ineffable. This also is so ineffable, that a thousand ideas of thought of the angels from their wisdom cannot present more than one idea of the thought of men from their wisdom ; thus nine hundred and ninety-nine ideas of the thought of angels cannot enter ; for they are supernatural. That this is the case, it has often been given me to know by lively experience. But, as was said before, no one can come into that ineffable wisdom of the angels, but by conjunction with the Lord, and according to it ; for the Lord only opens the spiritual degree and the celestial degree, and in those only who are wise from him ; and those are wise from the Lord, who cast out from themselves the devil, that is evil.

35. But let not any one believe, that a person has wisdom because he knows many things, and perceives them in a certain light, and can speak of them intelligently, unless it be con-

joined to love; for love by its affections produces it. If it is not conjoined to love, it is like a meteor in the air which vanishes, and like a falling star; but wisdom conjoined to love is like the permanent light of the sun, and like a fixed star. A man has the love of wisdom, in proportion as he has an aversion to the diabolical crew, which are the concupiscences of evil and falsity.

36. Wisdom, which comes by or according to perception, is the perception of truth from the affection of it, especially the perception of spiritual truth; for there are civil truth, moral truth, and spiritual truth. Those who are in the perception of spiritual truth from the affection of it, are also in the perception of moral and civil truth; for the affection of spiritual truth is the soul of them. I have sometimes discoursed about wisdom with the angels, who said, that wisdom is conjunction with the Lord, because the Lord is wisdom itself; and that a man comes into that conjunction who rejects, and in the same proportion only as he rejects, hell from himself. They said, that they represented to themselves wisdom as a magnificent and highly adorned palace, to which there is an ascent by twelve steps; and that no one comes to the first step, but from the Lord by conjunction with him; that every one ascends according to conjunction; and that as he ascends, he perceives that no one is wise from himself, but from the Lord; also, that the things concerning which he is wise, compared with those concerning which he is not, are as a few drops to a great lake. By the twelve steps to the palace of wisdom, are signified principles of good conjoined to those of truth, and principles of truth conjoined to those of good.

37. IV. *That a man becomes happier in proportion as he is more nearly conjoined to the Lord.* The same things which are said above, n. 32, 33, 34, of the degrees of life and of wisdom according to conjunction with the Lord, may also be said of the degrees of felicity; for felicities or beatitudes and delights ascend, as the superior degrees of the mind, which are called spiritual and celestial, are opened in a man; and these degrees, after his life in the world, increase to eternity.

38. No man who is in the delight of the concupiscences of evil can know any thing of the delight of the affections of good in which exists the angelic heaven; for these two kinds of delight are altogether opposite to each other in internals, and thence interiorly in externals, though in the surface itself there is but little difference. For every love has its delights, even the love of evil in those who are in concupiscences; as the love of committing adultery, of revenge, fraud, theft, outrage, and, in the most wicked, the love of blaspheming the holy things of the church, and spitting out their virulence against God. The source of these delights is the love of dominion from the love of

23

self. These delights are from the concupiscences which possess the interiors of the mind, flow from them into the body, and there excite uncleannesses, which titillate the fibres. Thus, from the delight of the mind, according to its concupiscences, arises delight of the body. Of what kind the unclean things are, which titillate the fibres of the body, it is given every one to know, after death, in the spiritual world. They are in general cadaverous, excrementitious, stercoraceous, nidorous, and urinous matters; for the hells abound with such unclean things; and that they are correspondences, see some passages in the treatise on THE DIVINE LOVE AND THE DIVINE WISDOM, n. 422, 423, 424. But such foul delights, after the subjects of them enter into hell, are turned into direful punishments. These things are stated, that the nature of the felicity of heaven, which is now to be spoken of, may be better understood; for every thing is known from its opposite.

39. The beatitudes, blessednesses, delights, and pleasantnesses,—in a word, the felicities of heaven, cannot be described in words, though in heaven they can be perceived by the sense; for what is perceived by the sense alone cannot be described, because it does not come within the ideas of thought, or consequently into words : since the understanding alone sees, and sees the things which are of wisdom or of truth, but not the things which are of love or of good; therefore those felicities are inexpressible. But still they ascend in a similar degree with wisdom; the varieties of them are infinite, and each of these ineffable. This I have heard, and have perceived. These felicities, however, enter as a man removes the concupiscences of the love of evil and falsity, as if of himself, but nevertheless of the Lord; for they are the felicities of the affections of good and truth, which are opposite to the concupiscences of the love of evil and falsity. The felicities of the affections of good and truth begin from the Lord, therefore from the inmost, thence diffusing themselves to the inferiors, even to the ultimates, and so filling the angel, and causing him to be as it were all delight. Such felicities, with infinite varieties, are in every affection of good and truth, especially in the affection of wisdom.

40. The delights of the concupiscences of evil, and those of the affections of good, cannot be compared; because the devil is inwardly in the delights of the concupiscences of evil, and the Lord is inwardly in the delights of the affections of good. If they are to be compared, the delights of the concupiscences of evil can only be compared with the lascivious delights of frogs in stagnant waters, and of serpents in stenches; but the delights of the affections of good may be compared to those of the mind in gardens and shrubberies. For things similar to what affect frogs and serpents, affect also those in the hells who are in the concupiscences of evil; and things similar to what affect the mind

24

in gardens and shrubberies, affect also those in the heavens who are in the affections of good : because, as was said above, correspondent unclean things affect the wicked, and correspondent clean things affect the good.

41. Hence it may appear, that in proportion as any one is more nearly conjoined to the Lord, he becomes happier. But this happiness rarely manifests itself in the world, because a man is then in a natural state, and what is natural does not communicate with what is spiritual by continuity, but by correspondences ; and this communication is only felt by a certain quiet and peace of mind, which is especially produced after combats against evils. When, however, a man puts off the natural and enters into the spiritual state, as is the case after his departure out of the world, then the felicity above described successively manifests itself.

42. V. *That a man, in proportion as he is more nearly conjoined to the Lord, appears to himself to be more distinctly at his own disposal, and perceives more evidently that he is the Lord's.* In judging from appearance, it might be supposed, that the nearer any one is conjoined to the Lord, the less he is free, or at his own disposal. There is such an appearance with all the wicked, as well as with those who believe from religion that they are not under the yoke of the law, and that no one can do good from himself ; for both these sorts of persons can see no otherwise, than that, not to be at liberty to think and to will evil, but only good, is not to be at one's own disposal ; and they conclude from the appearance in themselves, that because those who are conjoined to the Lord neither will nor can think and will evil, therefore this is to be not at their own disposal ; when, nevertheless, it is altogether the contrary.

43. There is infernal liberty, and there is celestial liberty. To think and to will evil, and, so far as civil and moral laws do not prevent, to speak and to do it, is from infernal liberty ; but to think and to will good, and, as far as opportunity is given, to speak and to do it, is from celestial liberty. Whatsoever a man thinks, wills, speaks, and does, from freedom, he perceives as his own, for a man derives all liberty from his love. Those therefore who are in the love of evil, perceive no otherwise, than that infernal liberty is real liberty, while those who are in the love of good, perceive that celestial liberty is real liberty ; and to each, consequently, the opposite appears to be servitude : yet it cannot be denied that only one of the two is liberty, for two kinds of liberty, in themselves opposite, cannot both be liberty ; nor can it be denied that to be led by good is liberty, and to be led by evil is servitude ; for to be led by good is to be led by the Lord, and to be led by evil is to be led by the devil. Now since every thing which a man does from freedom or liberty, appears to him as his own,—for, as was said above, it is of his love, and to act

25

from his love is to act from liberty,—it follows, that conjunction with the Lord causes a man to appear to himself free, consequently at his own disposal; and the nearer his conjunction with the Lord is, the more free he appears, consequently the more at his own disposal. The reason why he appears to himself *more distinctly* at his own disposal, is, that such is the Divine Love, that what is its own it wills to be another's, therefore to be men's and angels': all spiritual love is such, and especially Divine Love. Besides, the Lord never forces any one, because nothing to which any one is forced appears as his own, and what does not appear as his own cannot be made of his love, and so appropriated as his own. A man therefore is led by the Lord continually in freedom, and is also reformed and regenerated in freedom. But on this subject more will be said in what follows; and something also may be seen above, n. 4.

44. The reason, however, why a man, the more distinctly he appears to himself at his own disposal, the more evidently perceives that he is the Lord's, is, that in proportion as he is more nearly conjoined to the Lord, he becomes wiser, as was shown above, n. 34, 35, 36; and wisdom teaches this, and he also perceives it. The angels of the third heaven, because they are the wisest of the angels, also perceive this, and likewise call it liberty itself; but to be led by themselves they call servitude. They declare also the reason of this, namely, that the Lord does not flow immediately into the things which are of their perception and thought from wisdom, but into the affections of the love of good, and through the latter into the former; that they perceive the influx in the affection from which is derived their wisdom; that then all which they think from wisdom appears as from themselves, therefore as their own; and that by this reciprocal conjunction is effected.

45. As the Divine Providence of the Lord has for its end a heaven out of the human race, it follows that it has for its end the conjunction of the human race with him, concerning which see n. 28—31; also, that it has for its end that a man may be more and more nearly conjoined to him (see n. 32, 33), for thus he enters an interior heaven: also, that it has for its end, that a man by such conjunction may become wiser (see n. 34, 35, 36); and that he may become happier (see n. 37—41); because a man possesses heaven from wisdom, and according to it; and by it also felicity: and lastly, that it has for its end, that a man may appear to himself more distinctly as his own, and yet may perceive more evidently that he is the Lord's (see n. 42, 43, 44). All these things are of the Divine Providence of the Lord, because all these things constitute heaven, which is the end proposed.

THAT THE DIVINE PROVIDENCE OF THE LORD, IN ALL THAT IT DOES, HAS RESPECT TO WHAT IS INFINITE AND ETERNAL.

46. It is well known in the Christian world, that God is infinite and eternal; for in the doctrine of the trinity, which has its name from Athanasius, it is said that God the Father is infinite, eternal, and omnipotent; in like manner, God the Son, and God the Holy Ghost; and that nevertheless there are not three Infinites, Eternals, and Omnipotents, but one. From this it follows, that as God is infinite and eternal, nothing but infinite and eternal can be predicated of God. But what infinite and eternal is, cannot be comprehended by finite beings, and yet it can: it cannot be comprehended, because finite is not capable of infinite; and yet it can be comprehended, because there are abstract ideas given, by which it can be seen that things exist, though not what is their quality. Such ideas are given of infinite, as, that God, because he is infinite, or the Divine, because it is infinite, is *Esse* itself; that it is essence and substance itself; that it is love itself and wisdom itself, or that it is good itself and truth itself; therefore that it is itself, yea, that it is man himself: then also if it be said that infinite is all,—that Infinite Wisdom is Omniscience, and Infinite Power is Omnipotence. Still, however, these things fall but obscurely within the thought, and from being incomprehensible perhaps come to be denied; unless the things which thought derives from nature be abstracted from the idea, especially what it derives from those two things proper to nature, space and time; for these cannot but terminate ideas, and cause abstract ideas to be as nothing. But if these can be abstracted by a man as they are by an angel, then infinite can be comprehended by means of the things above mentioned; and it can also be comprehended that a man is something, because he was created by an infinite God who is all; and that a man is a finite substance, because he was created by an infinite God, who is substance itself; also, that a man is wisdom, because he was created by an infinite God who is wisdom itself, and so on; for unless the infinite God were all, substance itself, and wisdom itself, a man would not be any thing; therefore he would either be nothing, or only an idea of being, according to those visionaries who are called idealists. From what is shown in the treatise on THE DIVINE LOVE AND THE DIVINE WISDOM, it is evident, that the Divine Essence is love and wisdom, n. 28—39. That the Divine Love and the Divine Wisdom are substance itself and form itself; and that it is self-subsisting and sole-subsisting, n. 40—46. And that God created the universe and all things therein from Himself, and not from nothing, n. 282, 283, 284. Thence it follows, that every created thing, and

27

especially a man, and in him love and wisdom, are something. and not merely an idea of being; for if God was not infinite, there would be no finite; also, if infinite was not all, there would not be any thing: and if God had not created all things out of Himself, there would be nothing; in a word, WE ARE BECAUSE GOD IS.

47. Now, as the Divine Providence is the subject here treated of, and it is intended in this article to show how it has respect, in all that it does, to what is infinite and eternal, and as this cannot be set forth distinctly except in a certain order; therefore the order shall be as follows: I. That what is infinite in itself and eternal in itself is the same as what is divine. II. That what is infinite and eternal in itself cannot but have respect to what is infinite from itself in finites. III. That the Divine Providence, in all that it does, has respect to what is infinite and eternal from itself, especially in saving the human race. IV. That an image of what is infinite and eternal exists in the angelic heaven from the human race saved. V. That to have respect to what is infinite and eternal in forming the angelic heaven, in order that it may be before the Lord as one man, the image of himself, is the inmost end or purpose of the Divine Providence.

48. I. *That what is infinite in itself and eternal in itself is the same as what is divine*, may appear from what is shown in many places in the treatise on THE DIVINE LOVE AND THE DIVINE WISDOM. That what is infinite in itself and eternal in itself is divine, is grounded in the idea of the angels, they meaning by infinite no other than the divine *esse*, and by eternal the divine *existere*. But that what is infinite in itself and eternal in itself is divine, can be seen, and yet cannot be seen by men: it can be seen by those who think of infinite not from space, and of eternal not from time; but cannot be seen by those who think of infinite and eternal from space and time: therefore it can be seen by those who think more elevatedly, that is, more interiorly in the rational mind; but it cannot be seen by those whose thought is lower, that is, more exterior. Those, by whom it can be seen, think that infinity of space cannot exist, nor therefore infinity of time, which is eternity from which all things began, because that which is infinite is without a first and last end, or without bounds. They think also, that neither can there exist infinite from itself, because from itself supposes a limit and beginning, or a prior from which it is derived; consequently, that it is a vain thing to speak of infinite and eternal from itself, because that would be like speaking of *esse* from itself, which is contradictory; for infinite from itself would be infinite from infinite, and *esse* from itself would be *esse* from *esse*, and such infinite and *esse* would either be the same with infinite, or it would be finite. From

these and similar considerations, which can be seen interiorly in the rational mind, it is evident that there exist infinite in itself, and eternal in itself, and that both together are the Divine, from which are all things.

49. I know that many will say within themselves, How can any one comprehend interiorly in his rational mind any thing without space and without time; and that they not only are, but also that they constitute the all—the very thing from which all things are derived: but think interiorly, whether love or any affection thereof, or wisdom or any perception thereof, or even whether thought, is in space and in time; and you will find that they are not: and since the Divine is Love itself and Wisdom itself, it follows that the Divine cannot be conceived in space and in time, therefore neither can infinite. That this may be more clearly perceived, consider whether thought is in time and space. Suppose a progression of it during ten or twelve hours: may not this space of time appear as but of one or two hours, and may it not also appear as of one or two days? for it appears according to the state of the affection from which the thought is derived. If it is an affection of joy, in which time is not regarded, the thought of ten or twelve hours seems scarcely of one or two; but the reverse happens if the affection is of grief, in which time is attended to. Hence it is evident, that time is only an appearance according to the state of affection from which thought is derived. It is the same with the distance of space in thought, whether in walking, or in going a journey.

50. As angels and spirits are affections which are of love, and thoughts thence derived, consequently they also are not in space and time, but only in the appearance thereof. The appearance of space and time is to them according to the states of the affections, and thence of the thoughts. Therefore, when any one thinks of another from affection, intently desiring to see him or speak with him, the other actually presents himself. Hence it is, that there are present with every man spirits who are in a similar affection with him,—evil spirits with him who is in the affection of similar evil, and good spirits with him who is in the affection of similar good; and they are as really present as any one can be with company shut up in the same room. Space and time contribute nothing to presence; because affection and its consequent thought are not in space and time, and spirits and angels are affections and thoughts derived from them. That this is the case, it has been given me to know from lively experience of several years; and also from this circumstance, that I have conversed with many persons after death, as well with those in Europe and its various kingdoms, as with those in Asia and Africa, and their various kingdoms; and they were all near me: whereas, if they had been in space and time,

29

a journey must have intervened, and time for that journey. Indeed, every man knows this to be the case from something inherent in himself or in his mind, as was proved to me by this consideration,—that no one thought of any distance of space, when I related that I had conversed with any person who died in Asia, Africa, or Europe,—as for example, with Calvin, Luther, Melancthon, or with any king, governor, or priest, in a remote country; and it did not even enter into any one's thoughts to ask, How could he converse with those who lived there, and how could they come to him and be present, when nevertheless lands and seas intervene? From this consideration also it was evident to me, that no one thinks from space and time, when he thinks of those who are in the spiritual world. That, notwithstanding, they have an appearance of space and time, may be seen in the work on HEAVEN AND HELL, n. 162—169, 191—199.

51. From these considerations then it may appear, that infinite and eternal, consequently the Lord, is to be thought of without space and time; and that he can be so thought of, likewise that he is so thought of, by those who think interiorly in the rational mind; and that then infinite and eternal is the same with the Divine. Thus do angels and spirits think. By virtue of thought abstracted from time and space are comprehended the Divine Omnipresence and the Divine Omnipotence, and likewise the Divine from eternity, and not at all by thought in which is included an idea from space and time. Hence it is evident, that we can think of God from eternity, but never of nature from eternity; consequently that we can think of the creation of the universe by God, but not any thing at all of creation from nature; for space and time are proper to nature, but the Divine is without them. That the Divine is without space and time, may be seen in the treatise on THE DIVINE LOVE AND THE DIVINE WISDOM, n. 7—10, 69—72, 73—76, and elsewhere.

52. II. *That what is infinite and eternal in itself, cannot but have respect to what is infinite and eternal from itself in finites.* By infinite and eternal in itself is meant the Divine itself, as was shown in the preceding article. By finites are meant all things created from the Divine, and especially men, spirits, and angels; and to have respect to what is infinite and eternal from itself, is to respect the Divine, that is, himself, in them, as a man respects or beholds his image in a glass. That this is the case, is abundantly shown in the treatise on THE DIVINE LOVE AND THE DIVINE WISDOM, especially where it is demonstrated, that in the created universe there is an image of man, and that it is an image of what is infinite and eternal, n. 317, 318, therefore an image of God the Creator, that is, of the Lord from eternity. But it is to be understood, that the Divine in itself

30

is in the Lord, but the Divine from itself is the Divine from the Lord in things created.

53. For the better understanding of this, however, it may be expedient to illustrate it. The Divine cannot respect or regard any thing but what is divine, and cannot respect what is divine anywhere but in things created from itself. That such is the case, is evident from this consideration, that no one can respect another but from something of his own existing in himself; he who loves another, regards him from his own love in himself; he who is wise, regards another from his own wisdom in himself. He may see indeed that the other either does or does not love him, and that he is either wise or not wise; but this he sees from love and wisdom in himself; therefore he conjoins himself to him in proportion as the other's love for him corresponds with his love for the other, or in proportion as the other is wise like himself; for they thus act as one. It is the same with the Divine in itself; for the Divine in itself cannot respect itself from another, as from a man, spirit, or angel; for they have nothing of the all-creating Divine in itself, and to respect the Divine from another, in which there is nothing of the Divine, would be to respect the Divine from what is not divine, which is impossible. Hence it is, that the Lord is so conjoined to a man, spirit, and angel, that all which has relation to the Divine is not from them but from the Lord. For it is a known thing, that all the good and all the truth which any one has, is not from himself but from the Lord; and indeed that no one can even name the Lord, or utter his names, Jesus and Christ, but from him. From this then it follows, that infinite and eternal, which is the same with the Divine, respects all things infinitely in finite subjects, and that it conjoins itself to them according to the degree of the reception of wisdom and love in them. In a word, the Lord cannot have his mansion and dwell with a man and angel, but in his own, and not in their proprium, for that is evil; and if it were good, still it is finite, which in itself, and from itself, is not capable of infinite. From these considerations it is evident, that it can never be possible for finite to respect infinite, but that it is possible for infinite to respect what is infinite from itself in finite subjects.

54. It appears as if infinite could not be conjoined to finite, because there is no proportion between infinite and finite, and because finite is not capable of infinite; but nevertheless conjunction is given, as well because infinite out of itself created all things, according to what is shown in the treatise on THE DIVINE LOVE AND THE DIVINE WISDOM, n. 282, 283, 284, as because infinite cannot respect any thing else in finites but what is infinite from itself, and that this can appear with finite beings as in them. Thus is established a proportion between finite and

31

infinite, not from finite, but from infinite in finite; and thus also finite is capable of infinite, not finite in itself, but as if in itself, originating in infinite from itself in it. But of this more in what now follows.

55. III. *That the Divine Providence in all that it does has respect to what is infinite and eternal from itself, especially in saving the human race.* Infinite and eternal in itself is the Divine itself, or the Lord in himself; but infinite and eternal from itself is the proceeding Divine, or the Lord in others created out of himself, therefore in men and in angels, and this Divine is the same with the Divine Providence; for the Lord by the Divine from himself provides, that all things may be contained in the order in which and for which they were created; and as the proceeding Divine effects this, it follows that all that is the Divine Providence.

56. That the Divine Providence in all that it does has respect to what is infinite and eternal from itself, may appear from this consideration, that every created thing, from the First, who is infinite and eternal, proceeds to ultimates, and from ultimates to the First from whom it proceeded, as was shown in the treatise concerning THE DIVINE LOVE AND THE DIVINE WISDOM, in the part which treats of the creation of the universe; and as in all its progression, the First from which it is derived exists intimately, it follows, that the proceeding Divine or the Divine Providence, in all that it does, respects some image of what is infinite and eternal. This it does in all things; but in some in a manner evidently perceptible, and in others not. It presents that image in a manner evidently perceptible in the variety which exists in all things, and in the fructification and multiplication of all things. *An image of what is infinite and eternal in the variety of all things* appears in this, that there does not exist, nor can exist to eternity, any one thing the same with another. This is manifest to the eye in the faces of men from the first creation, and therefore also from their minds, of which their faces are the types, and also from their affections, perceptions, and thoughts, for of these the mind consists. Hence it is that there do not exist in the universal heaven, nor indeed can there exist to eternity, two angels or two spirits the same. The same is true in regard to every object of sight in both worlds, as well in the natural as in the spiritual: hence it may appear that the variety is infinite and eternal. *An image of what is infinite and eternal in the fructification and multiplication of all things*, is evident from the faculty which is inherent in seeds in the vegetable kingdom, and in prolification in the animal kingdom, especially in the spawn of fishes, which is such, that, if they were to fructify and multiply according to it, they would in an age fill the spaces of the whole world, and even of the universe; from which consideration it is evident, that, in

32

that faculty there lies concealed an effort to propagate itself to infinity : and as fructifications and multiplications have not failed from the beginning of creation, and will never fail to eternity, it follows that in that faculty there is also an effort to propagate itself to eternity.

57. It is the same in men as to their affections which are of love, and their perceptions which are of wisdom ; the variety f both these is infinite and eternal ; in like manner their fructifications and multiplications, which are spiritual. No man possesses affection and perception so like another as to be the same, nor is it possible to eternity. Moreover, affections can be fructified and perceptions multiplied without end. That sciences can never be exhausted, is well known. This faculty of fructification and multiplication without end, or to infinity and eternity, exists in things natural with men, in things spiritual with spiritual angels, and in things celestial with celestial angels. Affections, perceptions, and knowledges, are such not only in general, but also in every particular, even the least constituent thing. They are such, because they exist from what is infinite and eternal in itself, by what is infinite and eternal from itself. But since what is finite has not any thing of the divine in itself, therefore there is not any thing divine, not even the least, in a man or an angel as his own : for a man or an angel is finite, and merely a receptacle, which in itself is dead ; his living principle being from the proceeding Divine, which is joined to him by contiguity, and which appears to him as his own. That this is the case, will be seen in what follows.

58. The reason why the Divine Providence respects what is infinite and eternal from itself, especially in saving the human race, is, because the end of the Divine Providence is to form a heaven out of the human race, as was shown above, n. 37—45 ; and this being the end, it follows, that it is the reformation and regeneration of man, therefore his salvation, which the Divine Providence particularly regards, since heaven exists from those who are saved or regenerated. And as to regenerate a man is to unite in him good and truth, or love and wisdom, as they are united in the Divine which proceeds from the Lord, therefore the Divine Providence especially regards this in saving the human race ; the image of what is infinite and eternal not existing in a man, except in the marriage of good and truth. That the proceeding Divine effects this in the human race is known from those who, being filled with the proceeding Divine, which is called the Holy Spirit, have prophesied, of whom mention is made in the Word ; and from those who, being illuminated, see divine truths in the light of heaven ; and it is especially in the angels, who sensibly perceive the presence, influx, and conjunction thereof ; yet they perceive also, that such conjunction is no other than what may be called adjunction.

33

59. Although not heretofore known, the Divine Providence, in all its proceedings with a man, has respect to his eternal state; for it cannot regard any thing else, because the Divine is infinite and eternal, and the infinite and eternal, or the Divine, is not in time, consequently things future are present to it; and as the Divine is such, it follows, that in all and every thing which it effects, there is respect to eternity. Those, however, who think from time and space, perceive this with difficulty, not ily because they love temporal things, but because they think from what is present in the world, and not from what is present in heaven, the latter being as absent from them as the end of the earth. But those who are in the Divine, when they think from the present, think also from what is eternal, because they think from the Lord, saying with themselves, What is that which is not eternal? is not what is temporal comparatively as nothing, and does it not also become nothing when it is ended? Not so what is eternal, which alone is, because its being has no end. To think thus, is, while thinking from the present, to think at the same time from what is eternal; and when a man so thinks, and also lives accordingly, then the proceeding Divine in him, or the Divine Providence, in all its progress, respects the state of his eternal life in heaven, and leads him to it. That the Divine in every man, as well evil as good, regards what is eternal, will be seen in what follows.

60. IV. *That an image of what is infinite and eternal exists in the angelic heaven.* Among the things necessary to be known, is also the angelic heaven; for every one who has any religion thinks of heaven, and wishes to go thither; but heaven is not granted to any but those who know the way to it and walk therein. This way likewise may in some measure be known from a knowledge of the nature and quality of those who constitute heaven, and that no one becomes an angel or goes to heaven but he who takes with him the angelic principle out of the world, in which angelic principle there is a knowledge of the way derived from walking in it, and a walking in the way through a knowledge of it. In the spiritual world also there are actually ways, which extend towards every society of heaven, and towards every society of hell; and every one sees his way as from himself. The reason of this is, that there are ways there for every love, each opening that which leads to its associates; and no one sees any other ways than those of his own love. From this consideration it is evident, that angels are no other than celestial loves, for otherwise they would not have seen the ways leading to heaven. But this may appear more clear from a description of heaven.

61. Every spirit of a man is affection and thought thence derived; and as every affection is of love, and thought is of the understanding, every spirit is his own love and his own under-

34

standing ; which is the reason that when a man thinks only from his spirit, as he does when he meditates at home with himself, he thinks from the affection which is of his love. Hence it may appear, that when a man becomes a spirit, which is the case after death, he is the affection of his love, and no other thought but what is of his affection. He is an evil affection, which is cupidity, if he has been principled in the love of evil ; and a good affection, if he has been principled in the love of good ; and every one has a good affection in proportion as he has shunned evils as sins, or an evil affection, in proportion as he has not so shunned them. Now as all spirits and angels are affections, it is evident that the universal angelic heaven is nothing but the love of all the affections of good, and thence the wisdom of all the perceptions of truth. As, likewise, all good and truth is from the Lord, and the Lord is love itself and wisdom itself, it follows, that the angelic heaven is an image of him ; and as the Divine Love and the Divine Wisdom is in its form a man, it also follows, that the angelic heaven cannot be otherwise than in such a form. But more will be said of this in the following article.

62. The reason why the angelic heaven is an image of what is infinite and eternal, is, because it is an image of the Lord, who is infinite and eternal. The image of his infinity and eternity appears in this, that there are myriads of myriads of angels, of which heaven consists ; that they constitute as many societies as there are general affections of celestial love, and that each angel in every society is distinctly his own affection ; that from so many affections in general and in particular exists the form of heaven, which is as one before the Lord, just as a man is one ; and that this form is made more and more perfect to eternity, according to the increase of members, the union becoming more perfect in proportion as more enter the form of the divine love, which is the form of forms. From these considerations it is manifest, that an image of what is infinite and eternal is apparent in the angelic heaven.

63. From the knowledge of heaven afforded by this short description, it is evident, that affection, which is of the love of good, constitutes heaven in a man : but who knows this at the present day ? Who, indeed, knows what the affection of the love of good is, or that the affections of the love of good are innumerable, and even infinite ? For, as before observed, every angel is distinctly his own affection, and the form of heaven is the form of all the affections of the divine love there. No one can unite all these affections into that form, but he who is love itself and at the same time wisdom itself, and at once infinite and eternal ; for in all the form there is something of infinite and eternal ; it is infinite in its conjunction, and eternal in its perpetuity. If what is infinite and eternal were taken away from it, it would instantly fall in pieces. Who else can unite affections into

35   D

form,—who else, indeed, can unite one constituent thereof? for one constituent thereof cannot be united except from the universal idea of all, nor the universal idea of all, except from the particular idea of each. There are myriads of myriads who compose that form, and there are myriads who enter it every year, and will do so to eternity. All infants enter it, and as many adults as are affections of the love of good. From these considerations again may be seen an image of what is infinite and eternal in the angelic heaven.

64. V. *That to respect what is infinite and eternal in forming the angelic heaven, that it may be before the Lord as one man, the image of himself, is the inmost end or purpose of the Divine Providence.* That the universal heaven is as one man before the Lord, and in like manner every society in heaven; that in consequence every angel is in a perfect human form, and that this is the case because God the Creator, who is the Lord from eternity, is a man, may be seen in the work on Heaven and Hell, n. 59—86. Also, that hence there is a correspondence of all things of heaven with all things of man, n. 87—102. That the universal heaven is as one man, has not been seen by me, because the universal heaven cannot be seen by any but the Lord only; but that an entire society of heaven, greater or less, appears as one man, has sometimes been seen; and then it was told me, that the greatest society, which is heaven in its whole complex, appears in like manner, but before the Lord only; and that this is the reason why every angel is in all the particulars of his form a man.

65. As the universal heaven is in the sight of the Lord as one man, therefore heaven is distinguished into as many general societies as there are organs, viscera, and members in a man; and each general society into as many less general or particular societies as there are larger parts in each viscus or organ. From this it is evident what heaven is. Now as the Lord is perfect man, and heaven is the image of him, therefore being in heaven is called being in the Lord. That the Lord is perfect man may be seen in the treatise on the Divine Love and the Divine Wisdom, n. 11—13, and n. 285—289.

66. From these considerations, this arcanum, which may be called angelic, can in some measure be seen,—that every affection of good, and at the same time of truth, in its form is a man; for whatever proceeds from the Lord, derives from his divine love its being an affection of good, and from his divine wisdom its being an affection of truth. The affection of truth, which proceeds from the Lord, appears as perception, and thence thought of truth, in an angel and a man; because perception and thought are attended to, while the affection from which they proceed is but little observed, notwithstanding it proceeds from the Lord with the affection of truth as one.

36

67. Now as a man by creation is a heaven in its least form, and thence an image of the Lord ; and as heaven consists of as many affections as there are angels, and every affection in its form is a man, it follows, that it is the continual design of the Divine Providence, that a man should be made a heaven in form, and thence an image of the Lord : and this, being done by the affection of good and truth, that a man should be made that affection. But although this is the continual design of the Divine Providence, its inmost end or purpose is, that a man should be in a particular society in heaven, or in a certain part in the divine celestial man, for thus he is in the Lord. This is effected with those whom the Lord can lead to heaven ; and since he foresees this, he also continually provides that a man should be brought into a state to be led ; for every one who suffers himself to be led to heaven is prepared for his place in heaven.

68. Heaven, as was said above, is divided into as many societies as there are organs, viscera, and members in a man ; and in these, no one part can have any other place than its own : since, therefore, angels are such parts in the divine celestial man, and none are made angels but such as have been men in the world, it follows, that the man who suffers himself to be led to heaven is continually prepared by the Lord for his particular place, which is done by such an affection of good and truth as corresponds to it : and into this his proper place every man-angel is enrolled after his departure out of the world. This is the inmost purpose of the Divine Providence concerning heaven.

69. But the man who does not suffer himself to be led to and enrolled in heaven, is prepared for his place in hell ; for a man from himself continually tends to the lowest hell, but is continually withheld by the Lord ; and he who cannot be withheld is prepared for a certain place there, in which he is also enrolled immediately after his departure out of the world. This place is opposite to a certain place in heaven, for hell is in opposition to heaven ; therefore, as a man-angel, according to the affection of good and truth, has his place assigned him in heaven, so a man-devil according to the affection of evil and falsity, has his place assigned him in hell ; for two opposites, disposed in a similar situation against each other, are held in connection. This is the inmost purpose of the Divine Providence concerning hell.

THAT THERE ARE LAWS OF THE DIVINE PROVIDENCE WHICH ARE UNKNOWN TO MEN.

70. That there is a Divine Providence, is known ; but what the nature of it is, is not known. The reason why the nature of the Divine Providence is not known, is, that its laws are secret,

hitherto hid in wisdom among the angels. But they are now to be revealed, in order that what belongs to the Lord may be ascribed to him, and that a man may not have ascribed to him that which is not his : for most people in the world attribute all things to themselves, and to their own prudence ; or what they cannot so attribute, they call accidents and contingencies; not knowing that human prudence is nothing, and that accidents and contingencies are vain words. It is said that the laws of the Divine Providence are arcana, hitherto hid in wisdom among the angels ; the reason of which is, that in the Christian world the understanding in things divine is closed by religion, and it is thence become so dull and resisting in regard to such subjects, that a man cannot, because he will not, or will not because he cannot, understand any thing more of the Divine Providence than merely that it exists, or to reason whether it does exist or not, and likewise whether it is universal only, or also particular. The understanding, closed up by religion, could proceed no further in things divine. But as it is acknowledged in the church, that a man cannot from himself do good which in itself is really good, or from himself think truth which in itself is really truth ; and these are one with the Divine Providence, so that a belief in one depends upon a belief in the other ; therefore, lest one should be affirmed and the other denied, and so both fall to the ground, the nature of the Divine Providence is to be fully revealed. This however cannot be done, unless the laws be disclosed by which the Lord provides and governs what relates to the will and understanding of man : for these laws enable a man to know the nature and quality of Providence, and he, and only he, who knows its nature and quality, can acknowledge it, for in such case he sees it. This is the reason why the laws of the Divine Providence, hitherto hid in wisdom among the angels, are now revealed.

THAT IT IS A LAW OF THE DIVINE PROVIDENCE, THAT A MAN SHOULD ACT FROM LIBERTY ACCORDING TO REASON.

71. That a man has the liberty of thinking and willing as he pleases, but not the liberty of speaking whatsoever he thinks, or of doing whatsoever he wills, is well known. The liberty, therefore, which is here understood, is spiritual, and not natural liberty, except when they make one ; for to think and to will is spiritual, but to speak and to act is natural. They are also manifestly distinguished in a man ; for he can think what he does not speak, and will what he does not perform ; from which it is evident, that what is spiritual and what is natural in him are

distinguished from each other, so that he cannot pass from one to the other, but by a determination to do so. This determination may be compared to a door, which is first to be shut and opened; the door stands as it were open in those who think and will from reason, according to the civil laws of the kingdom and the moral laws of society, for they speak what they think, and do what they will; but it stands as it were shut in those who think and will contrary to those laws. He who attends to what he wills and to his consequent acts, will perceive that such a determination occurs, sometimes even several times in one discourse and in one action. This is premised, in order that it may be known, that by acting from liberty according to reason, is meant to think and will freely, and thence to speak and do freely, that which is according to reason.

72. But as there are few who know, that this can be a law of the Divine Providence, on this account especially, that a man has hereby also the liberty of thinking what is evil and false, and yet the Divine Providence continually leads a man to think and will what is good and true,—therefore, for the clearer perception of it, we shall proceed distinctly, and according to the following order: I. That a man has reason and free-will, or rationality and liberty; and that these two faculties are from the Lord in him. II. That whatever a man does from liberty, whether it be of reason or not, provided it be according to his reason, appears to him as his own act. III. That whatever a man does from liberty, according to his thought, is appropriated to him as his own, and remains. IV. That a man by these two faculties is reformed and regenerated of the Lord; and that without them he could not be reformed and regenerated. V. That a man by means of these two faculties can be reformed and regenerated, so far as he can be led by them to acknowledge, that all the truth and good which he does and thinks is from the Lord, and not from himself. VI. That the conjunction of the Lord with a man, and the reciprocal conjunction of a man with the Lord, is effected by these two faculties. VII. That the Lord preserves these two faculties in a man inviolable, and as sacred, in every proceeding of his Divine Providence. VIII. That therefore it is of the Divine Providence, that a man should act from liberty according to reason.

73. I. *That a man has reason and free-will, or rationality and liberty; and that these two faculties are from the Lord in him.* That a man has the faculty of understanding, which is rationality, and the faculty of thinking, willing, speaking, and doing that which he understands, which is liberty; and that these two faculties are from the Lord in him, was discussed in the treatise on THE DIVINE LOVE AND THE DIVINE WISDOM, n. 264—270, 425; and also above. But as several doubts may occur respecting both these faculties, when they are thought of, I am

39

desirous in this preliminary part to add a few observations concerning the liberty of acting according to reason in a man. It is first, however, to be observed, that all liberty is of love, insomuch that love and liberty are one; and since love is the life of a man, liberty also is of his life; for every delight enjoyed by a man is from his love, no delight being afforded from any other source; and to act from the delight of love is to act from liberty, for delight leads a man as a river does that which is borne away by its stream. Now as there are several kinds of love, some in agreement, and others contrary, it follows, that in like manner there are several kinds of liberty. They may however be reduced in general to three kinds,—natural, rational, and spiritual. Every man, by virtue of the hereditary principle received at his birth, has NATURAL LIBERTY; under the influence of which he loves nothing but himself and the world: his first life is nothing else; and as all evils exist from these two kinds of love, and thence also become objects of love, it follows, that to think and will evils is his natural liberty; and that when he has confirmed them in himself by reasonings, he does them from liberty according to his reason. When a man thus acts it is by virtue of the faculty called liberty; and when he thus confirms evils, it is by virtue of the faculty called rationality. For example: it is by virtue of the love in which a man is born, that he has the will to commit adultery, frauds, blasphemy, and revenge; and when he confirms these evils in himself, and thereby makes them lawful, he then, from the delight of the love of them, thinks and wills them freely as according to reason, and, so far as civil laws do not restrain, speaks of and does them. It is from the Divine Providence of the Lord, that a man is allowed so to do, because he has free-will or liberty. A man is in this liberty by nature, because by birth; and those are in this liberty who have confirmed it in themselves by reasonings from the delight of the love of self and of the world. RATIONAL LIBERTY is grounded in the love of fame for the sake of honor or interest. The delight of this love is to appear externally as a moral character. As a man loves this reputation, he does not defraud, or commit adultery, or indulge in a spirit of revenge or blasphemy; and as, by his reason, he confirms himself in abstinence from such crimes, he also from liberty, according to his reason, acts sincerely, justly, chastely, and friendly; indeed, from reason he can speak well in favor of such virtues. But if his rational faculty is only natural, and not at the same time spiritual, this liberty is only external and not internal liberty, for nevertheless he does not interiorly love those virtues, but only exteriorly, as before remarked, for the sake of reputation; and therefore the good actions which he does are in themselves not good. He can say also, that they ought to be done for the sake of the public good; but this he does not say from any love of the public good, but from the love of his own honor or interest; consequently, his liberty derives nothing from the love of the public good, neither does his reason, for it complies with his love. This rational liberty therefore is interior natural liberty; and, from the Divine Providence of the Lord, this liberty also is left to every one. SPIRITUAL LIBERTY is grounded in the love of eternal life. Into this love and its delight no one comes, but he who thinks that evils are sins, therefore does not will them, and at the same time looks to the Lord. As soon as a man does this, he is in that liberty; for no one has power not to will evils because they are sins, and therefore not to do them, but from an interior or superior liberty, which is from his interior or superior love. This liberty does not at first appear as liberty, but yet it is so; and afterwards it appears to be so, when a man acts from real liberty according to real reason, by thinking, willing, speaking, and doing what is good and true. This liberty increases, as natural liberty decreases and becomes subservient; and it joins itself with rational liberty, which it purifies. Every one may come into spiritual liberty, provided he be willing to think that there is an eternal life, and that the delight and blessedness of life in time for a time, is only as a transient shadow, compared with the delight and blessedness of life in eternity to eternity; and this a man may think if he chooses, because he possesses rationality and liberty, and because the Lord, from whom these two faculties are derived, continually gives him the power.

74. II. *That whatever a man does from liberty, whether it be of reason or not, provided it be according to his reason, appears to him as his own act.* What the rationality is, and what the liberty, which are proper to a man, cannot be known more clearly, than by a comparison of men with beasts; for the latter have not any rationality or faculty of understanding, or any liberty or faculty of willing freely, and thence have no understanding and will; but instead of understanding they have science, and instead of will, affection, both of which are natural: and as they have not those two faculties, therefore they have no thought, but instead of thought internal sight, which makes one with their external sight by correspondence. Every affection has its companion as a consort; the affection of natural love having science, the affection of spiritual love, intelligence, and the affection of celestial love, wisdom. For affection without its companion, or what may be called its connubial partner, is nothing; for it is like *esse* without *existere*, or like a substance without a form, of which nothing can be predicated. Hence it is, that in every created thing there is something which may be referred to the marriage of good and truth, as was abundantly shown above. In beasts there is a marriage of affection and science; the affection being that of natural good, and the science that of natural truth. Now as affection and science in beasts act entirely as

41

one, and their affection cannot be elevated above thei science, nor their science above their affection, and if they are elevated, they are elevated both together; and as they have no spiritual mind, to which or into the light and heat of which they can be elevated; therefore they have not the faculty of understanding or rationality, or the faculty of free-will or liberty, but only mere natural affection, with its science. Their natural affection is that of feeding themselves, of providing a habitation, of propagating their kind, and of shunning and flying from harm, with all the requisite science or knowledge; and such being their state of life, they cannot think within themselves, " I will do this, and will not do that," or, " I know, or do not know, such a thing," still less, " I understand such a thing, or I love such a thing;" but they are carried away of their particular affection by science, without rationality and liberty. The cause of their being so carried away is not from the natural, but from the spiritual world; for nothing exists in the natural world unconnected with the spiritual world, from which is every cause producing an effect. Something on this subject may be also seen below, n. 96.

75. It is otherwise with a man, who has not only the affection of natural love, but also the affection of spiritual love, and that of celestial love; for the human mind consists of three degrees, as was shown in the treatise concerning THE DIVINE LOVE AND THE DIVINE WISDOM, Part III.: a man can therefore be elevated from natural science into spiritual intelligence, and thence into celestial wisdom : and from intelligence and wisdom he can look up to the Lord, and thus be joined unto him, whereby he lives to eternity. But this elevation as to affection would not be possible, if he had not the faculty of elevating his understanding from rationality, and that of willing to do so from liberty. A man by these two faculties can think within himself concerning the things which with his bodily senses he perceives without himself, and can also think in a superior sphere concerning the things which he thinks of in an inferior sphere : for every one can say, " I thought this," or " I think this," also, " I willed this, and I will this," and likewise, " I understand this that it is so, I love this because it is such," and so on. Hence it is evident, that a man thinks as it were above his thought, which he sees as if it were below him. This power he derives from rationality and liberty,—from rationality in respect that he can think in a superior sphere, and from liberty in respect that from affection he wills so to think; for if he had not the liberty of so thinking, he would not have the will, or consequently the thought. Wherefore those who will not understand any thing but what is of the world and its nature, or what is moral and spiritual good and truth, cannot be elevated from knowledge or science into intelligence, and still less into

42

wisdom ; for they have obstructed those faculties ; and therefore they cause themselves to be men in no other respect than that from their inherent rationality and liberty they can understand if they will, and also that they have the power to will. From these two faculties a man has the power to think, and from thought to speak ; in other faculties men are but beasts, and often indeed from the abuse of these faculties become worse than beasts.

76. Every one from rationality not obscured may see or comprehend that a man, without an appearance that it is his own, cannot be in any affection of knowing, or in any affection of understanding ; for all delight and pleasure, therefore every thing of the will, is from the affection which is of love. Who can will to know and will to understand, unless he has some pleasure of affection ? And who can have the pleasure of affection, unless that by which he is affected appears as his own ? If it were none of his, but all of another's, that is, if a person from his own affections should infuse any thing into the mind of another, who had no affections of knowing and understanding as from himself, would the other receive it ? would he indeed be able to receive it ? would he not be as that which is called brute, or as a stock ? Hence it may plainly appear, that although every thing which a man perceives and thence thinks and knows, and according to perception wills and does, enters by influx, still it is of the Divine Providence of the Lord, that it should appear as the man's ; for otherwise, as before observed, he would receive nothing, therefore could not be gifted with any intelligence and wisdom. It is well known, that no good and truth is a man's, but all the Lord's, and yet that it appears to a man as his own ; and as all good and truth so appears, therefore all things also of the church and of heaven, consequently all things of love and wisdom, and of charity and faith, so appear ; and yet none of them is his. No one can receive them from the Lord, unless it appears to him that he perceives them as from himself. From these considerations this truth may be manifest, that whatsoever a man does from liberty, whether it be of reason or not of reason, provided it be according to his reason, appears to him as his own.

77. Who is not able to understand, by virtue of the faculty which is called rationality, that this or that good is useful to the community, and that this or that evil is noxious to the community ; as that justice, sincerity, and conjugal chastity, are beneficial to the community, and that injustice, insincerity, and whoredom committed with the wives of others, are injurious to the community ; consequently that these evils are in themselves mischievous, and that those various kinds of good are in themselves beneficial ? Who therefore, if he be so disposed, cannot make those species of good and evil the good and evil of his

43

reason, since he has both rationality and liberty ? His rationality and liberty also disclose themselves, appear, govern, and enable him to perceive and to have power, in proportion as, for the above reasons, he shuns those evils in himself; and in the same proportion as he does this, he respects those kinds of good, as a friend does his friends. From these circumstances it is in a man's power afterwards, by virtue of the faculty which is called rationality, to form conclusions respecting the various kinds of good which are useful to the community in the spiritual world, and respecting the various kinds of evil which are noxious there, provided that he perceives the different kinds of evils to be sins, and considers the different kinds of good to be works of charity. These conclusions, also, a man may make the conclusions of his reason, if he chooses, because he has rationality and liberty; and his rationality and liberty disclose themselves, appear, govern, and enable him to perceive and to possess power, in proportion as he shuns those evils as sins; and in proportion as he does this, he respects the good as charity, as one neighbour respects another mutually from love. Now as the Lord, for the sake of reception and conjunction, wills, that whatsoever a man does freely according to reason may appear to him as his own, and this is according to reason itself, it follows, that a man can, by virtue of reason, because it is for his eternal felicity, be willing to shun the above evils as sins, and, by imploring the divine power of the Lord, can effect what he wills.

78. III. *That whatever a man does from liberty according to his thought, is appropriated to him as his own, and remains.* The reason is, because the *proprium* of a man and his liberty make one. The *proprium* of a man is of his life, and what he does from his life, he does from liberty. Moreover, the *proprium* of a man is that which is of his love: for love is the life of every one, and what a man does from his life's love, he does from liberty. The reason why a man acts from liberty according to his thought is, that whatever is of the life or of the love of any one, is also the object of thought, and is by thought confirmed, and when it is confirmed, then he does it from liberty according to his thought. For whatsoever a man does, he does from the will by the understanding; and liberty is of the will, and thought is of the understanding. A man can also act from liberty contrary to reason; and again, not from liberty according to reason; but such acts are not appropriated to him, being only the acts of his lips and of his body, and not of his spirit and of his heart; yet the acts which are of his spirit and of his heart, when they are also made the acts of his lips and of his body, are appropriated to him: that this is the case might be illustrated by many considerations, but this is not the proper place for it. By being appropriated to a man is meant to enter into his life, and to be made of his ife, consequently to be made his *proprium*

44

That a man, however, has not any thing which is proper to himself, but that it appears to him as if it were so, will be seen in what follows. We shall here only observe, that all the good which a man does from liberty according to reason, is appropriated to him as his own, because, in thinking, willing, speaking, and acting, it appears to him as his own; nevertheless, good is not of a man, but is of the Lord in him, as may be seen above, n. 76. But how evil is appropriated to a man will be seen in its proper article.

79. It is also said, that whatever a man does from liberty according to his reason remains; for no one thing which a man has appropriated to himself can be eradicated, because it is made an object of his love and at the same time of his reason, or of his will and at the same time of his understanding, and thence of his life. It may be removed indeed, but not cast out; and when it is removed, it is transferred as it were from the centre to the circumference, and there abides. This is meant by its remaining. For example: if a man in his childhood and youth has appropriated to himself a certain evil by doing it from the delight of his love,—as, if he has defrauded, blasphemed, revenged, committed whoredom,—then as he has done these things from liberty according to his thought, he has also appropriated them to himself; but if he afterwards repents, shuns them, and considers them as sins which are to be abhorred, and thus from liberty according to reason desists from them, then there are appropriated to him the good principles to which those evils are opposite. These good principles then constitute the centre, and remove the evils towards the circumference further and further according to his aversion and abhorrence of them; but still they cannot be so cast out as to be said to be extirpated, although by such removal they may appear as if extirpated; which is effected by a man's being detained from evil and held in good by the Lord. This is the case with respect to all hereditary evil, and at the same time all actual evil of a man. I have also seen it proved by experience with some in heaven, who, because they were kept in good by the Lord, thought themselves to be without evils; but to prevent their thinking that the good in which they were was their own, they were let down from heaven and into their evils, till they acknowledged that they were in evils from themselves, but in good from the Lord; after which acknowledgment they were carried back into heaven. Let it be known therefore, that these good principles are no otherwise appropriated to a man, than as they are constantly of the Lord in him; and that in proportion as a man acknowledges this, the Lord grants that good may appear to him as his own, that is, that a man may appear to himself to love his neighbour or to have charity as from himself, to believe or to have faith as from himself, to do

45

good and to understand truth, and therefore to be wise as from himself; from which considerations every enlightened person may see, what and how strong is the appearance in which the Lord wills that a man should be; and the Lord wills this for the sake of his salvation, for no one without that appearance can be saved. On this subject, see also what is shown above, n. 42—45.

80. Nothing is appropriated to a man which he only thinks, nor yet that which he thinks to will, except he at the same time wills it to such a degree, that when opportunity is given he does it; and the reason is, that when a man does it from this ground, he does it from the will by the understanding, or from the affection of the will by the thought of the understanding. So long, however, as any thing is an object of the thought only, it cannot be appropriated, because the understanding does not join itself with the will, nor the thought of the understanding with the affection of the will; but the will and its affection join themselves with the understanding and its thought, as is shown abundantly in the treatise on THE DIVINE LOVE AND THE DIVINE WISDOM, Part the Fifth. This is meant by these words of the Lord: "Not that which goeth into the mouth defileth a man, but that which cometh out of the heart through the mouth, that defileth a man" (Matt. xv. 11, 17, 18, 19). By the mouth in a spiritual sense is meant the thought, because the thought speaks by the mouth; and by the heart in that sense is meant the affection which is of love. If a man thinks and speaks from this affection, then he defiles himself. By the heart also is signified the affection which is of love or of will, and by the mouth, the thought which is of the understanding, in Luke vi. 45.

81. The evils which a man thinks allowable, although he does them not, are also appropriated to him; allowableness in thought being from the will, for it is consent; therefore, when a man thinks any evil allowable, he loosens the internal restraint, respecting it, and is kept from doing it only by external restraints, which are fears; and because the spirit of the man favours such evil, therefore, when external restraints are removed, he does it freely; and in the mean time continually does it in his spirit. But on this subject see THE DOCTRINE OF LIFE FOR THE NEW JERUSALEM, n. 108—113.

82. IV. *That a man by these two faculties is reformed and regenerated by the Lord; and that without them he could not be reformed and regenerated.* The Lord teaches that unless a man be born again, he cannot see the kingdom of God, John iii. 3, 5, 7; but what it is to be born again, or to be regenerate, is known to few. The reason of this is, that it has not been known what love and charity are, nor therefore what faith is; for he who does not know what love and charity are, cannot

know what faith is; because charity and faith make one, like good and truth, and like affection which is of the will and thought which is of the understanding; concerning which union, see the treatise on THE DIVINE LOVE AND THE DIVINE WISDOM, n. 427—431, and THE DOCTRINE OF THE NEW JERUSALEM, n. 13—24; also see above, n. 3—20.

83. The reason why no man can enter into the kingdom of God unless he be born again, is, that a man hereditarily from his parents is born into evils of every kind, with the faculty of being made spiritual by the removal of those evils; and unless he be made spiritual, he cannot enter into heaven. To be made spiritual from natural, is to be born again, or to be regenerated. But in order that it may be known how a man is regenerated, these three things are to be considered: what his first state is, which is a state of damnation; what his second state is, which is a state of reformation; and what his third state is, which is a state of regeneration. *The first state of a man, which is a state of damnation*, every man has hereditarily from his parents, for he is thence born into the love of self and the love of the world, and into evils of every description from these two kinds of love as fountains. The delights of these kinds of love are the delights by which he is led, and these delights prevent him from knowing that he is in evils; for every delight of love is felt no otherwise than as good; and therefore also a man, unless he is regenerated, knows no other than that to love himself and the world above all things is essential good, and that to domineer over all, and possess the wealth of all others, is the supreme good. This is the source of all evil; for he regards no other person from a principle of love but himself alone; or if he regards another from a principle of love, it is as one devil regards another, or as one thief another, when they act as one. Those who confirm in themselves these kinds of love, and the evils flowing from them, from the delight thereof, remain natural and become sensual-corporeal; and in their own thought, which is that of their spirit, they are insane; but still, while they are in the world, they can speak and act rationally and wisely, being as men possessed of rationality and liberty; yet this also they do from a love of self and of the world. Such men after death, when they become spirits, cannot have any other delight than what they had in their spirits in the world, and that is the delight of infernal love, which is turned into what is unpleasant, dolorous, and direful, signified in the Word by torment and hell-fire. Hence it is evident that the first state of a man is a state of damnation; and that those are in it who do not suffer themselves to be regenerated. *The second state of a man, which is a state of reformation*, is, when a man begins to think of heaven from the joy that is therein, and thus to think of God, from whom he has the joy of heaven. At first, however, he thinks thus from

47

the delight of the love of self, heavenly joy being to him that delight; and so long as the delight of that love reigns, together with the delights of the evils flowing therefrom, he cannot understand otherwise than that to go to heaven is to pour out prayers, to hear preachings, to receive the Lord's supper, to give to the poor, to help the needy, to endow churches and hospitals, and such like things. Nor does a man in this state know otherwise than that barely to think the things that religion teaches effects salvation, whether it be that which is called faith, or that which is called faith and charity. The reason why he understands no other than that to think these things effects salvation, is, because he thinks nothing of the evils in the delights of which he is, and so long as their delights remain, the evils also remain; for their delights arise from the concupiscence of them, which continually inspires them and also produces them, when no fear operates to prevent it. So long as evils remain in the concupiscences, and thence in the delights of the love of them, there is neither any faith, charity, piety, nor worship, except only in externals; which appear before the world as if they were real, but yet are not. They may therefore be compared to waters flowing from an impure fountain, which cannot be drunk. So long as a man is such that he thinks of heaven and of God from religion, and nothing of evils as sins, he is still in his first state: but he comes into the second, or state of reformation, when he begins to think that there is such a thing as sin, and still more when he thinks that this or that is a sin, and when he explores it a little in himself, and does not will it. *The third state of a man, which is a state of regeneration,* takes up and continues the prior state; it begins when a man desists from evils as sins, proceeds as he shuns them, and is perfected as he fights against them; and then as he overcomes from the Lord he is regenerated. With the regenerate man the order of life is changed, and from natural he is made spiritual; for the natural principle separate from the spiritual is contrary to order, and the spiritual principle is according to order; therefore a regenerate man acts from charity, and makes what belongs to his faith conformable to his charity. But still he is only made spiritual in proportion as he is in truths; because every man is regenerated by truths, and a life according to them; for by truths he knows life, and by life he performs truths: he thus conjoins goodness and truth, which is the spiritual marriage, in which is heaven.

85. The reason why a man is reformed and regenerated by those two faculties which are called rationality and liberty, and that without them he cannot be reformed and regenerated, is, because by rationality he can understand and know what is evil and what is good, and thence what is false and what is true; and by liberty he can will that which he understands and

knows. But so long as the delight of the love of evil reigns, he cannot freely will what is good and true, and make them principles of his reason, therefore he cannot appropriate them to himself; for, as was shown above, the things which a man does from liberty according to reason, are appropriated to him as his own, and unless they are appropriated as his own, he is not reformed and regenerated. Then also he first acts from the delight of the love of goodness and truth, when the delight of the love of evil and false is removed; for two kinds of delight of love which are opposite to each other cannot exist at the same time. To act from the delight of love, is to act from liberty; and when reason favors the love, it is also to act according to reason.

86. Since a man, as well he who is wicked as he who is good, has rationality and liberty, so a wicked as well as a good man can understand truth and do good: but a wicked man cannot do so from liberty according to reason, whereas a good man can; because a wicked man is in the delight of the love of evil, and a good man is in the delight of the love of good. The truth therefore which a wicked man understands, and the good which he does, are not appropriated to him; but they are appropriated to a good man; and without appropriation as his own, reformation and regeneration do not take place. For evils with falsities are with the wicked as it were in the centre, and good principles with truths in the circumference; but good principles with truths are in the centre with the good, and evils with falsities in the circumference; and in both cases the things which are of the centre diffuse themselves to the circumference, as heat from fire in the centre, and cold from ice in the centre. Thus good in the circumference with the wicked is defiled by the evils of the centre, and evils in the circumference with the good are rendered mild by the good principles of the centre; and this is the reason why evils do not condemn a regenerate man, and good actions do not save an unregenerate man.

87. V. *That a man, by means of those two faculties, can be reformed and regenerated so far as he can be led by them to acknowledge, that all the truth and good which he thinks and does is from the Lord, and not from himself.* What reformation and regeneration are, was stated above; and also that a man, by the two faculties of rationality and liberty, is reformed and regenerated: and as this is effected by those faculties, it may be expedient to say something more concerning them. A man by virtue of rationality has power to understand, and by virtue of liberty has power to will, both as from himself; but the power of willing good from liberty, and thence of doing it according to reason, no one has but the regenerate. A wicked man can will only evil from liberty, and do it according to his thought, which by confirmations he makes as it were of reason; for evil

can be confirmed as well as good, but it is by fallacies and appearances, which, when they are confirmed, become falsities; and when evil is confirmed, it appears as of reason.

88. Every one, who has any thought from interior understanding, may see, that the power of willing and of understanding is not from a man, but from Him who has power itself, that is, who has power in its essence. Consider only, whence is power? Is it not from him who has it in its essential ground; that is, who has it in himself, and consequently from himself? Power therefore in itself is divine. To all power there will be leave, which is to be given, and thus a determination from what is interior or superior to self. The eye cannot see from itself, nor the ear hear from itself, neither can the mouth speak from itself, nor the hands act from themselves; there must be leave given, and thence determination from the mind. Nor can the mind think and will this or that from itself, unless there be something interior or superior by which it is determined to it. It is the same with the power of understanding and the power of willing; these cannot be given by any other than by Him who in and of himself is able to will and to understand. From such considerations it is evident, that those two faculties, which are called rationality and liberty, are from the Lord, and not from a man; and as they are from the Lord, it follows, that a man wills nothing from himself, and understands nothing from himself, but only as if it were from himself. That this is the case, every one may confirm in himself, who knows and believes that the willing of all good, and the understanding of all truth, is from the Lord, and not from man. That *a man cannot draw any thing from himself, and cannot do any thing from himself*, is taught by the Word in John iii. 27; xv. 5.

89. Now as all volition is from love, and all understanding is from wisdom, it follows, that to be able to will is from the divine love, and to be able to understand is from the divine wisdom, therefore, both from the Lord, who is divine love itself and divine wisdom itself. Hence it follows, that to act from liberty according to reason, is from no other source. Every one acts according to liberty, because liberty, like love, cannot be separated from volition; but in a man there exists an interior volition or interior will, and an exterior volition or exterior will, and he can act according to the exterior, and at the same time not according to the interior; in this case he acts the hypocrite and flatterer; and yet exterior volition is from liberty, because it is from the love of appearing otherwise than he is, or from the love of some evil which he intends from the love of his interior will. But, as was said above, a wicked man cannot from liberty according to reason do any thing but evil, for he cannot from liberty according to reason do good. He can indeed do good, but not from interior liberty, which is his

50

proper liberty, and from which his exterior liberty derives its quality of being not good.

90. It is said that a man can be reformed and regenerated in proportion as he can be led, by the above two faculties, to acknowledge that all the good and all the truth which he thinks and does is from the Lord, and not from himself. The reason why a man cannot acknowledge this but by those two faculties, is because they are from the Lord ; and they are of the Lord in him, as is evident from what was said above; it follows therefore, that a man cannot do this from himself, but from the Lord ; yet still he can do it as if it were from himself: this power the Lord gives to every one. Let it be supposed that he believes from himself; still, when he becomes wise, he will acknowledge that it is not from himself. Otherwise, the truth which he thinks, and the good which he does, are not true and good in themselves ; for the man, and not the Lord, is in them ; and the good in which a man is, if it be for the sake of salvation, is meritorious good ; but the good in which the Lord is, is not meritorious.

91. But that the acknowledgment of the Lord, and the acknowledgment that all good and all truth is from him, cause a man to be reformed and regenerated, is what few persons can see with the understanding ; for it may be thought, of what consequence is such acknowledgment, seeing that the Lord is omnipotent, and wills the salvation of all, and thence can and will effect it, if he be moved to compassion? But to think thus is not from the Lord, nor consequently is it from the interior light of the understanding, that is from any illumination ; therefore what acknowledgment operates, shall be here briefly explained. In the spiritual world, where spaces are appearances only, wisdom produces presence, and love produces conjunction ; and *vice versa.* There is given an acknowledgment of the Lord from wisdom, and there is given an acknowledgment of the Lord from love. The acknowledgment of the Lord from wisdom, which viewed in itself is only a knowledge of him, is given from doctrine ; and the acknowledgment of the Lord from love is given from a life according to doctrine ; the latter giving conjunction, but the former presence. This is the reason why those who reject doctrine concerning the Lord remove themselves from him ; and as they also reject life, they separate themselves from him : whereas those who do not reject doctrine, but life, are present, yet separated. They are like friends who converse together, but do not mutually love each other ; and like two, of which the one speaks with the other as a friend, but hates him as an enemy. That this is the case, is also known from the common idea, that he who teaches well and lives well, is saved, but not he who teaches well and lives ill ; and that he who does not acknowledge God, cannot be saved. From this consi-

deration it is evident, what sort of a religion it is, to think of
the Lord from faith, as it is called, and not to do any thing from
charity. Hence the Lord says, " Why call ye me Lord, Lord,
and do not the things which I say? Whosoever cometh to
me, and heareth my sayings, and doeth them, is like a man
that built a house, and laid the foundation on a rock : but he
that heareth, and doeth not, is like a man that without a foundation built a house upon the earth" (Luke vi. 46—49).

92. VI. *That the conjunction of the Lord with a man, and the
reciprocal conjunction of a man with the Lord, is effected by these
two faculties.* Conjunction with the Lord and regeneration are
one, for in proportion as any one is conjoined to the Lord, he is
regenerate : therefore, all that is said above of regeneration may
be said of conjunction, and what is here said of conjunction may
be said of regeneration. That there is a conjunction of the Lord
with a man, and a reciprocal conjunction of a man with the Lord,
the Lord himself teaches in John : "Abide in me, and I in you.
He that abideth in me, and I in him, the same bringeth forth
much fruit" (xv. 4, 5). "At that day ye shall know, that ye
are in me, and I in you" (xiv. 20). Any one may see from
reason alone, that there is no conjunction of minds unless it be
reciprocal, and that reciprocation conjoins. If one loves another, and is not loved in return, in this case, as the one
approaches the other retires ; but if he is loved in return, then
as one approaches the other approaches also, and conjunction is
effected : for love wills to be beloved ; this is inherent in it ; and
in proportion as it is beloved again, it is in itself and in its
delight. Hence it is evident, that if the Lord only loved a man,
and were not in his turn to be beloved by him, the Lord would
approach and he would retire ; thus the Lord would continually
will to meet the man and to enter in to him, and the man would
turn himself away and depart. With those who are in hell such
is the case, but with those who are in heaven there is a mutual
conjunction. As the Lord wills conjunction with a man for the
sake of his salvation, he provides also that in the man there should
be a reciprocal principle, by which the good which he wills and
does from liberty, and the truth which he thinks and speaks
from his will according to reason, should appear to him as being
from himself ; and that such good in his will and truth in his
understanding should appear as his own. Indeed, they appear
to a man as from himself, and as his own, altogether as if they
were so ; there is no distinction. Consider only whether a man
with any one of his senses perceives otherwise. Of this appearance as if from himself, see above, n. 74—77 ; and of appropriation as his own, n. 78—81 : the only difference is, that a man
ought to acknowledge that he does not do good and think truth
from himself, but from the Lord ; and, consequently, that the
good which he does and the truth which he thinks are not his

52

own. To think thus from some degree of love in the will, because it is the truth, effects conjunction; for thus a man looks to the Lord, and the Lord looks to him.

93. What the difference is between those who believe all good to be from the Lord, and those who believe good to be from themselves, it has been granted me to hear and to see in the spiritual world. Those who believe good to be from the Lord, turn their faces to him, and receive the delight and blessedness of good; but those who believe good to be from themselves, look to themselves, and think that they have deserved it; and as they look to themselves, they cannot but perceive the delight of their own good, which is not the delight of good, but the delight of evil; for a man's selfhood is evil, and the delight of evil perceived as good is hell. Those who have done good, and thought it was from themselves, if they do not after death receive the truth, that all good is from the Lord, mix with infernal genii, and at length act as one with them; whereas, those who receive that truth are reformed. But no others receive it except those who have respected God in their life: and to respect or look up to God in the life, is nothing else but to shun evils as sins.

94. Conjunction of the Lord with a man; and reciprocal conjunction of a man with the Lord, is effected by his loving his neighbour as himself, and loving the Lord above all things. To love his neighbour as himself, is nothing else than not to act insincerely and unjustly with him, not to hate him and burn with revenge against him, not to blaspheme and defame him, not to commit adultery with his wife, and not to do any other such like things against him. Who cannot see that those who do such things, do not love their neighbour as themselves? But those who refrain from such things, because they are evils against their neighbour and at the same time sins against God, deal sincerely, justly, friendly, and faithfully with their neighbour; and as the Lord does in like manner, a reciprocal conjunction is effected. When conjunction is reciprocal, whatsoever a man does to his neighbour, he does from the Lord, and whatsoever he does from the Lord is good; and then his neighbour is not to him the mere person, but good in the person. To love the Lord above all things, is nothing else than not to do evil to the Word, because the Lord is therein; or to do evil to the holy things of the church, because the Lord is therein; or to do evil to the soul of any one, because the soul of every one is in the hand of the Lord. Those who shun these evils as enormous sins, love the Lord above all things; but this none can do except such as love their neighbour as themselves, for love to the Lord and love to the neighbour are in conjunction.

95. Forasmuch as there is a conjunction of the Lord with

man, and of man with the Lord, therefore there are two tables
of the law, one for the Lord and the other for man. In proportion as a man as from himself, obeys the laws of his own
table, in the same proportion. the Lord enables him to obey the
laws of his table. But the man who does not keep the laws of
his own table, all of which relate to the love of his neighbour,
cannot keep the laws of the Lord's table, all of which relate to
the love of the Lord. How can a murderer, a thief, an adulterer, and a false witness, love the Lord? Does not reason
dictate, that to be such, and to love the Lord, is contradictory?
Is not the devil such a one, and can he do otherwise than hate
the Lord? But when a man turns away from murders, adulteries, thefts, and false testimony, as infernal, he can then love
the Lord ; for then he turns his face from the devil to the Lord,
and when he turns his face to the Lord, love and wisdom are
given him,—these principles entering into a man by his face,
and not by the hinder part of his head. As in this and in
no other manner conjunction with the Lord is effected, therefore those two tables are called the covenant, and a covenant
is between two.

96. VII. *That the Lord preserves these two faculties in a man
inviolable, and as sacred, in every proceeding of his Divine Providence.* The reasons are, that a man, without those two faculties,
would not have understanding and will, and, therefore, would
not be a man ; also, that a man, without those two faculties,
could not be conjoined to the Lord, and therefore, could not be
reformed and regenerated ; and further, that, without those two
faculties, he would not have immortality and eternal life.
That this is the case, may indeed be seen from the knowledge
respecting liberty and rationality (which are those two faculties),
which was given in the foregoing pages ; but it cannot be seen
clearly, unless the reasons be presented to the view as conclusions, wherefore it may be expedient to illustrate each. *That a
man, without those two faculties, would not have will and understanding, and, therefore, would not be a man :* for a man has will
from no other source than from the power of willing freely as
from himself; and freely to will, as from himself, is from the
faculty continually given him by the Lord, which is called
liberty ; and a man has understanding from no other source than
from the power as of himself to understand whether a thing be
of reason or not ; and to understand whether it be of reason
or not, is from that other faculty continually given him by
the Lord, which is called rationality. These faculties join themselves together in a man like the will and the understanding ;
for instance, because a man can will, he can also understand,
for volition is not given without understanding,—understanding
being its consort or companion, without which it cannot exist :
wherefore with the faculty which is called liberty, is given the

faculty which is called rationality. Further, if you take away volition from understanding, you understand nothing; and in proportion as you will, in the same proportion you can understand, provided there be at hand and at the same time are opened those assistances which are called knowledges, for these are like instruments in the hands of artificers. It is said that in proportion as you will you can understand, that is, in proportion as you love to understand; for will and love act as one. This indeed appears as a paradox; but it appears so to those only who do not love to understand, and therefore will not, and those who will not, say they cannot. But who they are that cannot understand, and who they that can with difficulty understand, will be shown in the following article. Without confirmation, it is evident, that if a man had not will from the faculty which is called liberty, and understanding from the faculty which is called rationality, he would not be a man. Beasts have not these faculties. It appears as if they could also will, and could understand, but they cannot; it is natural affection, which in itself is desire, with its concomitant science, which alone leads and prompts them to do what they do. There is indeed a civil and moral principle in their science; but they are not above science, because they have no spiritual principle, which enables them to perceive the moral principle, and thence to think it analytically. They can indeed be taught to do any thing; but this is only the natural principle, which adds itself to their science, and at the same time to their affection, and is reproduced either by sight or by hearing, but is never made a principle of thought, and still less of reason in them. Something on this subject may be seen above, n. 74. *That a man without those two faculties could not be conjoined to the Lord, and, therefore, could not be reformed and regenerated*, was shown above; for the Lord resides in those two faculties in men, in the wicked as well as in the good, and by them he joins himself to every man. Hence it is that a wicked man, as well as a good man, can understand, and has in his power the will of good and the understanding of truth; and it is from the abuse of those faculties that they are not in act. That the Lord resides in those faculties in every man, is owing to the influx of the will of the Lord, his desire to be received by a man, to make his abode with him, and to give him the felicities of eternal life. These things are of the will of the Lord, because they are of his divine love. It is this will of the Lord, which causes it to appear in a man that he of himself thinks, speaks, wills, and acts. That the influx of the will of the Lord produces this effect, may be confirmed by many particulars from the spiritual world; for sometimes the Lord fills an angel with his divine principle, so that the angel knows no other than that he is the Lord. In this manner were those angels filled who were seen

55

by Abraham Hagar, and Gideon, and who therefore called themselves Jehovah, as mentioned in the Word. So, also, one spirit can be filled by another, until he does not know but that he is the other, as has often been seen by me. Moreover, it is known in heaven that the Lord effects all things by volition, and that what he wills is done. Hence it is evident, that it is those two faculties by which the Lord conjoins himself to a man, and by which he causes a man to be reciprocally conjoined to him. But how a man by those two faculties is reciprocally conjoined, consequently, how by them he is reformed and regenerated, was mentioned before, and more will be said of it hereafter. *That a man without those two faculties would not have immortality and eternal life*, follows, from what has just been said,—that by them conjunction is effected with the Lord, and also reformation and regeneration. By conjunction a man has immortality, and by reformation and regeneration eternal life. And since by those faculties there is conjunction of the Lord with every man, with the wicked as well as the good, as before stated, therefore every man has immortality; but he alone has eternal life, that is, the life of heaven, in whom there is a reciprocal conjunction from inmost parts to ultimates. Hence may be seen the reasons why the Lord preserves those two faculties in man inviolable, and as sacred, in every proceeding of his Divine Providence.

97. VIII. *That therefore it is of the Divine Providence that a man should act from liberty according to reason.* To act from liberty according to reason, and to act from liberty and rationality, is the same thing, as is also to act from the will and the understanding; but it is one thing to act from liberty according to reason, or from liberty and rationality, and another to act from liberty itself according to reason itself, or from genuine liberty and genuine rationality. For the man who does evil from the love of evil, and confirms it in himself, acts indeed from liberty according to reason, but nevertheless his liberty is in itself not liberty, or not essential liberty, but it is infernal liberty, which is in itself slavery; and his reason is in itself not reason, but it is either spurious or false reason, or reason only appearing such from confirmations. Still, however, both are of the Divine Providence; for if the free power of willing evil, and of making it appear like reason by confirmations, were taken away from the natural man, liberty and rationality would perish, and at the same time the will and the understanding; and it would not be possible for him to be withdrawn from evils and reformed, or consequently to be conjoined to the Lord, and live to eternity. Wherefore the Lord guards liberty in a man, as a man guards the apple of his eye. But still the Lord by liberty continually withdraws a man from evils, and, so far as by liberty he can withdraw him, in the same degree by liberty he implants

goods: thus, successively, in place of infernal liberty he invests him with celestial liberty.

98. It was said above, that every man has a faculty of willing which is called liberty, and a faculty of understanding which is called rationality: it is, however, well to be observed, that these faculties are as it were inherent in a man, for the essential human principle resides in them; but, as before observed, it is one thing to act from liberty according to reason, and another to act from essential liberty according to essential reason. None act from essential liberty according to essential reason but those who have suffered themselves to be regenerated by the Lord: all others act from liberty according to their thought, which they make like reason. Nevertheless, every man, unless he be born an idiot or extremely stupid, may attain to essential reason, and thereby to essential liberty. The causes why he does not attain thereto are several, as will be seen in what follows. We shall here only point out to whom essential freedom or essential liberty, and, at the same time, essential reason or essential rationality, cannot be given, and to whom they are given with difficulty. Essential liberty and rationality cannot be given to those who are born idiots; or to those who afterwards become idiots, so long as they remain such. Essential liberty and rationality cannot be given to such as are born stupid and silly, or to some who become such from the torpor of idleness, or from sickness, which perverts or entirely closes the interiors of the mind, or from the love of a beastly life. Neither can essential liberty and rationality be given to those in the Christian world, who altogether deny the Lord's divinity and the sanctity of the Word, and have kept this denial confirmed in themselves to the end of life; for this is understood by the sin against the Holy Ghost, which is not forgiven in this world, or in that which is to come. Matt. xii. 31, 32. Neither can essential liberty and rationality be given in those who attribute all things to nature, and nothing to the Divine Being, and have made this a part of their faith by reasonings from visible objects: for all such are atheists. Essential liberty and rationality are given with difficulty in those who have confirmed themselves much in falses of religion; because the confirmer of what is false is the denier of truth. But those who have not so confirmed themselves may attain to true liberty and rationality, of whatsoever religion they may be; on which subject see what is adduced in *The Doctrine of the New Jerusalem concerning the Sacred Scripture*, n. 91—97. Infants and children cannot come into essential liberty and rationality before they grow up, because the interiors of the mind in a man are successively opened; and in the mean time they are like seeds in unripe fruit, which cannot germinate in the ground.

99. It was said, that essential liberty and rationality cannot

57

be given in those who have denied the Lord's divinity and the sanctity of the Word; or in those who have confirmed themselves for nature against the divine principle; and hardly in those who have confirmed themselves much in falses of religion: but still these have not lost those faculties themselves. I have heard atheists, that were become devils and satans, who understood arcana of wisdom as well as angels, yet only when they heard them from others; but when they returned into their own thoughts they did not understand them; the reason of which was that they would not. It was shown them that they also could will to understand them if the love and consequent delight of evil did not prevent them; and this also they understood when they heard it; yea, they affirmed that they could, and were able, but that they did not will to be able, because thereby they would not be able to will what they did will, which was evil from the delight of the concupiscence thereof. Such wonderful things in the spiritual world have I often heard; from which I was fully confirmed that every man has liberty and rationality, and that every one may come into essential liberty and rationality, if he shuns evils as sins. But the adult who does not come into essential liberty and rationality in the world can never come into them after death; for then whatever is the state of his life which has been acquired in the world, such it remains to eternity.

THAT IT IS A LAW OF THE DIVINE PROVIDENCE, THAT A MAN AS FROM HIMSELF SHOULD REMOVE EVILS AS SINS IN THE EXTERNAL MAN, AND THAT THUS AND NO OTHERWISE THE LORD CAN REMOVE EVILS IN THE INTERNAL MAN, AND THEN AT THE SAME TIME IN THE EXTERNAL.

100. EVERY one may see from reason alone, that the Lord, who is good itself and truth itself, cannot enter into a man unless the evils and falsities in him are removed; for evil is opposite to good, and falsity is opposite to truth; and two opposites never can be mixed, but when one approaches the other a combat ensues, which continues until one gives place to the other; that which gives place departing and the other succeeding. In such opposition are heaven and hell, or the Lord and the devil. Can any one think from reason that the Lord can enter where the devil reigns, or that heaven can be where hell is? Who does not see, by virtue of the rationality given to every man of sound mind, that, in order that the Lord may enter, the devil must be cast out, or in order that heaven may enter, hell is to be removed? This opposition is meant by the words of Abraham out of heaven to the rich man in hell: "Between us and you there

is a great gulf fixed, so that they which would pass from hence to you cannot ; neither can they pass to us that would come from thence" (Luke xvi. 26).   Evil itself is hell, and good itself is heaven, or, what is the same, evil itself is the devil, and good itself is the Lord ; and a man in whom evil reigns is a hell in its least form, and a man in whom good reigns is a heaven in its least form.   This being the case, how can heaven enter into hell, when between them so great a gulf is fixed that there is no passing from the one to the other ?   Hence it follows that hell is entirely to be removed, that the Lord may be able to enter with heaven.

101. But many, especially those who have confirmed themselves in faith separate from charity, do not know that they are in hell when they are in evils, nor do they know, indeed, what evils are, because they think nothing of them ; saying, that they are not under the yoke of the law, and therefore that the law does not condemn them ; also, because they cannot contribute any thing to their own salvation, that they cannot remove any evil from themselves ; and, moreover, that they cannot do any good from themselves.   These are they who omit to think of evil, and because they omit to think of it they are continually in it.   That these are they who are meant by the goats spoken of by the Lord in Matthew, ch. xxv., and of whom it is said, verse 41, " Depart from me, ye cursed, into everlasting fire, prepared for the devil and his angels," may be seen in the *Doctrine of the New Jerusalem concerning Faith*, n. 61—68.   For those who think nothing of evils in themselves, that is, who do not explore themselves, and afterwards desist from them, cannot but be ignorant what evil is, and then love it from the delight thereof; for he who does not know what evil is loves it, and he who omits to think of it is continually in it, being like a blind man who does not see ; for the thought sees good and evil as the eye sees what is beautiful and ugly ; and he is in evil who thinks and wills it, as well as he who believes that evil does not appear before God, and that it is forgiven if it appears, for thus he thinks that he is without evil.   If such persons abstain from doing evils, they do not abstain because they are sins against God, but because they are afraid of the laws and of their reputation ; thus they do evils in their spirit continually, for it is the spirit of man which thinks and wills ; and therefore that which a man thinks in his spirit in the world he does after his departure out of the world, when he becomes a spirit.   In the spiritual world, into which every man comes after death, it is not asked what has your faith been, or what your doctrine, but what has your life been ?. Thus the inquiry is concerning the nature and quality of the life ; for it is known that such as any one's life is, such is his faith, and such his doctrine ; because the life forms to itself doctrine, and forms to itself faith.

59

102. From what has just been said it may appear, that it is a law of the Divine Providence, that evils should be removed by a man, for without the removal of them the Lord cannot be conjoined to him, and lead him from self into heaven. But as it is not known, that a man ought as from himself to remove evils in the external man, and that unless he does this as from himself, the Lord cannot remove evils in him in the internal man, therefore we shall proceed to exhibit this to the view of reason in its light, in the following order. I. That every man has an external and an internal of thought. II. That the external of a man's thought is in itself such as is its internal. III. That the internal cannot be purified from the concupiscences of evil so long as evils in the external man are not removed, because they obstruct. IV. That evils in the external man cannot be removed by the Lord, but by means of the man. V. That therefore a man ought to remove evils from the external man as from himself. VI. That the Lord then purifies him from the concupiscences of evil in the internal man, and from evils themselves in the external. VII. That it is the continual endeavour of the Divine Providence of the Lord, to join a man to himself, and himself to a man, that he may be able to give him the felicities of eternal life; which cannot be done, except in proportion as evils with their concupiscences are removed.

103. I. *That every man has an external and an internal of thought.* By the external and internal of thought is here understood the same as by the external and internal man, which means nothing else but the external and the internal of the will and understanding, for the will and understanding make the man; and as these two manifest themselves in the thoughts, they are called the external and internal of thought. Now as it is not a man's body, but his spirit, which wills and understands, and thence thinks, it follows, that this external and internal is the external and internal of a man's spirit. Bodily action, whether exerted in speech or in work, is only an effect from the internal and external of a man's spirit; for the body is merely obedience.

104. That every man in an advanced age has an external and an internal of thought, therefore an external and an internal of will and understanding, or an external and an internal of the spirit, which is the same with the external and internal man, is evident to every one who attends to the thoughts and intentions of another from his speech or actions, and also to his own thoughts and intentions, when he is in company and when he is not; for any one may speak in a friendly manner with another in external thought, and yet be his enemy in internal thought; any one may speak of love towards his neighbour, and of love towards God, from external thought and at the same time from its affection, when, nevertheless, in his internal

thought he makes light of his neighbour, and does not fear God; any one also, from external thought and affection, may speak of the justice of civil laws, of the virtues of moral life, and of the things which relate to spiritual doctrine and life, and yet, from internal thought and its affection, when he is alone by himself, may speak against civil laws, against moral virtues, and against the things which relate to spiritual doctrine and life. This is the case with such as are in the concupiscences of evil, and still wish to appear before the world not to be in them. Most people also, whilst they hear others speaking, think with themselves, Do they think interiorly in themselves, as they express their thoughts in their speech? Are they to be believed or not? What is it they intend? It is known that flatterers and hypocrites have a double thought; for they can restrain themselves, and take care that their interior thought shall not be opened, and indeed can conceal it more and more interiorly, and as it were shut up the door lest it should appear. That exterior and interior thought is given to a man, is evidently manifest from this consideration, that he can from his interior thought see his exterior thought, and also reflect upon it, and judge of it, whether it be evil or not evil. This quality of his mind a man derives from the two faculties, which he has from the Lord, called liberty and rationality, from which, if he had not an external and an internal of thought, he could not perceive and see any evil in himself, and be reformed; neither could he even speak, but only utter sounds like a beast.

105. The internal of thought is from the life's love and its affections and consequent perceptions; while the external is from the things which are in the memory, and which are subservient to the life's love for confirmations and for means to attain its end. A man, from infancy to youth, is in the external of thought derived from the affection of knowing, which then makes his internal; and there transpires also something of concupiscence and thence of inclination derived from the life's love connate from his parents. But afterwards, as he lives, his life's love is formed, the affections and consequent perceptions of which make the internal of his thought; and from the life's love is produced the love of means, the delights of which, and the sciences excited thence from the memory, make the external of his thought.

106. II. *That the external of a man's thought is in itself such as is its internal.* That a man from head to foot is such as his life's love is, was shown above: here, therefore, it may be expedient to premise something concerning the life's love, before we proceed to speak of the affections, which, together with perceptions, make a man's internal, and of the delights of the affections, which, together with the thoughts, make his external. Loves are manifold; but there are two loves like lords

61

and kings—celestial love and infernal love. Celestial love is love to the Lord and towards the neighbour, and infernal love is the love of self and of the world. These loves are opposite to each other, as are heaven and hell; for he who is in the love of self and of the world wills not good to any one but himself, but he who is in love to the Lord and towards his neighbour wills good to all. These two loves are the loves of a man's life, but with much variety; celestial love is the life's love of those whom the Lord leads, and infernal love is the life's love of those whom the devil leads. But the life's love of no one can exist without derivations, which are called affections. The derivations of infernal love are affections of evil and of falsity, properly called concupiscences; and the derivations of celestial love are affections of good and truth, properly called dilections. The affections of infernal love, which properly are concupiscences, are as many as there are evils; and the affections of celestial love, which properly are dilections, are as many as there are goods. The love dwells in its affections, as a lord in his domain, or as a king in his kingdom. Its dominion or kingdom is over the things which belong to the mind, that is, which belong to the will and the understanding of a man, and thence to his body. The life's love of a man, by its affections and the perceptions thence derived, and by its delights and the thoughts thence derived, governs the whole man,—the internal of his mind by its affections and the perceptions thence derived, and the external of his mind by the delights of its affections and the thoughts thence derived.

107. The form of this government may in some measure be seen by comparisons. Celestial love with the affections of good and truth and the perceptions thence derived, and at the same time with the delights of these affections and the thoughts thence derived, may be compared to a beautiful tree with branches, leaves, and fruits. The life's love is that tree; the branches with the leaves are the affections of good and truth with their perceptions and the fruits are the delights of the affections with their thoughts. But infernal love, with its affections of evil and falsity, which are concupiscences, and at the same time with the delights of these concupiscences and the thoughts thence derived, may be compared to a spider and the web which encompasses it. The love itself, is the spider; the concupiscences of evil and falsity, with their interior wiles, are the retiform threads nearest to the seat of the spider; and the delights of these concupiscences, with deceitful machinations, are the more remote threads where flies are caught, entangled, and devoured.

108. From these comparisons may be seen indeed the conjunction of all things of the will and understanding, or of the mind of a man, with his life's love, but yet not rationally. Such conjunction may be seen rationally thus: There are every

where three things together which make one, and are called
end, cause, and effect; of which the life's love in a man is the
end, the affections with their perceptions are the cause, and the
delights of the affections with their thoughts are the effect; for
in such a manner as the end by the cause comes into effect, so
also love by its affections descends to its delights, and by its
perceptions to its thoughts. Effects are really in the delights
of the mind and their thoughts, when the delights are of the
will and the thoughts are of the understanding thence derived,
consequently, when there is a full consent therein. They are
in this case effects of the spirit, which, although they do not
come into bodily action, are still as it were in act, when there
is consent; and they are also then together in the body, and
dwell there with the life's love, and aspire after action, which is
produced when nothing hinders. Such are the concupiscences
of evil, and evils themselves in those who make evils allowable
in their spirit. Now as the end joins itself with the cause, and
by the cause with the effect, so the life's love joins itself with
the internal principle of thought, and by that with its external.
Hence it is evident, that the external of a man's thought is
in itself such as is its internal; for the end infuses all its quality
into the cause, and through the cause into the effect, there
being nothing essential in the effect but what is in the cause,
and through the cause in the end; and as the end is thus the
very essential principle which enters the cause and the effect,
therefore the cause and effect are called the middle end and the
ultimate end.

109. It appears sometimes as if the external of the thought
of a man was not in itself such as is its internal; but this happens because the life's love, with its internals about it, places
below itself a substitute which is called the love of means, and
appoints it to take heed and guard lest any thing of its concupiscences should appear; consequently that substitute (or
deputy) from the craftiness of its prince, which is the life's love,
speaks and acts according to the civil institutions of the kingdom, according to the morals of reason, and according to the
spirituals of the church, so cunningly indeed and ingeniously,
that no one sees but that persons are such as their speech and
actions seem to indicate; and at length, by encompassing th ·
selves with a veil, they scarcely know any otherwise themse.
Such are all hypocrites; and such are priests, who in their
hearts make light of their neighbour, and fear not God, yet
preach concerning the love of their neighbour and the love of
God; such are judges, who decide under the influence of bribes
and friendships, while they profess a zeal for justice, and speak
of judgment from reason; such are merchants, insincere and
fraudulent at heart, when they act sincerely for the sake of interest; such are adulterers, when from that rationality which

63

every man possesses they speak of the chastity of marriage, and so in other instances. But these same persons, if they strip the love of means, the substitute of their life's love, of the garments of purple and fine linen with which they have invested it, and clothe it in its domestic dress, then they think, and sometimes in communication with their intimate friends, who are in a similar life's love, even speak directly the contrary. It may be supposed, when from the love of means they have spoken so justly, sincerely, and piously, that then the quality of their internal thought was not in the external of their thought; but nevertheless it was, there being hypocrisy and the love of self and the world in those whose cunning it is, for the sake of honor or interest, to seek reputation by an outward appearance. This quality of the internal is in the external of their thought, when they so speak and act.

110. But with those who are in celestial love, the internal and external of thought, or the internal and external man, make one when they speak, nor do they know any difference. Their life's love, with its affections of good and their perceptions of truth, is as the soul in whatever they think, and thence speak and do. If they are priests, they preach from love towards their neighbour and love to the Lord; if they are judges, they judge from justice itself; if they are merchants, they act from sincerity itself; if they are married men, they love their wives from chastity itself; and so on. Their life's love also has a love of means, as its substitute, which it teaches and leads to act from prudence, and clothes in garments of zeal for the truths of doctrine and at the same time for the goods of life.

111. III. *That the internal cannot be purified from the concupiscences of evil so long as evils in the external man are not removed, because they obstruct,* follows from what was said above, that the external of a man's thought is in itself such as is the internal of his thought, and that they adhere together not only as one within, but also as from, the other; therefore one of them cannot be separated without the other. So it is with every external which is from an internal, with every posterior which is from a prior, and with every effect which is from a cause. Now, since concupiscences, together with craftiness, make the internal of thought with the wicked, and the delights of concupiscences, together with machinations, make the external of their thought, and the latter are joined with the former in one, it follows, that the internal cannot be purified from concupiscences so long as evils in the external man are not removed. It must be observed, that it is a man's internal will which is in concupiscences, and his internal understanding which is in craftiness; also, that it is his external will which is in the delights of concupiscences, and his external under-

64

standing which is in machinations from craftiness. Every one
may see that concupiscences and their delights make one, also
that craftiness and machinations make one, and that these four
are in one series, and make together, as it were, one bundle:
from which consideration it is again evident, that the internal,
which consists of concupiscences, cannot be cast out except by
the removal of the external, which consists of evils. Concupiscences by their delights produce evils; but when evils are
believed to be allowable, which happens by consent of the will
and understanding, then the delights and evils make one. That
consent is equivalent to act, is well known; and is also what
the Lord says : "Whosoever looketh on a woman to lust after
her hath committed adultery with her already in his heart"
(Matt. v. 28). It is the same with other evils.

112. Hence then, it may appear, that in order to a man's
being purified from the concupiscences of evil, evils are to be
entirely removed from the external man; for until this is done,
there is no outlet given to concupiscences, and if no outlet be
given to them, concupiscences remain within, breathe forth
delights from themselves, and so force a man to consent, consequently, to action. Concupiscences enter the body by the
external of thought; therefore when there is consent in the
external of thought, they are immediately in the body, the delight which is felt being there. That such as is the mind, such
is the body, consequently the whole man, may be seen in the treatise concerning THE DIVINE LOVE AND THE DIVINE WISDOM,
n. 362—370. The proposition under consideration may be illustrated by comparisons, and also by examples :—*By comparisons*
thus : concupiscences with their delights may be compared to
fire, which the more it is fomented the more it burns; and the
freer its course, the wider it spreads itself, until, if in a city,
it consumes the houses, and if in a wood, the trees. The concupiscences of evil are also compared in the Word to fire, and
evils proceeding from them to a conflagration. The concupiscences of evil with their delights appear likewise as fires in the
spiritual world; infernal fire being nothing else. They may
also be compared to deluges and inundations of waters, on the
removal of mounds or dykes. They may also be compared to
gangrenes and imposthumes, which bring death to the body as
they spread, or are not cured. *By examples*, it is clearly evident,
that if evils in the external man are not removed, concupiscences
with their delights increase and exuberate. A thief, in propor
tion as he practises stealing, has the concupiscence of stealing,
till at length he is unable to desist. The same is true of a
fraudulent person, in proportion as he defrauds. It is the same
also with hatred and revenge, with luxury and intemperance,
with fornication and blasphemy. It is well known that the love
of dominion grounded in the love of self increases in proportion

65

as it is indulged, and in like manner the love of possessing goods grounded in the love of the world; it appears as if there was no bound or end to them. From these considerations it is evident, that in proportion as evils in the external man are unremoved, the concupiscences thereof abound; and in proportion as evils are freed from restraint, concupiscences increase.

113. A man cannot perceive the concupiscences of his own evil. He perceives the delights of them indeed, but he reflects little upon them; for delights occupy the thoughts, and take away reflections; therefore if he did not from some other source know that they are evils, he would call them goods, and would commit them from liberty according to the reason of his thought; and when he does this, he appropriates them to himself. In proportion as he confirms them as allowable, he enlarges the court of his reigning love, which is his life's love. Its court is composed of concupiscences; for they are as it were its ministers and guards, whereby it governs the exteriors which constitute its kingdom. But such as the king is, such are his ministers and guards, and such is his kingdom: if the king is a devil, then his ministers and guards are insanities, and the people of his kingdom are falsities of every kind, which his ministers, whom they call wise, although they are insane, by reasonings from fallacies and by fantasies, make to appear as truths, and to be acknowledged as truths. Can such a state of a man be changed otherwise than by removing evils in the external man? So also the concupiscences which adhere to evils are removed; otherwise no egress is afforded to concupiscences, for they are shut in, like a besieged city, or as an ulcer skinned over.

114. IV. *That evils in the external man cannot be removed by the Lord but by means of the man.* In all Christian churches it is received as a doctrine that a man, before he approaches the holy communion, is to examine himself, to see and acknowledge his sins and to repent, by desisting from them and rejecting them because they are from the devil; and that otherwise his sins are not forgiven, and he is condemned. The English, although they are in the doctrine of faith alone, nevertheless, in the prayer at the holy communion, openly teach self-examination, the acknowledgment and confession of sins, repentance, and a new life, threatening those who do not comply in these words, that otherwise *the devil will enter into them as he did into Judas, and fill them with all iniquity, and destroy them body and soul.* The Germans, Swedes, and Danes, who are also in faith alone, teach the same in the prayer at the holy communion, threatening also that otherwise infernal punishment and eternal damnation will be incurred by reason of the mixture of what is sacred and profane. These things are read by the priest with a loud voice before those who are about to receive the Lord's supper, and are heard by them with a full acknowledgment that they

are true. Nevertheless, the same persons, when they hear a sermon the same day on faith alone, and then that the law does not condemn them because the Lord has fulfilled it for them; that from themselves they cannot do any good but what is meritorious, and thus that works have nothing of salvation in them, but faith only; they return home entirely forgetful of their former confession, and reject it in proportion as they think of the sermon on faith alone. Which doctrine now is true,—the latter or the former? (for two things contrary to each other cannot both be true)—that without an examination, knowledge, acknowledgment, confession, and rejection of sins, therefore without repentance, there is no remission of them, consequently no salvation, but eternal damnation; or that such things contribute nothing towards salvation, because full satisfaction for all the sins of men was made by the Lord through the passion of the cross for those who are in faith, and that those who are in faith only with a confidence that it is so, and in dependence on the imputation of the Lord's merit, are without sins, and appear before God like those who have their faces clean washed? From the above it is evident, that the common religion of all the churches in the Christian world is, that a man ought to examine himself, to see and acknowledge his sins, and afterwards to desist from them; and that otherwise there is no salvation, but condemnation. That this moreover is Divine Truth itself, is obvious from those passages in the Word in which men are commanded to repent; as from these: Jesus said, "Bring forth therefore fruits worthy of REPENTANCE." "Now also the axe is laid unto the root of the trees : every tree therefore which bringeth not forth good fruit is hewn down and cast into the fire" (Luke iii. 8, 9). Jesus said, "Except ye REPENT, ye shall all likewise perish" (Luke xiii. 3, 5). "Jesus preached the gospel of the kingdom of God; saying REPENT ye, and believe the gospel" (Mark i. 14, 15). Jesus sent forth his disciples, who "went out, and preached that men should REPENT" (Mark vi. 12). Jesus said unto the apostles, that they should preach "REPENTANCE AND REMISSION OF SINS AMONG ALL NATIONS" (Luke xxiv. 47). "John did preach the baptism of REPENTANCE FOR THE REMISSION OF SINS" (Mark i. 4; Luke iii. 3). Think on this subject also from some degree of understanding; and if you have any religion, you will see that repentance from sins is the way to heaven, that faith separate from repentance is not faith, and that those who are not in faith in consequence of not being in repentance are in the way to hell.

115. Those who are in faith separate from charity, and have confirmed themselves therein from the saying of Paul to the Romans, "that a man is justified by faith without the deeds of the law" (iii. 28), adore this saying as those who adore the sun, and become like those who, fixing their eyes steadily upon the

sun, whereby the sight becomes dim, do not see any thing in the midst of light; for they do not see what is understood there by the deeds of the law,—that they are not the commandments of the decalogue, but the rituals described by Moses in his books, which are everywhere there called the law; and, therefore, lest the commandments of the decalogue should be understood, he explains it by saying, " Do we then make void the law through faith? God forbid : yea, we establish the law" (verse 31 of the same chap.). Those who, from the above saying, have confirmed themselves in faith separate from charity, by looking at that passage as at the sun, do not see where Paul enumerates the laws of faith, that they are the very works of charity; and what is faith without its laws? Neither do they see where he enumerates evil works, saying that those who do them cannot enter into heaven. From which it is evident, how much blindness is induced from this one passage misunderstood.

116. The reason why evils in the external man cannot be removed but by means of the man is, because it is of the Divine Providence of the Lord that whatsoever a man hears, sees, thinks, wills, speaks, and does, should appear altogether as his own. That without this appearance a man would have no reception of divine truth, no determination to do good, no appropriation of love and wisdom, or of charity and faith, and thence no conjunction with the Lord, consequently no reformation and regeneration, and thereby salvation, is shown above, n. 71—95, and the following. That without this appearance it is evident there can neither be repentance from sins nor even faith; and that a man, without that appearance, is not a man, but is void of rational life like a beast. Let him who is so disposed consult his own reason, as to whether it does not appear that a man thinks from himself of good and truth, as well spiritual as moral and civil. Let him then receive this doctrinal,—that all good and truth is from the Lord, and nothing from the man : and will he not acknowledge this consequence, that a man ought to do good and think truth as from himself, but still to acknowledge that they are from the Lord; therefore, also, that a man ought to remove evils as from himself, but nevertheless to acknowledge that he does it from the Lord?

117. There are many who do not know that they are in evils, because they do not commit them in externals; for they are afraid of civil laws, as well as of the loss of reputation, and thus they acquire a custom and habit of shunning evils as detrimental to their honor and interest. But if they do not shun evils from a principle of religion, because they are sins, and against God, then the concupiscences of evils with their delights remain in them, like impure waters obstructed or stagnant. Let them explore their thoughts and intentions, and they will find these concupiscences, provided they know what

sin is. There are many such persons, who, having confirmed themselves in faith separate from charity, and because they believe that the law does not condemn, do not even attend to sins, and indeed doubt whether there be any such thing, or think that if there be, they are not such in the sight of God, because they are forgiven. Such also are natural moralists, who think civil and moral life, with the prudence belonging to it, effects all things, and the Divine Providence nothing. And, such are those who studiously affect the reputation and name of honesty and sincerity for the sake of honor or interest. But those who are such, and at the same time spurn religion, become after death spirits of concupiscences, who appear to themselves as if they were real men, but to others at a distance as priapuses ; and like owls they see in the dark, and not at all in the light.

118. From these considerations now follows the confirmation of Article V., which is, *that therefore a man ought to remove evils from the external man as from himself.* This may also be seen explained in THE DOCTRINE OF LIFE FOR THE NEW JERUSALEM, in three articles ; one of which is, that no one can shun evils as sins, so as interiorly to have an aversion for them, except by combats against them, n. 92—100 ; another, that a man ought to shun evils as sins, and to fight against them as from himself, n. 101—107 ; the third, that if any one shuns evils from any other cause than because they are sins, he does not shun them, but only causes them not to appear before the world, n. 108 —113.

119. VI. *That the Lord then purifies him from the concupiscences of evil in the internal man, and from evils themselves in the external.* The reason why the Lord purifies a man from the concupiscences of evil, when the man removes evils as from himself, is because the Lord cannot purify him until he does this ; for there are evils in the external man, and concupiscences of evil in the internal, and these cohere together like the roots of a tree to their trunk. Unless, therefore, the evils are removed, there is no opening ; for they obstruct and close the door, which cannot be opened by the Lord except by means of the man as was shown above. When a man does so open the door as from himself, then the Lord immediately extirpates the concupiscences. Another reason is, because the Lord acts upon the inmost of a man, and from the inmost upon the next in order, even to the ultimates ; and in the ultimates the man is entire. So long therefore as the ultimates are kept closed by the man himself, there cannot be any purification effected by the Lord, but only such an operation in the interiors as the Lord produces in hell, of which the man is a form who is in concupiscences and at the same time in evils ; and that operation is a disposition only that one may not destroy another, and

69

that goodness and truth may not be violated. That the Lord continually urges and presses that a man may open the door to him, is evident from his own words in the Revelation, "Behold, I stand at the door, and knock: if any man hear my voice and open the door, I will come in to him, and will sup with him, and he with me" (iii. 20).

120. A man knows nothing at all of the state of the interior of his mind, or of his internal man, and yet there are infinite things there, not one of which comes to his knowledge; for the internal of a man's thought, or his internal man, is his spirit itself, and in it there are things as infinite or innumerable as there are in a man's body. They must, indeed, be fully as innumerable; for a man's spirit is in its form a man, and all things thereof correspond to all the things of a man as to his body. Now, since a man has no knowledge from any sensation, how his mind or soul operates upon all things of his body jointly and severally, so neither does he know how the Lord operates upon all things of his mind or soul, that is, upon all things of his spirit. The operation is continual and the man has no share in it; but yet the Lord cannot purify him from any concupiscence of evil in his spirit or internal man, so long as he keeps his external closed. There are evils by which a man keeps his external closed, each of which appears to him as one, although there are infinite numbers in each; and when a man removes this seeming one, the Lord removes the infinite numbers in it. This is what is meant by the Lord's purifying a man from the concupiscences of evil in the internal man, and from evils themselves in the external.

121. It is thought by many, that merely to believe that which the church teaches, purifies a man from evils; and it is thought by some, that to do good purifies; by some, to know, speak, and teach such things as are of the church; by some, to read the Word and books of piety; by some, to frequent churches, to hear sermons, and especially to receive the holy supper; by some, to renounce the world, and study piety; by some, to confess themselves guilty of all sins; and so on. But, nevertheless, none of these things do at all purify a man unless he examines himself, perceives his sins, acknowledges them, condemns himself on account of them, and repents by desisting from them; and all these things he must do as from himself, but still from an acknowledgment of the heart that he does them from the Lord. Before they are done, the acts just mentioned avail nothing, for they are either meritorious or hypocritical; and they appear in heaven either before the angels like beautiful harlots smelling offensively from their defilement, like deformed women appearing handsome by means of paint, like actors and mimics on the stage, or like apes in human apparel. But when evils are removed, the acts before enumerated become

70

acts of the love, and then the doers thereof appear in heaven before the angels as beautiful men, and as their associates and companions.

122. But it should be well known, that a man in doing the work of repentance ought to look up to the Lord alone. If he looks up to God the Father only, he cannot be purified; nor if to the Father for the sake of the Son; nor if to the Son as a man only; for there is one God, and the Lord is he; for his divine and human essence constitute one person, as is shown in THE DOCTRINE OF THE NEW JERUSALEM CONCERNING THE LORD. In order that every one in the work of repentance might look to the Lord alone, he instituted the holy supper, which confirms, to those who repent, the remission of sins; and it confirms it, because in that supper or communion every one is kept looking to the Lord only.

123. VII. *That it is the continual endeavour of the Divine Providence of the Lord, to join a man to himself and himself to a man, that he may be able to give him the felicities of eternal life; which cannot be done, except in proportion as evils with their concupiscences are removed.* That it is the continual endeavour of the Divine Providence of the Lord to join a man to himself and himself to a man; that it is this conjunction which is called reformation and regeneration; and that a man has thence salvation, was shown above, n. 27—45. Who does not see that conjunction with God is salvation and eternal life? This is seen by every one who believes that men by creation are images and likenesses of God (Gen. i. 26, 27), and who knows what an image and likeness of God is. Who that has sound reason, when he thinks from his rationality, and wills to think from his liberty, can believe that there are three Gods, equal in essence, and that the Divine Esse or Divine Essence can be divided? That there is a trine in one God, may be thought and comprehended, as are comprehended the soul and body in an angel and in a man, and the sphere of life proceeding from them: and as this trine in one exists in the Lord only, it follows, that conjunction must be with him. Make use of your rationality, and at the same time of your liberty of thinking, and you will see this truth in its light, only first admitting, that there is a God, and that there is a heaven and eternal life. Now since God is one, and man by creation was made an image and likeness of him, and since, by infernal love, and its concupiscences and their delights, he came into the love of all evils, and thence destroyed in himself the image and likeness of God, it follows, that it is the continual endeavour of the Divine Providence of the Lord to conjoin a man to himself and himself to a man, and thus to make a man into his image. It follows also, that this is in order that the Lord may be able to give a man the felicities of eternal life, for such is the nature of the divine

71

love. But the reason why he cannot give those felicities, nor make a man an image of himself, unless a man as from himself remove sins in the external man, is, because the Lord is not only divine love, but also divine wisdom, and divine love does nothing but from and according to its divine wisdom. It is according to his divine wisdom that a man cannot be conjoined to the Lord, and so reformed, regenerated, and saved, unless he is permitted to act from liberty according to reason, for thereby a man is a man ; and whatsoever is according to the divine wisdom of the Lord, that also is of his Divine Providence.

124. To what has been said I will add two arcana of angelic wisdom, from which the nature of the Divine Providence may be seen. The first is, that the Lord never acts upon any particular principle in a man separately, but upon all together : the other is, that the Lord acts from inmost principles and from ultimate or lowest principles at the same time. *The reason why the Lord never acts upon any particular principle in a man separately, but upon all together,* is, because all things of a man are in such a connection, and by their connection in such a form, that they act not as several, but as one. It is known that a man is in such a connection, and by that connection in such a form as to his body ; and in a similar form, by virtue of the connection of the whole, is the human mind also, for that is the spiritual man, and is indeed truly a man. Hence it is that a man's spirit, which is his mind in the body, is a man in every particular of its form, and therefore after death a man is equally a man as in the world, with this difference only, that he has put off that covering which constituted his body in the world. Now, as the human form is such, that all its parts make a one which acts as one, it follows, that one part cannot be removed out of its place and changed as to its state, but in agreement with the rest ; for if one were removed out of its place and changed as to its state, the form which must act as one would suffer. From this it is evident, that the Lord never acts upon any particular part or principle, unless upon all together. Thus does he act upon the universal angelic heaven, because that in his sight is as one man ; so also does he act upon every angel, because every angel is a heaven in its least form ; and so also does he act upon every man, proximately upon all things of his mind, and through these upon all things of his body ; for a man's mind is his spirit, and according to its conjunction with the Lord is an angel, and his body is obedience. But it is to be well observed, that the Lord acts also singularly, yea most singularly upon every particular of a man, yet at the same time through all things of his form ; but he does not change the state of any part, or of any thing in particular, except so far as is suitable to the whole form. Of this, however, more will be said in what follows,

72

where it will be demonstrated, that the Divine Providence of the Lord is universal, because it is in particulars, and that it is particular because it is universal. *The reason why the Lord acts from inmost and from ultimate principles at the same time*, is, because in this way and no other all and singular things are contained in connection; intermediate principles depending successively upon the inmost even to the ultimate, and in ultimate principles they exist all together; for it is shown in the treatise ON THE DIVINE LOVE AND THE DIVINE WISDOM, part the third, that in the ultimate principle there is the simultaneous derived from the first of all principles. Hence also it is, that the Lord from eternity, or Jehovah, came into the world, and there put on and assumed the human nature in ultimate principles, that he might be from first principles and in ultimate at the same time; thus from first principles by ultimate might govern the universal world, and so save men; whom he is able to save according to the laws of his Divine Providence, which are also the laws of his divine wisdom. In this manner, therefore, is true, what is known in all Christian countries, that no mortal could have been saved, except the Lord had come into the world, respecting which THE DOCTRINE OF THE NEW JERUSALEM CONCERNING FAITH, n. 35, may be consulted. It is on this account that the Lord is called the First and the Last.

125. These angelic arcana are premised, in order that it may be comprehended, how the Divine Providence of the Lord operates, that he may conjoin a man to himself, and himself to a man. This is not effected upon a particular of a man separately, but upon the whole of him together; and it is done from his inmost and his ultimate principles at the same time. His life's love is the inmost of a man; the things which are in the external of his thought are the ultimates; and the things which are in the internal of his thought are the intermediates. The nature and quality of these principles, in a wicked man, was shown in the foregoing pages; from which consideration it is again evident, that the Lord cannot act from inmost and ultimate principles at the same time, except together with a man, for a man is together with the Lord in ultimate principles; therefore, as a man acts in ultimate principles, which are at his disposal, because subject to his free-will, so the Lord acts from his inmost principles, and upon the successive to the ultimate. The things which are in a man's inmost principles, and in the successive from the inmost to the ultimate, are altogether unknown to him, and therefore he is totally ignorant how and what the Lord works there; but since they cohere as one with the ultimate principles, it is not therefore necessary for a man to know more than that he ought to shun evils as sins, and look up to the Lord. In this and in no other way can his life's

love, which by birth is infernal, be removed by the Lord, and a love of celestial life be implanted in its place.

126. When the love of celestial life is implanted by the Lord in place of the love of infernal life, then, in place of the concupiscences of evil and falsity are implanted affections of good and truth, in place of the delights of the concupiscences of evil and falsity are implanted the delights of the affections of good, and in place of the evils of infernal love are implanted the goods of celestial love; then, also, instead of cunning is implanted prudence, and instead of thoughts of malice are implanted thoughts of wisdom. Thus a man is born again, and becomes a new man. What goods succeed in the place of evils, may be seen in The Doctrine of Life for the New Jerusalem, n. 67—73, 74—79, 80—86, 87—91. Also, that in proportion as a man shuns and turns away from evils as sins, he loves the truths of wisdom, n. 32—41; and that in the same proportion he possesses faith, and becomes spiritual, n. 42—52.

127. That it is according to the religion common in the universal Christian world, that a man should examine himself, perceive his sins, acknowledge them, confess them before God, and desist from them, and that this is repentance, remission of sins, and thence salvation, was shown above from the prayers read before the holy communion in all the Christian churches. The same may also appear from the creed that has its name from Athanasius, which likewise is received in the whole Christian world, and at the end of which are these words:—" The Lord shall come to judge the quick and the dead, at whose coming those that have done good shall go into life everlasting, and those that have done evil into everlasting fire."

128. Who does not know from the Word, that the life of every one after death is according to his actions? Open the Word, read it, and you will clearly see it; but in this case remove your thoughts from faith, and justification by it alone. That the Lord in his Word everywhere teaches this, let these few passages testify: " Every tree that bringeth not forth good fruit is hewn down, and cast into the fire. Therefore by their fruits ye shall know them" (Matt. vii. 19, 20). " Many will say to me in that day, Lord, Lord, have we not prophesied in thy name? and in thy name done many wonderful works? And then will I profess unto them, I never knew you: depart from me, ye that work iniquity" (Matt. vii. 22, 23). " Whosoever heareth these sayings of mine, and doeth them, I will liken him unto a wise man, which built his house upon a rock : but every one that heareth these sayings of mine, and doeth them not, shall be likened unto a foolish man, which built his house upon the sand" (Matt. vii. 24, 26 ; Luke vi. 46—49). " The Son

of Man shall come in the glory of his Father, and then he shall REWARD EVERY MAN ACCORDING TO HIS WORKS" (Matt. xvi. 27). " The kingdom of God shall be taken from you, and given to a nation BRINGING FORTH THE FRUITS THEREOF" (Matt. xxi. 43). " Jesus said, My mother and my brethren are these, which hear the word of God and DO IT" (Luke viii. 21). " Then ye shall begin to stand without and to knock at the door, saying, Lord, open unto us ; but he shall answer and say unto you, I know you not whence ye are ; depart from me all ye WORKERS of iniquity" (Luke xiii. 25—27). " And shall come forth, they that have done good, unto the resurrection of life ; and they that have done EVIL, unto the resurrection of damnation" (John v. 29). " We know that God heareth not SINNERS : but if any man be a worshipper of God, AND DOETH HIS WILL, him he heareth" (ix. 31). " If ye know these things, happy are ye if ye DO THEM" (John xiii. 17). " He that hath my commandments, and KEEPETH THEM, he it is that loveth me ; and I will love him, and will come to him, and will make my abode with him (John xiv. 15, 21—24). " Ye are my friends, IF YE DO whatsoever I command you. I have chosen you, that ye should BRING FORTH FRUIT, and that YOUR FRUIT should remain" (John xv. 14, 16). " The Lord said unto John, Unto the angel of the church of Ephesus write, I KNOW THY WORKS : I have against thee, that thou has left thy first LOVE, REPENT AND DO THE FIRST WORKS ; or else I will remove thy candlestick out of h s place" (Rev. ii. 1, 2, 4, 5). " Unto the angel of the church of Smyrna write, I KNOW THY WORKS" (Rev. ii. 8). " Unto the angel of the church in Pergamos write, I KNOW THY WORKS. REPENT" (Rev. ii. 12, 13, 16). " Unto the angel of the church in Thyatira write, I KNOW THY WORKS AND CHARITY ; AND THY LAST WORKS to be more than the first" (Rev. ii. 18). " Unto the angel of the church in Sardis write, I KNOW THY WORKS, that thou hast a name that thou livest, and art dead. I HAVE NOT FOUND THY WORKS PERFECT BEFORE GOD. REPENT" (Rev. iii. 1, 2, 3). " And to the angel of the church in Philadelphia write, I KNOW THY WORKS" (Rev. iii. 7, 8). " Unto the angel of the church of the Laodiceans write, I KNOW THY WORKS. REPENT" (Rev. iii. 14, 15, 19). " I heard a voice from heaven saying, Write, Blessed are the dead which die in the Lord from henceforth ; THEIR WORKS DO FOLLOW THEM" (Rev. xiv. 13). " A book was opened, which is the book of life, and the dead were judged, ALL ACCORDING TO THEIR WORKS" (Rev. xx. 12, 13). " Behold, I come quickly ; and my reward is with me, TO GIVE EVERY MAN ACCORDING TO HIS WORK" (Rev. xxii. 12). These passages are in the New Testament : there are still more in the Old, out of which I will adduce only this : " Stand in the gate of the Lord's house, and proclaim there this word : Thus saith Jehovah of hosts, the God of Israel, Amend your ways and

75

your doings; trust ye not in lying words, saying, The temple
of Jehovah, The temple of Jehovah, The temple of Jehovah are
these.   Will ye steal, murder, and commit adultery, and swear
falsely, and come and stand before me, in this house, which is
called by my name, and say, We are delivered to do all these
abominations? Is this house become a den of robbers? Behold,
even I have seen it, saith Jehovah" (Jer. vii. 2, 3, 4, 9, 10, 11).

THAT IT IS A LAW OF THE DIVINE PROVIDENCE, THAT A MAN SHOULD NOT BE FORCED BY EXTERNAL MEANS TO THINK AND WILL, AND SO TO BELIEVE AND LOVE THE THINGS WHICH ARE OF RELIGION; BUT THAT A MAN SHOULD LEAD, AND SOMETIMES FORCE HIMSELF TO IT.

129. THIS law of the Divine Providence follows from the
two preceding, which are, That a man should act from liberty
according to reason, of which see n. 71—99 : and this from
himself, although from the Lord, therefore as if from himself,
of which see n. 100—128.   And since to be forced is not to act
from liberty according to reason, and is not from himself, but
from what is not liberty and from another, therefore this law
of the Divine Providence follows in order after the two former.
Every one knows also that no person can be forced to think
that which he will not think, and to will that which he thinks
not to will; or therefore to believe that which he does not believe, and especially that which he will not believe ; or to love
that which he does not love, and especially that which he will not
love ; for a man's spirit, or his mind, is in full liberty to think,
will, believe, and love.   It is in this liberty by virtue of influx
from the spiritual world, which does not force, (for a man's
spirit or mind is in that world;) but not by virtue of influx
from the natural world, which is not received, unless they act
as one.   A man may be compelled to say, that he thinks and
wills such and such things, and that he believes and loves such
and such things ; but if they are not or do not become objects
of his affection and thence of his reason, he nevertheless does
not think, will, believe, and love them.   A man may be compelled also to speak in favour of religion, and to act according
to it ; but he cannot be compelled to think in favour of it from
any faith, and to will it from any love.   Every one also, in
kingdoms where justice and judgment are preserved, is restrained from speaking and acting against religion ; yet still,
no one can be forced to think and will in favour of it ; for it is
in the liberty of every one to think with hell, and to will in

76

favour of it, as likewise to think and will in favour of heaven. But reason teaches what the one is, and what the other; also what portion awaits the one, and what the other; and the will from reason has its option and election. Hence it may appear, that what is external cannot force what is internal: nevertheless, this is sometimes the case; but that to do so is hurtful, will be shown in the following order. I. That no one is reformed by miracles and signs, because they force. II. That no one is reformed by visions and by conversations with the dead, because they force. III. That no one is reformed by threats and punishments, because they force. IV. That no one is reformed in states which are not of rationality and liberty. V. That it is not contrary to rationality and liberty for a man to force himself. VI. That the external man is to be reformed by the internal, and not contrariwise.

130. I. *That no one is reformed by miracles and signs, because they force.* It has been previously shown, that a man has an internal and an external principle of thought; and that the Lord in a man flows through the internal of thought into its external and so teaches and leads him; also, that it is from the Divine Providence of the Lord, that a man should act from liberty according to reason; but both these laws of man's being would be nullified if miracles were performed, and the man by them were compelled to believe. That such would be the case, may be rationally seen thus: it cannot be denied that miracles induce a belief, and strongly persuade, that that is true which is said and taught by him who performs miracles; and that this at first so occupies the external of man's thought, as in a manner to fascinate and enchain it: but the man is hereby deprived of his two faculties, called rationality and liberty, by which he is enabled to act from freedom according to reason; and then the Lord cannot flow-in through the internal into the external of his thought, but only leaves him to confirm from his rationality that thing which by the miracle was made an object of his belief. The state of a man's thought is such, that from the internal thereof he sees a thing in the external as it were in a glass; for, as was said above, a man can see his thought, which can only be from interior thought. When he sees an object as in a glass, he can also turn it this way or that, and fashion it, till it appears to himself beautiful; and this object, if it be a truth, may be compared to a living and beautiful virgin or youth. But if the man cannot turn it this way or that, and so fashion it, but only believe it from persuasion induced by a miracle, in this case, if it be a truth, it may be compared to a virgin or youth cut out of stone or wood, in which there is no life. It may also be compared to an object constantly before the sight, which, itself only being seen, hides all that is on each side and behind it. It may also be compared

77

to one continual sound in the ear, which takes away the perception of harmony arising from several sounds. Such is the degree of blindness and deafness induced in the human mind by miracles. It is the same with every thing confirmed, which is not seen from some rationality before it is confirmed.

131. From these considerations it may appear, that faith induced by miracles is not faith, but persuasion; for there is nothing rational in it; still less any thing spiritual, it being merely external without any internal principle. It is the same with all that a man does from such persuasive faith, whether he acknowledge God, or worship him at home or at church, or perform acts of kindness. When a miracle alone leads a man to the acknowledgment of God, to worship, and to piety, he acts from the natural man, and not from the spiritual; for a miracle infuses faith by an external, and not by an internal way, therefore from the world, and not from heaven : but the Lord does not enter into a man by any other than by an internal way, which is by the Word, and by doctrine and preachings derived from the Word; and as miracles shut up this way, therefore at this day no miracles are wrought.

132. That such is the nature of miracles may plainly appear from those wrought before the Jewish and Israelitish people. Although they saw so many miracles in the land of Egypt, afterwards at the Red Sea, others in the desert, and especially upon Mount Sinai, when the law was promulgated, yet, in the space of a month, when Moses tarried upon that mountain, they made themselves a golden calf, and acknowledged it for Jehovah who brought them out of the land of Egypt (Exod. xxxii. 4, 5, 6). The same also may appear from the miracles wrought afterwards in the land of Canaan, notwithstanding which the people so often departed from the worship that was commanded; and from the miracles which the Lord wrought before them when he was in the world, notwithstanding which they crucified him. The reason why miracles were wrought among the Jews and Israelites was, because they were altogether external men, and were introduced into the land of Canaan merely that they might represent a church and its internal principles by the external things of worship; and a wicked man may be a representative as well as a good man. The external things of worship among them were rituals, all which signified spiritual and celestial things. Even Aaron, although he made the golden calf, and commanded the worship of it (Exod. xxxii. 2—5, 35), could, nevertheless, represent the Lord and his work of salvation. And as they could not, by the internal principles of worship, be led to represent these things, therefore they were led, yea forced and compelled to it, by miracles. The reason why they could not be brought to such representation by the internal principles of worship was, because they did not acknowledge

the Lord, although the whole Word, which was among them, treats of him only; and he who does not acknowledge the Lord cannot receive any internal worship. But, after the Lord manifested himself, and was received and acknowledged in the churches as the eternal God, miracles ceased.

133. The effect of miracles upon the good, however, is different from what it is upon the wicked. The good do not desire miracles, but they believe the miracles which are recorded in the Word; and if they hear any thing of a miracle, they attend no otherwise to it than as a light argument which confirms their faith, for they think from the Word, consequently from the Lord, and not from a miracle. It is otherwise with the wicked: they indeed may be driven and forced into faith, and even into worship and piety, but only for a short time; for their evils being shut in, the concupiscences thereof and the delights thence derived continually act against the external of their worship and piety; and in order that these evils may escape from confinement and break out, they think about the miracle, and at length call it a delusion or an artifice, or an operation of nature, and so return into their evils; and he who returns into his evils after worship, profanes the truths and goods of worship, and the lot of profaners after death is the worst of all. These are those who are meant by the Lord's words in Matt. xii. 43, 44, 45, whose last state is worse than their first. Besides, if miracles were to be wrought before those who do not believe in consequence of the miracles recorded in the Word, they must be continually performed, and constantly presented to their view. From these considerations, the reason may appear why miracles are not performed at this day.

134. II. *That no one is reformed by visions and by conversing with the dead, because they force.* Visions are of two kinds, divine and diabolical: divine visions are effected by representatives in heaven, and diabolical visions are effected by magic in hell. There are also fantastical visions, which are illusions of an abstracted mind. *Divine visions*, which, as was said, are produced by representatives in heaven, are such as the prophets had, who, when they were in them, were not in the body, but in the spirit; for visions cannot appear to a man when his body is awake. Therefore, when they appeared to the prophets, it is said also that they were then in the Spirit; as is plain from the following passages: Ezekiel says, "The Spirit took me up, and brought me in a VISION BY THE SPIRIT OF GOD into Chaldea. to them of the captivity; so the VISION that I had seen went up from me" (xi. 1, 24). Again, he says, that the Spirit lifted him up between the earth and the heaven, and brought him in the VISIONS OF GOD to Jerusalem (viii. 3). In like manner he was in a vision of God, or in the Spirit, when he saw four animals, which were cherubim (i. x.); as also when he saw the new

79

temple and the new earth, and an angel measuring them (xl. xlviii.). That he was then in the visions of God, he declares (xl. 2, 26); and that he was in the Spirit (xliii. 5). In a similar state was Zechariah, when he saw a man riding among the myrtle trees (i. 8); when he saw the four horns and a man with a measuring line in his hand (ii. 1, 3); when he saw a candle-stick and two olive trees (iv. 1, 3); when he saw a flying roll and an ephah (v. 1, 6); when he saw four chariots coming out from between two mountains, and horses (vi. 1, and following verses). In a similar state was Daniel, when he saw four beasts ascending out of the sea (vii. 1, and following verses); and when he saw the battle of the ram and the he-goat (viii. 1, and fol-lowing verses). That he saw these things in a vision of his spirit is stated in chap. vii. 1, 2, 7, 13; viii. 2; x. 1, 7, 8; and that the angel Gabriel was seen of him in a vision (ix. 21). John also was in a vision of the spirit, when he saw the things which he has described in the Revelation; as when he saw the seven candlesticks and the Son of Man in the midst of them (i. 12—16); when he saw a throne in heaven, and one sitting on the throne, and four animals, which were cherubim, round about it (iv.); when he saw the book of life taken by the Lamb (v.); when he saw horses coming forth out of the book (vi.); when he saw seven angels with trumpets (viii.); when he saw the bottomless pit opened, and locusts coming forth out of it (ix.); when he saw the dragon and his war with Michael (xii.); when he saw the two beasts, one coming out of the sea, and the other from the earth (xiii.); when he saw the woman sitting upon the scarlet beast (xvii.), and Babylon destroyed (xviii.); when he saw the white horse, and him that sat thereon (xix.); when he saw the new heaven and the new earth, and the holy Jerusalem coming down out of heaven (xxi.); and when he saw the river of the water of life (xxii.). That he saw these things in a vision of the Spirit is declared (i. 10; iv. 2; v. 1; vi. 1; xxi. 10). Such were the visions, which appeared out of heaven, before the sight of their spirit, and not before the sight of their body. Such visions do not exist at this day; for if they did, they would not be understood, because they are effected by rep-resentatives, the particulars of which signify internal things of the church, and arcana of heaven. That visions were also to cease when the Lord came into the world, is foretold by Daniel (xi. 24). *Diabolical visions* sometimes have existed, being induced by enthusiastic spirits and visionaries, who from the delirium they were in called themselves the Holy Ghost: but those spirits are now collected by the Lord, and cast into a hell separate from the hells of others. From what has been said it is evident, that no one can be reformed by any other visions than those which are recorded in the Word. There are also *fantas-tical visions*, but these are mere illusions of an abstracted mind.

80

134*. That neither can any one be reformed by speaking with the dead, is evident from the Lord's words concerning the rich man in hell, and Lazarus in the bosom of Abraham; for the rich man said, "I pray thee, father Abraham, that thou wouldst send Lazarus to my father's house: for I have five brethren; that he may testify unto them, lest they also come into this place of torment. Abraham said unto him, They have Moses and the prophets; let them hear them. But he said, Nay, father Abraham, but if one went unto them from the dead, they will repent. And he said unto him, If they hear not Moses and the prophets, neither will they be persuaded though one *rose* from the dead" (Luke xvi. 27—31). Speaking with the dead would have the same effect as miracles before-mentioned, viz.: that a man would be persuaded and compelled to worship for a short time; but as such compulsion deprives a man of rationality, and at the same time shuts in his evils, as was said above, the charm or internal restraint becomes dissolved, and the inclosed evils break out with blasphemy and profanation. This only happens, however, when spirits induce some dogmatic principle of religion, which is never done by any good spirit, still less by any angel of heaven.

135. Nevertheless, to speak with spirits, though rarely with angels of heaven, is allowed, and has been for many ages back; but when it is allowed, the spirits speak with a man in his mother tongue, and only a few words. Those, however, who speak by permission of the Lord, never say any thing which takes away the freedom of reason; nor do they teach; for the Lord alone teaches a man, though mediately through the Word in illumination, which will be spoken of presently. That this is the case, has been made known to me by experience. I have discoursed with spirits and angels now for several years; nor durst any spirit, neither would any angel, say any thing to me, much less instruct me, about any thing in the Word, or any doctrinal derived from the Word; but the Lord alone, who was revealed to me, and afterwards continually did and does appear before my eyes as the sun in which he is, even as he appears to the angels, taught me and illuminated me.

136. III. *That no one is reformed by threats and punishments, because they force.* It is known that the external cannot force the internal, but that the internal can force the external. It is also known, that the internal is so averse to force from the external, that it turns itself away; and also that external delights allure the internal to give its consent and its love: it may also be known, that there exists internal constraint and internal liberty. But all these points, although they are known, should, nevertheless, be illustrated; for there are many things which when they are heard are immediately perceived to be as stated, because they are truths, and they are thence affirmed; but if

81

not at the same time confirmed by reasons, they may be invalidated by arguments from fallacies, and at length denied. The things, therefore, which are now mentioned as known, are to be resumed and rationally confirmed. FIRST, *That the external cannot force the internal, but that the internal can force the external.* Who can be forced to believe and to love? It is no more possible for any one to be forced to believe, than to be forced to think that a thing is so and so when he does not think it so; and it is no more possible for any one to be forced to love, than to be forced to will that which he does not will; for belief is of the thought, and love is of the will. But the internal may be restrained by the external from speaking ill against the laws of the kingdom, the morals of life, and the sanctities of the church. The internal may be thus forced or restrained by threats and punishments, and also is and ought to be restrained; but such internal is not an internal properly human, but an internal that a man has in common with beasts, which also can be forced. The human internal resides above this animal internal; and it is the former which is here meant, and which cannot be forced. SECONDLY, *That the internal is so averse to force from the external, that it turns itself away.* The reason of this is, that the internal wills to be at liberty, and loves liberty; for liberty is of a man's love or of his life, as was shown above. Therefore when liberty perceives itself to be forced, it withdraws itself as it were within itself, and averts itself, regarding force as its enemy; for the love, which makes a man's life, is exasperated, and causes him to think, that thus he is not his own, consequently, that he does not live to himself. The reason why a man's internal is such, is grounded in the law of the Divine Providence of the Lord, that a man should act from liberty according to reason. Hence it is evident, that to force men to divine worship by threats and punishments, is hurtful. But there are some who suffer themselves to be forced to religion, and some who do not. Those who suffer themselves to be forced to religion are many of the papists; but it is the case with those in whose worship there is nothing internal, but all is external. Those who do not suffer themselves to be forced are many of the English nation, and hence it is that there is an internal in their worship; what is in the external is from the internal. The interiors of these latter, as to religion, appear in spiritual light like white clouds; but the interiors of the former, as to religion, appear in the light of heaven like dark clouds. Both these appearances are to be seen in the spiritual world, and whoever will may see them when he enters that world after death. Moreover, constrained worship shuts in evils, which then lie concealed like fire in wood under the ashes, which continues to kindle and spread till it breaks out into a flame; whereas worship which is not constrained, but spontaneous, does not shut in evils, which, therefore, are like fires that immediately burn out and are dispersed. From these considerations it is evident, that the internal has such a repugnance to restraint, that it averts itself. The reason why the internal can force the external, is, because the internal is as a master, and the external as a servant. THIRDLY, *That external delights allure the internal to give its consent and also its love.* Delights are of two kinds—those of the understanding and those of the will. The delights of the understanding are also delights of wisdom, and the delights of the will are also delights of love; for wisdom is of the understanding, and love is of the will. Now, since the delights of the body and its senses, which are external delights, act as one with the internal delights, which are of the understanding and the will, it follows, that as the internal refuses constraint from the external, insomuch as to turn itself away, so the internal gratefully beholds delight in the external, insomuch as to turn itself to it; thus is produced consent on the part of the understanding, and love on the part of the will. All infants in the spiritual world are introduced into angelic wisdom, and by it into celestial love, by delights and pleasantness from the Lord; first, by beautiful objects in houses and pleasant things in gardens; then, by representatives of spiritual things, which affect the interiors of their minds with pleasure; and, lastly, by truths of wisdom, and so by goods of love: thus continually by delights in their order; first, by the delights of the love of the understanding and its wisdom, and lastly, by the delights of the love of the will, which becomes their life's love, under which the other things, which have entered by delights, are kept subordinate. This is done, because all of the understanding and will is to be formed by the external before it is formed by the internal; all of the understanding and will being formed first by the things which enter through the senses of the body, especially the sight and hearing; but when the first understanding and the first will are formed, then the internal of thought regards them as the external of its thought, and either conjoins itself with them or separates itself from them; conjoining itself with them if they are delightful, and separating itself from them if they are not. But it ought to be well understood that the internal of the understanding does not join itself with the internal of the will, but that the internal of the will joins itself with the internal of the understanding, and causes a reciprocal conjunction; which, however, is formed by the internal of the will, and not at all by the internal of the understanding. Hence it is, that a man cannot be reformed by faith alone, but by the love of the will which forms faith to itself. FOURTHLY, *That there exists internal constraint and internal liberty.* Internal constraint exists with those whose worship is altogether external, and in no degree internal; for their internal is to think and will that to which their external is forced. Such are those whose worship is directed to men, both living and dead, and thence to idols, and who are in the faith of miracles. In these there is no internal, but what is, at the same time, external. But in those whose worship is internal, there exists internal constraint, of which there are two kinds, one from fear and another from love. Internal constraint from fear exists in those whose worship originates in the fear of infernal torment and its fire; but in this case the internal is not the internal of thought, before treated of, but the external of thought, which is here called internal, because it is of thought. The internal of thought, which was before treated of, cannot be forced or constrained by any fear; but it can be constrained by love and by the fear of losing it. The fear of God in a genuine sense is no other than this. To be constrained by love and by the fear of losing it, is to be constrained by oneself; and it will be afterwards seen, that to force oneself is not against liberty and rationality.

137. From this it may appear, what is constrained worship, and what is unconstrained. Constrained worship is corporeal, inanimate, obscure, and gloomy: corporeal, because it is of the body and not of the mind; inanimate, because there is no life in it; obscure, because there is no understanding in it; and gloomy, because there is no delight of heaven in it. But unconstrained worship, when it is genuine, is spiritual, living, lucid, and joyful: spiritual, because there is spirit from the Lord in it; living, because there is life from the Lord in it; lucid, because there is wisdom from the Lord in it; and joyful, because there is heaven from the Lord in it.

138. IV. *That no one is reformed in states which are not of rationality and liberty.* It was shown above, that nothing is appropriated to man but what he does from liberty according to reason; the cause of which is, that liberty is of the will, and reason of the understanding; and when a man acts from liberty according to reason, then he acts from his will through his understanding, and that which is done in conjunction of both is appropriated. Now since the Lord wills that a man should be reformed and regenerated, in order that he may enjoy eternal life or the life of heaven, and no one can be reformed and regenerated unless good be appropriated to his will, that it may be as it were his own, and truth to his understanding, that it likewise may be as it were his own; and since nothing can be appropriated to any one but what is from the liberty of his will according to the reason of his understanding, it follows, that no one is reformed in states which are not of liberty and rationality. There are several states which are not of liberty and rationality; but in general they may be referred to these: *States of fear, of misfortune, mental disorder, bodily sickness, ignorance, and*

blindness of the understanding; but of each of these states something shall be distinctly mentioned.

139. The reason why no one is reformed in A STATE OF FEAR, is, because fear takes away free-will and reason, or liberty and rationality ; for, while love opens the interiors of the mind, fear closes them, and when they are closed, a man thinks little, and only what offers itself to the mind and senses. Such is the effect of all kinds of fear which assail the mind. It was shown before, that a man has both an internal and an external of thought. Fear can never invade the internal of thought, this being always in freedom because it is in its life's love ; but it can invade the external of thought, and when it does this, the internal is closed, in which case the man can no longer act from liberty according to his reason, and therefore cannot be reformed. The fear which invades the external of thought and closes the internal is chiefly the fear of the loss of honour or of gain ; but the fear of civil punishments, and of external ecclesiastical punishments, does not close it, because these laws only prescribe punishments for those who speak and act against the civil institutions of a kingdom and the spiritual ones of the church, and not for those who think against them. The fear of infernal punishment indeed invades the external of thought, but only for some moments, hours, or days, and afterwards it is restored to liberty by the internal of thought, which is properly of a man's spirit and life's love, and is called the thought of the heart. But fear for the loss of honour and gain invades the external of a man's thought, and, when it invades it, closes the internal of thought above against the influx from heaven, and renders a man's reformation impracticable. The reason is, because the life's love of every man is by birth the love of self and of the world ; and the love of self makes one with the love of honour, and the love of the world makes one with the love of gain ; therefore when a man is in possession of honour or of gain, he, out of fear for the loss of them, confirms in himself means which are subservient to them, and which are as well of a civil as an ecclesiastical nature, both respecting government. He also that is not yet in possession of honour or gain, if he aspires to them, acts in like manner, but out of fear for the loss of reputation, which is valued for the sake of them. It is said that this fear invades the external of thought, and closes the internal above against influx from heaven ; and the latter is said to be closed when it acts entirely as one with the external ; for then it is not in itself, but in the external. Since, however, the loves of self and of the world are infernal loves, and the sources of all evils, of what nature the internal of thought is, in itself, with those in whom these loves reign or are the life's loves, appears evident; namely, that it is full of the concupiscences of evils of all kinds. This is unknown to those who, from the fear of the loss of dignity

and wealth, are in a powerful persuasion concerning the religion in which they are principled, especially a religion which involves the idea that they shall be worshiped as deities, and at the same time as Plutos in hell. These can burn as it were with zeal for the salvation of souls, and this nevertheless from infernal fire. As this fear especially takes away rationality itself and liberty itself, which are of celestial origin, it is evident that it is an obstacle to a man's being reformed.

140. The reason why no one is reformed in A STATE OF MISFORTUNE, if he then only thinks of God and implores assistance, is, because it is a state of constraint; and therefore when he comes into a state of liberty, he returns into the former state in which he had thought little if any thing about God. Not so those who had feared God before, while in a state of liberty. By the fear of God is meant a fear to offend him, and to offend him is to sin; and this is not really of fear but of love. Who that loves any one, does not fear to do him harm, and fear it the more in proportion as he loves him? Without this fear, love is lifeless and superficial, appertaining to the thought only, and not to the will. By states of misfortune are meant states of desperation from dangers, as in battles, duels, shipwrecks, falls, fires, imminent or unexpected loss of wealth, also loss of office, and thence of honour, and other similar cases. To think of God, in these only, is not from God but from self; for then the mind is as it were imprisoned in the body, therefore not in liberty, and thence not in rationality either, without which there cannot be reformation.

141. The reason why no one is reformed in A STATE OF MENTAL DISORDER, is, because disease of the mind takes away rationality, and thereby the liberty of acting according to reason; for a disordered mind is not sound, and it is the sound mind which is rational, and not the diseased mind. Such disorders of the mind are melancholy, spurious and false consciences, phantasies of various kinds, grief of mind from misfortunes, anxieties and anguish of mind arising from disease of the body, which are sometimes erroneously considered as temptations. Genuine temptations have for their object spiritual things, in which the mind is wise; but the former have for their object natural things, in which the mind is insane.

142. The reason why no one is reformed in A STATE OF BODILY SICKNESS, is, because reason then is not in a free state; for the state of the mind depends upon that of the body. When the body is sick, the mind also is sick, if from no other cause than its being removed from the world; for a mind removed from the world thinks indeed of God, but not from God, for it is not in the liberty of reason. A man has liberty of reason from this circumstance, that he is in the midst between heaven and the world, and can think from heaven and from the world,

86

also from heaven concerning the world, and from the world concerning heaven. When therefore a man is in sickness, and thinks of death, and of the state of his soul after death, he is not then in the world, but is abstracted in spirit, in which state alone no one can be reformed; but he may be confirmed by this, if he was reformed before he was visited with sickness. It is the same with those who renounce the world and all business in it, and give themselves up solely to thoughts concerning God, heaven, and salvation : but on this subject more elsewhere. Therefore, such persons, if they are not reformed before the sickness, become after it, if they die, such as they were before it : hence it is vain to think a person can repent, or receive any faith under sickness ; for there is nothing of action in such repentance, and nothing of charity in such faith ; therefore in both, all is of the mouth and nothing of the heart.

143. The reason why no one is reformed in A STATE OF IGNORANCE, is, because all reformation is effected by truths and a life according to them ; therefore, those who do not know truths cannot be reformed ; but if they desire truths from the affection thereof, they are reformed in the spiritual world after death.

144. Nor can persons be reformed in A STATE OF BLINDNESS OF THE UNDERSTANDING. They also are ignorant of truths, and consequently of life ; for the understanding must teach them, and the will do them ; and when the will does what the understanding teaches, it has life according to truths ; but when the understanding is blinded, the will also is closed, and does not from liberty according to reason any thing but the evil confirmed in the understanding, which is falsity. Religion also, as well as ignorance, blinds the understanding, when it teaches a blind faith ; and so does false doctrine : for as truths open the understanding, so falsities close it ; they close it above, but open it below, and the understanding, open only below, cannot see truths, but merely confirms whatever it wills, especially what is false. The understanding is also blinded by the lusts of evil. So long as the will is in such lusts, it forces the understanding to confirm them ; and so far as the lusts of evil are confirmed, the will cannot be in affections of good, and from them see truths, and so be reformed. For example : when a man is in the lust of adultery, his will, which is in the delight of his love, forces his understanding to confirm it, by saying What is adultery? Is there any harm in it? Is there not the same harm in the connection between husband and wife? Cannot children equally be born from adultery? Cannot a woman admit several without any harm? What has any spiritual consideration to do in this case? Thus does the understanding, which is then the harlot of the will, think ; and so stupid is it made by its whoredom with the will, that it can

87

not see that conjugial love is spiritual celestial love itself, which is an image of the love of the Lord and of the church, from which also it is derived, and thus that in itself it is holy, being essential chastity, purity, and innocence; that it makes men loves in form, for married pairs can love each other mutually from their inmost souls, and so form themselves into loves; and that adultery destroys this form, and with it the image of the Lord; and, what is horrible, that the adulterer mixes his life with the life of the husband in his wife, for a man's life is in the seed. As this is profane, therefore hell is called adultery, and on the contrary heaven is called marriage: the love of adultery also communicates with the lowest hell, but love truly conjugial with the inmost heaven; and the members of generation of both sexes also correspond to societies of the inmost heaven. These particulars are adduced, that it may be known how much the understanding is blinded when the will is in the lust of evil; and that in a state of blindness of the understanding no one can be reformed.

145. V. *That it is not contrary to rationality and liberty for a man to force himself.* It was shown before, that a man has an internal and an external of thought; that they are distinct as prior and posterior, or as superior and inferior; and that, as they are so distinct, they can act separately, and can act in conjunction. They act separately, when a man speaks and acts from the external of his thought otherwise than he interiorly thinks and wills; and they act in conjunction, when he speaks and does what he interiorly thinks and wills. The latter case is common with the sincere, but the former with the insincere. Now, since the internal and the external of the mind are so distinct, the internal can also combat with the external, and by that compel it to consent. Combat takes place when a man thinks evils to be sins, and therefore wills to desist from them; for when he desists, the door is opened, upon which the concupiscences of evil which besieged the internal of thought are cast out by the Lord, and in their place are implanted affections of good, and this in the internal of thought. But as the delights of the concupiscences of evil, which besiege the external of thought, cannot be cast out at the same time, therefore a combat takes place between the internal and the external of thought; the internal desiring to cast out those delights, because they are delights of evil, and do not accord with the affections of good, which the internal is now in, and instead of the delights of evil to introduce delights of good, which do accord. The delights of good are what are called goods of charity. From this contrariety arises a combat, which, if it becomes grievous, is called temptation. Now since a man is a man by virtue of the internal of his thought, this being the man's spirit itself, it is evident that a man forces himself, when he forces the external

of his thought to consent to or to receive the delights of his affections, which are goods of charity. That this is not contrary to rationality and liberty, however, but conformable to them, is evident; for rationality causes the combat, and liberty executes it. Liberty itself also, with rationality, resides in the internal man, and from the internal in the external. When, therefore, the internal conquers, which is the case when it has reduced the external to consent and obedience, then liberty itself and rationality itself are given to the man by the Lord; for then he is delivered by the Lord from infernal liberty, which in itself is slavery, and placed in celestial liberty, which in itself is real liberty, and he is privileged to associate with angels. That those are slaves who are in sins, and that the Lord makes those free who receive truth from him through the Word, he himself teaches in John viii. 31—36.

146. Let us take an example by way of illustration: suppose a man, who has perceived delight in frauds and clandestine thefts, to see and acknowledge that they are sins, and therefore to will to desist from them; when he desists, there arises a combat of the internal man with the external. The internal man is in the affection of sincerity, but the external as yet in the delight of defrauding; which delight, because it is altogether opposite to the delight of sincerity, does not recede, unless it is compelled, nor can it be compelled without a combat; and when he overcomes, the external man comes into the delight of the love of sincerity, which is charity; afterwards successively the delight of defrauding becomes undelightful to him. It is similar with other sins, as with adultery and fornication, revenge and hatred, blasphemy and lying. But the most difficult combat of all is that with the love of dominion from the love of self; he who subdues this, easily subdues other evil loves, because it is their head.

147. It shall also be briefly shown, in what manner the Lord casts out the concupiscences of evil which besiege the internal man from his birth, and plants affections of good in lieu of them, when a man as from himself removes evils as sins. It was shown above, that a man has a natural mind, a spiritual mind, and a celestial mind; that he is in the natural mind only so long as he is in the concupiscences of evil and their delights, and that so long the spiritual mind is shut; but as soon as, after self-examination, he acknowledges evils as sins against God because they are contrary to the divine laws, and therefore wills to desist from them, then the Lord opens the spiritual mind, and enters into the natural by the affections of truth and good; he also enters into the rational, and from it disposes into order the things which are below contrary to order, in the natural. It is this which appears to a man as a combat, and in those who have indulged much in the delights of evil, as temptation; for

89

it gives pain to the mind when the order of its thoughts is inverted. Now as the combat is against the things which are in the man himself, and which he feels as his own, and no one can fight against himself except from what is interior in himself, and from liberty there, it follows that the internal man then fights against the external, also that he does it from liberty, and that he forces the external to obedience; this, therefore, is to force himself. It is evident that this is not contrary to liberty and rationality, but according to them.

148. Moreover, every man wills to be free, and not to remove liberty but slavery from himself. Every boy, who is under a master, wills to be his own master, and so to be free. It is the same with every man-servant under his master, and every maid-servant under her mistress. Every virgin also wills to depart out of her father's house and marry, that she may act freely in her own house; and every youth who wills to work, or traffic, or exercise some office, while he is in servitude under others, wills to be emancipated, that he may be his own master. All those who serve of their own accord for the sake of liberty, force themselves: and in forcing themselves they act from liberty according to reason, but from interior liberty, from which exterior liberty is regarded as a servant. These considerations are adduced, in order to confirm the position, that for a man to force himself is not contrary to rationality and liberty.

149. One reason why a man does not in like manner desire to come out of spiritual servitude into spiritual liberty, is, that he does not know what spiritual servitude and spiritual liberty are. He has not the truths which teach it, and without them spiritual servitude is believed to be liberty, and spiritual liberty to be servitude. Another reason is, because the religion of the Christian world has closed the understanding, and the doctrine of faith alone has sealed it; for they have both placed about themselves, like an iron wall, this tenet, that theological things are transcendent, therefore are not to be approached from any rationality, and that they are for the blind and not for those who see. By this the truths have been hid which would teach what spiritual liberty is. A third reason is, because few examine themselves, and see their sins; and he who does not see them, and desist from them, is in the liberty of them, which is infernal liberty,—in itself servitude: and from this, to see celestial liberty, which is liberty itself, is like seeing light in darkness, and seeing under a black cloud that which is above it from the sun. Hence it is, that it is not known what celestial liberty is, and that the difference between this and infernal liberty is like the difference between what is alive and what is dead.

150. VI. *That the external man is to be reformed by the internal, and not contrariwise.* By the internal and the external man is meant the same as by the internal and the external of

thought, which have often been treated of before. The reason why the external is reformed by the internal, is, because the internal flows into the external, and not *vice versa*. That there is a spiritual influx into natural, and not the contrary, is known in the learned world; and that the internal man is first to be purified and renewed, and thereby the external, is known in the church. The reason why it is known, is, because the Lord and reason declare it; the Lord teaches it in these words: "Wo unto you, hypocrites! for ye make clean the outside of the cup and the platter, but within they are full of extortion and excess: thou blind Pharisee, cleanse first the inside of the cup and the platter, that the outside of them may be clean also" (Matt. xxiii. 25, 26). That reason declares it, is shown abundantly in the treatise on THE DIVINE LOVE AND THE DIVINE WISDOM: for what the Lord teaches, he also enables a man to perceive by reason, and this in two ways; one of which is, that he sees in himself that a thing is so and so, as soon as he hears it; and the other, that he understands it by reasons. To see in himself is in his internal man, and to understand by reasons is in his external man. Who, when he hears it declared, does not see in himself that the internal man is first to be purified, and by that the external? But he who does not receive a general idea of this by influx from heaven, may be led into a mistake when he consults the external of his thought; for from this alone no one sees otherwise than that external works, which are of charity and piety, are saving without internal principles. It is the same in other things; as that sight and hearing flow into thought, and smell and taste into perception, and thus that what is external flows into what is internal; when, nevertheless, it is quite the contrary. That things seen and heard appear to flow into the thought is a fallacy; for the understanding sees in the eye and hears in the ear, and not contrariwise. So it is in other cases.

151. But here it may be expedient to observe briefly in what manner the internal man is reformed, and thereby the external. The internal man is not reformed by knowing, understanding, and being wise, alone; or, consequently, by thinking alone; but by willing that which knowledge, intelligence, and wisdom teach. When a man knows, understands, and has wisdom to see, that there are a heaven and a hell, and that all evil is from hell, and all good from heaven; if then he does not will evil because it is from hell, but wills good because it is from heaven, he is in the first step of reformation, and in the entrance out of hell into heaven. When he advances further, and wills to desist from evils, he is in the second step of reformation, and is then out of hell, but not yet in heaven, which he sees above him. There must be this internal, in order that

a man may be reformed; but unless the external, as well as the internal, be reformed, the man is not reformed. The external is reformed by the internal, when the former desists from the evils which the latter does not will because they are infernal, and more so when he therefore shuns them and fights against them. Thus, the internal is to will, and the external is to do; for unless a person does that which he wills, there is within a principle which wills it not, and at length he comes not to will it. From these few considerations it may be seen, how the external man is reformed by the internal. This also is what is meant by the Lord's words to Peter: "Jesus said, If I wash thee not, thou hast no part with me. Peter saith unto him, Lord, not my feet only, but also my hands and my head. Jesus saith to him, He that is washed, needeth not save to wash his feet, but is clean every whit" (John xiii. 8, 9, 10). By washing is here meant spiritual washing, which is purification from evils: by washing the head and the hands is meant to purify the internal man, and by washing the feet is meant to purify the external. That when the internal man is purified, the external is to be purified is meant by these words: "He that is washed, needeth not save to wash his feet." That all purification from evils is from the Lord, is meant by these words: "If I wash thee not, thou hast no part with me." That washing among the Jews represented purification from evils; that this is signified by washing in the Word; and that by washing the feet is signified the purification of the natural or external man, is abundantly shown in the ARCANA CŒLESTIA.

152. Since every man has an internal and an external, and both are to be reformed in order that the man may be reformed; and since no one can be reformed except he examine himself, see, and acknowledge his evils, and afterwards desist from them, it follows, that not only is the external to be explored, but also the internal. If the external only is explored the man does not see any thing but what he has or has not actually committed; as, that he has not committed murder, adultery, or theft, or borne false witness, &c. Thus he explores the evils of his body, and not those of his spirit; and yet the latter are to be explored in order that any one may be reformed; for a man lives a spirit after death, and all the evils which are in him remain; and the spirit is no otherwise explored than by the man's attending to his thoughts, especially to his intentions, for these are thoughts from the will. In the will, evils are in their origin and root, that is, in their concupiscences and delights; and unless they are seen and acknowledged, the man is still in evils, although he may not have externally committed them. That to think from intention, is to will and to do, is evident from these words of the Lord: "Whosoever looketh on a woman, to lust after her,

92

hath committed adultery with her already in his heart" (Matt. v. 28). Such is the search of the internal man, by which the external man is essentially explored.

153. I have often wondered, that although the whole Christian world is informed that evils are to be shunned as sins, otherwise they are not remitted, and that if not remitted, there is no salvation, yet nevertheless scarce one in a thousand knows it. This was inquired into in the spiritual world, and it was found to be so; for every one in the Christian world is informed of it from the prayers read before those who receive the holy supper, it being plainly declared therein; and yet when they are asked whether they know this, they answer that they do not, and did not know it; the reason of which is, that they did not think about it, and most of them only thought of faith, and of salvation by it alone. I have also wondered, that faith alone so shuts the eyes, that those who have confirmed themselves in it, when they read the Word, see nothing of what is there said concerning love, charity, and works. It is as though they had smeared over all things in the Word with faith, as he who smears over a writing with paint, by which nothing which is underneath appears; or if any thing appears, it is absorbed by faith, and said to be faith.

THAT IT IS A LAW OF THE DIVINE PROVIDENCE, THAT A MAN SHOULD BE LED AND TAUGHT FROM THE LORD OUT OF HEAVEN BY THE WORD, AND BY DOCTRINE AND PREACHING FROM THE WORD, AND THIS IN ALL APPEARANCE AS FROM HIMSELF.

154. IN appearance a man is led and taught from himself, but in truth he is led and taught from the Lord only. Those who confirm in themselves the appearance, and not at the same time the truth, are not able to remove from themselves evils as sins; but those who confirm in themselves the appearance, and at the same time the truth, are able; for evils as sins are removed in appearance by man, and in truth by the Lord. The latter persons can be reformed, but the former cannot. Those who confirm in themselves the appearance, and not at the same time the truth, are all interior idolators; for they are worshipers of self and the world. If they have no religion, they become worshipers of nature, and thus Atheists; but if they have any religion, they become worshipers of men, and at the same time of images; and these are they who are meant in the first commandment of the decalogue, who worship other gods. But those who confirm in themselves the appearance,

93

and at the same time the truth, become worshipers of the Lord;
for the Lord elevates them from their proprium (or own proper
life), which is principled in appearance, and leads them into
light, in which is the truth, and which is the truth, and gives
them to perceive interiorly, that they are not led and taught of
themselves, but of the Lord.   The rational faculty of both these
descriptions of persons may appear to many as similar, but it is
dissimilar : the rational faculty of those who are principled in
appearance, and at the same time in the truth, is a spiritual
rational ; but the rational faculty of those who are principled in
appearance, and not at the same time in the truth, is a natural
rational.   The latter rational faculty may be compared to a garden as it is in the light of winter; while the spiritual rational
faculty may be compared to a garden as it is in the light of
spring.   But on this subject more will be stated, in the following
order.   I. That a man is led and taught of the Lord alone.
II. That a man is led and taught of the Lord alone by the angelic heaven and from it.   III. That a man is led of the Lord
by influx, and taught by illumination.   IV. That a man is
taught of the Lord by the Word, and by doctrine and preaching
from the Word, thus immediately by him alone.   V. That a
man is led and taught of the Lord in externals, to all appearance
as of himself.

155.   I. *That a man is led and taught of the Lord alone.*
This flows, as a universal consequence, from all that was shown
in the treatise concerning THE DIVINE LOVE AND THE DIVINE
WISDOM; as well from what is there demonstrated concerning
the divine love of the Lord and his divine wisdom, in part the
first; as from what is said concerning the sun of the spiritual
world, and the sun of the natural world, in part the second; and
also concerning degrees, in part the third; concerning the creation of the universe, in part the fourth; and concerning the creation of man, in part the fifth.

156.   The reason why a man is led and taught of the Lord
alone, is, because he lives from the Lord alone; for the will
of his life is led, and the understanding of his life is taught.
This, however, is contrary to appearance; for it appears to a
man as if he lived from himself, and yet the truth is, that he
lives from the Lord, and not from himself.   Now, since there
cannot be given to a man, so long as he is in the world, a sensible perception that he lives from the Lord only, because the
appearance that he lives from himself is not taken away from
him (for without it a man is not a man), therefore this must be
evinced by reasons, which are afterwards to be confirmed by experience, and lastly by the Word.

157.   That a man lives from the Lord alone, and not from
himself, may be evinced by these reasons : that there is one
only essence, one only substance, and one only form, from

which are all the essences, substances, and forms that are created; that the one only essence, substance, and form, is the divine love and the divine wisdom, from which are all things that have relation to love and wisdom in a man; that moreover it is good itself and truth itself, to which all things have relation; and that these are life, from which are the life of all things and all things of life: also, that the self-subsisting and sole-subsisting principle is omnipresent, omniscient, and omnipotent; and that this self-subsisting and sole-subsisting principle is the Lord from eternity, or Jehovah. FIRST, *That there is one only essence, one only substance, and one only form, from which are all the essences, substances, and forms that are created.* It was shown in the treatise on THE DIVINE LOVE AND THE DIVINE WISDOM, n. 44—46, and in part the second of the same work, that the sun of the angelic heaven, which is from the Lord, and in which is the Lord, is that sole or only substance and form, from which all things are created; and that nothing does exist, or can exist, which is not from it. That all things are from it by derivations, according to degrees, is shown there in part the third. Who does not perceive and acknowledge from reason, that there is one sole Essence, from which is all essence, or one sole *Esse*, from which is all *esse?* What can exist without an *Esse*, and what is that *Esse* from which is all *esse*, but *Esse* itself, and that which is *Esse* itself, is also the sole *Esse*, and in itself *Esse*. This being the case, and every one perceiving and acknowledging this from reason, or at least being capable of perceiving and acknowledging it, what else then follows but that this *Esse*, which is the Divine itself, which is Jehovah, is all in all things which are and exist? It is the same thing if it be said, that there is one sole substance, from which are all things; and since a substance without a form is nothing, it follows also, that there is one sole form, from which are all things. That the sun of the angelic heaven is that sole substance, and form; and how that essence, substance, and form, is varied in things created, is demonstrated in the above-mentioned treatise. SECONDLY, *That the one only essence, substance, and form, is the divine love and the divine wisdom; from which are all things that have relation to love and wisdom in man,* is also fully shown in the treatise on THE DIVINE LOVE AND THE DIVINE WISDOM. Whatever things in a man appear to live, have relation to the will and the understanding in him; and that these two principles constitute his life, every one from reason perceives and acknowledges. Why else is it so constantly said, I will this or I understand this, or I love this or I think this? And since a man wills what he loves, and thinks what he understands, therefore all things of the will have relation to love, and all things of the understanding to wisdom: and as these two principles cannot exist in any one from himself, but from him who is love itself

95

and wisdom itself, it follows that it is from the Lord from eternity or Jehovah. If this were not the origin of those principles, a man would be love itself and wisdom itself, therefore God from eternity, at which human reason itself is struck with horror. Can any thing exist but from what is prior to itself, and can this prior exist but from what is still prior to it, and thus finally from the first, which is in itself? THIRDLY: *That in like manner, it is good itself and truth itself, to which all things have relation.* It is received and acknowledged by every one who has reason, that God is good itself and truth itself, and that every thing good and true is from him; therefore, also, that what is good and true cannot come from any other source than from good and truth itself. These things are acknowledged by every rational man as soon as they are heard. When it is next said, that every thing of the will and understanding, or every thing of love and wisdom, or every thing of affection and thought with the man who is led of the Lord, has relation to good and truth, it follows, that all which such a man wills and understands, or which he loves and is wise in, or by which he is affected and which he thinks, is from the Lord. Hence it is, that every one in the church knows that every thing good and every thing true from a man, is in itself not good and true, but only that which is from the Lord. As this is a truth, it follows, that all that which such a man wills and thinks is from the Lord. That neither can a wicked man will and think from any other origin, will be seen in what follows. FOURTHLY, *That those principles are life, from which are the life of all things and all things of life,* is abundantly shown in the treatise on THE DIVINE LOVE AND THE DIVINE WISDOM. Human reason also, at the first hearing, receives and acknowledges, that all a man's life is of his will and understanding; for if the will and understanding be taken away, he does not live; or, what is the same, that all a man's life is of his love and his thought, for if love and thought be taken away, he does not live. Now because every thing of the will and understanding, or every thing of love and thought in a man is from the Lord, as was said above, it follows, that every thing of life is from him. FIFTHLY, *That the self-subsisting and sole-subsisting principle is omnipresent, omniscient, and omnipotent.* This also every Christian acknowledges from his doctrine, and every Gentile from his religion; hence also, every one, in whatever place he is, thinks that God is where he is, and that he should pray to God as present; and since every one so thinks, and so prays, it follows, that he cannot think otherwise than that God is every where, therefore omnipresent; in like manner, that he is omniscient and omnipotent; therefore every one praying to God implores from his heart, that he would lead him, because he is able to do so. Thus every one then acknowledges the divine omnipresence, omniscience, and omnipotence; he acknowledges, because he then turns his face to the Lord, from whom that truth then flows. SIXTHLY, *That this self-subsisting and sole-subsisting principle is the Lord from eternity, or Jehovah.* IN THE DOCTRINE OF THE NEW JERUSALEM CONCERNING THE LORD, it is shown, that God is one in essence and in person, and that that God is the Lord; that the divine itself, which is called Jehovah the Father, is the Lord from eternity; that the divine human is the Son conceived from his divine from eternity, and born in the world; and that the divine proceeding is the Holy Spirit. It is said to be self-subsisting and sole-subsisting, because it was stated before, that the Lord from eternity, or Jehovah, is life itself, being love itself and wisdom itself, or good itself and truth itself, from which are all things. That the Lord created all things out of himself, and not out of nothing, may be seen in the treatise on THE DIVINE LOVE AND THE DIVINE WISDOM, n. 282—284, n. 349—357. By the above considerations, this truth, that a man is led and taught of the Lord alone, is confirmed by reasons.

158. This same truth is confirmed, not only by reasons, but also by living perceptions among the angels, especially the angels of the third heaven. These perceive the influx of divine love and divine wisdom from the Lord; and because they perceive it, and from their wisdom know that these principles are life, therefore they say that they live from the Lord, and not from themselves; and they not only say this, but also love and desire that it may be so. Yet they are still in all appearance as if they lived from themselves, in a stronger appearance, indeed, than other angels; for as was shown above, n. 42—45, *in proportion as any one is more nearly conjoined to the Lord, he appears to himself more distinctly as his own, and perceives more evidently that he is the Lord's.* It has been granted me also to be in a similar perception and appearance now for many years; from which I am fully convinced, that I neither will nor think any thing from myself, but that it appears as from myself; and it is also given me to desire and love this. The same may be confirmed by many other considerations from the spiritual world, but these two may be sufficient at present.

159. That the Lord alone is life, is evident from these passages in the Word: "I am the resurrection and the life: he that believeth in me, though he were dead, yet shall he live" (John xi. 25). "I am the way, the truth, and the life" (John xiv. 6). "God was the Word. In him was life; and the life was the light of men" (John i. 1, 4). The Word there is the Lord. "As the Father hath life in himself, so hath he given to the Son to have life in himself" (John v. 26). That a man is led and taught of the Lord only, is evident from these passages: "Without me ye can do nothing" (John xv. 5). "A man can receive nothing, except it be given him from heaven" (John iii

97

27). "A man cannot make one hair white or black" (Matt. ▼ 36); by a hair in the Word is signified the least of all things.

160. That the life of the wicked is also from the same origin, will be demonstrated hereafter in its proper article. It will here only be illustrated by comparison. From the sun of the world flow both heat and light; and they flow alike into trees which bear evil fruit and into those which bear good fruit, and they vegetate and grow alike. The forms into which the heat flows, cause the difference; it is not the heat itself. It is similar with light, which is variegated in colours according to the forms into which it flows. There are beautiful and lively colours, and there are ugly and dull colours, yet still the light is the same. It is similar with the influx of spiritual heat, which in itself is love; and of spiritual light, which in itself is wisdom, from the sun of the spiritual world. The forms into which they flow, cause the difference, but not that heat which is love and that light which is wisdom in themselves. The forms into which they flow are human minds. From these considerations then it is evident, that a man is led and taught of the Lord alone.

161. But what the life of animals is, was shown above, namely, that it is a life of affection merely natural, with its concomitant science; and that it is a mediate life corresponding to the life of those which are in the spiritual world.

162. II. *That a man is led and taught of the Lord alone, by the angelic heaven, and from it.* It is said that a man is led of the Lord by the angelic heaven, and from it; but that it is by the angelic heaven, is according to appearance, whereas, that it is from it, is according to the truth. The reason why there is an appearance that it is by the angelic heaven, is, because the Lord appears above that heaven as the sun; and the reason why it is a truth that it is from that heaven, is, because the Lord in that heaven is as the soul in a man: for the Lord is omnipresent, and is not in space, as was shown before; therefore distance is an appearance, according to conjunction with him, conjunction being according to the reception of love and wisdom from him; and since no one can be conjoined to the Lord as he is in himself, therefore he appears to the angels at a distance as a sun: nevertheless he is in the universal angelic heaven like the soul in a man, and in like manner in every society of heaven, and in every angel there; for a man's soul is not only the soul of the whole, but also of each part of him. Since, however, it is from appearance that the Lord rules the universal heaven, and by it the world from the sun which is from him, and in which he is (concerning which sun see the treatise on THE DIVINE LOVE AND THE DIVINE WISDOM, Part II.); and since it is allowable for any man to speak from appearance, nor can he indeed do otherwise, therefore also it is allowable for any one, who is not principled in wisdom itself, to think, that the Lord

rules all and every thing from his sun, and also that he rules the world by the angelic heaven. From such appearance also the angels of the interior heavens think ; but the angels of the superior heavens, although they speak from appearance, think from the truth, which is that the Lord rules the universe from the angelic heaven, which is from himself. That the simple and the wise speak alike, but do not think alike, may be illustrated from the sun of the world. Of this sun all men speak from the appearance that it rises and sets ; but the wise, although they speak in like manner, still think that it stands immovable, which also is the truth, while the contrary is an appearance. The same may also be illustrated from appearances in the spiritual world ; for in that world there appear spaces and distances as in the natural world, but still they are appearances according to the dissimilitude of affections and thoughts thence derived. It is the same with the appearance of the Lord in his sun.

163. But how the Lord leads and teaches every man from the angelic heaven must be briefly explained. In the treatise on THE DIVINE LOVE AND THE DIVINE WISDOM, and above, in this treatise on THE DIVINE PROVIDENCE, also in the work on HEAVEN AND HELL, published in London in the year 1758, from things seen and heard, it is made known, that the universal angelic heaven appears before the Lord as one man, and in like manner each society in heaven, and that thence it is, that each particular angel and spirit is in a perfect human form. Moreover, in the above-named treatises it is shown, that heaven is not heaven from the *proprium* of the angels, but from the reception of divine love and divine wisdom from the Lord by the angels. Hence it may appear, that the Lord rules the universal angelic heaven as one man ; that that heaven, because it is a man, is the very image and likeness of the Lord ; that the Lord himself rules that heaven, as the soul rules its body ; and, because the universal human race is ruled by the Lord, that it is not ruled by heaven, but from heaven by the Lord, consequently from himself, because, as was said, he himself is heaven.

164. But as this is an arcanum of angelic wisdom, it can only be comprehended by the man whose spiritual mind is opened, such a man, by virtue of conjunction with the Lord, being an angel ; and by such a one, from what has been premised, the following particulars may be comprehended : 1. That all, men as well as angels, are in the Lord, and the Lord in them, according to conjunction with him, or, what is the same, according to their reception of love and wisdom from him. 2. That every one of these has his place appointed in the Lord, therefore in heaven, according to the quality of his conjunction with or reception of him 3. That every one in his place has his state distinct from the state of others ; and that from the common body he derives his task according to his situation, his function,

and his necessity, just in the same manner as does any particular part in the human body.   4. That every man is initiated into his place by the Lord according to his life.   5. That every man from infancy is introduced into that Divine Man, whose soul and life is the Lord, and that he is led and taught from his divine love according to his divine wisdom, in him and not out of him; but because liberty is not taken away from any man that he cannot otherwise be led and taught than according to reception as if from himself.   6. That those who receive are conducted to their places, through infinite windings and meanderings, as it were, nearly in the same manner as the chyle is conveyed through the mesentery and lacteal vessels into its receptacle, and thence through the thoracic duct into the blood, and so into its proper place.   7. That those who do not receive, are separated from those who are within the Divine Man, as excrement and urine are secreted and separated by a man.   These are arcana of angelic wisdom, which a man may in some measure comprehend; but there are many which he cannot.

165.   III. *That a man is led of the Lord by influx, and taught by illumination.*   The reason why a man is led of the Lord by influx, is, because to be led and also to flow-in are predicated of love and of the will; and the reason why he is taught of the Lord by illumination, is, because to be taught and to be illuminated are properly predicated of wisdom and of the understanding. It is well known that every man from his own love is led of himself, and according to it by others, and not by the understanding. He is led by the understanding and according to it, only when the love or the will makes the understanding: and when this is the case, it may also be said of the understanding, that it is led; but yet the understanding is not then led, but the will from which it is derived.   It is called influx, because it is customary to say, that the soul flows into the body, that influx is spiritual and not physical, and that a man's soul or life is his love or will, as was shown before; also, because influx is comparatively like the influx of the blood into the heart, and from the heart into the lungs.   That there is a correspondence of the heart with the will, and of the lungs with the understanding, and that the conjunction of the will with the understanding is like the influx of the blood out of the heart into the lungs, is shown in the treatise on THE DIVINE LOVE AND THE DIVINE WISDOM, n. 371—432.

166.   But the reason why a man is taught by illumination, is, because to be taught and also to be illuminated are predicated of the understanding; for the understanding, which is a man's internal sight, is no otherwise illuminated by spiritual light than as a man's eye or external sight is by natural light.   In like manner also both are taught; but the internal sight, which is of the understanding, by spiritual objects, and the external sight, which is of the eye, by natural objects.   There are spiritual

light and natural light, both alike as to external appearance, but unlike as to internal; for natural light is from the sun of the natural world, and thence in itself void of life; but spiritual light is from the sun of the spiritual world, and thence in itself living; it is this which illuminates the human understanding, and not natural light. Natural and rational illumination is not from the latter light, but from the former. It is called natural and rational illumination, because it is spiritual-natural; for there are three degrees of light in the spiritual world,—celestial light, spiritual light, and spiritual-natural light. Celestial light is a ruddy flaming light, and is with those who are in the third heaven; spiritual light is a white shining light, and is with those who are in the middle heaven; and spiritual-natural light is such as is the light of day in our world, and is with those who are in the last or lowest heaven, as well as with those who are in the world of spirits, which is midway between heaven and hell; but this light, in the latter world, is with the good like the light of summer, and with the wicked like the light of winter upon earth. It is to be observed, however, that all the light of the spiritual world has nothing in common with the light of the natural world; they being as different as life and death. From these considerations it is evident, that natural light, such as we have before our eyes, does not illuminate the understanding, but spiritual light. Men are ignorant of this, because heretofore they knew nothing of spiritual light. That spiritual light is in its origin divine wisdom, or divine truth, is shown in the work on HEAVEN AND HELL, n. 126—140.

167. As the light of heaven has now been spoken of, it may be expedient to say something also of the light of hell. This is also of three degrees: the light in the lowest hell being like the light of burning coals; the light in the middle hell like that from the flame of a wood fire; and the light in the highest hell like the light of candles, and to some like the light of the moon by night. These lights, however, are not natural, but spiritual; for all natural light is dead, and extinguishes the understanding. Those who are in hell have the faculty of understanding, which is called rationality, as was shown before, and rationality itself is from spiritual light, and not in the least from natural light; but the spiritual light which they have from rationality is turned into infernal light, as the light of day into the darkness of night. Yet all who are in the spiritual world, as well those who are in the heavens as those who are in the hells, see in their own light as clearly as man does in his by day; the reason of which is, that the eye of every one is formed for the reception of the light in which he is; consequently, the eyes of the angels of heaven for the reception of the light in which they are, and the eyes of the spirits of hell for the reception of their light. With the latter it is comparatively as with owls and

101

bats, which see objects as clearly in the night as other birds see them in the day ; for their eyes are formed for the reception of their own light. But the difference between these kinds of light appears clearly to those who look out of one light into another : as when an angel of heaven looks into hell, he sees nothing there but mere darkness ; and when a spirit of hell looks into heaven, he sees nothing there but darkness ; the reason of which is, that celestial wisdom is as darkness to those who are in hell; and, on the other hand, infernal insanity is as darkness to those who are in heaven. Hence it may appear, that such as a man's understanding is, such is his light ; and that every one comes into his own light after death, for he does not see in any other : and in the spiritual world, where all are spiritual even as to their bodies, the eyes of all are formed to see from their own light ; the life's love of every one making to itself an understanding, and so also a light ; for love is as the fire of life, from which is the light of life.

168. As few know any thing of the illumination, in which exists the understanding of the man who is taught of the Lord, therefore something must be said concerning it. There is interior and exterior illumination from the Lord, and there is also interior and exterior illumination from man. Interior illumination from the Lord is that by which a man at first hearing perceives whether what is said be true or not true ; and exterior illumination is derived thence in the thought. Interior illumination from man is from confirmation alone ; and exterior illumination from man is from science alone. But to speak of each more particularly : *A rational man by interior illumination from the Lord* immediately perceives, on hearing them, whether things are true or not ; as for example, that love is the life of faith, or that faith lives from love. A man from interior illumination also perceives this, that whatever a man loves he wills, and what he wills he does, consequently, that to love is to do : he also perceives this, that whatever a man believes from love, he likewise wills and does, consequently, that to have faith is also to do ; and likewise, that an impious man cannot have the love of God, or therefore the faith of God. A rational man also, from interior illumination, immediately perceives the following truths, when he hears them : viz. That God is one ; that he is omnipresent ; that every good is from him : also, that all things have relation to good and truth ; and that every thing good is from Good itself, and every thing true from Truth itself. These, and other similar truths, a man perceives interiorly in himself when he hears them : the reason of which is, that he has rationality, and this is in the light of heaven, which illuminates. *Exterior illumination* is that of the thought derived from interior illumination, and the thought is in this illumination in proportion as it remains in the perception which it has from interior

illumination, and at the same time possesses knowledges of things true and good, for from these it supplies itself with reasons for confirmation. The thought, by virtue of this exterior illumination, sees a thing on both sides,—on one side seeing the reasons which confirm it, and on the other the appearances which invalidate it: the latter it dispels, and the former it collects. But *interior illumination from man* is totally different: a man, by virtue of this illumination, sees a thing on one side, and not on the other; and when he has confirmed it, he sees it in a light similar in appearance to the light treated of above, but it is the light of winter. For example: a judge, who, in consequence of bribes and for the sake of interest, judges unjustly, after he has confirmed his judgment by the laws and by reasons, does not see any thing but justice in his judgment. Some see injustice; but, because they do not desire to see it, darken and blind themselves, and so do not see it. It is the same with a judge who passes judgment under the influence of friendship, from the desire of conciliating favour, and from the influence of connections. With persons of such a character, the same thing happens in respect to whatever they receive from the mouth of a man of authority, or from a man of reputation or fame, or in respect to whatever they have hatched out of their own self-derived intelligence. They are blind reasoners; for their sight is grounded in false principles, which they confirm; and falsity closes up the sight, and truth opens it. Such persons do not see any thing true from the light of truth, nor any thing just from the love of justice, but from the light of confirmation, which is infatuating light. They appear, in the spiritual world, like faces without a head, or like faces similar to human faces, behind which there are heads of wood; and they are called rational beasts, because they have rationality in their power. *Exterior illumination from man*, however, has place with those who think and speak from science alone impressed upon the memory; and these of themselves are but little able to confirm any thing.

169. Such are the different kinds of illumination, and thence of perception and thought. There is an actual illumination from spiritual light, although the illumination itself from that light does not appear to any one in the natural world, because natural light has nothing in common with spiritual light: but such illumination has sometimes appeared to me in the spiritual world, being seen among those who were in illumination from the Lord, as something luminous about the head, and ruddy, similar to the colour of the human face. With those who were in illumination from themselves, there was such a luminous appearance, not about the head, but about the mouth and above the chin.

170. Besides these illuminations there is also another, by

which it is revealed to a man in what faith, and in what intelligence and wisdom he is, which revelation is such that he himself perceives it in himself. He is admitted into a society where there is genuine faith, and where there are true intelligence and wisdom, and there the interior of his rationality is opened, from which he sees and even acknowledges of what kind are his faith, and his intelligence and wisdom. I have seen some returning thence, and have heard them confess that they had had no faith, although in the world they thought they had much, and in an eminent degree above others; and in like manner they confessed respecting their intelligence and wisdom. They were some of those who were principled in faith alone, and in no charity, and who were in self-derived intelligence.

171. IV. *That a man is taught of the Lord by the Word, and by doctrine and preachings from the Word, and thus immediately from him alone.* It was said and shown above, that a man is led and taught of the Lord alone, and that from heaven, and not by heaven, or by any angel there; and since he is led of the Lord alone, it follows, that he is led immediately, not mediately; but how this is done, is now to be explained.

172. In the DOCTRINE OF THE NEW JERUSALEM CONCERNING THE SACRED SCRIPTURE, it is shown, that the Lord is the Word, and that all doctrine of the church is to be drawn from the Word. Now, because the Lord is the Word, it follows, that the man who is taught from the Word, is taught of the Lord alone. But as this is difficult to be comprehended, it may be expedient to illustrate it in this order : 1. That the Lord is the Word, because the Word is from him and concerning him. 2. And because it is the divine truth of the divine good. 3. That thus to be taught from the Word, is to be taught from him. 4. And that this being effected mediately by preaching does not take away the immediate teaching. FIRST, *That the Lord is the Word, because it is from him and concerning him.* That the Word is from the Lord, is denied by no one in the church ; but that the Word is concerning the Lord alone, this indeed is not denied, but neither is it known : it is shown, however, in the DOCTRINE OF THE NEW JERUSALEM CONCERNING THE LORD, n. 1—7, and n. 37 —44 ; and in the DOCTRINE OF THE NEW JERUSALEM CONCERNING THE SACRED SCRIPTURE, n. 62—69, n. 80—90, n. 98, 99, 100. Now as the Word is from the Lord alone, and concerning the Lord alone, it follows, that when a man is taught from the Word, he is taught from the Lord, for the Word is divine. Who can communicate what is divine, and plant it in the heart, but the Divine Being himself, from whom it is, and of whom it treats? Wherefore, the Lord, where he speaks of his conjunction with his disciples, says, that they should abide in him, and his words in them (John xv. 7); that his words are spirit and life (John vi. 63); and that he maketh his abode with those who

keep his words, xiv. 20—24. To think, therefore, from the Lord, is to think from the Word, as by the Word. That all things of the Word have communication with heaven, is shown in THE DOCTRINE OF THE NEW JERUSALEM CONCERNING THE SACRED SCRIPTURE, from beginning to end; and, as the Lord is heaven, it is meant that all things of the Word have communication with the Lord himself. The angels of heaven have communication indeed, but this also from the Lord. SECONDLY, *That the Lord is the Word, because it is the divine truth of the divine good.* That the Lord is the Word, he teaches in John in these words: "In the beginning was the Word, and the Word was with God, and God was the Word: and the Word was made flesh, and dwelt among us," i. 1, 14. This passage has heretofore been no otherwise understood, than as implying that God taught men by the Word, therefore it has been explained by supposing it an elevated expression, involving that the Lord is not the Word itself; the reason of which is, that man did not know that by the Word is meant the divine truth of the divine good, or what is the same, the divine wisdom of the divine love. That these are the Lord himself, is shown in the treatise ON THE DIVINE LOVE AND THE DIVINE WISDOM, part the first; and that these are the Word, is shown in THE DOCTRINE OF THE NEW JERUSALEM CONCERNING THE SACRED SCRIPTURE, n. 1—86. How the Lord is the divine truth of the divine good, may also be briefly shown in this place. A man is not a man from his face and body, but from the good of his love and the truths of his wisdom; and because a man is a man by virtue of these principles, every man is also his own truth and his own good, or his own love and his own wisdom; and without these he is not a man. But the Lord is goodness itself and truth itself, or, what is the same, love itself and wisdom itself; and these are the Word, which in the beginning was with God, and which was God, and which was made flesh. THIRDLY, *That thus to be taught from the Word, is to be taught from the Lord himself,* because it is to be taught from goodness itself and truth itself, or from love itself and wisdom itself, which are the Word, as was said; but every one is taught according to the understanding of his love, and what is over and above does not remain. All those who are taught of the Lord in the Word, are instructed in a few truths in the world, but in many when they become angels; for the interiors of the Word, which are divine spiritual and divine celestial things, are implanted at the same time, but are not opened in a man till after his death, when in heaven, where he is in angelic wisdom, which, compared with human, and therefore with his former wisdom, is ineffable. That the divine spiritual and the divine celestial things which constitute angelic wisdom, are in all and every particular of the Word, may be seen in THE DOCTRINE OF THE NEW

JERUSALEM CONCERNING THE SACRED SCRIPTURE, n. 5—26. FOURTHLY, *That this being effected mediately by preaching does not take away the immediate teaching.* The Word cannot otherwise be taught than mediately by parents, masters, preachers, books, and especially by reading it; but still it is not taught from them, but by them from the Lord. This is also agreeable to what is known to preachers, who say, that they do not speak from themselves, but from the spirit of God; and that every thing true, as well as every thing good, is from God. They are able indeed to say this, and make it enter into the understanding of many, but not into the heart of any one; and that which is not in the heart, perishes in the understanding: by the heart is meant the man's love. It may hence be seen, that a man is led and taught of the Lord alone; and immediately from him, when from the Word. This is an arcanum of arcana of angelic wisdom.

173. That by the Word those also have light who are out of the church, and have not the Word, is shown in THE DOCTRINE OF THE NEW JERUSALEM CONCERNING THE SACRED SCRIPTURE, n. 104—113: and because a man has light through the Word, and from light has understanding, and this is the case with the wicked as well as the good, it follows, that from light in its origin there is light in its derivations, which are perceptions and thoughts on any subject whatever. The Lord says, that "without him they can do nothing" (John xv. 5); that "a man can receive nothing except it be given him from heaven" (John iii. 27); and that our "Father which is in heaven, maketh his sun to rise on the evil and on the good, and sendeth rain on the just and on the unjust" (Matt. v. 45). By sun is meant here, as elsewhere in the Word, in its spiritual sense, the divine good of the divine love, and by rain the divine truth of the divine wisdom. These are given to the evil and to the good, and to the just and to the unjust; for if they were not, no one would have perception and thought. That there is one sole life, from which all have life, was shown above; and perception and thought are of life; therefore from the same fountain from which is life, are also perception and thought. That all light, which makes the understanding, is from the sun of the spiritual world, which is the Lord, was abundantly shown above.

174. V. *That a man is led and taught of the Lord in externals to all appearance as of himself.* This is done in his externals, but not in his internals; no one knows how the Lord leads and teaches a man in his internals, any more than he knows how the soul operates in order that the eye may see, the ear hear, the tongue and the mouth speak, the heart impel the blood, the lungs respire, the stomach digest, the liver and pancreas distribute, the kidneys secrete, and innumerable other things. These do not come within a man's perception and sen-

sation; and it is similar with the things which are done of the Lord in the interior substances and forms of the mind, which things are infinitely more numerous. The operations of the Lord therein do not appear to a man; but their effects, which are many, do appear, and also some causes of the effects. These are externals in which the man is together with the Lord; and because externals make one with internals, for they cohere in one series, therefore no disposition can be made in internals by the Lord, otherwise than according to that which is made in externals by means of the man. Every one knows that a man thinks, wills, speaks, and acts to all appearance as from himself; and any one may see, that without such appearance a man would have no will and understanding, consequently no affection and thought, and also no reception of any thing good and true from the Lord. This being the case, it follows, that without such appearance there would be no knowledge of God, no charity and faith, consequently no reformation and regeneration, and therefore no salvation. From which it is evident, that this appearance was given to man by the Lord for all those uses; but principally that he might have a receptive and a reciprocal principle by which the Lord may be conjoined to him and he to the Lord, and that by such conjunction he may live to eternity. It is this appearance which is here meant.

.THAT IT IS A LAW OF THE DIVINE PROVIDENCE THAT A MAN SHOULD NOT PERCEIVE AND FEEL ANY THING OF THE OPERATION OF THE DIVINE PROVIDENCE, BUT YET SHOULD KNOW AND ACKNOWLEDGE IT.

175. THE natural man, who does not believe in the Divine Providence, thinks within himself, What is the Divine Providence, when I see that the wicked are promoted to honours, and acquire wealth more frequently than the good; that many such like things succeed with those who do not believe in the Divine Providence better than with those who do; and even that infidels and impious persons can occasion injuries, losses, and misfortunes, and sometimes death, to the faithful and pious, and this by craft and malice? The natural man also thinks to himself, Do not I see from experience itself, as in open day, that deceitful machinations, provided a man by ingenious cunning can make them appear to be faithful and just, prevail over fidelity and justice? What am I to think then of other cases, but that they are necessities, consequences, and fortuitous incidents, in which nothing from the Divine Providence appears? Are not necessities to be ascribed to nature? Are not consequences produced by causes flowing from natural or civil order?

And are not fortuitous incidents either derived from causes which are not known or from no causes at all? Such are the thoughts of the natural man, who attributes nothing to God, but all things to nature: for he who does not attribute any thing to God does not attribute any thing to the Divine Providence either, for God and the Divine Providence make one. But the spiritual man says or thinks with himself otherwise. Although, in thought, he does not perceive, or with his eyes see the Divine Providence in its operations, he nevertheless knows and acknowledges it. Now since the above-mentioned appearances and consequent fallacies have blinded the understanding, which cannot receive any sight unless the fallacies which induced blindness, and the false principles which induced darkness, be dispelled; and since this cannot be done except by truths, in which there is a power of dispelling false principles, therefore these truths are to be opened; but that this may be done distinctly, it may be expedient to observe the following order. I. That, if a man perceived and felt the operation of the Divine Providence, he would not act from liberty according to reason, nor would any thing appear to him as from himself. It would be the same if he foreknew events. II. That if a man plainly saw the Divine Providence, he would interfere with the order and tenor of its progress, and would pervert and destroy it. III. That if a man plainly saw the Divine Providence, he would either deny God or make himself a god. IV. That it is granted a man to see the Divine Providence on the back, and not in the face; also in a spiritual state, and not in a natural state.

176. I. *That if a man perceived and felt the operation of the Divine Providence, he would not act from liberty according to reason, nor would any thing appear to him as his own. It would be the same if he foreknew events.* That it is a law of the Divine Providence that a man should act from liberty according to reason; also, that whatever a man wills, thinks, speaks, and does, should appear to him as from himself; and that without such appearance no man would have any thing his own, or be his own man, therefore would have nothing proper to himself, and thus no imputation, without which it would be indifferent whether he should do evil or good, and whether he should have the faith of God or a persuasion from hell; in a word, that in such a case he would not be a man, was shown above under several articles to the evidence of the understanding. We shall now proceed to show, that if a man perceived and felt the operation of the Divine Providence, he would have no liberty of acting according to reason, and no appearance of acting as from himself, because if he perceived and felt it, he would also be led by it; for the Lord by his Divine Providence leads all, and a man does not lead himself except in appearance, as was also shown above; therefore if he had a lively perception and sensation of being

led, he would not be conscious of life and in such case would scarcely differ from a statue, when operated upon to utter sounds and to act. Supposing him, however, still conscious of life, yet he would only be led like one bound hand and foot, or like a horse before a cart. Who does not see, that in this case the man would have no liberty, and if he had no liberty, he would also have no reason; for every one thinks from liberty and in liberty, and whatever he does not think from liberty and in liberty, does not appear to him from himself, but from another. Indeed, if you weigh this interiorly, you will perceive that he would also have no thought, much less reason, and consequently would not be a man.

177. It is the continual operation of the Divine Providence of the Lord, to withdraw a man from evils: supposing now any one were to perceive and feel this continual operation, and yet were not to be led as one bound, would he not continually resist it, and in such case would he not either strive with God, or mix self with the Divine Providence? If he did the latter, he would make himself also God; if the former, he would loose himself from all bonds, and deny God. This is very evident, that there would be two powers continually acting against each other,—the power of evil from the man, and the power of good from the Lord; and when two opposites act against each other, then either one overcomes, or both perish; but in this case, if one overcomes, both perish; because the evil which is of the man does not receive good from the Lord in a moment, nor does the good from the Lord cast out the evil from the man in a moment; for if either the one or the other were done in a moment, life would not remain in the man. These and many other hurtful consequences would ensue, if a man were manifestly to perceive and feel the operation of the Divine Providence. But this will be clearly demonstrated by examples in what follows.

178. The reason, also, why it is not granted a man to foreknow events, is, that he may be able to act from liberty according to reason; for it is known, that whatever a man loves, he desires to effect, and leads himself to it by reason; also, that there is nothing that a man revolves in his reason which is not from a desire that it may come into effect by thought. If, therefore, he knew the effect or event from divine prediction, reason would become quiescent, and with reason, love; for love with reason terminates in the effect, and from that begins anew. It is the very delight of reason, that from love in the thought it may see the effect,—not in the effect, but before it, or not in the present, but in the future. Hence a man has what is called Hope, which in reason increases and decreases, as it sees or expects the event. This delight is fulfilled in the event, but afterwards is obliterated with the thought concerning the event; and it would be the same with an event foreknown. A man's

mind is continually in these three principles, which are called end, cause, and effect. If one of these is wanting, the human mind is not in its life. The affection of the will is the end from which; the thought of the understanding is the cause by which; and the action of the body, the speech of the mouth, or external sensation is the effect of the end by the thought. That the human mind is not in its life, when it is only in the affection of the will, and in nothing else, and in like manner when it is only in the effect, is evident to any one; therefore the mind has not any life from one of the principles separately, but from the three in conjunction. This life of the mind would be diminished and would recede in an event predicted.

179. Forasmuch as a foreknowledge of the future takes away the essential human principle, which consists in acting from liberty according to reason; therefore it is not granted any one to know the future, but every one is allowed to conclude concerning things to come from reason; and hence reason with all that appertains to it is in his life. It is on this account, that a man does not know his lot after death, or know any event before it is upon him; for if he knew, he would no longer think from his interior self how he should act or live, in order that it might happen, but would think only from his exterior self, that it would come to pass; and this latter state closes the interiors of the mind, in which the two faculties of his life, which are liberty and rationality, principally reside. The desire of foreknowing the future is connate with most people, but it derives its origin from the love of evil; it is therefore taken away from those who believe in the Divine Providence, and there is given them a confidence that the Lord will appoint their lot: hence they do not desire to foreknow it, lest by any means they should interfere with the Divine Providence. This the Lord teaches by many passages in Luke, chap. xii. 14—48. That this is a law of the Divine Providence, may be confirmed by many circumstances from the spiritual world. Most people, when they come into that world after death, desire to know their lot; but they are answered that their lot is in heaven if they have lived well, and in hell if they have lived ill. But as all, even the wicked, are afraid of hell, they ask what they are to do and to believe, that they may go to heaven. It is answered, that they may do and believe as they will, but they should know, that in hell they neither do what is good nor think what is true, but only in heaven; and they are told to inquire what is good and what is true, and to think the one and do the other, if they are able. Thus it is left to every one, in the spiritual world as well as in the natural world, to act from liberty according to reason; but as they have acted in this world, so they act in that; for the life of every one continues with him, and thence is his lot, because the lot is of the life.

180. II. *That if a man plainly saw the Divine Providence, he would interfere with the order and tenor of its progress, and would pervert and destroy it.* That this may enter distinctly into the perception of the rational and also of the natural man, it may be expedient to illustrate it by examples in this order. 1. That externals have such a connection with internals, that in every operation they make one. 2. That a man is only in some externals with the Lord, and if he were at the same time in internals, he would pervert and destroy all the order and tenor of the progress of the Divine Providence. But, as was said, these propositions shall be illustrated by examples. FIRST: *That external things have such a connection with internal things, that in every operation they make one.* The illustration in this case shall be taken from some particulars in the human body. In the whole and in every part of the human body there are externals and internals: the externals are called skins, membranes, and coverings: the internals are forms of nervous fibres and blood-vessels, variously composed and united. The covering which infolds them, by fibres sent out from itself, enters into all the interiors even to the inmost parts; and thus the external, which is the covering, connects itself with all the internals, which are organic forms consisting of fibres and vessels. From this it follows, that as the external acts or is acted upon, the internals also act or are acted upon; for there is a perpetual infolding together, or union of the whole. Only take some common covering in the body, as for example the PLEURA, which is the common covering of the breast, or of the heart and lungs, and examine it with an anatomical eye, or, if you have not made this your study, consult anatomists, and you will learn that this common covering, by various circumvolutions, and afterwards by derivations from itself, finer and finer, enters into the most interior parts of the lungs, even to the smallest bronchial ramifications, and into the follicles themselves, which are the beginnings of the lungs,—not to mention its progress afterwards by the trachea into the larynx towards the tongue; from which it is evident, that there is a perpetual connection of the outmost with the inmost, and therefore as the outmost acts or is acted upon, so also the interiors from the inmost act or are acted upon. This is the reason, that when that outmost covering, which is the pleura, has either a defluxion or inflammation, or is full of ulcers, the lungs labour from their inmost parts; and if the disease increases, all action of the lungs ceases, and the man dies. It is the same with every other part of the body, as with the PERITONÆUM, the common covering of all the abdominal viscera, and also with the coverings about each; as with the stomach, the liver, the pancreas, the spleen, the intestines, the mesentery, the kidneys, and the organs of generation in both sexes. Take any of these parts, and either examine it yourself and you

111

will see, or consult those who are skilled in the science, and you will hear. For example, take the liver, and you will find that there is a connection of the peritonæum with the covering of that viscus, and by that covering with its inmost substance; for there are thence perpetual branchings forth, and insertions towards the interiors, and thus continuations to the inmost parts, and thence a folding together of the whole, which is such, that when the covering acts or is acted upon, the whole form in like manner acts or is acted upon. It is the same with the rest. The reason is, that in every form, what is common and what is particular, or what is universal and what is singular, by a wonderful conjunction act as one. That in spiritual forms, and in the changes and variations of their state, which have relation to the operations of the will and understanding, the case is the same as in natural forms and their operations, which have relation to motion and action, will be seen below. Now as a man, in some external operations, is together with the Lord, and the liberty of acting according to reason is not taken away from any one, it follows, that the Lord cannot in internals act otherwise than as together with the man in externals; therefore if a man does not shun and avoid evils as sins, the external of the thought and will must be vitiated and diseased, and at the same time their internal, comparatively as the pleura from its disease which is called pleurisy, in consequence of which the body dies. SECONDLY, *That if a man were at the same time in internals, he would pervert and destroy all the order and tenor of the Divine Providence.* This also may be illustrated by examples from the human body: if a man knew all the operations of both the brains upon the fibres, of the fibres upon the muscles, and of the muscles upon actions, and from a knowledge thereof were to dispose all things as he disposes his actions, would he not pervert and destroy all? If a man knew how the stomach digests, the viscera about it perform their task, elaborating the blood, and distributing it for all the business of life, and had the disposition of the same as he has in externals,—in the case, for example, of eating and drinking,—would he not pervert and destroy all? When he cannot dispose the external, which appears as one, but destroys it by luxury and intemperance, what would be the case if he were also to dispose internals, which are infinite? Lest a man, therefore, by any will of his should enter into them, and make them subject to himself, the internals are entirely exempted from his will, except the muscles, which constitute the covering; and moreover it is not known how these act: it is only known that they do act. The same may be said in respect to the other parts of the body; as if a man were to dispose the interiors of his eye to see, the interiors of his ear to hear, the interiors of his tongue to taste, the interiors of his skin to feel, the interiors of his heart to contract,

112

the interiors of the lungs to respire, the interiors of the mesentery to distribute the chyle, the interiors of the kidneys to secrete, the interiors of the organs of generation to propagate, the interiors of the womb to perfect the embryo, and so on, would he not by infinite means pervert and destroy in these the order of progression of the Divine Providence? That a man is in externals is well known; as that he sees with the eye, hears with the ear, tastes with the tongue, feels with the skin, respires with the lungs, contributes to propagation, &c. Is it not enough that he is acquainted with externals, and may dispose them for the health of the body and mind? When he cannot do this, what would he do if he were also to dispose internals? Hence then it may appear, that if a man manifestly saw the Divine Providence, he would interfere with the order and tenor of its progress, and pervert and destroy it.

181. The reason why it is the same in the spiritual things of the mind as in the natural things of the body, is because all things of the mind correspond to all things of the body; therefore also the mind actuates the body in externals, and in things general, at its pleasure. It actuates the eye to see, the ears to hear, the mouth and the tongue to eat and to drink, and also to speak, the hands to act, the feet to walk, and the organs of generation to propagate. The mind not only actuates the externals to do these things, but also the internals in all their series, the ultimate or outmost from the inmost, and the inmost from the ultimate: thus, while it actuates the mouth to speak, it actuates the lungs, the larynx, the glottis, the tongue, the lips, and each distinctly to its function at once, and also the face conformably. Hence it is evident, that the same which was said of the natural forms of the body may be said of the spiritual forms of the mind, and what was said of the natural operations of the body may be said of the spiritual operations of the mind; therefore as a man disposes externals, the Lord disposes internals,—consequently, in one way if the man of himself disposes externals, and in a different way if he disposes them of the Lord, and at the same time as if of himself. A man's mind is also in every particular of its form a man, for it is his spirit, which after death appears a man altogether as in the world; and consequently there are similar things in both. Thus, what was said of the conjunction of externals with internals in the body, is also to be understood of the conjunction of externals with internals in the mind; with this difference only, that the one is natural and the other spiritual.

182. III. *That if a man manifestly saw the Divine Providence, he would either deny God or make himself a god.* The merely natural man says within himself, What is the Divine Providence? Is it any thing else or any thing more than a word among the vulgar received from the priest? Who sees

113

any thing of it? Is it not prudence, wisdom, cunning, and malice, from which all things are effected in the world? As to other things derived thence, are they not necessities and consequences, and also, in many cases, contingencies? Does the Divine Providence lie concealed in these things? How can it be in craft and cunning? And yet it is said that the Divine Providence operates in all things. Cause me therefore to see this, and I will believe it. Can any one believe it until he sees it? Thus speaks the merely natural man, but not so the spiritual man. The latter, because he acknowledges God, acknowledges also the Divine Providence, and likewise sees it: but he cannot manifest it to any one who thinks only in nature from nature; for such a one cannot elevate his mind above nature, and see in the appearances of it any thing of the Divine Providence, or conclude any thing concerning it from the laws of nature, which are also laws of the Divine Wisdom: therefore if he manifestly saw it, he would infuse it into nature, and thus not only veil it over with fallacies, but also profane it; instead of acknowledging it, he would deny it; and he who in his heart denies the Divine Providence also denies God. It must be thought either that God governs all things, or that nature does.: he who thinks that God governs all things, thinks that they are governed by love itself and wisdom itself, therefore by life itself; but he who thinks that nature governs all things, thinks that they are governed by natural heat and natural light, which nevertheless are in themselves dead, because they are from a dead sun. Does not that which is really living govern what is dead, or can that which is dead govern any thing? If you think that what is dead can give life to itself, you are insane; for life must be from life.

183. That if a man manifestly saw the Divine Providence and its operation, he would deny God, appears not probable, because it seems that if any one saw it manifestly, he could not but acknowledge it, and consequently, acknowledge God; but yet it is altogether otherwise. The Divine Providence never acts in unity with the love of a man's will, but continually against it; for a man from his hereditary evil always pants towards the lowest hell, whereas the Lord by his Providence continually withholds him, and draws him out thence, first to a milder hell, then from hell, and, lastly, to himself in heaven. This operation of the Divine Providence is perpetual; and therefore if a man manifestly saw this retraction and abduction, he would be angry, accounting God as his enemy, and from the evil of his *proprium* would deny him. Lest, therefore, a man should know this, he is kept in liberty, whereby he knows no other than that he leads himself. But examples may serve for illustration: a man, by hereditary disposition, desires to become great, and also to become rich, and in proportion as these loves are unrestrained, he

desires to be greater and richer, and at length the greatest and richest of all : nor thus would he be quiet, but would desire to become greater than God himself, and to possess the very heaven. This cupidity lies deeply concealed in hereditary evil, and thence in a man's life, and in his life's nature. The Divine Providence does not take away this evil in a moment; for if it were taken away in a moment, the man would die; but it is taken away tacitly and successively, without the man's knowing any thing of it. This is effected by his being permitted to act according to thought, which he makes the thought of his reason, and then being withdrawn by various means, as well rational as civil and moral : thus, so far as he can be withdrawn in liberty, he is withdrawn. Nor can evil be taken away from any one, unless it appear, be seen, and acknowledged; like a wound which is not healed except it be opened. If, therefore, a man knew and saw that the Lord, by his Divine Providence, thus operates against his life's love, from which he has his chief delight, he could not but run counter to it, be exasperated, contend against, speak harsh things, and at length from his own evil remove the operation of the Divine Providence, by denying it, and thus denying God; especially if he saw his success opposed, himself cast down from dignity, and deprived of opulence. It is however to be observed, that the Lord never withholds a man from seeking after honours and acquiring wealth, but from the cupidity of seeking after honours for the sake of eminence only, or for the sake of self; in like manner, from acquiring wealth for the sake of opulence only, or for the sake of the wealth; but when he withdraws a man from these, he introduces him into the love of uses, that he may respect eminence, not for the sake of self, but for the sake of uses, therefore, that it may be of uses and thence of himself, and not first of himself and thence of uses : the same is true in regard to opulence. That the Lord continually humbles the proud, and exalts the humble, he himself teaches in many places of the Word; and what he there teaches, that also is of his Divine Providence.

184. The case is the same with other evils in which a man is principled from hereditary disposition ; as with adulteries, frauds, revenges, blasphemies, and other such like; all which can be removed no otherwise than by the liberty of thinking and willing them being left, that so the man may remove them as from himself, which nevertheless he cannot do unless he acknowledges the Divine Providence, and implores that it may be effected by it. Without this liberty, and the Divine Providence at the same time, those evils would be like poison shut in, and not voided, which would shortly spread and occasion the death of all parts : and they would be like a disease of the heart itself, from which the whole body in a short time dies.

115

185. That this is true, cannot better be known than from the case of men after death in the spiritual world, where the greatest part of those who in the natural world became great and rich, and in honours as well as in riches respected themselves alone, at first speak of God and of the Divine Providence, as if they acknowledged them in their hearts; but as they then manifestly see the Divine Providence, and from it their final portion, which is to be in hell, they connect themselves with devils there, and then not only deny God, but also blaspheme; coming at length into such a delirium, that they acknowledge the more powerful of the devils for their gods, and desire nothing more ardently than that they themselves also may be deified.

186. The reason why a man would run counter to God, and also deny him, if he manifestly saw the operations of his Divine Providence, is, because a man is in the delight of his love, and this delight constitutes his very life; therefore when he is kept in the delight of his life, he is in his freedom, for freedom and that delight make one. Did he perceive therefore, that he is continually drawn away from his delight, he would be exasperated as against him who wished to destroy his life, and would regard him as an enemy. In order to prevent this, the Lord does not manifestly appear in his Divine Providence, but tacitly leads a man by it, as an imperceptible tide or prosperous current does a ship. From this a man knows no other than that he is constantly in his own *proprium*, for with that liberty makes one. Hence it is evident, that liberty appropriates to a man that which the Divine Providence introduces, which would not be the case if the latter manifested itself. To be appropriated is to become of the life.

187. IV. *That it is granted a man to see the Divine Providence on the back, and not in the face; also in a spiritual state, and not in a natural state.* To see the Divine Providence on the back and not in the face, is to see it after and not before; and to see it from a spiritual state and not from a natural state, is to see it from heaven and not from the world. All those who receive influx from heaven, and acknowledge the Divine Providence—especially those who by reformation are made spiritual, —when they see events in a certain wonderful series, do, as it were, from interior acknowledgment see and confess a Providence. These do not desire to see it in the face, that is, before it exists; for they are afraid lest their own will should enter into any thing of its order and tenor. Not so those who do not admit any influx from heaven, but only from the world, especially those who from the confirmation of appearances in themselves are made natural: these do not see any thing of the Divine Providence from behind or after it, but they want to see it in the face, or before it exists; and as the Divine Providence operates by means, and means are effected through man or through the

world, therefore, whether they see it before or after, they attribute it either to man or to nature, and thus confirm themselves in the denial of it. The reason why they so attribute it, is, because their understanding is closed above and open only below; consequently, shut towards heaven and open towards the world; and it is not permitted to see the Divine Providence from the world, but from heaven. I have sometimes thought within myself whether such persons would acknowledge the Divine Providence, if their understanding was opened above, and they saw as in clear day that nature in itself is dead, and that human intelligence in itself is nothing, but that it is only from influx that both these appear to be; and I perceived that those who have confirmed themselves in favour of nature and human prudence would not acknowledge it, because the natural light flowing in from beneath would immediately extinguish the spiritual light flowing in from above.

189. The man who is made spiritual by the acknowledgment of God, and wise by the rejection of his *proprium*, sees the Divine Providence in the universal world, and in all and every particular thereof. If he looks at natural things he sees it; if he looks at civil things he sees it; if he looks at spiritual things he sees it; and this as well in the simultaneous as in the successive order of things,—in ends, in causes, in effects, in uses, in forms, in things great and small; especially in the salvation of men; as, that Jehovah gave the Word, that by it he taught men concerning God, concerning heaven and hell, and concerning life eternal.; and that he came into the world himself, that he might redeem and save men. These, and more things of a similar kind, and the Divine Providence in them, does a man see from spiritual light in natural light. But the merely natural man sees nothing of these things: he is like one who beholds a magnificent temple, and hears a preacher illuminated in divine things, and says, when returned home, that he saw nothing but a stone building, and heard nothing but articulate sounds: or he is like a near-sighted man who goes into a garden furnished with all kinds of fruits, and then comes home and declares that he saw only a wood and trees. Such persons also, after death, when they become spirits, if they are taken up into the angelic heaven, where all things are in forms representative of love and wisdom, see nothing of such objects, or even of their existence; as I have perceived with respect to several who denied the Divine Providence.

190. There are many constant or fixed things, which were created in order that things inconstant or unfixed might exist: such are the stated times of the rising and setting of the sun and moon, and also of the stars; the darkening of them by interpositions, which are called eclipses; heats and lights from them; the seasons of the year, which are called spring, summer,

117

autumn, and winter; and the times of the day, which are morning, noon, evening, and night; also the atmospheres, waters, and earths considered in themselves; the vegetative faculty in the vegetable kingdom, and together with it the prolific faculty in the animal kingdom, and likewise the things which are constantly produced from these, when they are put in action according to the laws of order. These and many other things are provided by creation, that things infinitely various may exist; for variety cannot exist except in things constant, stated, and certain. But examples will illustrate this. The various things of vegetation would not exist, if the rising and setting of the sun, and the heat and light thence proceeding, were not constant. Harmonies are of infinite variety: but they would not exist, if the atmospheres in their laws, and the ears in their form, were not constant. The varieties of sight, which are also infinite, would not exist, unless the ether in its laws, and the eye in its form, were constant; nor, in like manner, colours, unless the light were constant. It is the same with thoughts, speech, and actions which also are of infinite variety, and which would not exist, except the organic parts of the body were constant. Must not a house be constant, that various things may be done therein? in like manner, a temple, that various particulars of divine worship, sermons, instructions, and meditations of piety, may be performed therein? and so in other things. As to what relates to the varieties themselves, which are produced in things constant, stated, and certain, they go on *ad infinitum*, and have no end; yet, in all and singular the things of the universe, there never exists one entirely the same with another, or can exist in the succession of things to eternity. Who disposes these varieties, which go on to infinity and eternity, that they may be in order, but He who created things constant, to the end that such varieties might exist therein? And who can dispose the infinite varieties of life among men, but He who is life itself, that is, love itself and wisdom itself? Without his Divine Providence, which is as a continual creation, could the infinite affections and the thoughts of men thence derived, and thus the men themselves, be so disposed as to make one,—evil affections and the thoughts thence derived, one devil which is hell; and good affections and the thoughts thence derived, one Lord in heaven? That the universal angelic heaven is in the sight of the Lord as one man, who is the image and likeness of himself, and that the universal hell is in opposition as one man-monster, has been said and shown occasionally before. These observations are made, because some natural men, even from things constant and stated, which are necessary to the end that various things may exist in them, catch at arguments in their delirium in favour of nature and self-derived prudence.

118

THAT SELF-DERIVED PRUDENCE IS NOTHING, AND ONLY AP-PEARS AS IF IT WAS, AND ALSO OUGHT SO TO APPEAR; BUT THAT THE DIVINE PROVIDENCE FROM THINGS THE MOST SINGULAR IS UNIVERSAL.

191. THAT self-derived prudence is nothing, is altogether contrary to appearance, and therefore contrary to the belief of many; and because it is so, no one who from appearance is in the belief that human prudence does every thing, can be convinced but by reasons of deeper investigation, which are to be taken from causes. Such appearance is an effect, and its causes discover whence it is. In this preliminary part something shall be said of the common opinion concerning this matter. Contrary to appearance is this tenet which the church teaches,—that love and faith are not from man but from God, as also wisdom and intelligence, consequently prudence likewise, and every thing good and true in general. When these tenets are received, it must also be admitted, that self-derived prudence is nothing, but only appears as if it was. Prudence is from no other source than intelligence and wisdom, and these two are from no other source than the understanding and thought thence derived of what is good and true. This is received and believed by those who acknowledge the Divine Providence, and not by those who acknowledge human prudence alone. Now either what the church teaches must be true, that all wisdom and prudence is from God, or what the world teaches, that all wisdom and prudence is from man. Can they be reconciled in any other way than by saying that what the church teaches is true, and what the world teaches is an appearance? For the church confirms what it teaches from the Word, and the world what it teaches from its *proprium;* but the Word is from God, and *proprium* is from man. Since prudence is from God, and not from man, therefore a Christian man, when he is in devotion, prays that God would lead his thoughts, intentions, and actions, adding also, because from himself he cannot: such a one also, when he sees any one doing good, says that he was inclined to it by God, and other similar things. Can any one so speak, unless he then interiorly believes it? and to believe it interiorly is from heaven; but when he thinks within himself, and collects arguments in favour of human prudence, he can believe the contrary, and this is from the world. Internal belief, however, prevails with those who acknowledge God in their hearts, and external belief with those who do not acknowledge God in their hearts, however they may do it with their mouths.

192. It was said, that no one, who from appearance is in the belief that human prudence does every thing, can be convinced except by reasons of deeper investigation, which are to

be deduced from causes; therefore, that reasons deduced from causes may be evident to the understanding, it is expedient to present them in their order, which will be as follows. I. That all a man's thoughts are from the affections of his life's love, and that there do not and cannot exist any thoughts at all without those affections. II. That the affections of a man's life's love are known to the Lord only. III. That the affections of a man's life's love are led of the Lord by his Divine Providence, and at the same time his thoughts, from which human prudence is derived. IV. That the Lord by his Divine Providence connects together the affections of the whole human race into one form, which is human. V. That thence heaven and hell, which are from the human race, are in such a form. VI. That those who have acknowledged nature alone and human prudence alone, constitute hell; and those who have acknowledged God, and his Divine Providence, constitute heaven. VII. That all these things cannot be effected, unless it appears to a man that he thinks and disposes things from himself.

193. I. *That all a man's thoughts are from the affections of his life's love, and that there do not and cannot exist any thoughts at all without those affections.* What the life's love is, what the affections and thoughts thence derived, and from these the sensations and actions which exist in the body, are in their essence, was shown above in this treatise, and also in that which is called ANGELIC WISDOM CONCERNING THE DIVINE LOVE AND THE DIVINE WISDOM, particularly in Part I. and Part V. Now since from these things are the causes from which human prudence flows as an effect, it is necessary that some of them should be adduced here also; for the things which are written in another place cannot be connected so continuously with the things which are written after them, as if the same are recalled and placed in view. Above, in this treatise, and in that before mentioned concerning THE DIVINE LOVE AND THE DIVINE WISDOM, it is demonstrated, that in the Lord there are divine love and divine wisdom; that these two are life itself; that from these two a man has will and understanding,—from the divine love will, and from the divine wisdom understanding; that to these two principles the heart and lungs in the body correspond; and thence it may appear, that as the pulsation of the heart, together with the respiration of the lungs, governs the whole man as to his body, so the will, together with the understanding, governs the whole man as to his mind; that thus there are two principles of life in every man, one natural and the other spiritual, and that the natural principle of life is the pulsation of the heart, and the spiritual principle of life the will of the mind; and that each adjoins to itself a consort, with which it cohabits, and with which it performs the functions of life, the heart conjoining to itself the lungs, and the will con-

120

joining to itself the understanding. Now, since the soul of the will is love, and the soul of the understanding is wisdom, both from the Lord, it follows, that love is the life of every one, and that according to the nature of its conjunction with wisdom, such is the life: or, what is the same, that the will is the life of every one, and that according to the nature of its conjunction with the understanding such is the life. But on this subject see more in a preceding part of this treatise, and especially in THE ANGELIC WISDOM CONCERNING THE DIVINE LOVE AND THE DIVINE WISDOM, in Part I. and Part V.

194. In these two treatises it is also demonstrated, that the life's love produces from itself subordinate loves, which are called affections, and which are exterior and interior; and that these taken together make as it were one dominion or kingdom, in which the life's love is lord or king. It is also demonstrated, that those subordinate loves or affections adjoin to themselves consorts, each its own,—the consorts of the interior affections being called perceptions, and those of the exterior affections being called thoughts; that each cohabits with its own consort, and discharges the functions of its life; and that there is a conjunction of both, like that of the essence of life with the existence of life, which is such, that one is not any thing but in conjunction with the other: for what is the essence of life unless it exists, and what is the existence of life but from its essence? also, that the conjunction of life is like that of sound and harmony, or of sound and speech, and in general like that of the pulsation of the heart and the respiration of the lungs; which conjunction is such that one without the other is not any thing, but that one by conjunction with the other becomes something. Conjunctions must either be in them, or are produced by them. Take sound for example: he is mistaken who thinks that sound is any thing, unless there be something in it which distinguishes. Sound also corresponds to affection in a man; and as there is in it always something which distinguishes, therefore from the sound or tone of a man's voice in speaking, is known the affection of his love, and from its variation, which is speech, is known his thought. Hence it is, that the wiser angels, merely from the sound or tone of voice of him who speaks, perceive his life's loves, together with certain affections which are derivations. These things are adduced, in order that it may be known, that there does not exist any affection without its thought, or any thought without its affection. But more may be seen on the subject above in this treatise, and in THE ANGELIC WISDOM CONCERNING THE DIVINE LOVE AND THE DIVINE WISDOM.

195. Now, as the life's love has its delight, and the wisdom thereof has its pleasantness, and in like manner every affection—which in its essence is a subordinate love derived from the life's love, as a stream from its fountain, or as a branch

121

from its tree, or as an artery from its heart—has its delight, and thence every perception and thought its pleasantness; it therefore follows, that those delights and pleasantnesses constitute a man's life. What is life without its delight and pleasantness? It is not any thing animate, but inanimate. Diminish delight and pleasantness, and you will grow cold or torpid; take them away, and you will expire and die. From the delights of the affections, and the pleasantnesses of the perceptions and thoughts, is derived the vital heat. Since every affection has its delight, and the thought thence derived its pleasantness, it may be plainly seen whence are good and truth, and also what they are in their essence. Good is to every one that which is the delight of his affection, and truth that which is the pleasantness of his thought thence derived: for every one calls that good which from the love of his will he feels delightful, and that true which from the wisdom of his understanding he thence perceives as pleasant. They both flow from the life's love, as water from a fountain, or as blood from the heart; and taken together are like a tide or atmosphere in which dwells the whole human mind. These two, delight and pleasantness, are spiritual in the mind, but natural in the body; and as existing in both they constitute a man's life. Hence it is evident what that is in a man which is called good, and what that which is called true; also, what that is in a man which is called evil, and what that which is called false; namely, that that is evil to him which destroys the delight of his affection, and that false which destroys the pleasantness of his thought thence derived. It is further evident, that evil from its delight and falsity from its pleasantness, may be called and thought good and true. Goods and truths are indeed changes and variations of state in the forms of the mind, but these are only perceived and exist by their delights and pleasantnesses. These things are stated, that it may be known what affection and thought are in their life.

196. Now, since it is not a man's body, but his mind which thinks, and thinks from the delight of its affection; and since a man's mind is his spirit, which lives after death, it follows that a man's spirit is nothing but affection, and thought thence derived. That there cannot exist any thought without affection, is very evident from spirits and angels in the spiritual world; for all there think from the affections of their life's love, the delight thereof encompassing every one as his atmosphere; and all there are connected according to the spheres emanating from their affections through their thoughts. The character and quality, also, of every one is known from the sphere of his life. Hence it may appear, that all thought is from affection, and that it is the form of its affection. It is the same with the will and the understanding; the same with good and truth; and the same with charity and faith.

197. II. *That the affections of a man's life's love are known to the Lord alone.* A man knows his thoughts and thence his intentions, because he sees them in himself; and as all prudence is from them, he sees that also in himself. If in this case his life's love is the love of self, he comes into the pride of self-derived intelligence, and ascribes prudence to himself, collecting arguments in favour of it, and so receding from the acknowledgment of the Divine Providence. It is similar if the love of the world is his life's love; but then he does not recede in the same degree. From these considerations it is evident, that these two loves ascribe all things to the man and his prudence; and, if examined more interiorly, nothing to God and his providence. Therefore when persons of that description happen to hear it stated as the truth, that human prudence is nothing, and that it is the Divine Providence alone which governs all things, they laugh at it if they are absolute atheists; but if they retain any thing of religion in the memory, and it is affirmed to them that all wisdom is from God, they acknowledge it indeed at first hearing, but yet inwardly in their spirit deny it. Such particularly are priests, who love themselves better than God, and the world better than heaven, or, what is the same thing, who worship God for the sake of honours and interest, and yet preach that charity and faith, every thing good and true, likewise all wisdom, and even all prudence, are from God, and nothing from man. In the spiritual world I once heard two priests disputing with a certain royal legate concerning human prudence, whether it be from God or from man; and their dispute was warm. They all three in their hearts thought alike, namely, that human prudence does every thing, and the Divine Providence nothing; but the priests, who were then under the influence of theological zeal, said that nothing of wisdom and prudence is from man; and when the legate replied, that at that rate there would be no thought from man either, they said that there was none. As it was perceived by the angels, however, that these three were of the same opinion, the legate was told to put on the garments of a priest, and think himself a priest, and then to speak: he accordingly did put them on, and thought as he was desired; and then he declared loudly that there never can be any wisdom or prudnce in a man but from God, and defended himself with his usual eloquence, full of rational arguments. Afterwards they said to the two priests also, Put off your garments, and put on the garments of political ministers, and think yourselves such: they did so, and then at the same time thought from their inner selves, and spoke from arguments which they had before cherished inwardly in favour of human prudence against the Divine Providence. As these three were in a similar faith, they subsequently became intimate friends and entered together into the path of self-derived prudence, which leads to hell.

198. It was shown above, that a man has not any thought, except from some affection of his life's love, and that thought is nothing else than the form of affection. Since, therefore, a man sees his thought, and cannot see his affection, for he feels the latter, it follows, that it is from sight, which is in appearance, that he concludes self-derived prudence to do every thing; and not from affection, which does not come into sight, but into sensation. For affection only manifests itself by a certain delight of thought and pleasure of ratiocination concerning it, and then this pleasure and delight make one with thought in those who are in the belief of self-derived prudence from the love of self or the love of the world; and thought flows in its delight as a ship in the current of a river, to which the sailor does not attend, but only to the sails which he expands.

199. A man can reflect, indeed, upon the delight of his external affection, when it acts as one with the delight of any bodily sense; but yet he does not reflect that that delight is from the delight of his affection in thought. For example: when a fornicator sees a harlot, his eyes sparkle with the fire of lasciviousness, and from it he feels delight in the body; but yet he does not feel the delight of his affection or concupiscence in thought, but as something of cupidity in the body. It is the same with a robber in the woods, when he sees travellers; a pirate in the sea, when he sees ships; and so with others. That these delights govern his thoughts, and that his thoughts are nothing without them, is evident; but he thinks that they are only thoughts, when nevertheless thoughts are nothing but affections composed into forms by his life's love, that they may appear in the light; for all affection is in heat, and all thought in light. These are affections of external thought, which manifest themselves indeed in the sensation of the body, but rarely in the thought of the mind: but the affections of internal thought, from which the external exist, never manifest themselves to a man. Of these he knows no more than a traveller sleeping in a carriage does of his journey, or than a man feels the circumrotation of the earth. Now, since a man knows nothing of the things which are transacted in the interiors of his mind, which are so infinite that they cannot be defined by numbers, and yet the few externals which come to the sight of his thought are produced from interiors, and the interiors are regulated of the Lord alone by his Divine Providence, and those few externals by the Lord in conjunction with the man; how can any one say, that his own prudence does every thing? If you were only to see one idea of thought disclosed, you would see more stupendous things than tongue can utter. That in the interiors of a man's mind there are such infinite things as cannot be defined by numbers, is evident from the infinite number of things in the body, from which nothing comes to the sight and sense but

124

action alone in much simplicity, to which, nevertheless, concur thousands of moving or muscular fibres, thousands of nervous fibres, thousands of blood-vessels, and thousands of pulmonary vessels, which must co-operate in every action, thousands of things in the brains and in the spinal marrow; and there are many more still in the spiritual man, which is the human mind: all the things whereof are forms of affections, and of perceptions and thoughts thence derived. Does not the soul which disposes interior things dispose actions also by virtue thereof? A man's soul is nothing but the love of his will, and the love of his understanding thence derived: such as this love is, such is the whole man; and he is made such according to the disposition in externals in which he is concerned with the Lord. Therefore if he attributes all things to himself and to nature, his soul becomes the love of self; but if he attributes all things to the Lord, his soul becomes the love of the Lord: and the latter love is celestial, but the former infernal.

200. Now, since the delights of a man's affections carry him from inmost things by the interiors to the exteriors, and at length to the outermost, which are in the body, as the airs and currents carry a ship; and since nothing of them appears to the man but what is done in the outermost of the mind and of the body, how can a man claim to himself what is divine from this circumstance alone, that those few outermost things appear to him as his own? Still less ought he to claim to himself what is divine, when he knows from THE WORD, that a man cannot take any thing from himself, except it be given him from heaven; and knows from REASON, that that appearance is granted him, in order that he may live a man, see what is good and evil, choose one or the other, and appropriate to himself that which he chooses, that there may be a possibility of his being joined reciprocally to the Lord, reformed, regenerated, saved, and of his living to eternity. That this appearance was granted to man that he might act from liberty according to reason, thus as if from himself, and not hang down his hands and wait for influx, was stated and shown above. Hence follows the confirmation of that which was to be demonstrated thirdly, *That the affections of a man's life's love are led of the Lord by his Divine Providence, and at the same time his thoughts, from which human prudence is derived.*

201. IV. *That the Lord by his Divine Providence connects together the affections of the whole human race into one form, which is the human.* That this is a universal of the Divine Providence, will be seen in the subsequent paragraph. Those who ascribe all things to nature, likewise ascribe all things to human prudence; for those who ascribe all things to nature deny God in their hearts, and those who ascribe all things to human prudence, deny the Divine Providence in their hearts: one is

not separable from the other. Yet both these sorts of persons for the sake of their reputation, and for fear of losing it, profess with their mouths that the Divine Providence is universal or general, but that the singulars of it rest with man; and that these singulars in their complex are understood by human prudence. But think within yourself, what is universal providence, when singulars are separated from it? Is it any thing more than a bare word? For that is called universal which is formed of singulars connected together, as that is common which exists from particulars. If, therefore, you separate singulars, what then is the universal but like something which is empty within, consequently like a surface within which there is nothing, or like a complex containing nothing? If it should be alleged, that the Divine Providence is a universal government, and that nothing is governed, but only kept in its connection, while the things which relate to government are disposed by others, can this be called a universal government? No king has such a government as this; for if a king were to allow his subjects to govern every thing in his kingdom, he would be no longer a king, but would only be called a king, therefore would have only a nominal and not a real dignity. Such a king cannot be said to hold the government, much less universal government. Providence with God is called prudence with man: as there cannot be said to be universal prudence in a king who has reserved to himself no more than the name, in order that his kingdom may be called a kingdom, and thus kept together; so neither could there be said to be a universal Providence, if men from their own prudence were to provide every thing. It is the same with the name of universal providence, and of universal government, as spoken in relation to nature, when it is understood that God created the universe, and endued nature with a power of producing all things from herself: what is universal providence in this case, but a metaphysical term, or a mere sound without meaning? And of those who attribute to nature every thing that is produced, and to human prudence every thing that is done, yet profess with their mouths that God created nature, many think no otherwise of the Divine Providence than as of an empty sound. But the case really is, that the Divine Providence exists in the most minute particulars of nature, and in the most minute particulars of human prudence, and by governing these particulars, governs universally.

202. The Divine Providence of the Lord is universal from things the most particular in this, that he created the universe, to the end that an infinite and eternal creation might exist therein from himself; and this creation exists by the Lord's forming from men a heaven, which appears before him as one man, in the image and likeness of himself. That heaven formed from men is such in the sight of the Lord, and that this was

126

the end of creation, was shown above, n. 27—45 : and that the Divine, in all that it does, has respect to what is infinite and eternal, n. 56—69. The infinite and eternal to which the Lord has respect in forming his heaven out of men, is, that it may be enlarged to infinity and eternity ; and thus that he may constantly dwell in the end of his creation. This creation which the Lord provided by the creation of the universe is infinite and eternal, and in this creation he is constantly engaged by his Divine Providence. Who that knows and believes from the doctrine of the church, that God is infinite and eternal—(*for the doctrine of all the churches in the Christian world holds, that God the Father, God the Son, and God the Holy Ghost, is infinite, eternal, uncreate, and omnipotent ; see the Athanasian Creed*) —can be so void of reason as not to assent, when he hears that God cannot do otherwise than respect infinity and eternity in his great work of creation,—(for how can he act otherwise when he acts from himself?)—and also that he respects this in the human race, out of which he forms his own heaven ? What else then can the Divine Providence have for its end, but the reformation and salvation of the human race ? And no one can be reformed of himself by his own prudence, but of the Lord by his Divine Providence : hence it follows, that except a man is led by the Lord every moment, even every the most minute point of time, he departs from the way of reformation, and perishes. Every change and variation of state of the human mind changes and varies something in the series of things present, and thereby of things consequent : what then must it not do in the progression to eternity ? It is like an arrow shot from a bow, which, if its direction at first should decline ever so little from the mark, would diverge immensely at the distance of a mile or more ; so would it be if the Lord, every the least moment, did not lead and govern the state of human minds. This the Lord does according to the laws of his Divine Providence ; according to which it is also necessary, that it should appear to a man as if he led himself ; but the Lord foresees how he will lead or guide himself, and continually provides accordingly. That the laws of permission are also laws of the Divine Providence ; that every man may be reformed and regenerated ; and that there does not exist any such thing as predestination, will be seen in what follows.

203. Since, therefore, every man lives after death to eternity, and according to his life here has his place assigned to him either in heaven or in hell, and both these, as well heaven as hell, must be in such a form as to act as one, as was said before ; and since no one can occupy any other place in that form but his own ; it follows, that the human race throughout the whole world is under the auspices of the Lord, and that every one, from his infancy even to the end of his life, is led of him in the

most minute particulars, and his place foreseen, and at the same time provided. From which considerations it is evident, that the Divine Providence of the Lord is universal, because it is in the most minute particulars; and that this is the infinite and eternal creation which the Lord has provided for himself by the creation of the universe. Of this universal providence a man does not see any thing; and if he did, it could not appear to him otherwise than as the scattered heaps and collections of materials, out of which a house is to be formed, appear to those who pass by; but by the Lord it is seen as a magnificent palace, the building and enlarging of which is continually going on.

204. V. *That heaven and hell are in such a form.* That heaven is in the human form, has been made known in the work concerning HEAVEN AND HELL, published in London in 1758, n. 59—102; also in the treatise concerning THE DIVINE LOVE AND THE DIVINE WISDOM; and in some parts of this treatise; it is therefore unnecessary to give it further confirmation. It is said that hell also is in the human form, but it is in a monstrous human form, such as is that of the devil, by whom is meant hell in its whole complex. It is in the human form, because those also who are there were born men, and have moreover those two human faculties which are called liberty and rationality, although they have abused their liberty to will and to do evil, and their rationality to think and confirm it.

205. VI. *That those who have acknowledged nature alone and human prudence alone, constitute hell; and those who have acknowledged God and his Divine Providence constitute heaven.* All who lead an evil life interiorly acknowledge nature and human prudence alone; for such acknowledgment lies inwardly concealed in all evil, however it may be covered by things good and true; these being borrowed garments, or like perishable decorations of flowers, strewed over evil lest it should appear in its nakedness. That all who lead an evil life interiorly acknowledge nature and human prudence alone, is not known because of that common covering by which it is hid from view; but that they do nevertheless acknowledge them, may appear from the origin and cause of such acknowledgment, for the purpose of discovering what it may be expedient to explain, whence and what self-derived prudence is; then, whence and what the Divine Providence is; afterwards, who and what kind of persons they are who favor the latter, and also those who favor the former; and lastly, that those who acknowledge the Divine Providence are in heaven, and those who acknowledge self-derived prudence are in hell.

206. WHENCE AND WHAT *self-derived prudence is.* It is from a man's proprium which is his nature, and is called his soul, derived from the parent. This proprium is the love of self and

128

the love of the world thence derived, or the love of the world and the love of self thence derived. The love of self is such, that it regards itself only, and looks upon others either as vile or of no account; or if it respects any person or thing, it is only so long as they honour and worship itself. Just like the effort to fructify and propagate, which is contained in a seed, there lies concealed in the inmost of self-love a desire to become great, to be made a king if possible, and then if possible to be deified. Such is a devil, because he is essentially the love of self, being such that he adores himself, and favours no one who does not also adore him. He hates another devil like himself, because he wishes himself alone to be adored. As no love can exist without its consort, and the consort of love or of the will in a man is called the understanding, therefore when the love of self inspires its love into the understanding its consort, it there becomes conceit, which is the conceit of self-derived intelligence, from which self-derived prudence proceeds. Now, since the love of self desires to be sole lord of the world, consequently a god, therefore the concupiscences of evil, which are derivations thence, have from it life in themselves, as have in like manner the perceptions of concupiscences, which are all sorts of craft and cunning; and as have also the delights of concupiscences which are evils, and their thoughts which are falses. All these are like servants and ministers of their lord, and act at his command, not knowing that they do not act, but are acted upon, being acted upon by the love of self through the conceit of self-derived intelligence. Hence it is that self-derived prudence, by virtue of its origin, lies concealed in every evil. The reason why an acknowledgment of nature alone also lies concealed therein, is, because self-love has closed as it were its upper window, or sky-light, by which there is an open communication with heaven, and the side windows also, lest it should see and hear that the Lord alone governs all things, that nature in herself is void of life, that a man's proprium is hell, and consequently that the love of the proprium is the devil: then, having shut the windows, it is in the dark, and there makes a fire for itself, by which it sits down with its consort; and they reason like friends in favour of nature against God, and in favour of self-derived prudence against the Divine Providence.

207. WHENCE AND WHAT *the Divine Providence is*. It is the divine operation in the man who removes the love of self; for self-love, as before said, is the devil, and concupiscences and their delights are the evils of his kingdom, which is hell. These being removed, the Lord enters with affections of neighbourly love, and opens the man's sky-light, and then his side windows, causing him to see that there is a heaven, a life after death, and everlasting happiness; and by means of the spiritual light and at the same time spiritual love then flowing in causes

129

him to acknowledge that God by his Divine Providence governs all things.

208. WHO AND WHAT *kind of persons those are who favour the latter, and also those who favour the former.* Those who acknowledge God and his Divine Providence, are like the angels of heaven, who dislike to be led of themselves, and love to be led of the Lord : and a sign of their being led of the Lord, is, that they love their neighbour. But those who acknowledge nature and their own prudence, are like infernal spirits, who dislike to be led of the Lord, and love to be led of themselves. These, if they are persons of distinction in a kingdom, desire to have dominion in all things. So, also, if they are primates of the church. If they are judges, they pervert judgment, and exercise dominion over the laws. If men of learning, they apply scientifics to confirm the proprium of man and nature. If they are merchants, they act as thieves : if husbandmen, as robbers. They are all enemies of God, and deriders of the Divine Providence.

209. It is wonderful, that when heaven is opened to such, and they are told that they are mad, and their madness is also made manifest to their perception, which is done by influx and illumination, they still, from indignation, shut heaven against themselves, and look down to the earth, under which is hell. This is the case with such of them in the spiritual world as are still out of hell, and yet of such a disposition ; from which circumstance is evinced the error of those who think, If I were to see heaven, and hear the angels speak to me, I should acknowledge. Their understanding however acknowledges ; but if their will does not at the same time, they nevertheless do not acknowledge ; for the love of the will infuses into the understanding whatever it chooses, and not *vice versa ;* obliterating indeed every thing in the understanding which is not from itself.

210. VII. *That all these things cannot be effected, unless it appears to a man that he thinks and disposes from himself.* That in case it did not appear to a man, as if he lived from himself, and thus thought and willed, spoke and acted as from himself, he would not be a man, is fully demonstrated in the preceding pages : from which it follows, that if a man did not dispose, as if from his own prudence, all things appertaining to his function and life, he could not be guided and regulated by the Divine Providence ; for he would be like one standing with his hands hanging down, his mouth open, his eyes shut, and his breath indrawn, in expectation of influx. He would therefore divest himself of humanity, which consists in the perception and sensation that he lives, thinks, wills, speaks, and acts as if from himself ; and at the same time he would divest himself of his two faculties, liberty and rationality, by which he is distinguished from beasts. That without such

appearance no man would possess receptibility and reciprocality, or therefore immortality, is demonstrated above in this treatise, and also in that on the DIVINE LOVE AND THE DIVINE WISDOM. Therefore, if you desire to be led by the Divine Providence, use prudence, as a servant and minister, who may faithfully dispense the goods of his master. This prudence is the talent given to the servants to traffic with, of which they are to render an account (Luke xix. 13—25; Matt. xxv. 14—31). Prudence itself appears to a man as his own, and is believed to be his own, so long as he keeps shut up within himself that most inveterate enemy of God and the Divine Providence, self-love, which dwells in the interiors of every man from his birth. If you do not know him,—for he desires not to be known,—he dwells securely, and guards the door, lest a man should open it, and he should thus be cast out by the Lord. That door is opened by a man, when, as if from himself, he shuns evils as sins, with an acknowledgment that he does so from the Lord. It is this prudence with which the Divine Providence acts as one.

211. The reason why the Divine Providence operates so secretly, that scarcely any one knows that it exists, is, in order that a man may not perish; for a man's proprium which is his will, never acts as one with the Divine Providence. A man's proprium has an innate enmity against it; for it is that serpent which seduced our first parents, of which it is written, "I will put enmity between thee and the woman, and between thy seed and her seed: it shall bruise thy head" (Gen. iii. 15). The serpent is evil of every kind: his head is self-love: the seed of the woman is the Lord: the enmity is between a man's self-love and the Lord, therefore also between a man's self-derived prudence and the Lord's Divine Providence; for self-derived prudence is continually lifting up its head, and the Divine Providence is continually keeping it down. If a man felt this, he would be enraged and exasperated against God, and would perish: but while he does not feel or perceive it, he may be enraged and exasperated against men, against himself, and likewise against fortune, and yet not perish. Hence it is, that the Lord by his Divine Providence continually leads a man in freedom, and being in freedom, it appears no otherwise to him than that he is led by his own proprium. To lead in freedom one who is in opposition to him that leads, is like raising from the earth a great resisting weight with pulleys, by which means the weight and resistance are not felt; or as, when any one is in the power of an enemy, whose intention is to put him to death, which he does not then know, and a friend contrives his escape through unknown ways, and afterwards discovers to him the enemy's intention.

212. Who does not talk of fortune, and who does not

131

acknowledge it, because he talks of it, and because he knows something of it by experience? But who knows what it is? That it is something, because it is and exists, cannot be denied; and nothing can be and exist without a cause; but the cause of this something or of fortune is not known. Yet lest it should be denied, merely from ignorance of that cause, take dice, or cards, and play with them, or consult players: which of them denies fortune? for they play with it, and it with them, in a wonderful manner. Who can oppose it, if it is obstinate? Does it not in such case make a jest of prudence and wisdom? When you throw the dice and shuffle the cards, does it not seem as if it knew and disposed the evolutions and motions of the hands, to favour one more than another, from some certain cause? Can this cause exist from any other source, than the Divine Providence in ultimates, where, by constant, and inconstant things, it deals wonderfully with human prudence, and at the same time conceals itself? That the Gentiles formerly acknowledged Fortune, and that those of Italy also built a temple for her at Rome, is well known. Concerning this fortune, which is, as was said, the Divine Providence in ultimates, many things have been made known which it is not permitted me to reveal; and from which it was evinced to me, that it is not an illusion of the mind, or a sporting of nature, or something without a cause, for that is not any thing; but that it is an ocular testification, that the Divine Providence is in the most minute particulars of a man's thoughts and actions. When the Divine Providence operates in the smallest particulars of matters so mean and trifling, what must it not do in the particulars of things not mean and trifling, such as the affairs of peace and war upon earth, and those of salvation and everlasting life in heaven!

213. But I know that human prudence brings over the rational faculty to take part with it, more than with the Divine Providence, because the latter does not appear, and the former does. It can be more easily conceded that there is one sole life, which is God, and that all men are recipients of life from him, as was abundantly shown before; and this nevertheless amounts to the same thing, because prudence is of life. Who does not reason in favour of human prudence and nature, when he reasons from the natural or external man? Whereas, who does not reason in favour of the Divine Providence and of God, when he reasons from the spiritual or internal man? But write, I pray you, two books (I speak this to the natural man), one in favour of self-derived prudence, another in favour of nature, and fill them with plausible, probable, and likely arguments, such as in your opinion are solid; and when you have done, put them into the hand of any angel, and I know that there will be written under them these few words: They are all appearances and fallacies.

132.

THAT THE DIVINE PROVIDENCE HAS RESPECT TO THINGS ETERNAL, AND NOT TO THINGS TEMPORARY, EXCEPT SO FAR AS THEY ACCORD WITH THINGS ETERNAL.

214. THAT the Divine Providence has respect to things eternal, and not to things temporary, except so far as they accord with things eternal, or make one with them, is to be demonstrated in the following order :—I. That temporary things relate to dignities and riches, therefore to honours and emoluments, in this world. II. That eternal things relate to spiritual honours and riches, which are of love and wisdom, in heaven. III. That things temporary and eternal are separated by man, but joined by the Lord. IV. That the conjunction of things temporary and eternal is the Divine Providence of the Lord.

215. I. *That temporary things relate to dignities and riches, therefore to honours and emoluments, in this world.* There are many temporary things, but yet they all relate to dignities and riches. By temporary things are meant those which either perish with time, or cease with a man's life in this world only ; but by eternal things are meant those which do not perish and cease with time, therefore not with the life in this world. Since all temporary things, as was observed, have relation to dignities and riches, it is important that the following points should be understood ; namely, what and whence are dignities and riches : what is the nature of the love of them for their own sake, and what the nature of the love of them for the sake of use : that these two loves are distinct from each other, as hell is from heaven : that the difference between these loves is difficult to be known : but of each of these distinctly. FIRST, *What and whence are dignities and riches.* Dignities and riches were totally different in the earliest ages from what they afterwards successively became. Dignities in the most ancient times were no other than such as exist among parents and their children, which were dignities of love, full of respect and veneration in the latter for the former, not because they received from them birth, but instruction and wisdom, which is a second birth, in itself spiritual, because it was the birth of their spirit. This was the only dignity in the earliest ages, because then nations, families, and houses dwelt separately, and were not formed into kingdoms as in the present day. It was the father of the family in whom that dignity resided. Those times were called by the ancients the golden age. After those times, however, the love of governing, from the sole delight of that love, successively crept in ; and because enmity and hostility against those who would not submit arose at the same time, therefore nations, families, and houses assembled themselves together from necessity, and set over themselves one whom at first they called a judge, afterwards a prince, and lastly a king and an emperor.

133

Then also they began to fortify themselves by towers, bulwarks, and walls. From the judge, prince, king, or emperor, as from the head into the body, a lust of dominion spread itself like a contagion among many, and thence arose degrees of dignities, with honours, conformable to them; and with them self-love, and the pride of self-derived prudence. The case was similar with regard to the love of riches. In the most ancient times, when nations and families dwelt distinctly from each other, there was no other love of riches than that of possessing the necessaries of life, which they procured for themselves by flocks and herds, and by fields, pastures, and gardens, from which they derived subsistence. Among their necessaries of life were also reckoned decent houses, furnished with all kinds of utensils, and likewise clothing. The care and management of all these things was the business of the parents, children, men-servants, and maid-servants in the house. But after the love of dominion began to prevail, and destroyed this state of society, the love of possessing wealth beyond their necessities also invaded mankind, and grew to such a height as to produce a desire of possessing the wealth of all. These two loves are connected as it were by consanguinity; for he who desires to rule over all things, desires also to possess all, that thus all persons may become his servants, and he their sole lord and master. This is plainly manifested among those of the popish religion, who have exalted their dominion even into heaven, unto the throne of the Lord, upon which they have placed themselves, and who covet also the riches of the whole earth, and amass treasures without end. SECONDLY, *What is the nature of the love of dignities and riches for their own sake, and what the nature of the love of them for the sake of use.* The love of dignities and honours for the sake of dignities and honours, is the love of self, properly the love of dominion arising from the love of self; and the love of riches and wealth, for the sake of riches and wealth, is the love of the world, properly the love of possessing the goods of others by any art whatever: but the love of dignities and riches for the sake of uses, is the love of uses, which is the same with the love of our neighbour; for that for the sake of which a man acts, is the end which he has in view, and is first or primary, while other things are means, and are secondary. With respect to the love of dignities and honours for their own sakes, which is the same with self-love, properly with the love of dominion from the love of self, it is the love of a man's proprium, and a man's proprium is all evil. Hence it is that a man is said to be born in all evil, and that his hereditary disposition is nothing but evil. A man's hereditary disposition is his proprium, in which he is, and into which he comes by self-love, principally by the love of dominion grounded in the love of self; for the man who is principled in that love, has respect to nothing but himself, and so immerses his thoughts

134

and affections into his proprium. Hence it is that in the love of self there dwells a love of doing evil; the reason of which is, that the man does not love his neighbour, but himself only; and he who loves himself alone, sees others as without himself, or as vile, or of no account, and despises them in comparison with himself, whilst he makes light of doing them mischief. It is from this cause that he who is in the love of dominion from the love of self scruples not to defraud his neighbour, to commit adultery with his neighbour's wife, to slander him, to breathe revenge against him even unto death, to treat him cruelly, and the like. A man derives such evil dispositions from this circumstance, that the devil himself, with whom every one principled in self-love is conjoined, and by whom he is led, is nothing else than the love of dominion from the love of self; and he who is led of the devil, that is, of hell, is led into all the above evils, and is continually led by the delights of those evils. Hence it is, that all who are in hell have a desire to do mischief to every one; but those who are in heaven have a desire to do good to every one. From this opposition exists that middle state, in which a man is placed, and in which he is as it were in an equilibrium, so that he can turn himself either to hell or to heaven; and in proportion as he favours the evils of self-love, he turns himself to hell, and in proportion as he removes those evils from himself, he turns himself to heaven. It has been granted me to feel of what kind and how great is the delight of the love of dominion from the love of self. I was let into it in order that I might know it; and it was such, that it exceeded all the delights in the world. It was a delight of the whole mind from its inmost to its ultimate faculties, but was only felt in the body as a certain pleasure and gladness swelling in the breast. It was also granted me to perceive, that from this delight, as from their fountain, flow the delights of all evils, as adultery, revenge, fraud, blasphemy, and every thing that is wicked in general. There is a similar delight also in the love of possessing the wealth of others by any art whatever, and in the concupiscences which are derivations from it; but yet not in the same degree, unless it be joined to the love of self. With respect to dignities and riches, however, that are loved not for their own sake, but for the sake of uses, such love is not the love of dignities and riches, but the love of uses, to which dignities and riches are subservient as means; and this love is celestial: but of it more in what follows. THIRDLY, *That those two loves are distinct from each other as heaven and hell*, is evident from what has now been said; to which I will add, that all those who are in the love of dominion from the love of self, whoever they be, whether great or small, are in hell as to their spirit; and that all who are in that love, are in the love of all evils, which if they do not commit, they still in their spirit think them allowable, and

135

therefore do them in the body, when the consideration of dignity and honour, and the fear of the law, do not prevent. And what is more, the love of dominion from the love of self conceals deeply within it hatred against God, consequently against the divine things of the church, and especially against the Lord. If persons influenced by this love acknowledge a God, they do it only with their mouths; and if they acknowledge the divine things of the church, they do it only for fear of losing credit. The reason why this love inmostly conceals in it hatred against the Lord, is, because it is the inmost tendency of it to desire to be a god, for it worships and adores itself alone; hence it is, that if any one honours it so much as to say that it has divine wisdom, and is the deity of the world, it loves such a one in its heart. It is otherwise with the love of dignities and riches for the sake of uses; for this love is celestial, because, as has been observed, it is the same with the love of our neighbour. By uses are meant goods, and therefore by performing uses, is meant doing good; and by doing uses or good, is meant serving others and ministering to them. Those who do so, although they are in dignity and opulence, yet respect such dignity and opulence only as means of performing uses, consequently of serving and ministering. These are those who are meant by these words of the Lord: " Whosoever will be great among you, let him be your minister; and whosoever will be chief among you, let him be your servant" (Matt. xx. 26, 27). These also are those to whom dominion in heaven is entrusted by the Lord; for to them dominion is the means of performing uses, or doing good, consequently of serving; and when uses or good are the ends, or objects of the love, then it is not they who have dominion, but the Lord, for all good is from him. FOURTHLY, *That the difference between them is difficult to be known*, is, because most of those who are in dignity and opulence also perform uses; but it is not known whether they perform them for the sake of themselves, or for the sake of the uses; and the less so, because in the love of self and of the world, there is more of the fire and ardour of performing uses than in those who are not in the love of self and the world. The former, however, perform uses for the sake of fame or interest, therefore for the sake of themselves; but those who perform uses for the sake of uses, or good for the sake of good, do not perform them from themselves, but from the Lord. The difference between them is difficult to be known by a man, because he does not know whether he is led by the devil or the Lord. He who is led by the devil, performs uses for the sake of himself and the world; but he who is led by the Lord, does it for the sake of the Lord and of heaven; and all those perform uses from the Lord who shun evils as sins, while all those perform uses from the devil who do not shun evils as sins; for evil is the devil, and use or good is the Lord

136

Hereby and no otherwise is the difference known. Both in their external form appear alike, but in their internal form they are totally unlike. One is like gold which contains within it dross; the other is like gold which is within pure gold. One also is like artificial fruit, which in its external form appears like fruit gathered from a tree, when nevertheless it is coloured wax, which has within it dust or resin; the other is like excellent fruit, delightful to the taste and smell, which has within it seeds.

216. II. *That eternal things relate to spiritual honours and riches, which are of love and wisdom in heaven.* As the natural man calls the delights of self-love, which are also the delights of the concupiscences of evil, goods, and also confirms himself in the notion that they are goods, he therefore calls honours and riches divine blessings; but when this natural man sees that the wicked, as well as the good, are advanced to honours and promoted to riches, and still more when he sees that the good are in contempt and poverty, and the wicked in glory and opulence, he thinks within himself, What is the meaning of this? It cannot be of the Divine Providence, for if the Divine Providence governed all things, it would load the good with honours and wealth, and afflict the wicked with poverty and contempt, and thus compel the wicked to acknowledge that there is a God and a Divine Providence. But the natural man, unless illuminated by the spiritual man, that is, unless he is at the same time spiritual, does not see that honours and riches may possibly be blessings, and that possibly also they may be curses; or, that when they are blessings they are from God, and when they are curses they are from the devil. That honours and wealth are also given by the devil is known, for thence he is called the prince of this world. Now since it is not known when honours and riches are blessings, and when they are curses, it shall therefore be shown, in this order: 1. That honours and riches are blessings, and that they are curses. 2. That honours and riches, when they are blessings, are spiritual and eternal; and that when they are curses, they are temporary and perishing. 3. That the honours and riches which are curses, in comparison with those which are blessings, are as nothing to everything, or as that which does not exist in *itself*, to *that which* does exist in itself.

217. These three points are now to be separately illustrated. FIRST, *That honours and riches are blessings, and that they are curses.* Common experience testifies, that the pious as well as the impious, or the just as well as the unjust, that is, the good as well as the evil, are in dignities and riches; yet it cannot be denied by any one, that the impious and unjust, that is, the wicked, go to hell, and the pious and just, that is, the good, to heaven. This being true, it follows, that dignities and riches,

137

or honours and wealth, are either blessings or curses ; and that with the good they are blessings, and with the wicked curses. In the work concerning HEAVEN AND HELL, published in London in the year 1758, n. 357—365, it is shown, that in heaven and also in hell there are rich as well as poor, and great as well as little; from which it is evident, that dignities and riches, with those who are in heaven, were in this world blessings, and, with those who are in hell, were in this world curses. But whence it is that they are blessings, and whence that they are curses, every one may know, if he thinks a little on the subject from reason; namely, that they are blessings with those who do not place their hearts in them, and that they are curses with those who do place their hearts in them. To place the heart in them, is to love self in them; and not to place the heart in them, is to love uses and not self in them. The nature and quality of the difference between these two loves, was explained above, n. 215; to which may be added, that dignities and wealth seduce some, and do not seduce others. They seduce, when they excite the loves of a man's proprium, which is the love of self; and that this is the love of hell, which is called the devil, was also shown above; but they do not seduce, when they do not excite that love. The reason why the wicked as well as the good are advanced to honours and promoted to wealth, is, because the wicked as well as the good perform uses; but the wicked do so for the sake of the honour and interest of their own persons, and the good for the sake of the honour and interest of the thing itself. The latter respect the honour and interest of the thing itself as principal causes, and the honour and interest of their own persons as instrumental causes; but the wicked respect the honour and interest of their own persons as principal causes, and the honour and interest of the thing itself as instrumental causes. Yet who does not see, that the person, his function, and honour, are for the sake of the office which he administers, and not the contrary? Who does not see that a judge is for the sake of justice, a magistrate for the sake of the community, and a king for the sake of the kingdom, and not *vice versa?* Therefore also, according to the laws of a kingdom, every one is in dignity and honour suitable to the dignity of his office and the functions belonging to it; and there is a difference between them like that which exists between what is principal and what is instrumental. He who attributes the honour of his office to himself, or to his own person, appears in the spiritual world, when the same is represented, like a man with his body inverted, having his feet upward, and his head downward. SECONDLY, *That dignities and riches, when they are blessings, are spiritual and eternal, and when they are curses, are temporary and perishing.* There are dignities and riches in heaven as well as in this world; for there

138

are governments there, consequently administrations and functions, and there are also commercial dealings, consequently riches, because there are societies and communities. The universal heaven is distinguished into two kingdoms, one of which is called the celestial, the other the spiritual kingdom, and each kingdom into innumerable societies, greater and smaller, all which, and all in which, are disposed in order according to the differences of love and the wisdom therefrom derived; the societies of the celestial kingdom according to the differences of celestial love, which is love to the Lord; and the societies of the spiritual kingdom according to the differences of spiritual love, which is love towards their neighbour. As there are such societies, and all who compose them have been men in the world, consequently retain in them the loves in which they were principled in the world,—with this difference, that in another world they are spiritual, and that the dignities and riches themselves are spiritual in the spiritual kingdom, and celestial in the celestial kingdom,—it follows as a consequence, that those who have greater love and wisdom than others, have greater dignities and riches than others, and these are those to whom dignities and riches were blessings in this world. Hence may appear, what is the nature of spiritual dignities and riches, namely, that they belong to the thing and not to the person. Persons, indeed, who are in dignity in heaven, are in magnificence and glory, like that of kings upon earth; but yet they do not regard the dignity itself as any thing, but the uses, in the exercise and administration of which they are engaged. They receive every one the honours of his dignity, but they do not attribute them to themselves, but to the uses: and as all uses are from the Lord, they attribute them to the Lord, from whom they are derived. Such therefore are spiritual dignities and riches, which are eternal. But it is otherwise with those to whom dignities and riches in this world were curses. These, since they attributed them to themselves, and not to uses, and since they did not desire that uses should govern them, but that they should govern uses, which they only regarded as such so far as they were subservient to their own honour and glory, are therefore in hell, where they are vile drudges in contempt and misery; for which reason, as these dignities and riches perish, they are called temporary and perishing. Concerning both the latter and the former the Lord teaches as follows: "Lay not up for yourselves treasures upon earth, where moth and rust corrupt, and where thieves break through and steal: but lay up for yourselves treasures in heaven, where neither moth nor rust doth corrupt, and where thieves do not break through nor steal. for where your treasure is, there will your heart be also" (Matt. vi. 19, 20, 21). THIRDLY, *That dignities and riches which are curses, compared with those which are blessings, are as*

139

nothing to every thing, or as that which does not exist in itself, to that which does exist in itself. Every thing which perishes and becomes nothing is inwardly in itself nothing : outwardly indeed it is something, and even appears to be much, and to some every thing, so long as it lasts, but in itself it is not. It is like a surface within which there is not any thing; or like a theatrical performer who appears in a king's apparel only till the play is ended. But that which remains to eternity is in itself something perpetually, therefore every thing; and moreover It Is, because it does not cease to be.

218. III. *That things temporary and eternal are separated by man, but are joined by the Lord.* The reason of this is, that all things appertaining to a man are temporary, from which circumstance a man may be called temporary ; and all things appertaining to the Lord are eternal, whence the Lord is called eternal. Temporary things are those which have an end and perish, but eternal things are those which have no end, and do not perish. That these two cannot be joined together, except by the infinite wisdom of the Lord, therefore that they can be joined together by the Lord, and not by man, every one can see. But that it may be known, that these two are separated by a man, and joined by the Lord, it shall be demonstrated in the following order. 1. What are temporary things and what eternal things. 2. That a man is in himself temporary and the Lord is in himself eternal; that therefore nothing can proceed from a man but what is temporary, and nothing from the Lord but what is eternal. 3. That temporary things separate from themselves eternal things, and that eternal things join to themselves temporary things. 4. That the Lord joins a man to himself by appearances. 5. And by correspondences.

219. These propositions are severally to be illustrated and confirmed by themselves. FIRST, *What are temporary things, and what eternal things.* Temporary things are all those which are proper to nature, and thence proper to a man. Things proper to nature are especially spaces and times, both subject to limit and termination; and the things which are thence proper to a man, are those of his proper will and his proper understanding, which are thence of his affection and thought, especially the things which are of his own prudence; which things, it is well known, are finite and limited. But things eternal are all things which are proper to the Lord, and from him are as it were proper to a man. Things proper to the Lord are all infinite and eternal, therefore without time, consequently without limit and without end. The things which are thence as it were proper to a man, are in like manner infinite and eternal; but nothing of these is of the man, but of the Lord alone in him. SECONDLY, *That a man is in himself temporary, and the Lord is in himself eternal; that therefore nothing can*

proceed from a man but what is temporary, and nothing from the Lord but what is eternal. That a man is in himself temporary, and the Lord in himself eternal, was stated above. Since nothing can proceed from any one but that which is in him, it follows, that nothing can proceed from a man but what is temporary, and nothing from the Lord but what is eternal; for infinite cannot proceed from finite, and to suppose that it can is a contradiction; nevertheless infinite can proceed from finite, yet not from finite itself, but from infinite through it. So, on the other hand, finite cannot proceed from infinite, and to suppose this is also a contradiction: yet finite can be produced by infinite, but this is not to proceed, but to be created; on which subject see THE ANGELIC WISDOM CONCERNING THE DIVINE LOVE AND THE DIVINE WISDOM, from beginning to end. Therefore if finite proceeds from the Lord, as is the case in many things with a man, it does not proceed from the Lord, but from the man; and it may be said to proceed from the Lord through the man, because it so appears. This may be illustrated by these words of the Lord: "Let your communication be, Yea, yea; Nay, nay; for whatsoever is more than these, cometh of evil" (Matt. v. 37). Such is the communication of all in the third heaven; for they never reason concerning things divine, whether they be so or not, but see in themselves from the Lord, that they are so or not so. Reasoning concerning things divine, whether they be so or not, arises from the reasoner's not seeing them from the Lord, but desiring to see them from himself; and that which a man sees from himself is evil. But yet the Lord wills, not only that a man should think and speak of things divine, but also reason concerning them, to the end that he may see that they are so or not so; and such thought, discourse, or reasoning, provided it has for its end that he may see the truth, may be said to be from the Lord in him; but it is from the man, until he sees truth, and acknowledges it. In the mean time it is from the Lord alone, that a man is capable of thinking, speaking, and reasoning; for this he can do by virtue of his two faculties called liberty and rationality, which he possesses from the Lord alone. THIRDLY, *That temporary things separate from themselves eternal things, and that eternal things join to themselves temporary things.* By temporary things separating from themselves eternal things, is meant, that a man who is temporary does so from the temporary things in himself; and by eternal things joining to themselves temporary things, is meant, that the Lord who is eternal, does so from the eternal things in himself, as was said above. In the preceding pages it was shown, that there is a conjunction of the Lord with a man, and a reciprocal conjunction of the man with the Lord; yet that the reciprocal conjunction of the man with the Lord is not from the man, but from the Lord; also that a man's will is in oppo-

141

sition to the Lord's will, or, what amounts to the same, that a man's self-derived prudence is in opposition to the Lord's Divine Providence; from which considerations it follows, that a man, from his own temporary things, separates from himself the eternal things of the Lord, but that the Lord joins eternal things to the man's temporary things, that is, joins himself to the man and the man to himself. As this subject has been fully treated of before, it is not necessary to add any further confirmation of it. FOURTHLY, *That the Lord joins a man to himself by appearances:* for it is an appearance that a man from himself loves his neighbour, does good, and speaks truth. If these things were not to appear to a man as from himself, he would not love his neighbour, or do good, or speak truth, therefore would not be conjoined to the Lord; but as love, good, and truth are from the Lord, it is evident that the Lord joins a man to himself by appearances. This appearance, however, and the conjunction of the Lord with a man, with the reciprocal conjunction of the man with the Lord thereby, are abundantly treated of above. FIFTHLY, *That the Lord joins a man to himself by correspondences.* This is done by means of the Word, the literal sense of which consists of mere correspondences. That by that sense there is a conjunction of the Lord with a man, and a reciprocal conjunction of the man with the Lord, is shown in THE DOCTRINE OF THE NEW JERUSALEM CONCERNING THE SACRED SCRIPTURE, from beginning to end.

220. IV. *That the conjunction of things temporary and eternal in a man is the Divine Providence of the Lord.* As the subjects involved in this proposition cannot fall within the first perception of the understanding, except they be previously reduced to order, and unfolded and demonstrated according to it, therefore the arrangement of them shall be as follows. 1. That it is from the Divine Providence, that a man by death puts off things natural and temporary, and puts on things spiritual and eternal. 2. That the Lord by his Divine Providence joins himself to things natural by things spiritual, and to things temporary by things eternal, according to uses. 3. That the Lord joins himself to uses by correspondences, and so by appearances according to confirmations by a man. 4. That such conjunction of things temporary and eternal is the Divine Providence. But these points may be placed in a clearer light by explanations. FIRST, *That it is from the Divine Providence, that a man by death puts off things natural and temporary, and puts on things spiritual and eternal.* Things natural and temporary are extremes and ultimates (or the outermost and last or lowest things), into which a man first enters, which he does when he is born, to the end that he may afterwards be introduced into things interior and superior; for extremes and ultimates are the continents (or those which contain or keep the whole

142

together); and these exist in the natural world. Hence it is that no angel or spirit was immediately created such, but all were first born men, and so introduced: therefore, they have extremes and ultimates, which in themselves are fixed and stated, within which and by which their interiors can be retained in their state of connection. A man first puts on the grosser substances of nature, his body consisting of them; but these he puts off by death, and retains the purer substances of nature, which are next to what is spiritual, and which then are his continents. Besides, in extremes or ultimates, are all things interior or superior together, as was shown before in its proper place; therefore every operation of the Lord is from primary and ultimate things at once, consequently in full. But as the extremes and ultimates of nature cannot receive things spiritual and eternal, for which the human mind is formed, as they are in themselves, and yet a man is born that he may be made spiritual and live to eternity, therefore he puts them off, and retains only interior natural things, which are convenient, and accord with things spiritual and celestial, and serve them as continents. This is effected by the rejection of temporary and natural ultimates, which is the death of the body. SECONDLY, *That the Lord by his Divine Providence joins himself to things natural by things spiritual, and to things temporary by things eternal, according to uses.* Natural and temporary things are not only those which are proper to nature, but also those which are proper to men in the natural world. Both these a man puts off by death, and puts on things spiritual and eternal corresponding to them. That he puts on these according to uses, is fully shown in the foregoing pages. The natural things which are proper to nature, relate in general to time and space, and in particular to the objects which are seen upon earth. These a man relinquishes by death, and in place of them receives things spiritual, which are similar as to their outward aspect or appearance, but not as to their internal quality and essence; which subject also is treated of above. The temporary things which are proper to men in the natural world, relate in general to dignities and riches, and in particular to the necessities of each individual, which are food, clothing, and habitation. These also are put away and left by death, and these things put on and received which are similar to them as to their outward aspect or appearance, but not as to their internal quality and essence. All these derive their internal quality and essence from the uses of things temporary in the world; and uses are the goods which are called goods of charity. Hence it may appear, that to things natural and temporary the Lord by his Divine Providence joins things spiritual and eternal, according to uses. THIRDLY, *That the Lord joins himself to uses by correspondences, and so by appearances according to the confirmations of them by a*

143

man. As this point cannot but seem obscure to those who have not yet acquired a clear notion respecting the nature of correspondence and appearance, it must be illustrated by example and thus explained. All things in the Word are mere correspondences of things spiritual and celestial, and, because they are correspondences, they are also appearances; that is, all things in the Word are divine goods of the divine love, and divine truths of the divine wisdom, which are naked in themselves, but clothed in the literal sense of the Word; therefore they appear like a man invested with a garment corresponding to the state of his love and wisdom; from which it is evident that if a man confirms in himself appearances, it is just as if he were to believe that garments are men. Thus, appearances become fallacies. It is otherwise if a man searches after truths, and sees them in appearances. Now as all the uses, or truths and goods of charity, which a man does to his neighbour, he does either according to appearances or according to the truths themselves in the Word, if he establishes the confirmation of them in himself according to appearances, he is in fallacies, but if according to truths, he does as he ought to do. Hence it may appear, what is meant by the Lord's joining himself to uses by correspondences, and so by appearances, according to the confirmations of them by a man. FOURTHLY, *That such conjunction of things temporary and eternal is the Divine Providence.* That this may be presented to the understanding in some degree of light, it is expedient to illustrate it by two examples,—by one which concerns dignities and honours, and by another which concerns riches and possessions. Both these in their external form are natural and temporary, but in their internal form spiritual and eternal. Dignities with their honours are natural and temporary, when a man has respect to himself personally in them, and not to the state and uses; for then he cannot but think interiorly with himself, that the state is for the sake of him, and not he for the state. He is like a king who thinks that his kingdom and all the people in it are for him, and not he for the kingdom and the people of which it consists. But the same dignities with their honours are spiritual and eternal, when a man considers himself personally as subservient to the state and to uses, and not them to him. If he does this, he is in the truth and in the essence of his dignity and honour, but if the other, then he is in correspondence and appearance, which if he confirms in himself, he is in fallacies, and no otherwise in conjunction with the Lord than as those who are in falsities and evils derived therefrom; for fallacies are falsities with which evils join themselves. Such persons do indeed perform uses and do good; but it is from themselves, and not from the Lord; therefore, they put themselves in the place of the Lord. It is the same with regard to riches and possessious, which also are natural and temporary, as well as spiritual and eternal. Riches and possessions are natural and temporary with those who have respect to them alone, and to themselves in them, and in these two place all their pleasure and delight; but they are spiritual and eternal with those who have respect to good uses in them, and have in these an interior pleasure and delight. With the latter, the exterior pleasure and delight also is made spiritual, and the temporary is made eternal; therefore also after death they dwell in heaven, and in palaces there, the utensils of which are resplendent with gold and precious stones; but these nevertheless they regard no otherwise than as externals deriving their splendour and transparency from internals, which are uses, and from them they have essential pleasure and delight, which in themselves are the bliss and happiness of heaven. A contrary lot falls to those who have had respect to riches and possessions solely for their own sake and for the sake of self, therefore for the sake of externals and not at the same time of internals, consequently according to appearances and not according to their essences. Such persons, when they put off these things, as is the case when they die, put on the internals thereof, which, since they are not spiritual, cannot be otherwise than infernal; for either the one or the other principle is in them, as both cannot be there together. Hence, instead of riches they experience poverty, and, instead of possessions, misery. By uses are meant, not only the necessaries of life, which relate to food, clothing, and habitation for a man and his family, but also the good of his country, of society, and of his fellow-citizens. Such a good is commerce, when the love of it is the end, and that of money the means subservient, provided the merchant shuns and avoids frauds and evil arts as sins; but not so when the love of money is the end, and that of commerce the means subservient to it; for this is avarice, which is the root of all evils, as may be seen in Luke xii. 15, and the parable concerning it, verse 16—21.

THAT A MAN IS NOT ADMITTED INTERIORLY INTO THE TRUTHS OF FAITH AND THE GOODS OF CHARITY, EXCEPT SO FAR AS HE CAN BE KEPT IN THEM TO THE END OF LIFE.

221. It is well known in the Christian world, that the Lord wills the salvation of all, and also that he is omnipotent; therefore many thence conclude, that he is able to save every one, and does save those who implore his mercy, especially those

who implore it by the received form of faith,—that God the
Father would have mercy for the sake of his Son,—particularly
if, at the same time, they pray that they may receive that faith.
That the case is altogether different, however, will be seen in
the last article of this treatise, where it will be explained, that
the Lord cannot act against the laws of his Divine Providence,
because to act against them would be to act against his divine
love and his divine wisdom, consequently against himself; and
where also it will be seen, that such immediate mercy is not
possible, because man's salvation is effected by means, according
to which no one can lead a man, but He who wills the salvation
of all, and is, at the same time, omnipotent, consequently the
Lord. The means by which a man is led by the Lord, are what
are called the laws of the Divine Providence, among which is
this, that a man is not admitted interiorly into the truths of
wisdom and the goods of love, except so far as he can be kept
in them to the end of life. But that this may be evident to
reason, it shall be explained in the following order. I. That a
man may be admitted into the wisdom of spiritual things, and
also into the love of them, and yet not be reformed. II. That
if a man afterwards recedes from them, and runs counter to
them, he profanes what is sacred. III. That there are several
kinds of profanation, but that this kind is the worst of all.
IV. That therefore the Lord does not admit a man interiorly
into the truths of wisdom, and at the same time into the goods
of love, except so far as he can be kept in them to the end
of life.

222. I. *That a man may be admitted into the wisdom of
spiritual things, and also into the love of them, and yet not be
reformed.* The reason is, because a man has rationality and
liberty. By rationality he can be elevated into wisdom almost
angelic, and by liberty into a love not unlike angelic love;
nevertheless, such as is the love, such is the wisdom: if the
love is celestial and spiritual, the wisdom also becomes celestial
and spiritual; but if the love is diabolical and infernal, the wisdom also is diabolical and infernal. The latter, indeed, may
then appear in its external form, and consequently before others,
as celestial and spiritual; but in its internal form, which is its
very essence, it is diabolical and infernal, not outwardly but
inwardly. That it is such, does not appear to men, because
they are natural, and see and hear naturally, and the external
form is natural; but it does so appear to angels, because they
are spiritual, and the internal form is spiritual. Hence it is
evident, that a man might be admitted into the wisdom of
spiritual things, and also into the love of them, and yet not be
reformed; but in this case only into the natural, and not into
the spiritual love of them. The reason is, because a man can
admit himself into natural love, but the Lord alone can admit

146

bim into spiritual love; and those who are admitted into the latter are reformed, but those who are only admitted into the former are not reformed; for these last are for the most part hypocrites, and many of them of the order of Jesuits, who interiorly do not believe any thing divine, but exteriorly play with divine things after the manner of soothsayers.

223. By much experience in the spiritual world it has been made known to me, that a man possesses in himself the faculty of understanding the arcana of wisdom, like the angels themselves; for I have seen fiery devils, who, when they heard arcana of wisdom, not only understood them, but also spoke them from their own rationality: as soon however as they returned to their diabolical love, they did not understand them, but instead of them things contrary thereto, which were insanities, and which they then called wisdom. It has even been permitted me to hear that when they were in a state of wisdom, they laughed at their own insanity, and when they were in a state of insanity, they laughed at wisdom. A man who has been such in this world, when after death he becomes a spirit, is generally admitted into alternate states of wisdom and insanity, that he may distinguish the one from the other. But although from wisdom they see their insanity, yet when their option is given them, as it is to every one, they put themselves into a state of insanity, love it, and then hate a state of wisdom: the reason of which is, that their internal was diabolical, and their external as if it were divine. These are those who are meant by devils who pretend to be angels of light; and by him, who at the marriage had not on a wedding garment, and was cast into outer darkness, Matt. xxii. 11, 12, 13.

224. Who cannot see, that it is the internal from which the external exists; consequently, that the latter has its essence from the former? And who does not know by experience, that the external is able to appear otherwise than according to its essence from the internal? This is manifestly the case with hypocrites, flatterers, and dissemblers. And that a man can assume a character not his own in externals, is evident from players and mimics; for they can represent kings, emperors, and even angels, in their tone of voice, speech, face, and gesture, as though they were really such; when nevertheless they are nothing but imitators. These observations are made, because a man in a similar manner can act the sycophant in matters of a civil and moral nature as in those of a spiritual nature; and it is well known, also, that many do so. As, therefore, the internal in its essence is infernal, and the external in its form appears spiritual, when nevertheless the external derives its essence from the internal, as before observed, it may be asked where that essence lies concealed in the external. It does not appear in the gesture, in the tone of voice, in the speech,

147   x

or in the face; but yet it lies concealed interiorly in all the four That it lies interiorly concealed in them, is evident from the case of such persons in the spiritual world; for when a man goes out of the natural into the spiritual world, which he does when he dies, he leaves his externals with his body, and retains his internals which he had treasured up in his spirit; and then, if his internal was infernal, he appears a devil, such also as he had been as to his spirit when he lived in the world. Who does not acknowledge, that every man leaves externals with his body, and enters into internals when he becomes a spirit? To this I may add, that in the spiritual world there is a communication between the affections and the thoughts derived from them, whence no one can speak otherwise than as he thinks; also, that every one there changes his face, and becomes like his affection, so that it is apparent what he is from his face also. Hypocrites are sometimes permitted to speak otherwise than as they think; but the sound of their voice is altogether discordant to the interiors of their thoughts, and from such discordance they are discovered. Hence it may appear, that the internal lies concealed interiorly in the tone, speech, face, and external gesture; and that this is not perceived by men in the natural world, but manifestly by angels in the spiritual world.

225. From these considerations, then, it is evident, that a man, so long as he lives in the natural world, can be admitted into the wisdom of spiritual things, and also into the love of them; and that this may and can be done, with those who are merely natural, as well as with those who are spiritual; yet with this difference, that the latter are reformed by them, but the former are not. It may also appear as if the merely natural loved wisdom; but they love it no otherwise than as an adulterer loves a noble courtesan, with whom he speaks flatteringly, to whom he presents rich garments, and of whom, nevertheless, he thinks with himself at home, that she is nothing but a vile whore, whom I will make believe that I love her, because she favours my lust; but if she does not favour it, I will reject her. His internal man is this adulterer, and his external man is this woman.

226. II. *That if a man afterwards recedes from them, and runs counter to them, he profanes what is holy.* There are several kinds of profanation of what is holy, which will be noticed in the following article: but this kind is the most grievous of all; for those who are profaners of this kind, become after death no longer men. They live indeed, but continually in a fantastical delirium, and appearing to themselves to be flying on high, and when they are still they play with fantasies, which seem to them as things real; and as they are no longer men, they are not called he and she, but it: even when they are seen in the light of heaven, they appear like skeletons, some like

148

skeletons of a bony colour, some fiery, and some dry. That those who are guilty of this kind of profanation become such after death, is not known in the world; and it is not known because the cause of it is not known. The cause of it is, that when a man first acknowledges divine things, and believes them, and afterwards recedes and denies them, he then mixes holy with profane things; which, when mixed, cannot be separated otherwise than by the destruction of the whole. But that this may be more clearly perceived, it shall be explained in the following order: 1. That whatever a man thinks, speaks, and does from his will, is appropriated to him and remains,—as well good as evil. 2. That the Lord by his Divine Providence continually provides and disposes, that evil may be by itself, and good by itself, so that they may be separated. 3. That this cannot be done, if a man first acknowledges the truths of faith, and lives according to them, and afterwards recedes from and denies them. 4. That he then mixes good and evil in such a manner that they cannot be separated. 5. And as good and evil with every man are to be separated, and in such a one cannot be separated, therefore he is destroyed as to every thing truly human.

227. These are the causes why a thing so enormous exists; but as these causes are in obscurity from ignorance respecting them, they shall be explained, in order that they may be evident to the understanding. FIRST, *That whatever a man thinks, speaks, and does from his will, is appropriated to him and remains, —as well good as evil.* This was shown above, n. 78—81. For a man has an external or natural memory, and an internal or spiritual memory: in the latter is inscribed every thing that he had thought, spoken, and done from his will in the world, and that so perfectly as to every particular, that no one thing is wanting. This memory is the book of his life, which after death is opened, and according to which he is judged. Concerning this memory more is adduced from my own experience, in the work ON HEAVEN AND HELL, n. 461—465. SECONDLY, *But that the Lord by his Divine Providence continually provides and disposes, that evil may be by itself, and good by itself, so that they may be separated.* Every man is both in evil and in good; for he is in evil from himself, and in good from the Lord: and he cannot live unless he is in both. For if he were in himself alone, and so in evil only, he would not have any life: nor if he were in the Lord alone, and so in good only, would he have any life; for a man in *the latter kind of life* would be as it were suffocated, continually gasping for breath, or like one in the agonies of death; and in *the former kind of life* he would be extinct, for evil without any good is in itself dead; therefore every man is in both. But the difference is, that one is interiorly in the Lord, and exteriorly as if in himself; while the other is interiorly in himself, but exteriorly as if in the Lord

149

The latter is in evil, and the former in good, yet each is in both good and evil. The reason why this is also the case with a wicked man, is, because he is in the good of civil and moral life, and also exteriorly in some good of spiritual life; and is kept besides in rationality and liberty by the Lord, in order that he may have the power of being in good: this is the good by which every man, even the wicked, is led of the Lord. From these considerations it may be seen, that the Lord separates evil and good, that the one may be interior and the other exterior, and so provides that they may not be mixed. THIRDLY, *But that this cannot be done, if a man first acknowledges the truths of faith, and lives according to them, and afterwards recedes and denies them.* This is evident from what has now been said; first, that every thing which a man thinks, speaks, and does from the will, is appropriated to him and remains; and, secondly, that the Lord by his Divine Providence continually provides, and so disposes things, that good may be by itself, and evil by itself, and that they may be separated. Moreover, they are separated by the Lord after death: from those who are interiorly evil and exteriorly good, the good is taken away, and they are thus left in their evil; but the case is reversed with those who are interiorly good, and exteriorly like other men have acquired wealth, sought after dignities, been delighted with various worldly things, and have favoured some concupiscences; for in these, nevertheless, good and evil are not mixed, but separate, as internal and external; thus in their external form they have been, in many respects, like the wicked, yet not in their internal form. So, also, on the other hand, in the wicked who, in their external form, have appeared like the good, in regard to piety, divine worship, words, and actions, and yet, in their internal form, have been wicked, the evil is separated from the good. But in those who have first acknowledged the truths of faith, and lived according to them, and afterwards have run counter, and rejected them, especially if they have denied them, goods and evils are no longer separated, but mixed together; for such a man has appropriated to himself good, and has also appropriated to himself evil, and so has joined and mixed them. FOURTHLY, *That in this case he mixes good and evil in such a manner that they cannot be separated*, follows from what has just now been said; and if evil cannot be separated from good, and good from evil, he can neither be in heaven nor in hell. Every man must be either in one or the other; he cannot be in both; for in that case he would be one while in heaven, and another while in hell; when in heaven he would act in favour of hell, and when in hell he would act in favour of heaven, and so destroy the life of all who were about him,—the celestial life in the angels, and the infernal life in the devils,—whereby the life of every one would perish; for the life of every one must be his own, no one living in a life foreign to his own, still less in one that is opposite. Hence it is, that in every one after death, when he becomes a spirit or a spiritual man, the Lord separates good from evil and evil from good,—good from evil in those who are interiorly in evil, and evil from good in those who are interiorly in good; which is according to his own words: "Whosoever hath, to him shall be given, and he shall have more abundance; but whosoever hath not, from him shall be taken away even what he hath" (Matt. xiii. 12; xxv. 29; Mark iv. 25; Luke viii. 18; xix. 26). FIFTHLY, *As good and evil in every man are to be separated, and in such a one cannot be separated, therefore he is destroyed as to every thing truly human.* What is truly human every one has from rationality, so that if he will, he can see and know what is true and what is good, and as was shown before, can also will, think, speak, and do good from liberty; but this liberty with its rationality is destroyed in those who have mixed good and evil in themselves; for they cannot from good see evil, or from evil know good, because they make one: they have therefore no longer the faculty or power of rationality, nor consequently have they any liberty. This is the reason why, as was said above, they are as mere fantastical delirious beings and no longer appear as men, but like bones covered with skin, and therefore when they are named, they are not called he or she, but it. Such is the lot of those who in this manner mix things holy with profane: but there are several kinds of profanation, which are not of this nature, to be noticed in the subsequent article.

228. No man thus profanes things holy who does not know them; for he who does not know them, cannot acknowledge them, and afterwards deny them: those therefore who are without the Christian world, and do not know any thing of the Lord, and of redemption and salvation by him, do not profane the holiness thereof, when they do not receive it, or even when they speak against it. Neither do the Jews themselves profane it; because from their infancy they have refused to receive and acknowledge it. It would be otherwise if they received and acknowledged, and afterwards denied it, which however is very rare; for many of them acknowledge it exteriorly and deny it interiorly, being like hypocrites. Those however profane things holy, by mixing them with what is profane, who first receive and acknowledge them, and afterwards depart from them and deny them. Their receiving and acknowledging them in their infancy and childhood is of no account, for this all Christians do, because at that age they do not receive and acknowledge the things which are of faith and charity from any rationality and liberty, that is, in the understanding from the will, but only from memory and the authority of masters: and if they live according to them, it is out of blind obedience; but if,

151

when a man comes into the use of his rationality and liberty, which he does successively as he grows up, he then acknowledges truths and lives according to them, and afterwards denies them, he mixes things holy and profane, and instead of a man, becomes such a monster as was described above. If a man is in evil, however, from the time he becomes possessed of rationality and liberty, that is, from the time he begins to think for himself, even to the period of youth, and afterwards acknowledges the truths of faith and lives according to them, provided he then abides in them to his life's end, he does not mix them; for the Lord then separates the evils of his former life from the goods of his latter life: this is the case with all who repent. But of this more in what follows.

229. III. *That there are several kinds of profanation of what is holy, and that this kind is the worst of all.* In the most common or general sense, by profanation is meant all impiety, therefore by profaners are meant all impious persons, who in their hearts deny God, the sanctity of the Word, and consequently the spiritual things of the church, which are sanctity itself, and concerning which they also speak impiously. Of such profaners, however, we are not here treating, but of those who profess to believe in God, who maintain the sanctity of the Word, and who acknowledge the spiritual things of the church, and yet do this for the most part with their mouths only. The reason why these are guilty of profanation, is, because what is holy from the Word is in and with them, and this, which is in them and which constitutes some part of their understanding and will, they profane; but in the impious, who deny the Divine Being and all things divine, there is nothing holy for them to profane. They are profaners indeed, but are not the profane.

230. The profanation of what is holy is meant in the second commandment of the Decalogue, by, Thou shalt not profane the name of thy God; and that it ought not to be profaned is meant in the Lord's Prayer, by, Hallowed be thy Name. What is understood by the name of God, is scarcely known by any in the Christian world; the reason of which is, because it is not known that in the spiritual world there are not names as in the natural world, but that every one is named according to the quality of his love and wisdom; for as soon as any one comes into society or association with others, he is immediately named according to his quality there. He is named by spiritual language, which is such, that it can give a name to every thing, because each letter in its alphabet signifies a thing; and several letters joined into a word, which constitute the name of a person, include the entire state of the thing. This is one of the wonderful things in the spiritual world. Hence it is evident, that by the name of God in the Word is signified God, with every

thing divine which is in him, and proceeds from him; and as the Word is the proceeding divine, it is the name of God; as, likewise, all the divine things, which are called spiritual things of the church, are from the Word, they are also the name of God. From these considerations it may be seen what is meant in the second commandment in the Decalogue by *Thou shalt not profane the name of God*, and in the Lord's Prayer, by *Hallowed be thy name*. Similar is the signification of the name of God and of the Lord, in many places of the Word in both Testaments, as in Matt. vii. 22; x. 22; xviii. 5, 20; xix. 29; xxi. 9; xxiv. 9, 10; John i. 12; ii. 23; iii. 17, 18; xii. 13, 28; xiv. 14, 15, 16; xvi. 23, 24, 26, 27; xvii. 6; xx. 31; besides other places, and very many in the Old Testament. He who knows this signification of name, may know what is signified by these words of the Lord: "He that receiveth a prophet in the name of a prophet shall receive a prophet's reward; and he that receiveth a righteous man in the name of a righteous man shall receive a righteous man's reward; and whosoever shall give to drink unto one of these little ones a cup of cold water only in the name of a disciple, he shall in no wise lose his reward" (Matt. x. 41). He who, by the name of a prophet, a righteous man, and a disciple, here understands only a prophet, a righteous man, and a disciple, does not understand any other than barely the literal sense, nor does he know what is the reward of a prophet, the reward of a just man, and the reward of a cup of cold water given to a disciple, when, nevertheless, by the name and the reward of a prophet is meant the state and felicity of those who are in divine truths; by the name and the reward of a righteous man, the state and felicity of those who are in divine goods; and by a disciple, those who are in some spiritual things of the church, a cup of cold water being something of truth. That the quality of the state of love and wisdom, or of goodness and truth, is signified by name, is also evident from these words of the Lord: "He that entereth in by the door is the shepherd of the sheep. To him the porter openeth; and the sheep hear his voice: and he calleth his own sheep by name, and leadeth them out" (John x. 2, 3). To call his sheep by name, is to teach and lead every one who is in the good of charity, according to the state of his love and wisdom. By the door is meant the Lord, as is evident from verse 9th of the same chapter; "I am the door: by me if any man enter in, he shall be saved." From which it is evident, that the Lord himself is to be approached, in order that any one may be saved; and that he who approaches him is the shepherd of the sheep; but he who does not approach him is a thief and a robber, as it is said in the first verse of that chapter.

231. Since by the profanation of what is holy is meant profanation by those who are acquainted with the truths of faith

153

and the goods of charity from the Word, and also in some measure acknowledge them, and not by those who are not acquainted with them, or by those who from impiety entirely reject them; therefore what follows is said not of the latter, but of the former. The kinds of profanation by these are several, some lighter and some more grievous than others: but they may be referred to these seven. THE FIRST KIND OF PROFANATION IS COMMITTED BY THOSE *who jest from the Word, and concerning the Word, or from and concerning the divine things of the church.* This is done by some persons from a bad habit, by taking names or forms of speech out of the Word, and introducing them into unseemly and sometimes filthy discourse; which cannot but be connected in some degree with a contempt of the Word. Yet the Word in the whole and in every particular is divine and holy; for every Word thereof contains in its bosom something divine, by which it has communication with heaven. This kind of profanation however is lighter, or more grievous, in proportion to the acknowledgment of the sanctity of the Word, and the indecency of the discourse into which it is introduced by those who make a jest of it. A SECOND KIND OF PROFANATION IS COMMITTED BY THOSE *who understand and acknowledge divine truths, and yet live contrary to them.* Those however profane them more lightly who only understand them, while those who acknowledge them also profane them more grievously; for the understanding only teaches, much in the same manner as a preacher teaches, and does not conjoin itself with the will from itself; but acknowledgment conjoins itself; for nothing can be acknowledged without the consent of the will. Nevertheless, this conjunction is various, and the profanation is according to the conjunction, when the life is contrary to the truths which are acknowledged. For example, if any one acknowledges that revenge and hatred, adultery and fornication, fraud and deceit, blasphemy and lies, are sins against God, and yet commits them, such a one is in the more grievous degree of this kind of profanation; for the Lord says, "The servant that knew his Lord's will, and did not according to his will, shall be beaten with many stripes" (Luke xii. 47). And in another place, "If ye were blind, ye should have no sin; but now ye say, We see; therefore your sin remaineth" (John ix. 41). But it is one thing to acknowledge appearances of truth, and another to acknowledge genuine truths. Those who acknowledge genuine truths, and yet do not live according to them, appear in the spiritual world without the light and heat of life in the tone of their voice and speech, as if they were mere sloths. A THIRD KIND OF PROFANATION IS COMMITTED BY THOSE *who apply the literal sense of the Word to confirm evil loves and false principles.* The reason of this is, because a confirmation of what is false is a negation of the truth, and a

154

confirmation of evil is a rejection of good. The Word contains in its bosom nothing but divine truth and divine good; and this in the ultimate sense, which is the literal sense, does not appear in genuine truths, except where it teaches concerning the Lord and the essential way of salvation, but in truths clothed, which are called appearances of truth; therefore this sense may be wrested to confirm heresies of many kinds. But he who confirms evil loves, offers violence to divine goods; and he who confirms false principles, offers violence to divine truths. This latter violence is called the falsification of truth; the former, the adulteration of good. They are both understood by bloods in the Word; for the spiritual holiness, which is also the spirit of truth proceeding from the Lord, is interiorly in every particular of the literal sense of the Word; and this holiness is violated when the Word is falsified and adulterated. That this is profanation is evident. A FOURTH KIND OF PROFANATION IS COMMITTED BY THOSE *who with their mouths speak things pious and holy, and also in their tone of voice and gesture counterfeit affections of the love of such things, yet in their hearts do not believe and love them.* Most of these are hypocrites and Pharisees, from whom after death every truth and good is taken away, and then they are sent into outer darkness. Of this kind, those who have confirmed themselves against what is divine, and against the Word, thence also against the spiritual things of the Word, sit silent in that darkness, impotent of speech, and desirous to babble about things pious and holy, as they did in the world, but they are not able; for in the spiritual world every one is forced to speak as he thinks, and a hypocrite wishes to speak otherwise than as he thinks, consequently there is an opposition in the mouth, by reason of which he can only mutter. Hypocrites, nevertheless, are lighter or more grievous, according to confirmations against God, and reasonings exteriorly in favour of God. A FIFTH KIND OF PROFANATION IS COMMITTED BY THOSE *who attribute to themselves things divine.* These are those who are meant by Lucifer in Isaiah xiv. By Lucifer is there meant Babel, as may appear from the 4th and 22d verses of that chapter, where also their lot is described. The same are likewise meant and described by the whore sitting upon the scarlet coloured beast, in Revelation xvii. Babel and Chaldea are mentioned in many parts of the Word: by Babel is there meant the profanation of good, and by Chaldea the profanation of truth, both in those who attribute to themselves things divine. A SIXTH KIND OF PROFANATION IS COMMITTED BY THOSE *who acknowledge the Word, and yet deny the Lord's divinity.* These are called in the world Socinians, and some of them Arians: the lot of both these is, that they invoke the Father, and not the Lord; and continually pray the Father, some of them also for the sake of the Son, that they may be

155

admitted into heaven, but in vain, until they become without hope of salvation; and they are then let down into hell among those who deny God.   These are meant by those who blaspheme the Holy Ghost, who will not be forgiven either in this world, or in that which is to come (Matt. xii. 32).   The reason of this is, because God is one in person and in essence, in whom there is the trinity, and this God is the Lord; and as the Lord is also heaven, and consequently those who are in heaven are in the Lord, therefore those who deny the Lord's divinity cannot be admitted into heaven, and be in the Lord.   That the Lord is heaven, and that consequently those who are in heaven are in the Lord, was shown above.   A SEVENTH KIND OF PROFANATION IS COMMITTED BY THOSE *who first acknowledge divine truths, and live according to them, and afterwards recede and deny them.* This is the worst kind of profanation, because such persons mix things holy and profane in such a manner that they cannot be separated, and yet in order to their admission into either heaven or hell, they must be separated; and as in such persons this cannot be effected, all the intellectual and voluntary human faculty is destroyed, and, as was said before, they become no longer men.   It is nearly the same with those who in their hearts acknowledge the divine things of the Word and the church, and entirely immerse them in their proprium, which is the love of having dominion over every thing, and respecting which much has been said above; for these after death, when they become spirits, will not be led by the Lord, but entirely by themselves: when their love is not restrained, they desire to rule not only over heaven, but also over the Lord; and because they cannot do so, they deny the Lord, and become devils.   It is to be observed, that the life's love, which is also the ruling love, remains in every one after death, and cannot be removed.   The profane of this kind are meant by the lukewarm, of whom it is thus written in the Revelation : " I know thy works, that thou art neither cold nor hot: I would thou wert cold or hot.   So then because thou art neither cold nor hot, I will spew thee out of my mouth" (iii. 15, 16).   This kind of profanation is also thus described by the Lord in Matthew: " When the unclean spirit is gone out of a man, he walketh through dry places, seeking rest, but findeth none.   Then he saith, I will return into the house from whence I came out; and when he is come, he findeth it empty, swept, and garnished.   Then goeth he, and taketh with himself seven other spirits more wicked than himself, and they enter in and dwell there : and the last state of that man is worse than the first" (xii. 43, 45).   The conversion of a man is here described by the unclean spirit's going out of him; his returning to his former evils, after casting out things true and good, is described by the return of the unclean spirit with seven others more wicked than himself into the house, which he found garnished for him ; and the profanation of what is holy by what is profane, is described by the last state of that man being worse than the first. The same is understood by the passage in John, where Jesus said to him that was healed in the pool of Bethesda, " Sin no more, lest a worse thing come unto thee " (v. 14). That the Lord provides, that a man may not interiorly acknowledge truths, and afterwards recede from them and become profane, is meant by these words : " He hath blinded their eyes, and hardened their heart; that they should not see with their eyes, or understand with their heart, and be converted, and I should heal them " (John xii. 40). Lest they should be converted and I should heal them, signifies, lest they should acknowledge truths and then recede, and so become profane. For the same reason the Lord spoke by parables, as he himself says (Matt. xiii. 13). The Jews being forbid to eat fat and blood (Lev. iii. 17 ; vii. 23, 25), signified that they were not to profane things holy ; for fat signified divine good, and blood divine truth. That a man being once converted ought to continue in good and truth to the end of his life, the Lord teaches in Matthew. Jesus said, " He that endureth to the end shall be saved " (x. 22 ; also in Mark xi i. 13).

232. IV. *That therefore the Lord does not admit a man interiorly into the truths of wisdom, and at the same time into the goods of love, except so far as he can be kept in them to the end of life.* In demonstrating this we must proceed distinctly, for two reasons ; first, because it nearly concerns the salvation of mankind ; secondly, because on a knowledge of this law depends a knowledge of the laws of permission; to be treated of in the following section. It nearly concerns the salvation of mankind ; because, as was observed before, he who first acknowledges the divine things of the Word, and thence those of the church, and afterwards recedes from them, very grievously profanes what is holy. Therefore that this arcanum of the Divine Providence may be disclosed in such a manner, that the rational man may see it in its true light, it shall be unfolded in the following series. 1. That evil and good cannot exist together in a man's interiors, nor consequently the falsity of evil and the truth of good at the same time. 2. That good and the truth of good cannot be infused by the Lord into a man's interiors except in proportion as evil and the falsity of evil is thence removed. 3. If good with its truth were infused there before, or in a greater degree than that in which evil with its falsity is removed, the man would recede from good and return to his evil. 4. That when a man is in evil, many truths may be infused into his understanding, and treasured up in his memory, without being profaned. 5. But that the Lord by his Divine Providence most especially provides, that they be not received thence by the

157

will, before or in greater proportion than that in which the man removes evils in the external man as if of himself. 6. That if they were received sooner, or in greater proportion, the will would adulterate the good, and the understanding would falsify the truth, by mixing them with evils and falsities. 7. That therefore the Lord does not admit a man interiorly into the truths of faith and the goods of love, except so far as he can be kept in them to the end of life.

233. In order therefore that this arcanum of the Divine Providence may be disclosed in such a manner that the rational man may see it in his light, the things which have now been adduced shall be severally explained. FIRST, *That evil and good cannot exist together in a man's interiors, nor consequently can the falsity of evil and the truth of good.* By a man's interiors is meant the internal of his thought, of which he does not know any thing before he comes into the spiritual world and its light, which is the case after death. In the natural world, this can only be known from the delight of his love in the external of his thought, and from evils themselves when he explores them in himself; for, as was shown above, the internal of thought in a man coheres with the external of thought in so close a connection, that they cannot be separated; but of this more may be seen above. Good and the truth of good, and evil and the falsity of evil, are mentioned, because good cannot exist without its truth nor evil without its falsity, they being connubial partners or consorts; for the life of good is from its truth, and the life of truth from its good: it is the same with evil and its falsity. That in a man's interiors there cannot exist evil with its falsity and at the same time good with its truth, may be seen by the rational man without explanation; for evil is opposite to good, and good is opposite to evil, and two opposites cannot exist together. There is also in all evil an inherent hatred against good, and in all good an inherent love of defending itself against evil, and of removing the same from it; from which it follows, that the one cannot dwell with the other. If they were together, a conflict and combat would first arise, and destruction would follow; which also the Lord teaches in these words: " Every kingdom divided against itself is brought to desolation; and every city or house divided against itself shall not stand. He that is not with me is against me; and he that gathereth not with me scattereth abroad" (Matt. xii. 25, 30); and in other places. No one can at the same time " serve two masters; for either he will hate the one and love the other" (Matt. vi. 24). Two opposites cannot exist together in one substance or form, without its being distracted and perishing. Were one to advance and approach the other, they would separate themselves altogether like two enemies, of which one would retire within his camp or fortifications, and the other would remain without.

This is the case with evils and goods in a hypocrite, who possesses both; but evil is within, and good without, and thus they are separate and not mixed. From these things it is plain, that evil with its falsity, and good with its truth, cannot exist together. SECONDLY, *That good and the truth of good cannot be infused by the Lord into a man's interiors, except in proportion as evil and the falsity of evil is thence removed.* This is a necessary consequence of what precedes; for since evil and good cannot exist together, good cannot be implanted before evil is removed. It is affirmed of a man's interiors, by which is meant the internal of thought; and in the interiors which are here treated of, either the Lord or the devil must dwell. The Lord is there after reformation, and the devil before it; therefore, in proportion as a man suffers himself to be reformed, the devil is cast out, but in proportion as he does not suffer himself to be reformed, the devil remains. Who may not see that the Lord cannot enter so long as the devil is there? and he is there so long as the man keeps the door closed by which he is brought into communication with the Lord. That the Lord enters, when the man opens that door, he himself teaches in the Revelation: "I stand at the door, and knock; if any man hear my voice and open the door, I will come in to him, and will sup with him, and he with me" (iii. 20). The door is opened by the man's removing evil, which he does by shunning and avoiding it as infernal and diabolical; for whether it be called evil, or the devil, it is the same thing; and, on the other hand, whether you say good, or the Lord, it is the same thing; for the Lord dwells inwardly in all good, and the devil in all evil. Hence the truth of this position is evident. THIRDLY, *If good with its truth were infused before, or in a greater degree than that in which evil and its falsity is removed, the man would recede from good and return to his evil.* The reason of this is, because evil would prevail; and that which prevails, conquers, if not at the time, yet afterwards. While evil continues to prevail, good cannot be introduced into the inmost apartments of the mind, but only into the outer courts, because, as was said, evil and good cannot exist together; and that which is only in the outer courts is removed by its enemy which is in the inner apartments, whereby there is a recession from good and a return to evil, which is the worst kind of profanation. Besides, the very delight of a man's life is to love himself and the world above all things; and this delight cannot be removed in a moment, but must be done successively. According to the proportion of this delight which remains in a man is the prevalence of evil; and this evil can be removed no otherwise than by making the love of self to become the love of uses, and admitting the love of rule, not for the sake of self, but for the sake of being useful; for so uses constitute the head, the love of self or the love of rule

159

at first constituting the body under that head, and afterwards the feet upon which he walks. Who does not see that good constitutes the head, and that when it constitutes the head, the Lord is there, good and use being one? Who does not see, that if evil constitutes the head, the devil is there; and that, as civil and moral good, and also spiritual good in its external form, are nevertheless to be received, these then constitute the feet, and the soles of the feet, and are trampled upon? Since, therefore, the state of a man's life is to be inverted, so that what is above may be placed below, and this inversion cannot be effected in a moment (for that supreme delight of life, which proceeds from the love of self and thence of dominion, cannot be diminished except successively, and so changed into the love of uses), for this reason good cannot be introduced by the Lord before or in a greater degree than that in which evil is removed; and if it were infused sooner, or in greater quantity, the man would recede from good and return to his evil. FOURTHLY, *That when a man is in evil, many truths may be introduced into his understanding, and treasured up in his memory, without being profaned.* The reason of this is, because the understanding does not flow into the will, but the will into the understanding; and as the understanding does not flow into the will, many truths may be received by it, and be stored up in the memory, yet not be mixed with the evil of the will, and thus what is holy may not be profaned. Besides, it is incumbent on every one to learn truths from the Word, or from preachings, to deposit them in the memory, and to think of them; for it is the duty of the understanding, from the truths in the memory, and which thence enter into the thought, to teach the will, that is, the man, what he ought to do; this therefore is a principal means of reformation: when truths are only in the understanding and thence in the memory, they are not within the man, but without him. A man's memory may be compared with the ruminatory stomach in which certain animals deposit their food, which, so long as it is there, is not within their body, but without it; but as soon as they bring it up thence, and swallow it, it enters into the life and nourishes the body. In a man's memory, however, the provision stored up is not material but spiritual, namely, truths, and in itself consists of knowledges; and in proportion as the man, by the exercise of his thinking principle, which is a kind of rumination, takes in thence, his spiritual mind is nourished. It is the love of the will which has a desire, and as it were an appetite, for truths thus deposited, causing them to be imbibed and converted into nourishment. If that love is evil, it has a desire and as it were an appetite for unclean things; but if good, it has a desire, and as it were an appetite for clean things; and those things which do not agree with it, it separates, puts away, and casts out, which is effected by various means. FIFTHLY, *But that the Lord by his Divine Providence most especially provides that they be not received thence by the will before or in greater proportion than that in which the man removes evil in the external man as if of himself ;* for that which is from the will enters into the man, is appropriated to him, and becomes a principle of his life ; and in the life itself, which the man has from the will, evil and good cannot exist together, for in such case he would perish. But both may be in the understanding, and are there called falsities of evil or truths of good, yet not together ; for in such case the man would not be able to know evil from good or good from evil ; but they are distinguished and separated there like a house into interior and exterior apartments. When a wicked man thinks and speaks good things, he thinks and speaks exteriorly, but when evil things, interiorly ; wherefore when he speaks good things, his speech issues as it were from the wall of the house, and may be compared to fruit which is fair on the outside but worm-eaten and rotten within, and also to the outside shell of a dragon's egg. SIXTHLY, *That if they were received sooner and in greater proportion, the will would adulterate the good, and the understanding would falsify the truth, by mixing them with evils and their consequent falsities.* When the will is in evil, it then adulterates good in the understanding, and good adulterated in the understanding is evil in the will, for it confirms the persuasion that evil is good, and *vice versa.* Evil does thus with all good, which is opposite to itself ; it likewise falsifies the truth, because the truth of good is opposite to the falsity of evil : this the will does in the understanding, and not the understanding from itself. Adulterations of good are described in the Word by adulteries, and falsifications of truth by whoredoms. These adulterations and falsifications are effected by reasonings from the natural man, which is in evil, and they are also effected by confirmations from the appearances of the literal sense of the Word. Self-love, which is the head of all evils, is more ingenious than other loves in adulterating goods and falsifying truths ; and this it does by the abuse of rationality, which every man has from the Lord, the wicked as well as the good. It can indeed by confirmations cause evil to appear altogether as good and falsity as truth. What can it not do, when it can confirm, by a thousand arguments, that nature created herself, that she then created men, beasts, and vegetables of all kinds ; and further, that by influx from her interior self she causes men to live, to think analytically, and to understand wisely ! The reason why self-love excels in the art of confirming whatever it chooses, is, because its most outward surface is constituted by a certain splendour of light variegated into divers colours ; which splendour is that love's glory of acquiring wisdom, and by that also eminence and dominion. But when this love has confirmed such tenets, it then becomes so blind, that it does not see otherwise than that a man is a beast, that they think alike, and, indeed, that if a beast could also speak, it would be a man in another form.   If it be led by any persuasion to believe that something of a man lives after death, it is then so blind that it thinks beasts do the same, and that this something living after death is only a subtile exhalation of life, like vapor, which nevertheless relapses into its dead body; or that it is a vital something without sight, hearing, and speech, consequently blind, deaf, and dumb, hovering about and thinking; besides many other insane ideas, which nature, though in herself void of life, inspires into its fantasy.   Such is the effect of self-love, which viewed in itself is the love of a man's proprium; and a man's proprium, as to its affections, which are all natural, is not unlike the life of a beast, and as to its perceptions, which proceed from those affections, is not unlike an owl.   He therefore who continually immerses his thoughts in his proprium, cannot be elevated out of natural light into spiritual light, nor see any thing of God, of heaven, and of life eternal.   Since this love is of such a nature, and yet excels in the art of confirming whatever it chooses, therefore with the same art it can also adulterate the good things of the Word, and falsify its truths, when constrained through any kind of necessity to confess them.   SEVENTHLY, *That therefore the Lord does not admit a man interiorly into the truths of wisdom and the goods of love, except so far as he can be kept in them to the end of life.*   The Lord thus restrains a man, lest he should fall into that most grievous kind of profanation of things holy, which is treated of in this article.   On account of this danger, the Lord also permits evils of life, and many heresies relating to worship; concerning the permission of which the reader is referred to what is shown in the subsequent sections.

THAT THE LAWS OF PERMISSION ARE ALSO LAWS OF THE DIVINE PROVIDENCE.

234. THERE are not any laws of permission by themselves, or separate from the laws of the Divine Providence, but they are the same; therefore it is said that God permits, by which is not meant that he wills, but that he cannot prevent such a thing, on account of the end proposed, which is salvation. Whatever is done to the end that salvation may be effected, is according to the laws of the Divine Providence; for, as before observed, the Divine Providence keeping this end continually in view constantly proceeds in a manner different from a man's will and contrary thereto; therefore, in every moment of its opera-

tion or in every step of its progression, when it perceives a man to deviate from this end, it directs, turns, and disposes him, according to its laws, by withdrawing him from evil, and leading him to good. That this cannot be done without permitting evil, will be seen in what follows. Besides, nothing can be permitted without a cause, and the cause exists only in some law of the Divine Providence, which law explains why the thing is permitted.

235. He who does not at all acknowledge the Divine Providence, does not in his heart acknowledge God; but instead of God he acknowledges nature, and instead of the Divine Providence, human prudence. That this is the case is not apparent, because a man can think in two different ways, and also speak in different ways: he can think and speak one thing from his interior self, and another thing from his exterior self; like a hinge on which a door can be turned both ways,—one way when a person comes in, and another when he goes out; and like as a sail can turn a ship in different directions, according to the manner in which it is expanded by the mariner. Those who have confirmed themselves in favour of human prudence, in such a manner as to deny the Divine Providence, whatever they see, hear, and read, while they are under the influence of this their own way of thinking, do not observe or attend to any thing else; nor indeed can they, because they receive nothing from heaven, but only from themselves; and as they form conclusions from appearances and fallacies alone, and do not see any thing else, they can swear that it is so. If also they acknowledge nature alone, they can be angry with the defenders of the Divine Providence, provided they be not priests, of whom they think that they are led to such defence in compliance with their particular tenets and function.

236. We shall now proceed to enumerate some things which are of permission, and yet according to the laws of the Divine Providence, from which the merely natural man confirms himself in favour of nature against God, and in favour of human prudence against the Divine Providence; as, when he reads in the Word, that the wisest of men, Adam, and his wife, suffered themselves to be seduced by a serpent, and that God did not avert this by his Divine Providence;—that their first son, Cain, slew his brother Abel, and God did not then withhold him by speaking to him, but only denounced a curse against him after the act;—that the Israelitish nation worshiped a golden calf in the wilderness, and acknowledged it as the god which brought them out of the land of Egypt, yet Jehovah saw this from Mount Sinai, not far off, and did not prevent it;—also, that David numbered the people, and a pestilence was therefore sent among them, by which many thousands of men perished; and that God did not send the prophet Gad to him before the act,

but after it, to denounce punishment;—that Solomon was permitted to establish idolatrous worship, and many kings after him to profane the temple and the holy things of the church;—and, lastly, that that nation was permitted to crucify the Lord. In these and many other passages in the Word, he who acknowledges nature and human prudence sees nothing but what makes against the Divine Providence; therefore he can use them as arguments to deny it, if not in his exterior thought which is nearest to speech, yet in his interior thought which is remote from it.

237. Every worshiper of himself and of nature confirms himself against the Divine Providence, when he sees so many impious persons in the world, and so many of their impieties, in which at the same time some glory, and on account of which, nevertheless, they receive no punishments from God. Still more does he confirm himself against the Divine Providence, when he sees that wicked machinations, cunning, and deceit succeed, against the pious, the just, and the sincere; and that injustice triumphs over justice, in judgments and affairs of business. He confirms himself especially, when he sees the impious advanced to honours, and made nobles and primates; that they moreover abound in riches, and live elegantly and magnificently; while, on the other hand, the worshipers of God are in contempt and poverty. He likewise confirms himself against the Divine Providence, when he thinks how wars are permitted, by which so many men are slaughtered, and so many cities, nations, and families plundered; moreover, that victory inclines to the side of prudence, and not always in favour of justice; and that it makes no difference whether the general be a good or a wicked man; besides other such like circumstances; all of which are permissions according to the laws of the Divine Providence.

238. The same natural man confirms himself against the Divine Providence, when he takes a view of the religious persuasions of various nations; seeing that there are some who know nothing at all of God; some who worship the sun and moon; some also who worship idols and graven images even of monsters; and some who worship dead men. When, in addition to these, he thinks of the Mahometan religion, which is received by so many empires and kingdoms; and considers that the Christian religion prevails only in the smallest quarter of the habitable globe, called Europe; that even there it is in a state of division; that there are some of its professors who claim to themselves divine power, and desire to be worshiped as gods; that they invoke dead men; that there are some also who place salvation in certain words which they think and speak, and not in any good they do; and that there are few who live according to their own religion;—besides taking into account the great number of heresies which have heretofore prevailed, and some

which exist at this day, such as those of the Quakers, Moravians, Anabaptists, and others; also, that Judaism still continues;—from these things, the denier of the Divine Providence concludes, that religion in itself is not any thing, but yet that it is necessary, because it serves as a restraint.

239. To these arguments more may at this day be added, by which those who think inwardly in favour of nature and human prudence may still more strongly confirm themselves in their sentiments ; as, that the whole Christian world has acknowledged three gods, not knowing that God is one in person and in essence, and that that God is the Lord ; also that heretofore it was not known, that in every particular of the Word there is a spiritual sense, and that therein its holiness consists ;—further, that it was not known, that essential Christian religion consists in shunning evils as sins ;—and that hitherto it was not known, that a man lives as a man after death ;—for the favorers of nature may say with themselves, and among each other, If these things are true, why has the Divine Providence not revealed them till now ?

240. All the particular things which are recited in the numbers 237, 238, and 239, are adduced to the end that it may be seen, that all and singular the things which occur in the world, as well to the wicked as the good, are of the Divine Providence ; consequently, that the Divine Providence operates in the most minute particulars of the thoughts and actions of men, and that thereby it operates universally. As however this cannot be seen therein except each particular be explained separately, therefore they shall be briefly explained in the order in which they were adduced, beginning with n. 236.

241. I. *That the wisest of men, Adam, and his wife, suffered themselves to be seduced by a serpent, and that God did not prevent this by his Divine Providence.* The reason of this is, because by Adam and his wife are not meant the first of all the men that were created in this world, but the men of the most ancient church, whose new creation or regeneration is described at the beginning of Genesis. Their new creation or regeneration itself is signified by the creation of heaven and earth in the first chapter; their wisdom and intelligence, by the garden of Eden ; and the end of that church, by their eating of the tree of knowledge. For the Word internally is spiritual, containing within its bosom arcana of divine wisdom ; and in order that these arcana may be contained therein, it is written by mere correspondences and representations. From these correspondences and representations it is evident, that the men of that church, who in its beginning were the most wise, and in its end, by reason of the pride of their self-derived intelligence, the most wicked, were not seduced by any serpent, but by self-love, there denoted by the head of the serpent, which is to be

165

bruised by the seed of the woman, that is, by the Lord. Who cannot see from reason, that the things to be understood are different from what are there historically recorded in the letter? For who can comprehend, that the creation of the world could have been such as it is there described? The learned are therefore much puzzled to explain what is contained in the first chapter, and confess, after all, that they do not understand it. It is said, moreover, that in their garden or Paradise there were placed two trees, the one of life, and the other of knowledge, and these for a stumbling-block; also, that barely by eating of the latter, they sinned so greatly, that not only they, but the whole human race, their posterity, became subject to damnation; and that a serpent was able to seduce them; besides other circumstances, as, that the woman was created out of a rib of the man; that after their fall they knew that they were naked, and covered themselves with fig-leaves, when coats of skins were given them to clothe their bodies; and that cherubim were placed with a flaming sword to keep the way of the tree of life. All these things are representatives, by which are described the establishment of the most ancient church, its state of perfection, its decline, and lastly, its destruction. The concealed meaning of all the things contained in the spiritual sense, which resides in every particular of the Word, may be seen explained in THE ARCANA COELESTIA on the books of Genesis and Exodus, published in London; from which also it may appear, that by the tree of life is there understood the Lord with respect to his Divine Providence, and that by the tree of knowledge is understood man with respect to his self-derived prudence.

242. II. *That their first-born son, Cain, slew his brother Abel, and God did not prevent it by speaking to him, but only cursed him after the act.* Since by Adam and his wife is meant the most ancient church, as above observed, therefore by Cain and Abel, their first sons, are meant two essentials of the church, which are love and wisdom, or charity and faith,—by Abel, love and charity, and by Cain, wisdom or faith, specifically wisdom separate from love, or faith separate from charity; and wisdom, as also faith, separate, is of such a nature, that it not only rejects love and charity, but also annihilates them, and so slays its brother. That faith separate from charity has this effect, is well enough known in the Christian world: see THE DOCTRINE OF THE NEW JERUSALEM CONCERNING FAITH. The curse of Cain involves the spiritual state into which those who separate faith from charity, or wisdom from love, come after death. Yet that wisdom or faith might not therefore perish, a mark was set upon Cain, lest he should be slain; for love does not exist without wisdom, nor charity without faith. As by these circumstances nearly the same things are represented, as by eating of the tree of knowledge, therefore they follow in

order after the description of Adam and his wife. Those also who are in faith separate from charity, are in self-derived intelligence; and those who are in charity, and thereby in faith, are in intelligence from the Lord, and thus in the Divine Providence.

243. III. *That the Israelitish nation worshiped a golden calf in the wilderness, and acknowledged it as the god which brought them out of the land of Egypt; yet Jehovah saw this from Mount Sinai, not far off, and did not prevent it.* This was done in the wilderness of Sinai near the Mount. That Jehovah did not withhold the Israelites from that wicked idolatry, is conformable with all the laws of the Divine Providence which have before been set forth, and also with those which follow. This evil was permitted them that they might not all perish; for the children of Israel were brought out of Egypt that they might represent the Lord's church; which they could not have done, unless the Egyptian idolatry had been first rooted out of their hearts; and this could not have been done, except they had been left to themselves to act according to that which was in their hearts, and so to have it removed by a grievous punishment. What is further signified by that idolatrous worship, and by the threat that they should be totally rejected, and that a new nation should be raised up out of Moses, may be seen in THE ARCANA CŒLESTIA, on Exodus xxii., where this subject is treated of.

244. IV. *That David numbered the people, and a pestilence was therefore sent among them, by which many thousands of men perished; and that God did not send the prophet Gad to him before the act, but after it, to denounce punishment.* He who confirms himself against the Divine Providence may also think and revolve in his mind various things on this matter, particularly, why David was not forewarned, and why the people were so grievously punished for the king's transgression. That David was not forewarned, is conformable to the laws of the Divine Providence previously set forth, especially the two which are explained, n. 129—153; and n. 154—174. That the people were so grievously punished for the king's transgression, and seventy thousand of them cut off by the pestilence, was not owing to the king, but to the people; for it is written: " Again the anger of the Lord was kindled against Israel, therefore he moved David against them, saying, Go number Israel and Judah" (2 Sam. xxiv. 1).

245. V. *That Solomon was permitted to establish idolatrous worship.* This was in order that he might represent the Lord's kingdom or church, with all the religions in the universal world; for the church established with the Israelitish and Jewish nations was a representative church, and therefore all the judgments and statutes of that church represented spiritual things of the

167

church, which are its internals. The people themselves represented the church, the king represented the Lord,—David, the Lord who was about to come into the world, and Solomon, the Lord after his coming; and since the Lord after the glorification of his humanity had power over heaven and earth, as he himself says (Matt. xxviii. 18), therefore Solomon who represented him appeared in glory and magnificence, was in wisdom above all the kings of the earth, and also built the temple. He moreover permitted and established the religious worship of many nations, by which were represented the various religious principles prevailing in the world. The like is signified by his wives, which were seven hundred in number, and by his concubines, which amounted to three hundred, 1 Kings xi. 3; for wife in the Word signifies a church, and concubine a religious principle. Hence it may appear why Solomon was appointed to build the temple, by which the Lord's divine humanity was signified (John ii. 19, 21), and also the church; likewise, why he was permitted to establish idolatrous worship, and to have so many wives. That by David in many passages in the Word is meant the Lord, who was to come into the world, may be seen in THE DOCTRINE OF THE NEW JERUSALEM CONCERNING THE LORD, n. 43, 44.

246. VI. *That many kings after Solomon were permitted to profane the temple and the holy things of the church.* This was because the people represented the church, and their king the head of them; and as the Israelitish and Jewish nation were of such a nature, that they could not long represent the church, for they were idolaters at heart, therefore they receded successively from representative worship, by perverting all things of the church, so that in the end they vastated it. This was represented by profanations of the temple by their kings, and by their idolatries; the vastation of the church itself by the destruction of the temple, by the carrying away of the Israelitish people, and the captivity of the Jewish people in Babylon. This was the cause of the above permission; and whatever is done from any cause, is done from the Divine Providence of the Lord according to some of its laws.

247. VII. *That that nation was permitted to crucify the Lord.* The reason of this was, because the church among that nation was totally vastated, and become such, that they not only did not know and acknowledge the Lord, but also hated him: nevertheless, all that they did to him was according to the laws of his Divine Providence. That the passion of the cross was the last temptation, or last combat, by which the Lord fully overcame the hells, and fully glorified his humanity, may be seen in THE DOCTRINE OF THE NEW JERUSALEM CONCERNING THE LORD, n. 12, 13, 14, and in THE DOCTRINE OF THE NEW JERUSALEM CONCERNING FAITH, n. 34, 35.

248. Thus far we have explained the particulars above recited, n. 236, which are some passages out of the Word, whereby a natural man, who reasons against the Divine Providence, may confirm himself in such reasoning; for, as before observed, whatever such a man sees, hears, and reads, he can take up as an argument against Providence. Few, however, confirm themselves against the Divine Providence from the things contained in the Word; but many do so from the things which are extant before their eyes, as mentioned in n. 237, which shall now in like manner be explained.

249. I. *That every worshiper of self and of nature confirms himself against the Divine Providence, when he sees so many impious persons in the world, and so many of their impieties, in which, at the same time, some glory, and on account of which, nevertheless, they receive no punishment from God.* All impieties, and all glorying therein, are permissions, the causes of which are laws of the Divine Providence. Every man may freely, indeed most freely, think whatever he will, as well against God as in favour of God; and he who thinks against God is rarely punished in the natural world, because there he is always in a state capable of reformation; but he is punished in the spiritual world after death, for then he can no longer be reformed. That the laws of the Divine Providence are the cause of permissions, is evident from those above set forth, if they are reviewed and examined, namely, That a man ought to act from liberty according to reason; concerning which see n. 71—97 above. That a man ought not to be forced by external means to think and will, and so to believe and love the things which are of religion, but that he ought to lead and sometimes to force himself to it; concerning which see n. 129—174. That self-derived prudence is nothing, and only appears as if it was, and also ought so to appear; but that the Divine Providence from things the most particular is universal, n. 191—213. That the Divine Providence has respect to things eternal, and not to temporary things, except so far as they make one with things eternal, n. 214—220. And that a man is not admitted interiorly into the truths of faith and goods of charity, except so far as he can be kept in them to his life's end; concerning which see n. 221—233. That the causes of permissions are laws of the Divine Providence, will also be evident from what follows; as, from this consideration, that evils are permitted to the end that salvation may be effected; from this, that the Divine Providence is continual, as well with the wicked as the good; and, lastly, from this, that the Lord cannot act against the laws of his Divine Providence, because to act against them would be to act against his divine love and wisdom, consequently against himself. These laws, if they be compared, may show the reasons why impieties are permitted by the Lord, and not punished when they exist in thought only, also rarely when they exist in intention, or when in the will, and not in act. Yet every evil is followed by its punishment, for it is as if evil had its punishment inscribed upon it, which the impious man suffers after death. By the considerations here adduced, may also be explained the reason of the following position stated in n. 237: *That the worshiper of self and of nature confirms himself still more against the Divine Providence, when he sees that wicked contrivances, cunning, and deceit, succeed against the pious, the just, and the sincere; and that injustice triumphs over justice in judgments and affairs of business.* All the laws of the Divine Providence are necessities; and since necessities are the causes why the above evil things are permitted, it is evident that, to the end that a man may live as a man, the liberty of doing such things cannot be taken away from him by the Lord, except mediately by the Word, and especially by the precepts of the Decalogue, with those who acknowledge all kinds of murders, adulteries, thefts, and false testimony to be sins; but with those who do not acknowledge such things to be sins, the same is effected mediately by civil laws, and the fear of punishment thence incurred; also mediately by moral laws, and fear of the loss of character, honour, and interest. By these means the Lord leads the wicked, yet only from doing such things, and not from thinking and willing them; but by the former means he leads the good, not only from doing evils, but also from thinking and willing them.

250. II. *That the worshiper of self and of nature confirms himself against the Divine Providence, when he sees the impious promoted to honours, and made nobles and primates; that they moreover abound in wealth, and live elegantly and magnificently, while the worshipers of God remain in contempt and poverty.* The worshiper of self and of nature thinks dignities and riches the supreme and sole felicities which can be given, consequently the real and essential felicities. If, in consequence of having been initiated into divine worship in his infancy, he thinks any thing of God, he calls them divine blessings; and so long as from these blessings he does not aspire to any thing higher, he thinks that there is a God, and worships him; but in this worship there lies hid a motive which he himself does not then know,—that he may be promoted by God to still higher dignities and more abundant wealth; and if he attains thereto, his worship declines more and more to exteriors, till it comes to nothing, and at length he makes no account of God, and denies him. The effect is the same, if he be cast down from the dignity and opulence on which he had placed his heart. To the wicked then, what are dignities and riches but stumbling-blocks? Not so to the good, because they do not place their hearts thereon, but on the uses or goods, for the doing of which

170

dignities and riches serve as means. Therefore, from the promotion of the impious to dignities and riches, and their being made nobles and primates, no one but a worshiper of self and of nature can confirm himself against the Divine Providence. Besides, what is greater or lesser dignity, and greater or lesser opulence? Is it any thing in itself, but only something imaginary? Is one more prosperous and happy than the other? Is the dignity of a noble, or even of a king or an emperor, after a year's duration, considered any otherwise than as something common, which no longer makes his heart dilate with joy, and may even become vile in his sight? Are men, by virtue of their dignity, in any greater degree of happiness, than those who are in less dignity, or than those even who are in the least of all, such as husbandmen and their servants? May not these latter be in a greater degree of happiness, when they are prosperous and contented with their lot? Who is more restless at heart, more frequently fretted, or more grievously enraged, than a lover of himself? This is the case as often as he is not honoured according to the pride of his heart, or when any thing does not succeed according to his wish and pleasure. What then is dignity, if it be not to some use and purpose, but an idea? Can such an idea exist in any other thought, than in that about self and the world? And is it any thing in itself but an idea, that the world is every thing and eternity nothing? We will here add a few observations concerning the reason why the Divine Providence permits the wicked at heart to be promoted to dignities, and to acquire wealth. The impious, or wicked, can equally as well perform uses as the pious or good, indeed, with greater ardour, for they consider themselves in uses, and honours they consider as uses; therefore in proportion to the prevalence of self-love, is kindled the lust of doing uses with a view to their own glory. Such fire does not operate with the pious or good, unless it be kindled from below by the consideration of honour; for which reason the Lord rules the impious at heart, who are in dignities, by the love of fame, and thereby excites them to perform uses to the community or their country, to the society or city in which they dwell, and also to their neighbour or fellow-citizen: for the Lord's kingdom is a kingdom of uses; and where there are only a few who perform uses for the sake of being useful, he causes the worshipers of self to be advanced to offices of pre-eminence, in which they are all excited by self-love to do good. Suppose there were any infernal kingdom in this world (although there is not any such), in which the love of self only prevailed, self-love being the devil himself, would not every member of it perform uses from the fire of self-love, and the splendour of his own glory, more than in any other kingdom? All such have in their mouths nothing but the public good, and in their hearts nothing but their own good;

171

and as every one in such case looks up to his prince that he may be made greater, for he aspires to be greatest, can such a one see that there is a God, whilst he is encompassed by the smoke as it were of a conflagration, which no spiritual truth in its light can pervade? I have seen that smoke about the hells of such. Seek every method of information, and inquire how many of those, who at this day aspire to dignities in the kingdoms of the earth, are any other than lovers of self and of the world. You will scarcely find fifty in a thousand who are influenced by the love of God, and among these only a few aspire to dignities. Since then they are so few in number who are influenced by the love of God, and so many who are influenced by the love of self and of the world, and since the latter loves, from the nature of their fires, are more productive of uses, than the love of God is, from its fire, how can any one confirm himself against Divine Providence from the circumstance of the wicked being in greater pre-eminence and opulence than the good? This view is also confirmed by these words of the Lord: "And the Lord commended the unjust steward, because he had done wisely: for the children of this world are in their generation wiser than the children of light. And I say unto you, make to yourselves friends of the mammon of unrighteousness; that, when ye fail, they may receive you into everlasting habitations" (Luke xvi. 8, 9). What is meant by these words, in the natural sense, is evident: but, in the spiritual sense, by mammon of unrighteousness are meant the knowledges of things good and true which the wicked possess, and which they use solely for the purpose of acquiring to themselves dignities and riches. It is these knowledges, of which the good, or the children of light, are to make to themselves friends, and which are to introduce them into everlasting habitations. That there are many who love themselves and the world, and few who love God, the Lord also teaches in these words: "Wide is the gate, and broad is the way, that leadeth to destruction, and many there be which go in thereat; because strait is the gate, and narrow is the way, which leadeth unto life, and few there be that find it" (Matt. vii. 13, 14). That dignities and riches are either curses or blessings, and with whom they are such, may be seen above, n. 217.

251. III. *That the worshiper of self and of nature confirms himself against the Divine Providence, when he considers that wars are permitted, by which so many men are slaughtered, and their possessions plundered.* It is not from the Divine Providence that wars exist, because they are connected with murders, depredations, violences, cruelties, and other enormous evils, which are diametrically contrary to Christian charity; but still they cannot but be permitted, because the life's love of man, since the time of the most ancient people, who are meant by Adam and his wife (treated of above, n. 241), is become of such a nature,

172

that he desires to have dominion over others, and at length over all, and wishes to possess worldly wealth, and at length all the wealth in the world. These two loves cannot be held in bonds; since it is according to the Divine Providence, that every one should be allowed to act from liberty according to reason, concerning which see above, n. 71 to 97; and without permissions, a man cannot be led by the Lord from evils, consequently cannot be reformed and saved; for if evils were not permitted to break out, a man would not see them, therefore would not acknowledge them, and could not be induced to resist them. Hence it is that evils cannot be restrained from appearing by any regulation of the Divine Providence; for in that case, they would remain shut in, and like the diseases called cancer and mortification, would spread, and consume every thing vital in the man. For a man is by birth like a little hell, between which and heaven there is a perpetual disagreement. No man can be drawn out of his hell by the Lord, unless he sees that he is there, and wishes to be delivered; and this cannot be done without permissions, the causes of which are laws of the Divine Providence. This is the reason why there are wars of greater or lesser extent;—lesser wars between the possessors of lands and lordships and their neighbours, and greater wars between the monarchs of kingdoms and their neighbours. Their being greater or lesser makes no other difference than that the lesser are kept within certain bounds by the laws of their particular nation, and the greater by the law of nations; and that, although the lesser as well as the greater are desirous of going beyond their laws, the lesser cannot, and the greater can, yet still within the limits of a certain possibility. That the greater wars, notwithstanding they are connected with slaughter, depredations, violence, and cruelty, are not prevented by the Lord from being carried on by kings and generals, neither in their beginning nor in their progress, until in the end the power of one or the other is so reduced that they are in danger of destruction, is owing to several causes, which are hid in the treasury of divine wisdom. Some of these have been revealed to me; among which is the following,—that all wars, although they are of a civil nature, are representative of states of the church in heaven, and are correspondences. Such were all the wars which are described in the Word, and such also are all wars at this day. The wars described in the Word are those which were carried on by the children of Israel with various nations, as with the Amorites, the Ammonites, the Moabites, the Philistines, the Syrians, the Egyptians, the Chaldeans, the Assyrians; and when the children of Israel, who represented the church, departed from their precepts and statutes, and fell into the evils which were signified by those nations (for each particular nation, with which the children of

173

Israel waged war, signified some particular kind of evil), then they were punished by that nation. For example, when they profaned the holy things of the church by foul idolatries, they were punished by the Assyrians and Chaldeans, because by Assyria and Chaldea is signified the profanation of what is holy. What is signified by the wars with the Philistines may be seen in THE DOCTRINE OF THE NEW JERUSALEM CONCERNING FAITH, n. 50—54. Similar things are represented by wars at this day, wherever they are; for all the things which are done in the natural world correspond with spiritual things in the spiritual world, and all spiritual things concern the church. It is not known in this world, which kingdoms in Christendom represent the Moabites and Ammonites, which the Syrians and Philistines, and which the Chaldeans and Assyrians, and the others with whom the children of Israel carried on war; nevertheless there are kingdoms in Christendom which represent those people. But what is the quality of the church upon earth, and what are the evils into which it falls, and on account of which it is punished with wars, cannot at all be seen in the natural world, because in that world appear externals only, which do not constitute the church; but it is seen in the spiritual world, where internals appear, which do constitute the church; and there all are conjoined according to their various states. The conflicts of those in the spiritual world correspond to wars, which on both sides are governed correspondently by the Lord according to his Divine Providence. That wars in this world are governed by the Divine Providence of the Lord, is acknowledged by the spiritual man, but not by the natural man, except when a feast is appointed on account of a victory; and then upon his knees he can give thanks to God who has given the victory; and he can also offer up a few ejaculations before he goes to battle; but when he returns to himself, he either ascribes the victory to the prudence of the general, or to some measure or incident in the midst of the battle, which they had not thought of, and by which nevertheless the victory was decided. That the Divine Providence, which is called fortune, operates in the most minute particulars even of trifling things, may be seen above, n. 212; and if you acknowledge the Divine Providence in such things, much more should you acknowledge it in the concerns of war. Successes and advantages obtained in war are commonly called the fortune of war; and this is the Divine Providence operating especially in the counsels and designs meditated by the general, although he at the time, and afterwards, may ascribe the whole to his own prudence. This he may do if he pleases, for he is at full liberty to think either in favour of the Divine Providence or against it, and, indeed, either in favour of God or against him; but he ought to know, that not the smallest particular of his counsels or mediated measures is from himself: they all flow from heaven, or from hell,—from hell by permission, and from heaven by the Divine Providence.

252. IV. *That the worshiper of self and of nature confirms himself against the Divine Providence, when he thinks, according to his perception, that victories declare on the side of prudence, and not always on the side of justice; and that it makes no difference whether the general be a good or a wicked man.* The reason why it seems as if victory declared on the side of prudence, and sometimes not on the side of justice, is, because a man judges from appearance, and favours one party more than another; and that which he favours he can confirm by reasonings. Nor does he know, as before observed, that the justice of the cause in heaven is spiritual, and in this world natural; and that they are joined by a connection of things past and to come, which are known only to the Lord. That it makes no difference whether the general be a good or a wicked man, is owing to the same cause which is assigned above, n. 250, namely, that the wicked perform uses as well as the good, and, indeed, from the fire peculiar to themselves, more ardently than the good; especially in wars, because a wicked man is more crafty and cunning in devising deceitful contrivances, and from the love of glory receives pleasure in killing and plundering those whom he knows and declares to be enemies, which is not the case with a good man, who is only influenced by prudence and zeal in defending himself, and rarely in invading others. It is the same with the spirits of hell, and the angels of heaven; the former assaulting and the latter defending themselves. Hence may be deduced this conclusion, that it is allowable for any persons to defend their country and associates against invading enemies, even by means of wicked generals; but it is not allowable to make themselves enemies without a cause. When a desire for glory alone is the cause, it is in itself diabolical, for this springs from self-love.

253. Thus far have been explained the things adduced above, n. 237, by which the merely natural man confirms himself against the Divine Providence: we will now proceed to explain those which follow, in n. 238, relating to the religions of many nations, which can also serve the merely natural man as arguments against the Divine Providence; for he says in his heart, How can so many discordant religions exist, and why not one true religion throughout all the world, if, as is shown above, the Divine Providence has for its end a heaven out of the human race, n. 27—45? But hear, I beseech you: All who are born men, whatever may be their religion, are capable of being saved, provided they acknowledge a God, and live according to the commandments of the Decalogue, which are, not to kill, not to commit adultery, not to steal, not to bear false witness, because

175

to do such things is contrary to religion, therefore contrary to God. In such persons there is the fear of God and the love of their neighbour,—the fear of God, because they think that to do such things is to act against God; and the love of their neighbour, because to kill, to commit adultery, to steal, to bear false witness, and to covet their neighbour's house and his wife, is to act against their neighbour. These persons, since they respect God in their lives, and do no evil to their neighbour, are led by the Lord; and those who are so led, are also taught according to their religion concerning God and their neighbour; for those who so live, love to be taught, but those who live otherwise, do not love to be taught. As they love to be taught, therefore, after death also, when they become spirits, they are instructed by the angels, and willingly receive such truths as are contained in the Word. On this subject something may be seen in THE DOCTRINE OF THE NEW JERUSALEM CONCERNING THE SACRED SCRIPTURE, n. 91—97; and 104—113.

254. I. *That the merely natural man confirms himself against the Divine Providence, when he considers the religions of various nations, and that there are some who are totally ignorant of a God, some who adore the sun and moon, and some also who adore idols and graven images.* Those who from these circumstances deduce arguments against the Divine Providence, are not acquainted with the arcana of heaven, which are innumerable, and of which scarcely any come to our knowledge: for among these arcana this is one, that a man is not taught immediately from heaven, but mediately; on which subject, see above, n. 154—174. Since he is taught mediately, and the gospel could not by emissaries be extended to all who inhabit the whole earth, although some religion could be handed down by various means even to the Gentiles who are in the remote corners of the earth, therefore this was effected by the Divine Providence; for no man has any religion from himself, but through some other person, who either knows from the Word, or has learned by tradition from others, that there is a God, that there are a heaven and a hell, and a life after death, and that God is to be worshiped in order that man may be made happy. That religion has been made known over the whole earth from the ancient Word, and afterwards from the Israelitish Word, may be seen in THE DOCTRINE OF THE NEW JERUSALEM CONCERNING THE SACRED SCRIPTURE, n. 101—103; and that without the Word no one could have known any thing of God, of heaven and hell, or of a life after death, much less any thing of the Lord, may be seen, n. 114—118 of the same tract. When once a religion is implanted in any nation, the people are led by the Lord according to the precepts and tenets of their religion; and the Lord provides that in every religion there shall be precepts

similar to those in the Decalogue ; as, that God should be worshiped, and his name not profaned, that festivals should be observed, parents honoured, murder, adultery, and theft, not committed, and false testimony not given. The nation which makes these precepts divine, and from a principle of religion lives according to them, is saved, as was said above, n. 253. And most of the nations, which are even remote from the Christian world, consider these laws, not as civil, but as divine, and hold them sacred. That a man is saved by a life according to these precepts, may be seen in THE DOCTRINE OF THE NEW JERUSALEM FROM THE PRECEPTS OF THE DECALOGUE, from beginning to end. Among the arcana of heaven there is this also,— that the angelic heaven is in the sight of the Lord as one man, of whom the Lord is the soul and life, and that this divine man is in every particular of his form a man, not only as to his external, but also as to his internal members and organs, which are many, and likewise as to the skin, membranes, cartilages, and bones : none however of these parts in that man are material, but all are spiritual. And it is provided by the Lord, that those to whom the gospel cannot reach, but only some religion, may likewise have a place in that man, that is, in heaven, by constituting the parts called the skin, membranes, cartilages, and bones ; and that they may live equally as well as others in heavenly joy : for it makes no difference whether a person be in such joy as is experienced by the angels of the highest heaven, or in such as is experienced by the angels of the lowest heaven, since every one, who is received into heaven, enters into the supreme or full joy of his heart ; and greater than that he cannot support, for thereby he would be suffocated. The case is similar to a husbandman in comparison with a king : the former may be in a state of the greatest happiness, when he goes clad in a new suit of coarse worsted apparel, and sits down to a table furnished with plain and wholesome food ; and he would be distressed at heart, if he were to be clothed like a king in purple, silk, gold, and silver, and if a table were set out for him, with expensive and exquisite delicacies of various kinds, and generous wines. From which consideration it is evident, that the last as well as the first in heaven, have celestial felicity, each in his degree ; and consequently that those also enjoy such felicity, who are without the Christian world, provided they shun evils as sins against God, because they are contrary to religion. There are some few, who are totally ignorant with respect to God ; but that these, if they have lived a moral life, are instructed after death by angels, and in their moral life receive a spiritual principle, may be seen in the DOCTRINE OF THE NEW JERUSALEM CONCERNING THE SACRED SCRIPTURE, n. 116. It is the same with those who worship the sun and moon, and think that God is therein. They know no

177

otherwise, and therefore it is not imputed to them as a sin, for the Lord says, " If ye were blind," that is, if ye did not know, " ye would have no sin " (John ix. 41). But there are many who worship idols and images, even in the Christian world ; and this, indeed, is idolatrous, yet not in all ; for there are some to whom images serve as means of exciting them to think of God. By virtue of influx from heaven, those who acknowledge God, wish to see him ; and those who cannot, like those who are interiorly spiritual, elevate the mind above things sensual, awaken in themselves an idea of him from a statue or a graven image. Those who do this, and do not adore the image itself as a god, if also they live according to the precepts of the Decalogue from a principle of religion, are saved. Hence it is evident, that as the Lord wills the salvation of all, he has also provided that every one, if he lives well, may have some place in heaven. That heaven before the Lord is as one man ; that thence heaven corresponds to all and singular the things appertaining to man ; and that there are also some who represent the skin, the membranes, cartilages, and bones, may be seen in the work concerning HEAVEN AND HELL, published in London 1758, n. 59—102 : also in the ARCANA CŒLESTIA, n. 5552—5556 ; and above, n. 201—204.

255. II. *That the merely natural man confirms himself against the Divine Providence, when he reflects upon the Mahometan religion, and considers that it is received by so many empires and kingdoms.* That this religion is received by a greater number of kingdoms than the Christian religion, may be matter of scandal to those who think of the Divine Providence, and at the same time imagine that no one can be saved except he be born a Christian, and in a country where the Word is possessed, by means of which the Lord is known. But the Mahometan religion is no matter of scandal to those who believe that all things are of the Divine Providence. These inquire wherein such Providence can be traced, and they discover it. It is perceived in this, that the Mahometan religion acknowledges the Lord to be the Son of God, the wisest of men, and the greatest of prophets, who came into the world to teach men ; and most Mahometans therefore consider the Lord as greater than Mahomet. That it may be better understood that this religion was raised up by the Divine Providence of the Lord, for the purpose of destroying the idolatry of many nations, the subject shall be considered in an orderly arrangement, beginning with some observations concerning the origin of idolatries. Previous to the religion of Mahomet, the worship of idols was common over the whole earth ; the reason of which was, that the churches, before the Lord's coming, were all representative churches. Such was the Israelitish church ; and the tabernacle, the garments of Aaron, the sacrifices, all things appertaining to the temple at Jerusalem,

and also the statutes, were representative. The ancients also understood the science of correspondences, which is the science of representations, the peculiar science of their wise men, and was cultivated particularly in Egypt, whence they had their hieroglyphics. By this science, they knew what was signified by animals of all kinds, what by trees of all kinds, and what by mountains, hills, rivers, and fountains; what also by the sun, moon, and stars; and as all their divine worship was representative, consisting of mere correspondences, therefore they celebrated it upon mountains and hills, also in groves and gardens. For the same reason they consecrated fountains, turned their faces towards the east in their adoration of God, and also made themselves carved images of horses, oxen, calves, lambs, even of birds, fishes, and serpents, and placed them in their houses and other places, in a certain order, according to the spiritual things of the church to which they corresponded or which they represented. They placed similar things in their temples, that they might recall to their memories the holy things which they signified. In process of time when the science of correspondences was lost, their posterity began to worship the images themselves as sacred, not knowing that their ancestors saw nothing sacred in them, and that they were only so according to the correspondences they represented and thence signified. Thus arose the idolatries which filled the whole earth, as well Asia with its adjacent islands, as Africa and Europe. In order that all these idolatries might be extirpated, it was permitted by the Divine Providence of the Lord, that, in accommodation to the genius of the eastern nations, there should arise a new religion, in which there might be something out of both Testaments of the Word, and which might teach that the Lord came into the world, that he was the greatest prophet, the wisest of all, and the Son of God. This was effected by Mahomet, from whom that religion is called the Mahometan religion. It was raised up by the Divine Providence of the Lord, in accommodation, as was observed, to the genius of the eastern nations, to the end that it might destroy the idolatries which at that time so generally prevailed, and give the inhabitants of those countries some knowledge of the Lord, before they came into the spiritual world; and such religion would not have been received by so many kingdoms, or have had power to extirpate their idolatries, if it had not been accommodated and adapted to the ideas and mode of life prevailing amongst them all. The reason why they did not acknowledge the Lord as the God of heaven and earth, was because the eastern nations acknowledged a God the Creator of the universe, but could not comprehend that he himself came into the world, and took upon him the human nature. Nor is this comprehended by Christians, who, therefore, in thought, separate his divinity from his humanity, placing his divinity

179   M

beside the Father in heaven, and his humanity they know not where. Hence it may be seen, that the Mahometan religion also had its origin in the Divine Providence of the Lord; and that all persons of that religion, who acknowledge the Lord as the Son of God, and at the same time live according to the precepts of the Decalogue, which they also possess, by shunning evils as sins, are received into that heaven which is called the Mahometan heaven. This is also divided into three heavens,— the supreme, middle, and lowest. In the supreme heaven are those who acknowledge the Lord to be one with the Father, and consequently to be the only God; in the second heaven, those who renounce a plurality of wives, and live with one only; and in the ultimate heaven, those who are initiated. More concerning this religion may be seen in THE CONTI- NUATION CONCERNING THE LAST JUDGMENT AND THE SPIRITUAL WORLD, n. 68—72, where the Mahometans and Mahomet are treated of.

256. III. *That the merely natural man confirms himself against the Divine Providence, when he sees that the Christian religion is received only in the smallest quarter of the habitable globe, called Europe, and that there it is divided.* The reason why the Christian religion is established only in the smallest quarter of the habitable globe, called Europe, is, because it was not so well accommodated to the genius of the eastern nations, as the Mahometan religion which is mixed, as was shown above; and a religion is not received by those to whom it is not accom- modated. For example: a religion which forbids the having of more than one wife, is not received, but rejected, by those who for some ages back have been addicted to polygamy; and it is the same with respect to some other things prohibited by the Christian religion. Nor does it signify whether it be received by a greater or a smaller part of the world, provided there be a people who are in possession of the Word: for thence light is received even by those who are out of the church, and have not the Word, as is shown in THE DOCTRINE OF THE NEW JERU- SALEM CONCERNING THE SACRED SCRIPTURE, n. 104—113; and what is wonderful, where the Word is read with devotion, and the Lord is worshiped from the Word, there the Lord is, with heaven. The reason is, because the Lord is the Word, and the Word is divine truth, which constitutes heaven; and therefore the Lord says, "Where two or three are gathered together in my name, there am I in the midst of them" (Matt. xviii. 20). This may be effected with the Word by the Europeans in many parts of the habitable globe, because they have communication with the whole world; and either read the Word or teach from it everywhere. This may appear like a fiction, but it is never- theless true. The reason why the Christian religion is divided, is, because it is derived from the Word, which is written by

mere correspondences, and correspondences are for the most part appearances of truth, in which, nevertheless, genuine truths lie concealed. Therefore, as the doctrine of the church is to be drawn from the literal sense of the Word, which is of such a nature, there could not but exist in the church disputes, controversies, and dissensions, with respect especially to the meaning of the Word, but not with respect to the Word itself, and the Lord's divinity itself; for it is everywhere acknowledged that the Word is holy, and that the Lord is Divine, and these two are the essentials of the church; therefore, also, those who deny the Lord's divinity, as those who are called Socinians, are excommunicated from the church; and those who deny the sanctity of the Word, are not reputed as Christians. To this I will add a memorable circumstance relating to the Word, from which it may be concluded, that the Word interiorly is divine truth itself, and most interiorly the Lord. When any spirit opens the Word, and rubs his face or his clothes with it, then, merely by being rubbed with it, they shine as bright as the moon or a star, and this in the sight of all whom he meets: this is a proof that there is nothing in the world more holy than the Word. That the Word is written by mere correspondences, may be seen in THE DOCTRINE OF THE NEW JERUSALEM CONCERNING THE SACRED SCRIPTURE, n. 5—26; that the doctrine of the church is to be deduced from the literal sense of the Word, and confirmed by it, n. 50—61; that heresies may be derived from the literal sense of the Word, but that to confirm them is hurtful, n. 91—97; and that the church exists from the Word, and that its quality is according to its understanding of the Word, n. 76—79.

257. IV. *That the merely natural man confirms himself against the Divine Providence, because in many kingdoms, where the Christian religion is received, there are some who claim to themselves divine power, and desire to be worshiped as gods; and because they invoke dead men.* They say, indeed, that they have not arrogated to themselves divine power, and that they do not desire to be worshiped as gods; but yet they say that they can open and shut heaven, and remit and retain sins, consequently can save and condemn men, which is the prerogative of divinity itself; for the Divine Providence has nothing for its end but the reformation and thereby the salvation of mankind. This is its continual operation with every one; and salvation cannot be effected except by an acknowledgment of the Lord's divinity, and confidence that it is wrought by him, when a man lives according to his commandments. Who cannot see that this is the Babylon described in the Revelation, and the Babel treated of in many parts of the prophets? That this also is meant by Lucifer in Isaiah xiv. is evident from the 4th and 22d verses of that chapter, in which are the following words:

181

"Thou shalt take up this proverb against the king of Babylon" (verse 4): afterwards, "I will cut off from Babylon the name and remnant" (verse 22); from which it is evident, that Babylon is there signified by Lucifer, of whom it is said, "How art thou fallen from heaven, O Lucifer, son of the morning! For thou hast said in thy heart, I will ascend into heaven; I will exalt my throne above the stars of God: I will sit also upon the mount of the congregation, in the sides of the north: I will ascend above the heights of the clouds: I will be like the Most High" (verses 12, 13, 14). That they invoke dead men, and pray to them for succour, is well known. It is affirmed that they invoke them, because the invocation of them is established by a papal bull, confirming the decree of the Council of Trent, in which it is openly said that they are to be invoked: yet who does not know that God alone ought to be invoked, and not any dead man? But it shall now be stated why the Lord permitted such things. That he permitted them for a certain end, which is salvation, cannot be denied; for it is well known, that without the Lord there is no salvation. This being the case, there was a necessity that the Lord should be preached from the Word, and the Christian church thereby established; but this could not be effected except by leaders who should act with zeal, and there were no others qualified, than such as were heated, as it were, with zeal, from the fire of self-love. This fire first excited them to preach the Lord and teach the Word; and from this their primitive state it is, that Lucifer is called the son of the morning (verse 12). But as they came to see, that they should be able to obtain dominion by means of the holy things of the Word and the church, self-love, by which they were first excited to preach the Lord, broke out from within, and at length exalted itself to such a height, that they transferred all the divine power of the Lord to themselves, not leaving him any. This could not be prevented by the Divine Providence of the Lord; for had it been prevented, they would have proclaimed the Lord not to be God, and the Word not to be sacred, and would have become Socinians or Arians, and thus have destroyed the whole church; which, whatever may be the character of its rulers, still remains among the people who are under them. For all those of that religion also, who approach the Lord, and shun evils as sins, are saved; for which reason there are many celestial societies from them in the spiritual world; and it is also provided, that there should be among them a nation which has not submitted to the yoke of such a dominion, and which considers the Word as sacred. This is the noble French nation. But what was the consequence? When self-love, which is Lucifer, had exalted its dominion even unto the throne of the Lord, had removed him thence, and placed itself upon it, it could not do otherwise than profane all things appertaining to the Word and the church; and to prevent this, the Lord so ordered it of his Divine Providence, that those who were under its influence should depart from the worship of him, invoke dead men, pray to their images, kiss their bones, prostrate themselves at their sepulchres, forbid the Word to be read, place the sanctity of divine worship in masses not understood by the vulgar, and sell salvation for money; because, if they had not done these things, they would have profaned the holy things of the Word and the church; for, as was shown in the preceding paragraph, none can profane things sacred but those who are acquainted with them. Therefore, that they may not profane the most holy supper, it is of the Divine Providence of the Lord that they should divide it, giving the bread to the people, and drinking the wine themselves; for the wine in the holy supper signifies holy truth, and the bread, holy good; but when they are divided, the wine signifies truth profane, and the bread good adulterated. It is provided, also, that they should make it corporeal and material, and account this doctrine to be a primary tenet of religion. He who attends to these particulars, and considers them in some illumination of mind, may see the wonderful operation of the Divine Providence, in guarding the holy things of the church, and saving all who are capable of being saved, snatching as it were out of the fire those who will suffer themselves to be snatched away.

258. V. *That the merely natural man confirms himself against the Divine Providence from this circumstance, that among those who profess the Christian religion, there are some who place salvation in certain words which they think and speak, and not in any good they do.* That persons of this description are such as make salvation to consist in faith alone, and not in a life of charity, consequently, who separate faith from charity, is shown in THE DOCTRINE OF THE NEW JERUSALEM CONCERNING FAITH; and also, that they are meant in the Word by the Philistines, the dragon, and the goats. That such a doctrine is also permitted, is of the Divine Providence, in order that the Lord's divinity and the sanctity of the Word might not be profaned. The Lord's divinity is not profaned, when salvation is placed in the uttering of these words, "That God the Father will have mercy for the sake of his Son, who suffered on the cross, and made satisfaction for us;" for by using this form of words, they do not approach the Lord's divinity, but his humanity, which they do not acknowledge to be divine. The Word also is not profaned; because they do not attend to those passages where mention is made of love and charity, of doing good, and of works. All these, they say, are contained in the faith of the above form of words; and those who confirm themselves herein, say to themselves, The law does not condemn me, nor therefore does evil; and good does not save me, because good from myself

183

is not good; therefore they are like those who do not know any truth from the Word, and on that account cannot profane it. But faith in the above form of words is not confirmed by any except those who from self-love are in the pride of self-derived intelligence, and who are not Christians in their hearts, but only desire to seem such. That nevertheless the Lord's Divine Providence continually operates for the salvation of those with whom faith separated from charity is made the ground of religion, shall now be shown. It is of the Lord's Divine Providence, that although religion is made to consist in this faith, still every one knows that such faith does not save, but a life of charity with which faith acts as one: for in all the churches where this religion is received, it is taught, that there is no salvation, except a man examine himself, perceive his sins, acknowledge them, repent, desist from them, and lead a new life. This is read with much zeal before all those who approach the holy supper; and it is added, that unless they do this, they mix things holy and profane, and cast themselves into eternal damnation; and in England, indeed, that unless they do this, the devil will enter into them as he did into Judas, and destroy them both soul and body. Hence it is evident, that every one in the churches where faith alone is received, is nevertheless taught that evils are to be shunned as sins. Every one also who is born a Christian, knows that evils are to be shunned as sins, because the Decalogue is put into the hands of every boy and girl, and is taught by parents and masters. All the subjects of a kingdom, likewise, particularly the common people, are examined by the priest, out of the Decalogue, which they have learned by heart, what they know of the Christian religion, and are admonished to do the things therein contained. At such times, they are never told by any priest that they are not under the yoke of that law, or that they cannot do the things therein commanded, because they cannot do any good from themselves. The Athanasian Creed is also received by the whole Christian world; and what is said in the last part of it is acknowledged, namely, that the Lord will come to judge both the quick and the dead, when those who HAVE DONE GOOD will enter into everlasting life, and those who HAVE DONE EVIL into everlasting fire. In SWEDEN, where the religion of faith alone is received, it is also plainly taught, that there is no faith separate from charity, or without good works; and in a certain memorial annexed and inserted in all the books of the Psalms, which is entitled *Impediments or Stumbling Blocks to the Impenitent* (OBOTFERDIGAS FOERHINDER), there are these words: "Those who are rich in good works show thereby that they are rich in faith, because when faith is saving it operates by charity; for justifying faith never exists alone and separate from good works; as there is no good tree without fruit, no sun without light and

184

heat, and no water without moisture." These few things are adduced that it may be known, that although the religion of faith alone is received, yet the goods of charity, which are good works, are everywhere taught; and that this is of the Lord's Divine Providence, lest the common people should thereby be seduced. I have heard Luther, with whom I have sometimes conversed in the spiritual world, curse Solifidianism, and say, that when he established it, he was warned by an angel of the Lord not to do it; but that he thought within himself, that if he did not reject works, no separation from the Roman Catholic religion would be effected; for which reason he confirmed that faith, contrary to the warning he had received.

259. VI. *That the merely natural man confirms himself against the Divine Providence, because there have been, and still are, so many heresies in the Christian world, such as those of the Quakers, Moravians, Anabaptists, and others ;* for he can think within himself, that if the Divine Providence, by means of its operation in every particular, were universal, and had in view the salvation of all, it would have established one true religion throughout the world, and not have suffered it to be divided, much less torn to pieces by heresies. But use your reason, and, if you are able, reflect with more elevation of mind; then tell me, can a man be saved unless he be first reformed? For he is born into the love of self and of the world; and as these loves do not contain in them any love towards God, or towards his neighbour, except for the sake of self, he is also born into all kinds of evils: for, is there a single spark of love or mercy in those loves? Does he make any account of defrauding another, blaspheming him, hating him even to death, committing adultery with his wife, and raging against him when he is in a revengeful humour? because as the thing nearest to his heart is, that he may be supreme over all, he consequently considers others in comparison with himself as vile, and of no estimation. In order that such a one may be saved, must he not first be drawn away from these evils, and so be reformed? That this cannot be effected except in conformity to several laws, which are laws of the Divine Providence, is fully shown above. These laws are for the most part unknown, and yet they are laws of the divine wisdom, and at the same time of the divine love, against which the Lord cannot act; for to act against them, would be to destroy man, and not to save him. Read over again the laws which have been adduced, consider them, and you will perceive this. Since therefore it is conformable to those laws, that there should not be any immediate influx from heaven, but mediate through the Word, through doctrines and preachings; and since the Word, that it might be divine, could not be written except by mere correspondences, it follows, that dissensions and heresies are inevitable, and that the permission of

185

these is also according to the laws of the Divine Providence; especially, when the church itself had assumed for its essentials such things as belong to the understanding only, thus to doctrine; and not to the will, thus to the conduct of life. When the things which have relation to life are not made essentials of the church, then a man with respect to his understanding is in mere darkness, and gropes about like a blind man, who is ever stumbling, and falling into ditches; for the will must see in the understanding, and not the understanding in the will; or, what amounts to the same, the life and its love must lead the understanding to think, speak, and act, and not the contrary; for were the contrary the case, the understanding might from an evil, and even from a diabolical love, catch at whatever might impress the senses, and enjoin the will to do it. From these considerations it may be seen whence dissensions and heresies exist. It is however provided, that every one, in whatever heresy he may be with respect to his understanding, may still be reformed and saved, provided he shuns evils as sins, and does not confirm heretical falsities in himself; for by shunning evils as sins the will is reformed, and by the will the understanding, which then first emerges out of darkness into light. There are three essentials of the church,—an acknowledgment of the Lord's divinity, an acknowledgment of the holiness of the Word, and the life which is called charity. Every man's faith is conformable to his life, that is, his charity. From the Word he has a knowledge of what his life ought to be, and from the Lord he has reformation and salvation. If these three had been held as essentials of the church, intellectual dissensions would not have divided it, but only have varied it; as the light varies colours in beautiful objects, and as a variety of jewels constitutes the beauty of a kingly crown.

260. VII. *That the merely natural man confirms himself against the Divine Providence, because Judaism still continues;* that is, because the Jews, after the lapse of so many ages, are not converted, although they live among Christians, and do not according to the predictions in the Word confess the Lord, and acknowledge him as the Messiah, who, as they imagine, is to lead them back into the land of Canaan, but constantly persist in denying him, and yet it continues well with them. But those who think thus, and for that reason call in question the Divine Providence, do not know that by the Jews in the Word are meant all who are of the church and acknowledge the Lord, and that by the land of Canaan, into which it is said they are to be introduced, is meant the Lord's church. The reason, however, why they persevere in denying the Lord, is, because they are of such a disposition, that if they were to receive and acknowledge the Lord's divinity, and the holy things of his church, they would profane them; therefore the Lord says of

them, "He hath blinded their eyes, and hardened their heart; that they should not see with their eyes, or understand with their heart, and be converted, and I should heal them" (John xii. 40; Matt. xiii. 14; Mark iv. 12; Luke viii. 10; Isaiah vi. 9, 10). It is said, lest they should be converted, and I should heal them, because if they had been converted and healed, they would have been guilty of profanation; and it is a law of the Divine Providence, as was shown above, n. 221—233, that no one is interiorly admitted by the Lord into the truths of faith and the goods of charity, except so far as he can be kept in them to the end of life; and were it not so, he would profane things holy. This nation is preserved, and scattered over a great part of the earth, for the sake of the Word in its original language, which they hold more sacred than Christians do; and in every particular of the Word is the divinity of the Lord, for it is divine truth united to divine good, which proceeds from the Lord, and by which the Word is the conjunction of the Lord with the church and the presence of heaven, as is shown in THE DOCTRINE OF THE NEW JERUSALEM CONCERNING THE SACRED SCRIPTURE, n. 62—69; and there is the presence of the Lord and of heaven wherever the Word is read with devotion. This is the end which the Divine Providence has in view, in preserving and dispersing them over a great part of the world. What is the nature of their lot after death, may be seen in THE CONTINUATION CONCERNING THE LAST JUDGMENT AND THE SPIRITUAL WORLD, n. 79—82.

261. These then are the circumstances adduced above, n. 238, by which the natural man does or may confirm himself against the Divine Providence: there follow some others, mentioned above, n. 239, which may also serve the natural man as arguments against the Divine Providence, and may likewise occur to the minds of others, and suggest some doubts; these are,—

262. I. *That a doubt may be inferred against the Divine Providence, because the whole Christian world worship God under three persons, which is, three gods; and because hitherto they have not known that God is one in person and in essence, in whom there is a trinity, and that that God is the Lord.* The reasoner concerning the Divine Providence may say, Are not three persons three Gods, when each person by himself is God? Who can think otherwise; or who, indeed, does think otherwise? Athanasius himself could not think otherwise; and therefore, in the creed which has its name from him, he says, "As we are compelled by the Christian verity to acknowledge every person by himself to be God and Lord, so are we forbidden by the Catholic religion to say there be three Gods or three Lords;" by which words nothing else can be understood, than that we ought to acknowledge three Gods and three Lords, but that we

187

ought not to say there are three Gods and three Lords. Who can possibly have a perception of one God, who is not also one in person? If it be alleged, that it is possible to have such a perception, provided you think that the three persons have one essence,—who from thence does or can perceive any thing else, than that in such case they are unanimous, and consenting, but yet that they are three Gods? and if a man elevates his thoughts, he says within himself, How can the divine essence, which is infinite, be divided? and how can it from eternity beget another, and even produce a third, who proceeds from both? It may be said, that this is to be believed, and ought not to be thought of; but who does not think of that which he is told he ought to believe? and how otherwise can there be any acknowledgment, which is the essence of faith? Did not Socinianism and Arianism, which reign in the hearts of more people than you imagine, take their rise from thinking of God as of three persons? A belief in one God, and that that one God is the Lord, constitutes the church; for in him there is a divine trinity. That this is true, may be seen in THE DOCTRINE OF THE NEW JERUSALEM CONCERNING THE LORD, from beginning to end. But what is thought of the Lord at this day? Is it not thought that he is God and man,—God from Jehovah his Father, of whom he was conceived, and man from the Virgin Mary, of whom he was born? Who thinks, that God and man in him, or his divinity and his humanity, are one person, and that they are one as the soul and body are one? Does any one know this? Ask the doctors of the church, and they will say that they have not known it, when, nevertheless, it is the doctrine of the Church received throughout the whole Christian world, which is as follows: "Our Lord Jesus Christ, the Son of God, is God and man; and although he be God and man, yet he is not two, but one Christ; one, by taking of the manhood into God; one altogether, by unity of person; for as the soul and flesh is one man, so God and man is one Christ." This is taken from the creed of Athanasius. The reason why they have not known it, is, because when they read it, they did not think of the Lord as God, but only as a man. If the same be asked whether they know of whom he was conceived,—whether of God the Father, or of his own divinity,—they will answer that he was conceived of God the Father, for this is according to Scripture. Are not the Father and he one then, as the soul and body are one? Who can think that he was conceived of two divinities, and if of his own divinity, that this was his Father? If you ask them again, What is your idea of the Lord's divinity, and what of his humanity? they will say that his divinity is from the essence of the Father, and his humanity from the essence of the mother, and that his divinity is with the Father. If you then ask, where is his humanity, they will make no

188

answer; for they separate in idea his divinity from his human
ity, and make his divinity equal to that of the Father, and his
humanity similar to that of another man ; not knowing, that in
so doing, they also separate soul and body; nor seeing the
contradiction, that in this case he would have been born a rational man from the mother alone. In consequence of the idea
entertained concerning the Lord's humanity, that it was like
that of another man, it is now come to pass, that a Christian
cannot without difficulty be led to think of *A Divine Human
Being*, although it should be said that the Lord's soul or life
was from conception, and is, Jehovah himself. Collect these
reasons now, and consider whether there be any other God of
the universe than the Lord alone, in whom is the all-creating
Divine itself which is called the Father, the Divine Human
which is called the Son, and the Divine Proceeding which is
called the Holy Spirit ; thus, that God is one in person and in
essence, and that that God is the Lord. If you insist and say,
that the Lord himself named three in Matthew, saying, "Go and
teach all nations, baptizing them in the name of the Father, and
of the Son, and of the Holy Ghost" (xxviii. 19); I answer, it is
evident from the preceding and following verses, that he said
this, in order that it might be known that in himself now glorified there was a divine trinity. In the verse immediately preceding, he says, that all power was given to him in heaven and
in earth ; and in the succeeding verse, that he would be with
them until the consummation of the age; consequently, he speaks
of himself alone, and not of three. Now, with respect to the
Divine Providence, and the reason why it has permitted Christians to worship one God under three persons, which amounts to
the same as three Gods, and that hitherto they have not known
that God is one in person and essence, in whom there is a trinity,
and that that God is the Lord,—the reason does not exist in
the Lord, but in man himself. The Lord taught it manifestly
in his Word, as may appear from all the passages quoted in
THE DOCTRINE OF THE NEW JERUSALEM CONCERNING THE LORD ;
and he also taught it in the doctrine of all the churches, in
which it is insisted that his divinity and his humanity are not
two, but one person, united like soul and body. But the reason
why they divided his divinity and humanity, and made his
divinity equal to that of Jehovah the Father, and his humanity
equal to that of another man, was, because the church after its
establishment lapsed into Babylon, which transferred to itself
the divine power of the Lord ; yet, that it might not be called
divine power, but human, they made the Lord's humanity similar to that of another man. Afterwards also, when the church
was reformed, and faith alone received as the only means of
salvation (which is, that God the Father would have mercy for
the sake of his Son), the Lord's humanity could not be viewed

189

in any other light. The reason why it could not, is, that no one can approach the Lord, and acknowledge him in his heart as the God of heaven and earth, but he who lives according to his commandments. In the spiritual world, where every one is obliged to speak as he thinks, no one can even name Jesus, unless he has lived in the world as a Christian; and this from his Divine Providence, lest his name should be profaned.

263. But in order that what has now been said may appear more clearly, I will add what is adduced in THE DOCTRINE OF THE NEW JERUSALEM CONCERNING THE LORD, towards the end, n. 60, 61, which is as follows: "That God and man in the Lord are, according to the doctrine stated, not two, but one person, and altogether one, as the soul and body are one, appears clearly from many declarations of the Lord himself; as, that the Father and he are one; that all things of the Father are his, and all his the Father's; that he is in the Father, and the Father in him; that all things are given into his hand; that he has all power; that he is the God of heaven and earth; that he who believes in him has eternal life; and that the wrath of God abides on him who does not believe in him: moreover, that he ascended into heaven, both as to his divinity and his humanity, and that, with respect to both, he sits on the right hand of God, which means that he is Almighty; besides many passages from the Word, concerning his divine humanity, which are copiously quoted in the former part of this work, and all of which testify, that *God is one as well in person as in essence, that in him is a trinity, and that that God is the Lord.* The reason why these things relative to the Lord are now for the first time made publicly known, is, because it is foretold in the Revelation (xxi. and xxii.) that a new church, in which this doctrine will hold the chief place, should be established by the Lord at the end of the former. This church is what is meant by the New Jerusalem there mentioned, into which none can enter but those who acknowledge the Lord alone as the God of heaven and earth: therefore this church is there called the WIFE OF THE LAMB. I am also enabled to declare, that the universal heaven acknowledges the Lord alone; and that whoever does not acknowledge him is not admitted therein. For heaven derives all that makes it heaven solely from the Lord; and it is the acknowledgment of this, from love and faith, which causes all its inhabitants to be in the Lord, and the Lord in them; as he himself teaches in John: 'At that day ye shall know that I am in my Father, and ye in me, and I in you' (xiv. 20). And again: 'Abide in me, and I in you. I am the vine, ye are the branches: he that abideth in me, and I in him, the same bringeth forth much fruit: for without me ye can do nothing. If a man abide not in me, he is cast out' (xv. 4, 5, 6; xvii. 22, 23). The reason why this doctrine concerning the Lord

was not seen from the Word before, is, because if it had, it still would not have been received, in consequence of the last judgment's not being accomplished. Man, while in the world, stands in the midst between heaven and hell; and before the last judgment, the power of hell prevailed over that of heaven; whence, had this doctrine been seen before, the devil, that is, hell, would have plucked it from the heart, and would, moreover, have profaned it. This state of predominance on the part of hell, was altogether crushed by the last judgment, which is now accomplished. Since which event, that is, now, it is in the power of every one, who desires it, to become enlightened and wise."

264. II. *That a doubt may be inferred against the Divine Providence, because heretofore it was not known that in every particular of the Word there is a spiritual sense, and that therein its holiness consists:* for it may be suggested as a doubt against the Divine Providence, Why is this revealed now for the first time, and why by this or that person, and not by any primate of the church? But whether he be a primate or the servant of a primate, is according to the good pleasure of the Lord, who knows both the one and the other. The reason why that sense of the Word was not revealed before, is, I. Because, if it had been, the church would have profaned it, and thereby have profaned the sanctity of the Word itself. II. That the genuine truths also, in which the spiritual sense of the Word consists, were not revealed by the Lord, till after the last judgment was performed, and a new church, which is meant by the Holy Jerusalem, was about to be established by the Lord. These articles, however, shall be examined separately. FIRST, *That the spiritual sense of the Word was not revealed before, because if it had, the church would have profaned it, and thereby have profaned the sanctity of the Word itself.* The church, not long after its establishment, was converted into Babylon, and afterwards into Philistea; and Babylon does indeed acknowledge the Word, but yet contemns it, saying, that the Holy Ghost inspires them in their supreme judgment, equally as much as it inspired the prophets. They acknowledge the Word for the sake of the vicarship founded on the Lord's words to Peter; but yet they contemn it, because it does not accord with their views. For that reason, also, it is taken from the people, and hid in monasteries, where there are but few who read it; therefore, if the spiritual sense of the Word, in which is the Lord, and at the same time all angelic wisdom, had been revealed, the Word would have been profaned, not only as is now the case, in its ultimates, which are contained in the literal sense, but also in its internal or inmost meaning. Philistea, by which is meant faith separate from charity, would also have profaned the spiritual sense of the Word, because, as was shown before, it places

191

salvation in certain words which are to be thought and spoken, and not in any good that is to be done; thus making that a saving principle which is not saving, and removing the understanding from things which ought to be believed. And what have such persons to do with the light in which is the spiritual sense of the Word? Would it not be turned by them into darkness? When the natural sense is turned into darkness, what would the spiritual sense be? Is there any one of those who have confirmed themselves in faith separate from charity, and in justification by it alone, that desires to know what is the good of life, or, what is love to the Lord and towards their neighbour, or what is charity, what the goods of charity, what good works, and what it is *to do*, yea, what faith is in its essence, or any genuine truth that constitutes it? They write volumes, and confirm nothing but what they call faith, saying that all the things above recited are contained in that faith. From which it is evident, that if the spiritual sense of the Word had been revealed before, the case would have been according to what the Lord says in Matthew: "If thine eye be evil, thy whole body shall be full of darkness; if, therefore, the light that is in thee be darkness, how great is that darkness!" (vi. 23). By eye, in the spiritual sense of the Word, is meant the understanding. SECONDLY, *That the genuine truths also, of which the spiritual sense of the Word consists, were not revealed by the Lord, till after the last judgment was accomplished, and the New Church, which is meant by the Holy Jerusalem, was about to be established by the Lord.* It is foretold by the Lord in the Revelation, that after the last judgment is accomplished, genuine truths are to be revealed, a new church established, and the spiritual sense of the Word disclosed. That the final judgment is now accomplished, is shown in a small work concerning the LAST JUDGMENT, and in THE CONTINUATION of that work; and that this is meant by the heaven and earth which are to pass away, mentioned in the Revelation, xxi. 1. That genuine truths are then to be revealed, is foretold by these words in the Revelation: "He that sat upon the throne said, Behold, I make all things new" (verse 5; also, chap. xix. 17, 18; xxi. 18—21; xxii. 1, 2). That the spiritual sense of the Word is then to be revealed is foretold in chap. xix. 11—16, and it is denoted by the white horse, upon which he who sat was called the Word of God, who was the Lord of lords, and King of kings; on which subject the little work concerning THE WHITE HORSE may be consulted. That by the Holy Jerusalem is meant the New Church, which was then to be established by the Lord, may be seen in THE DOCTRINE OF THE NEW JERUSALEM CONCERNING THE LORD, n. 62—65, where it is demonstrated. Hence then it is evident, that the spiritual sense of the Word was to be revealed for a New Church, which will acknowledge and worship the Lord alone, hold his Word sacred, love divine truths, and reject faith separated from charity. In relation to this sense of the Word more may be seen in THE DOCTRINE OF THE NEW JERUSALEM CONCERNING THE SACRED SCRIPTURE, n. 5—26; as, what the spiritual sense of the Word is, n. 5—26; that there is a spiritual sense in all and every particular of the Word, n. 9—17; that it is by virtue of the spiritual sense that the Word is of divine inspiration and holy in every single expression, n. 18, 19; that the spiritual sense of the Word has been heretofore unknown, and why it was not revealed before, n. 20—25; and that henceforth the spiritual sense of the Word will be opened to none but those who are principled in genuine truths from the Lord, n. 26. From these considerations, then, it may appear that it is of the Lord's Divine Providence that the spiritual sense has been concealed from the world until the present age, and has hitherto been preserved in heaven among the angels, who derive their wisdom from it. This sense was known, and also cultivated, among the ancients who lived before Moses; but as their posterity converted the correspondences, of which their Word and consequently their religion solely consisted, into various idolatries, and the Egyptians into magic, it was, for the reasons above-mentioned, closed or shut up, by the Divine Providence of the Lord, first among the children of Israel, and afterwards among the Christians, and is now first opened for the Lord's New Church.

265. III. *That a doubt may be inferred against the Divine Providence, because heretofore it was not known that the very essence of the Christian religion consists in shunning evils as sins.* That this is the very essence of the Christian religion is shown in THE DOCTRINE OF LIFE FOR THE NEW JERUSALEM, from beginning to end; and because faith separated from charity is the only obstacle to its being received, that also is treated of. It is said that heretofore it was not known that the very essence of the Christian religion consists in shunning evils as sins, because almost everybody is ignorant of this, and yet every one is taught it, as may be seen above, n. 258. The reason why almost everybody is ignorant of it, is, because Solifidianism has erased it from the mind; for this teaches that faith alone saves, and not any good work or good of charity; also, that they are no longer under the yoke of the law, but at liberty. Those who frequently hear such doctrines, no longer think of any evil of life, or of any good of life; for every man by nature is inclined to embrace that idea, and when it is once embraced, he no longer thinks of the state of his life. This is the reason why the above is not known. That it is not known was discovered to me in the spiritual world. I questioned above a thousand who were newly arrived from this world, whether they knew

that the essence of religion consisted in shunning evils as sins: and they said that they did not know it; that it was a new thing never before heard of; but that they had heard they could not do any good from themselves, and were not under the yoke of the law.   When I asked, if they did not know that it was a man's duty to examine himself, to see his sins, repent of them, and lead a new life; that otherwise sins are not forgiven, and if sins are not forgiven there is no salvation; and that this was read aloud to them as often as they received the holy supper; they answered, that they did not attend to those things, but only to this, that by means of the Lord's Supper their sins are forgiven, and that faith, without their knowledge, operates the rest.   Again I asked, Why did you teach your children the Decalogue?   Was it not that they might know what evils are sins which are to be shunned?   Was it that they might only know and believe, and not act accordingly?   Why then do you say that this is a new thing?   To this they could make no other answer than that they knew it, and yet did not know it, and that they never thought of the seventh commandment when they committed adultery, or of the eighth when they committed theft or acted fraudulently, and so on; much less, that such things are contrary to the divine law, and consequently offences against God.   When I mentioned several things from the doctrines of the churches, and from the Word, in confirmation of my assertion, that to shun evils as sins, and hold them in aversion, is the very essence of the Christian religion, and that every one is gifted with faith in proportion as he shuns and holds them in aversion, they were silent; but they were confirmed in the truth of it when they saw that all were examined as to their lives, and judged according to their actions, and no one according to his faith unconnectedly with his life, because the faith of every one is conformable to his life.   The reason why the Christian world for the most part did not know this, exists in that law of the Divine Providence whereby every one is left to act from liberty according to reason, which see above, n. 71—99, and n. 100—128; also in the law, whereby it is appointed that no one is taught immediately from heaven, but mediately through the Word, doctrine, and preachings out of it, concerning which see above, n. 154—174: and likewise in all the laws of permission, which also are laws of the Divine Providence.   More may be seen above respecting these, n. 258.

274.   IV. *That a doubt may be inferred against the Divine Providence, because it was not known heretofore that a man lives as a man after death, and this was not discovered till now.* The reason why this was not known, is, because in those who do not shun evils as sins, there lies inwardly concealed a belief that a man does not live after death, and therefore they think it of no importance whether it be said that a man lives after

death, or that he will rise again at the day of judgment. If one happens to have any belief in a resurrection, he says to himself, I shall not fare worse than others; for if I go to hell, I shall have many to accompany me, and also if to heaven. Yet all who have any religion have in them an inherent knowledge that men live after death. The idea that they live as souls, and not as men, takes place with those, and with those only, who are infatuated by their own self-derived intelligence. That every one who has any religion in him has an inherent knowledge that a man lives after death, may appear from the following considerations. 1. Who thinks otherwise when he is dying? 2. What panegyrist, in his lamentation over the dead, does not send them to heaven, place them among the angels, in conversation with them, and partaking their joys? Not to mention the apotheosis of some. 3. Who among the vulgar does not believe, that when he dies, if he has lived well, he shall go to a heavenly Paradise, be clothed in a white garment, and enjoy life everlasting? 4. Where is the preacher who does not say these things, or the like, to those who are on their death-bed? And when he says them, he believes them himself, provided he does not at the time think of the last judgment. 5. Who is there that does not believe that his children are in heaven, and that he shall see his wife, whom he has loved, after death? Who ever supposes they are spectres, much less that they are souls or minds hovering about in the universe? 6. Who contradicts, when any thing is said of the lot and state of those who have passed from time to eternity? I have told many of the state and lot of such and such persons, and I have never yet heard any one say, that their lot was not yet decided, but that it would be so at the last judgment. 7. Who, when he sees angels painted or carved, does not acknowledge that they are such? Who ever imagines at such times that they are spirits without a body, airs, or clouds, as some of the learned do? 8. The papists believe their saints to be men in heaven, and others elsewhere, the Mahometans think the same of their dead; so do the Africans more especially, and in like manner many other nations: what then ought not reformed Christians to do, who know it from the Word? 9. It is also owing to this knowledge, inherent in every one, that some aspire after immortal fame; for this knowledge is converted into the love of such fame with some, and makes them heroes and valiant in war. 10. Inquiry was made in the spiritual world, whether this knowledge is inherent in all; and it was found, that it is so in the spiritual idea of all, which is of the internal thought, but not so in their natural idea, which is of the external thought. From these considerations it may appear, that no one ought to entertain any doubt against the Divine Providence, because he thinks it is now first discovered that men live after death. It is only a man's sensual mind which desires to see and touch what is to be believed; and he whose thoughts are not elevated above this is involved in darkness with respect to the state of his life.

THAT EVILS ARE PERMITTED FOR A CERTAIN END, WHICH IS SALVATION.

275. If a man were born in the love in which he was created, he would not be in any evil, nor, indeed, would he know what evil is; for he who has not been, and thence is not in evil, cannot know what it is. If it should be said to him that this or that is evil, he would not believe it possible. This is the state of innocence, in which Adam and his wife Eve were; and their nakedness, of which they were not ashamed, signified that state. The knowledge of evil after the fall is meant by eating of the tree of the knowledge of good and evil. The love in which man was created is the love of his neighbour, that he may wish him as well as he wishes himself, and even better, and that he may be in the delight of that love when he does good to him, just as a parent is in doing good to his children. This love is truly human; for in it there is something spiritual, whereby it is distinguished from natural love, which is common to brute animals. If a man were born into this love, he would not be born in the darkness of ignorance, as is now the case with every man, but in a certain light of knowledge, and thence of intelligence also, into which he would shortly enter, and indeed he would at first creep like a quadruped, but with an innate endeavour to raise himself upon his feet; for although he would creep, he would not look down to the ground, but upwards to heaven, and would, as it would be in his power to do, lift himself upright.

276. But when the love of the neighbour was turned into the love of self, and this latter increased, then human love was turned into animal love, and man from being man became a beast, with this difference, that he could think that which he felt in the body, rationally distinguish one thing from another, could be instructed, made a civil and moral, and at length a spiritual man; because, as was observed, a man has a spiritual principle, by which he is distinguished from brute animals; for by it he can know what is civil evil and good, what is moral evil and good, and also, if he will, what is spiritual evil and good. When the love of the neighbour was turned into self-love, man could no longer be born into the light of science and intelligence, but into the darkness of ignorance, because he was born totally

in the ultimate of life, which is called the corporeal sensual principle; but from it he could by instruction be introduced into the interiors of the natural mind, something spiritual always attending. The reason why he is born in the ultimate of life, which is called the corporeal sensual principle, and consequently in the darkness of ignorance, will be seen in what follows. That the love of the neighbour and the love of self are opposite, any one may see; for the former wishes well to all from itself, but the latter wishes well to itself alone from all. A man in the love of his neighbour desires to serve all; but he who is in self-love desires to be served by all : the former considers all as his brothers and friends, but the latter considers all as his servants, and if they do not serve him, as his enemies : in a word, he considers himself alone, and others scarcely as men, whom in his heart he values less than his horses and dogs; and as he thinks them so vile, he makes no account of injuring them; whence proceed hatred and revenge, adultery and fornication, thefts and frauds, lies and blasphemies, rage, cruelty, and the like. These are the evils in which every man is by birth. That these are permitted for a certain end, which is salvation, shall be demonstrated in the following order. I. That every man is in evil, and that he is to be withdrawn from evil that he may be reformed. II. That evils cannot be removed unless they appear. III. That in proportion as evils are removed, they are remitted. IV. That thus the permission of evil is for the sake of salvation as the end.

277. I. *That every man is in evil, and that he is to be withdrawn from evil that he may be reformed.* That every man has hereditary evil, and that therefrom he is in the concupiscence of many evils, is well known in the church. Thence it is that a man from himself cannot do good; for evil does not do good, except it be such good as has evil lurking within it; which evil consists in his doing good for the sake of self, and thus doing what is good only in appearance. That this evil is hereditary from parents is well known. It is said to be from Adam and Eve; but this is a mistake: for every one is born into it from his parent, that parent from his parent, and so on, every one from his own parent respectively; and thus it is successively transferred from one to another, by which it is increased and augmented abundantly, and is transmitted to posterity. Thence it is, that in man there is no health, or nothing sound, but that he is one entire mass of evil. Who is there that feels that to love himself more than others is evil, and who, therefore, knows that there is any evil in it; when, nevertheless, it is the head of all evils? That it is inherited from fathers, grandfathers, and great-grandfathers, is evident from many circumstances which are generally known; as from the similarity of faces in houses, families, and, indeed, in whole nations, by which they

197

are distinguishable, faces being the types of minds, and the state of minds being conformable to their affections, which are of love. Sometimes, also, the face of the grandfather returns in the grandchild, or great-grandchild. I can tell from seeing the face only, whether a person is a Jew or not ; also, from what stock some other people are derived ; and I doubt not but there are others who can do the same. If the affections, which are of love, are thus derived and transmitted from parents, it follows that it is the same with evils, because these appertain to the affections. The cause of this resemblance shall now be explained : the soul of every one is from his father, and is only clothed with a body from his mother. That the soul is derived from the father, not only follows as a consequence from what has been said above, but is evident from other circumstances ; as, that the child of a negro or Moor, by a white or European woman, is born black, and *vice versa ;* and especially that the soul is in the see l, for from it impregnation is effected, and it is that which is clothed with a body from the mother ; the seed being the primitive form of the love in which the father is,—the form of his ruling love, with its proximate derivations, which are the inmost affections of that love. These affections are in every one clothed in the decencies of moral life, and the goods which are partly of civil and partly of spiritual life ; and these constitute the external of life even with the wicked. Every infant is born into this external of life, and hence it is that it is amiable ; but as a man grows up and advances to mature age, he passes from that external to interiors, and at length to the ruling love of his father. If his father's ruling love was evil, his love also becomes evil, unless tempered and bent by means of education ; and even then, as will be shown in what follows, evil is not extirpated, but only removed. Hence it is evident that every man is in evil.

277. That a man is to be withdrawn from evil, in order that he may be reformed, is evident without explanation ; for he that is in evil in the world, is in evil after he goes out of it ; and therefore if evil be not removed in the world, it cannot be removed afterwards. Where the tree falls, there it lies ; so also it is with a man's life. As it was at his death, such it remains. Every one also is judged according to his actions ; not that they are enumerated, but because he returns to them, and does the like again ; for death is a continuation of life, with this difference, that then the man cannot be reformed. All reformation is effected in a plenary manner, that is, in primaries and in ultimates at the same time ; and ultimates are reformed in this world conformably to primaries ; but they cannot be so afterwards, because the ultimates of life, which a man carries with him after death, are quiescent, and conspire, that is, act as one, with his interiors.

278. II. *That evils cannot be removed except they appear.*
It is not meant that a man is to do evils that they may appear,
but that he is to examine himself, not his actions only, but also
his thoughts, and as to what he would do if he were not afraid
of the laws and of infamy; especially, what evils he considers
in his spirit as allowable, and does not look upon as sins, for
these he still commits. In order that a man may explore himself, understanding is given him, and this separate from the
will; that he may know, understand, and acknowledge what is
good and what evil, and may also see the quality of his will, or
what he loves and what he covets. That a man may see this,
his understanding is gifted with superior and inferior, or interior
and exterior thought, that from his superior or interior thought
he may see what his will is doing in his inferior or exterior
thought. This he sees as a man sees his face in a glass; and
when he sees it, and knows what sin is, he may, if he implores
the help of the Lord, not will it, but shun it, and afterwards
act against it; if not freely, still he may force himself to it by
combat, and at length hold it in aversion and abominate it:
then, and not before, he perceives and also feels that evil is evil
and good is good. This, then, is examining or exploring himself, seeing his sins, acknowledging them, confessing them, and
afterwards desisting from them. As however there are few who
know that the very essence of the Christian religion consists in
this, because those only who do so have charity and faith, are
led of the Lord, and do good from him, something shall be said
of those persons who do not do so, and yet think they have
religion in them. They are the following: 1. Those who confess themselves guilty of all sins, and do not search out any one
sin in themselves. 2. Those who omit such inquiry from a
principle of religion. 3. Those who, on account of worldly
matters, do not think of sins, and consequently do not know
them. 4. Those who favour them, and therefore cannot know
them. 5. That in all these persons sins do not appear, and
therefore cannot be removed. 6. Lastly, the hitherto unknown
cause shall be laid open why evils cannot be removed, without
the search, appearance, acknowledgment, confession thereof,
and resistance thereto.

These points however shall be viewed separately, because
they are fundamentals of the Christian religion on man's part.
FIRST, *Of those who confess themselves guilty of all sins, and do
not search out any sin in themselves.* Such a one says, I am a
sinner; I was born in sin; there is no health in me from head
to foot; I am nothing but evil. Good God, have mercy upon
me, forgive me, purify me, save me; cause me to walk in purity
of life, and in the way of uprightness,—and the like; yet he
does not examine himself, and consequently does not know any
evil; and no one can shun that which he does not know, much

199

less fight against it. After his confession, he also thinks himself clean and washed, when nevertheless he is unclean and unwashed from head to foot; for the confession of all is the quieting or laying asleep of all, and at length the blinding of all: it is like something general without any particular, which is nothing. SECONDLY, *Of those who omit such inquiry from a principle of religion.* They are such especially as separate charity from faith: for such a one says to himself, Why should I inquire whether it be evil or good?—why, whether it be evil, since evil does not condemn me? and why, whether it be good, since good does not save me? It is faith alone, thought of and pronounced with confidence and assurance, which justifies and purifies from all sin: and when I am once justified, I am pure in the sight of God. I am indeed in evil; but God wipes this away as soon as it is produced, and so it appears no more;—not to mention other notions of the same kind. But who does not see, if he opens his eyes, that such are empty words, having no substance in them, because they have no good in them? Who may not think and speak thus, even with confidence and assurance, when at the same time he thinks of hell and eternal damnation? Does such a one desire to know any thing else. whether it be true, or whether it be good? Of truth he says, what is truth but that which confirms such a faith? Of good he says, what is good but that which is in me from this faith? But in order that it may be in me, I will not do it as from myself, because that is meritorious, and meritorious good is not real good. Thus he omits all things, until he does not know what evil is; and what then can he search out or see in himself? In this case, is not his state such, that the fire of the concupiscences of evil being inclosed, consumes his interiors, and devastates them even to the gate, which he keeps shut lest the fire should appear? It is opened, however, after death, and then appears in the sight of every one. THIRDLY, *Of those who, on account of worldly matters, do not think of sins, and consequently do not know them.* These are such as love the world above all things, and admit no truth which may withdraw them from the falsities of their religion. Such a one says to himself, What have I to do with this? I do not love to think of it. Thus they reject truth as soon as they hear it, and if they hear it, suffocate it. The case is nearly the same with them when they hear preachings, of which they retain only some of the words, but not any of the substance. As truths are treated by them in this manner, they do not know what good is, for truth and good act as one; and by good which is not grounded in truth no discovery is made of evil, except that it also may be called good, which is effected by reasoning from falsities. These are those who are meant by the seed which fell among thorns, of whom the Lord says, "Some fell among thorns; and the thorns sprung up and choked them.". These also are those who "hear the Word, and the care of this world, and the deceitfu. ness of riches, choke the Word, and it becometh unfruitful" (Matt. xiii. 7, 22 ; Mark iv. 7, 14 ; Luke viii. 7, 14). FOURTHLY, *Of those who favour sins, and therefore cannot know them.* These are those who acknowledge God, and worship him according to the usual forms, but confirm themselves in the idea that any evil, which is a sin, is not a sin ; for they disguise it by fallacies and appearances, and so hide its enormity ; having done which, they favour it, and make it friendly and familiar to them. It is said that those who acknowledge God do this ; because others do not consider any evil as a sin, every sin being an offence against God. But this shall be illustrated by examples. He does not consider evil as sin who is covetous of money, and makes any species of fraud allowable, by reasons which he fabricates. It is the same with him who confirms himself in the lawfulness of revenge against enemies, and of committing depredations upon those who are not enemies in war. FIFTHLY, *That in these persons sins do not appear and therefore cannot be removed.* All evil which does not appear kindles itself, being like fire among wood under the ashes ; it is also like corrupted matter in a wound which is not laid open ; for all evil which is obstructed increases, and does not cease until the whole is consummated. Therefore, lest any evil should be obstructed, it is permitted that every one should think either in favour of God or against God, in favour of the holy things of the church, or against them, and should not be punished for the same in this world. Concerning this evil the Lord says in Isaiah : "From the sole of the foot, even unto the head, there is no soundness in it ; but wounds, and bruises, and putrefying sores : they have not been closed, neither bound up, neither mollified with ointment. Wash you, make you clean ; put away the evil of your doings from before mine eyes ; cease to do evil ; learn to do good." Then "although your sins be as scarlet, they shall be as white as snow ; though they be red like crimson, they shall be as wool. But if ye refuse and rebel, ye shall be devoured by the sword" (i. 6, 16, 18, 20). To be devoured by the sword, signifies, to perish by the falsity of evil. SIXTHLY, *The reason, hitherto concealed, why evils cannot be removed without being explored, appearing, being acknowledged, confessed, and resisted.* In the preceding pages it is mentioned, that the universal heaven is arranged into societies according to the affections of good opposite to the concupiscences of evil. Every man, with respect to his spirit, is in some society,—in a celestial society if he is in the affection of good, and in an infernal society if he is in the concupiscence of evil. He does not know this while he lives in the world ; but yet as to his spirit he is in some society, without which he could not live, and through

201

which he is governed by the Lord. If he is in an infernal society, he can only be brought out of it by the Lord, according to the laws of his Divine Providence, among which this is one, that a man must see that he is there, must desire to depart, and must himself endeavour to do it from himself. This he can do while he is in the world, but not after death; for then he abides to all eternity in the society into which he introduced himself when in the world.. This is the reason why a man ought to examine himself, to see and acknowledge his sins, to repent of them, and then to persevere to the end of his life. That this is the case, I could fully and satisfactorily confirm by abundant experience; but to produce proofs from experience does not belong to this place.

279. III. *That in proportion as evils are removed, they are remitted.* It is an error of the present age, to suppose that evils are separated from a man, and even cast out, when they are remitted; and that the state of a man's life can be changed in a moment, even to its opposite, so that, from being wicked, he can be made good, consequently brought out of hell, and instantly translated to heaven, by the immediate mercy of the Lord. Those however who entertain this belief and opinion, do not in the least know what evil and good are, or any thing of the state of a man's life. They are altogether ignorant that the affections, which are of the will, are mere changes and variations of the state of the purely organic substances of the mind; that the thoughts, which are of the understanding, are mere changes and variations of their form; and that the memory is the permanent state of these changes. From a knowledge of these things, it may be clearly seen, that no evil can be removed except successively; and that the remission of evil is not its removal. These things are here asserted in a summary way only; but unless they are demonstrated, although they may be acknowledged, they cannot be comprehended; and that which is not comprehended, is merely like a wheel turned about by the hand; therefore the propositions above mentioned shall be demonstrated separately in the same order in which they are adduced. First, *That it is an error of the present age, to suppose that evils are separated, and even cast out, when they are remitted.* That no evil into which a man is born, and which he actually imbibes, is separated from him, but that it is only removed so that it shall not appear, has been made known to me from heaven. Before that, I was in the belief entertained by most people in this world, that when evils are remitted, they are cast out, and are washed off and wiped away, as dirt from the face by water. This however is not the case with evils or sins; they all remain; and, when they are remitted after repentance, are removed from the middle to the sides,—that which is in the middle, as it is directly under the inspection,

appearing as in the light of day, and that which is at the sides appearing in the shade, and sometimes as it were in the darkness of night. And because evils are not separated, but only removed, that is, put away to the sides, and a man may be transferred from the middle to the circumference, it may also happen, that he can return to his evils, which he thought rejected ; for a man is of such a nature, that he can pass from one affection to another, and sometimes to an opposite one, thus, from one middle or centre to another, the affection which predominates constituting the middle or centre while the man is in it, for he is then in the delight and in the light of it. There are some men who, after death, are taken up by the Lord into heaven, because they have led a good life, but who still carry with them a belief, that they were cleansed and pure from sins, and, therefore, not in a state of guilt. These are at first clothed in white garments according to such persuasion, white garments signifying a state of purification from evils ; but afterwards they begin to think, as they did in the world, that they are washed clean as it were from all evil, and, therefore, begin to boast that they are no longer sinners like others, which persuasion it is difficult to separate from a certain exultation of mind, and some degree of contempt for others in comparison with themselves ; therefore, in order that this imaginary belief may be removed, they are then remanded from heaven, and let into the evils which they had contracted in the world, it being shown them, at the same time, that they are in hereditary evils, of which they knew nothing before. When they have been thus forced to acknowledge, that their evils are not separated from them, but only removed, so that of themselves they are impure, and, indeed, nothing but evil, that it is by the Lord that they are detained from evils, and kept in goods, and that this appears to them as from themselves, they are again taken up by the Lord into heaven. SECONDLY, *That it is an error of the present age to suppose that the state of a man's life can be changed in a moment, so that from being wicked he can be made good, consequently brought out of hell, and instantly translated into heaven, by the immediate mercy of the Lord.* Those are in this error who separate charity from faith, and place salvation in faith alone ; for they imagine that the bare thinking and uttering of the words in which that faith is conveyed, provided it be done with confidence and assurance, justifies and saves ; an effect which is also supposed by some to be momentaneous, and if not before, about the last hour of a man's life. Such persons cannot but think, that a man's state of life may be changed in a moment, and that he may be saved by immediate mercy. That the mercy of the Lord however is not immediate, and that a man from being wicked cannot be made good in a moment, or be led out of hell and translated into

203

heaven, but by continual operations of the Divine Providence from his infancy to the end of his life, will be seen in the last section of this treatise. We will here only observe, that all the laws of the Divine Providence have for their end the reformation and thereby the salvation of man, consequently the inversion of his state, which by birth is infernal, to its opposite, which is celestial; and that this can only be effected progressively, as a man, receding from evil and its delight, enters into good and its delight. THIRDLY, *That those who entertain this belief, do not in the least know what is evil and what is good :* for they do not know, that evil is the delight of the concupiscence of acting and thinking contrary to divine order, while good is the delight of the affection of acting and thinking according to divine order; that there are myriads of concupiscences, which as ingredients enter into and compose every evil; that there are myriads of affections, which, in like manner, enter into every good as its ingredients and compose it; and that these myriads of concupiscences and affections exist in such order and connection in a man's interiors, that it is not possible to change one, without at the same time changing the whole. Those who do not know this, may think or believe that evil, which appears to them as an entire one, can easily be removed, and that good, which also appears as a one, can be introduced into its place. These, as they do not know what evil is, and what good is, cannot but suppose that there is such a thing as momentaneous salvation, and immediate mercy; but that these are not possible, will be seen in the last section of this treatise. FOURTHLY, *That those who believe in momentaneous salvation and immediate mercy, do not know that the affections, which are of the will, are mere changes of the state of the purely organic substances of the mind ; that the thoughts, which are of the understanding, are mere changes and variations of their form ; and that the memory is the permanent state of those changes and variations.* Who does not assent to the affirmation that affections and thoughts exist only in substances and their forms, which are the subjects of them? and as they exist in the brain, which is full of substances and forms, they are called forms purely organic. No one, who thinks rationally, can do otherwise than laugh at the fantasies of those who suppose that affections and thoughts do not exist in substantiate subjects, but that they are vapours modified by heat and light, like figures appearing in the air or ether: for thought can no more exist separate from its substantial form, than vision can exist without its form, which is the eye; hearing without its form, which is the ear; or taste without its form, which is the tongue. Inspect the brain, and you will see innumerable substances and fibres, and that every part of it is organized. What need is there of any other than this ocular proof? But it may be asked, What is affection, and what is

204

thought, in their substantiate sub ects? A satisfactory answer may be deduced from all and every thing in the body, where there are many viscera, each fixed in its particular situation, and all performing their functions by changes and variations of their state and form. It is well known that they are severally engaged in their respective operations,—the stomach, the intestines, the kidneys, the liver, pancreas, and spleen, and likewise the heart and lungs, each in its respective office; all these operations being effected only intrinsically or within themselves, and to be effected intrinsically is to be effected by variations of state and form. Hence it may appear, that the operations of the purely organic substances of the mind are of a similar nature, with this difference only, that those of the organic substances of the body are natural, while those of the organic substances of the mind are spiritual, and that both act together as a one by correspondences. There can be no ocular demonstration of the changes and variations of state and form in the organic substances of the mind, which are affections and thoughts; but yet they may be seen, as it were, in a glass, by the changes and variations of the state of the lungs in speaking and singing, there being a correspondence; for the sound of the voice in speaking and singing, and also the articulations of sound, which are the words in speech and the modulations of the voice in singing, are effected by the lungs; and sound corresponds to affection, and speech to thought. Sound and speech are also produced by affection and thought, and this by means of changes and variations of the state and form of the organic substances of the lungs, and from the lungs by the trachea or wind-pipe in the larynx and glottis, afterwards in the tongue, and, lastly, in the lips. The first changes and variations of the state and form of sound are produced in the lungs, the second in the trachea and larynx, the third in the glottis by various openings of its orifice, the fourth in the tongue by its various applications to the palate and teeth, and the fifth in the lips by disposing them in various forms. Hence it may appear, that the mere changes and variations of the state of organic forms, successively continued, produce sounds and their articulations, which are speech and singing. Now as sound and speech are produced from no other source than the affections and thoughts of the mind,—for from the latter the former exist, and never without them,—it is evident that the affections of the will are changes and variations of the state of the purely organic substances of the mind, and that the thoughts of the understanding are changes and variations of the form of those substances; similar to what takes place in the lungs. Since affections and thoughts are mere changes in the state of the forms of the mind, it follows that the memory is no other than the permanent state thereof; for all changes and variations of state in organic substances are of such a nature, that when once they become habitual, they are permanent. Thus the lungs are habituated to produce various sounds in the trachea, to vary them in the glottis, to articulate them in the tongue, and to modify them in the mouth; and when those organs are once habituated to them, such sounds are in them, and can be reproduced. That these changes and variations are infinitely more perfect in the organs of the mind than in the organs of the body, is evident from what is said in the treatise concerning THE DIVINE LOVE AND THE DIVINE WISDOM, n. 119—204, where it is shown, that all perfections increase and ascend with degrees, and according to them. On this subject more may be seen below, n. 319.

280. To suppose that when sins are remitted, they are also removed, is likewise an error of this age. Those are in this error who suppose their sins to be remitted by the sacrament of the Lord's Supper, although they have not removed them from themselves by repentance; and those also are in this error who think to be saved by faith alone, as well as those who think to be saved by dispensations from the Pope. All these believe in immediate mercy and momentaneous salvation. When, however, this proposition is reversed it becomes a truth, namely, that when sins are removed they are also remitted : for repentance must precede remission, and without repentance there is no remission; therefore the Lord commanded his disciples to preach repentance for the remission of sins (Luke xxiv. 27); and John preached the baptism of repentance for the remission of sins (Luke iii. 3). The Lord remits the sins of all men : he does not accuse and impute : yet he can only take them away according to the laws of his Divine Providence; for since he said to Peter (who asked him how often he should forgive his brother when he sinned against him, whether till seven times) that he ought to forgive him not only seven times, but seventy times seven (Matt. xviii. 21, 22), what then will not the Lord do, who is Mercy itself?

281. IV. *That thus the permission of evil is for a certain end, which is salvation.* It is well known that a man is in full liberty to think and will, but not in full liberty to speak and act whatever he thinks and wills : for he may think as an Atheist, deny God, and blaspheme the holy things of the Word and the church; he may even desire in word and deed utterly to destroy them; but this is prevented by civil, moral, and ecclesiastical laws; and he therefore inwardly cherishes such impious and wicked desires by thinking and wishing, and also intending them, but not by doing them. A man, who is not an Atheist, is also at full liberty to think on many things which are of evil, as frauds, lasciviousness, vindictiveness, and other insanities, which at times he also does. Who cannot believe that unless a

man had full liberty, he not only could not be saved, but would even totally perish? Hear now the cause of this. Every man from his birth is in evils of many kinds. These evils are in his will, and the things which are in the will are loved; for that which a man wills from his interior he loves, and that which he loves he wills; and the love of the will flows into the understanding, there causing its delight to be felt. Hence it comes into the thoughts, and also into the intentions. If, therefore, a man were not permitted to think according to the love of his will, which is hereditarily inherent in him, that love would continue shut up, and would never appear to him; and that love of evil which does not appear is like an enemy lying in wait, or like corrupted matter in an ulcer, poison in the blood, and rottenness in the breast, which, if kept inclosed, will produce death. But when a man is permitted to think upon the evils of his life's love, so far even as to intend them, they are cured by spiritual means, as diseases are by natural means. What a man's quality would be were he not permitted to think according to the delights of his life's love, shall now be shown. He would no longer be a man, for he would lose the two faculties which are called liberty and rationality, in which humanity itself consists; the delights of the above evils would occupy the interiors of his mind to such a degree, that they would open the door of it; and then he could not help speaking and acting in conformity with those evils; thus his insanity would not only be known to himself, but would also appear to the world; and at length he would not have the sense to cover his nakedness. But to prevent this being the case, he is permitted to think and will his hereditary evils, but not to speak and do them. In the mean time he learns things civil, moral, and spiritual, which also enter into his thoughts, and remove these insanities; and thereby he is healed by the Lord; but yet no farther than to know how to keep the door shut, unless he also acknowledge a God, and implore his assistance, that he may be able to resist the above evils; and so far as he then resists, he does not admit them into his intentions, and at length, not even into his thoughts. Since then a man is at liberty to think as he pleases, to the end that his life's love may come forth from its lurking place into the light of his understanding, and since otherwise he would not know any thing of his own evil, and consequently would not know how to expel it, it follows that it would increase in him to such a degree that there would be no possibility of amendment in him, and scarcely in his children, if he had any; for the evil of the parent is transmitted to his offspring. The Lord, however provides that this may not be the case.

282. The Lord could heal the understanding in every man and so cause him to think not evil, but good, and this by means of various fears, by miracles, by speaking with the dead, and

207

by visions and dreams ; but to heal the understanding only is merely to heal the man outwardly ; for the understanding with its thought is the external of a man's life, and the will with its affection is its internal. The healing of the understanding alone, therefore, would be like a palliative, by which the interior malignity is closed up and prevented from coming out ; so that it consumes first the neighbouring parts and afterwards the more remote, till the whole is mortified. It is the will itself which is to be healed, not by influx of the understanding into it, because· that never takes place, but by instruction and exhortation from the understanding. If the understanding alone were healed, the man would become like a dead body embalmed, or covered over with fragrant aromatics and roses, which in a short time would contract such a stench from the corpse that no one could come near it. Such would be the case with celestial truths in the understanding, if the evil love of the will were obstructed.

283. The reason why a man is permitted to think evils, even so far as to·intend them, is, as was observed, that they may be removed by considerations of a civil, moral, and spiritual nature ; as is the case when he thinks that they are contrary to justice and equity, to honesty and decency, and to goodness and truth, therefore contrary to the tranquillity, pleasure, and happiness of life. By these three considerations the Lord heals the love of a man's will ; and at first, indeed, by fear, afterwards by love. Still, however, evils are not separated and cast out from the man, but only removed and put away to the sides ; and when they are there, and good is in the centre, they do not appear : for whatever is in the centre is directly under inspection, and is seen and perceived : but it should be known that although good is in the centre, yet the man is not therefore in good, unless the evils which are at the sides tend downwards and outwards ; if they look upwards or inwards, they are not removed ; for they still endeavour to return to the centre : they turn and look·downwards or outwards, when the man shuns his evils as sins, and still more when he has an aversion to them ; for he then condemns and devotes them to hell, and causes them to look thitherward.

284. A man's understanding is a recipient of good as well as of evil, and of truth as well as of falsity, but not .his will, which must be either in evil or in good ; it cannot be in both ; for the will is the man himself, and therein is his life's love. But good and evil in the understanding are separated, like internal and external ; hence a man may be interiorly in evil, and exteriorly in good. Still, however, when a man is reformed, good and evil are committed, and there then exists a conflict or combat, which, if grievous, is called temptation, but if not, is like the fermentation of wine or wort. In such case, if good

overcomes, evil with its falsities is removed to the sides, as the lees fall to the bottom of a vessel, and good becomes like generous wine after fermentation, or clear liquor ; but if evil overcomes, good with its truth is removed to the sides, and it becomes turbid and foul like unfermented wine or liquor. The comparison of fermentation is used because leaven in the Word signifies the falsity of evil, as in Hosea vii. 4 ; Luke xii. 1 ; and other places.

THAT THE DIVINE PROVIDENCE IS EQUALLY WITH THE WICKED AND THE GOOD.

285. IN every man, whether he be good or evil, there are two faculties, one of which constitutes the understanding and the other the will. The faculty which constitutes the understanding consists in his being able to understand and think, and thence is called rationality ; and that which constitutes the will consists in his being able freely to think, and thence also to speak and act, provided it be not contrary to reason or rationality ; for to act freely is to act as often as he wills, and according as he wills. Since these two faculties are perpetual, and continual from primaries to ultimates in all and every particular which a man thinks and does, and are not in the man from himself, but from the Lord, it follows that there is the Lord's presence with and in these faculties in each particular, even in the most minute particulars of a man's understanding and thought as well as of his will and affection, and thence in the most minute particulars of his speech and actions. Remove these faculties from the smallest particular, and you will not be able to think or speak it as a man. That a man is a man by virtue of these two faculties, that he can thereby think and speak, perceive goods and understand truths, not only such as are civil and moral, but also such as are spiritual, and can be reformed and regenerated,—in a word, that he can be joined to the Lord, and thereby live eternally, was abundantly shown above ; and it was also shown that these two faculties are possessed not only by good men, but also by the wicked. Now as these faculties are from the Lord, and are not appropriated to a man as his own, for that which is divine cannot be appropriated to a man as his own, but can be adjoined to him, and thence appear as his ; and as this divine in a man exists in the most minute particulars appertaining to him, it follows, that the Lord governs things the most particular, in a wicked as well as in a good man ; and it is the government of the Lord which is called the Divine Providence.

209

286. Now as it is a law of the Divine Providence that a man should act freely according to reason, that is, from the two faculties, liberty and rationality; as it is also a law of the Divine Providence, that what he does should appear to the man as from himself, consequently as his own; and as it is moreover a law, that evils are to be permitted to the end that he may be led out of them, it follows, that a man may abuse these faculties, and from liberty according to reason confirm whatever he will; for he can make whatever he will a persuasion of his reason, whether it be reasonable in itself or not. Therefore some say, What is truth? Cannot I make true whatever I will? and does not also the world do so? Yet he that can do this does it by reasonings. Assume a proposition the most false, and tell an ingenious person to confirm it, and he will do so. For example, tell him to prove that a man is a beast; or that the soul is like a little spider in its web, governing the body as the spider does by its threads; or that religion is nothing but a bond of constraint; and he will prove any of these propositions, till it will appear true. And what is easier? for he does not know what is an appearance or what is a falsity, which from a blind belief is assumed as a truth. Hence it is that a man cannot see this truth, that the Divine Providence operates in the most minute particulars of the understanding and will, or what amounts to the same thing, in the most minute particulars of the thoughts and affections of every man, the wicked as well as the good. He confounds himself principally by supposing that in this case evils also would be from the Lord; nevertheless, that not the least evil is from the Lord, but that it is from man, by means of his confirming in himself the appearance that he thinks, wills, speaks, and acts from himself, will be seen in what now follows; which, that it may be clearly understood, shall be demonstrated in this order. I. That the Divine Providence, not only with the good, but also with the wicked, is universal in things the most particular; and yet that it is not in their evils. II. That the wicked continually lead themselves into evils, but that the Lord continually withdraws them from evils. III. That the Lord cannot entirely lead the wicked out of evil, and into good, so long as they consider self-derived intelligence to be all, and the Divine Providence nothing. IV. That the Lord governs hell by opposites, and the wicked who are in the world he governs in hell as to interiors, but not as to exteriors.

287. I. *That the Divine Providence, not only with the good, but also with the wicked, is universal in things the most particular, and yet that it is not in their evils.* It was shown above that the Divine Providence is in the minutest particulars of men's thoughts and affections; by which it is meant that a man can think and will nothing from himself, but that all he thinks and wills, and thence speaks and does; is by influx,—by influx from

heaven if it is good, and by influx from hell if it is evil; or, what amounts to the same, that good is by influx from the Lord, and evil from man's proprium. I know, however, that this is difficult to be comprehended; because a distinction is made between that which flows in from heaven, or from the Lord, and that which flows in from hell, or from man's proprium; while it is said, notwithstanding, that the Divine Providence is in the minutest particulars of a man's thoughts and affections, so that he can think and will nothing from himself; and because it is said, that he can also think and will from hell, and from his proprium, this appears like a contradiction; but yet it is not. That it is not a contradiction will be seen in what follows, after some things are premised which will illustrate this matter.

288. All the angels of heaven confess that no one can think from himself, but only from the Lord; but all the spirits of hell affirm that no one can think from any other than himself; though sometimes it has been shown to the latter, that not one of them thinks from himself, or can do it, but that thought flows in. In vain, however, was this shown them, for they would not receive it. Experience however shall teach, first, that the whole of thought and affection, even in the infernal spirits, flows in from heaven; but that influent good is there turned into evil, and truth into falsity, thus every thing into its opposite. This was proved by the following experiment. There was let down out of heaven a certain truth from the Word; it was received by those who were in the superior hells, sent down from them to the inferior hells, and so on to the lowest; in its passage it was successively turned into falsity, and at length into such falsity as was directly opposite to that truth. Those among whom it was so changed thought the falsity from themselves, and knew no otherwise; when, nevertheless, what they thought was that truth descending from heaven so falsified and perverted in its way to the lowest hell. I have heard that this was done three or four times. The case is the same with good, which in its descent from heaven is progressively turned into evil opposite to such good. Thence it was evident, that truth and good proceeding from the Lord, when received by those who are in falsity and evil, is changed, and passes into another form, so that its first form does not appear. Thus it is with every wicked man; for such a one as to his spirit is in hell.

289. It has often been manifested to me that no one in hell thinks from himself, but from others about him, and those also not from themselves, but still from others; and that thoughts and affections make an orderly progression from one society to another, without any one's knowing otherwise than that they are from himself. Some, who supposed they thought and willed from themselves, were sent into a society, all communication being cut off with their neighbours, to whom also their thoughts

used to extend themselves, and they were detained therein. They were then told to think otherwise than the spirits of that society thought, and to force themselves to think contrary to it, but they confessed that they found it impossible. This was done by many, and among others with Leibnitz, who was also convinced, that no one thinks from himself, but from others, and that neither do those others think from themselves, but all by influx from heaven, and heaven by influx from the Lord. Some, when they meditated on this matter, said that it was astonishing, and that scarce any one would be led to believe it, because it is quite contrary to appearance, but that yet they could not deny it, because it was fully proved. Nevertheless, in their state of astonishment, they said, that at this rate they are not in fault when they think evil; also, that thus it would seem as if evil were from the Lord; and, moreover, that they did not comprehend how the Lord alone could cause all to think so differently. But these three points shall be explained in what follows.

290. To the experience already adduced this also shall be added. When it was granted me by the Lord to speak with spirits and angels, this arcanum was immediately revealed to me; for it was told me out of heaven, that like others I believed that I thought and willed from myself, when nevertheless it was not from myself, but if good, from the Lord, and if evil, from hell. That this was the case was also demonstrated to me in a lively manner by various thoughts and affections induced, and I was enabled successively to perceive and feel it; therefore afterwards, as soon as any evil stole into my will, or any falsity into my thoughts, I inquired whence it came, when it was discovered to me; and moreover it was permitted me to speak with those who infused it, to rebuke them, and to drive them away, that they might retire, thus withdraw their evil and falsity, and keep it to themselves, no longer infusing any such thing into my thoughts. This has been done a thousand times; and in this state I have now remained for many years, and still continue in it; yet I seem to myself, entirely like others, to think and will from myself, for it is of the Lord's Divine Providence that it should so appear to every one, as was shown above in its proper place. Novitiate spirits wonder at this my state; for it seems to them as if I did not think and will any thing from myself, and therefore that I am like something empty; but I opened this arcanum to them; and moreover that I also think more interiorly, and perceive what flows into my exterior thought, whether it be from heaven or from hell; that I reject the latter and receive the former; and that still I seem to myself, just as they do, to think and will from myself.

291. That all good is from heaven, and all evil from hell, is not unknown in the world. It is known to every one in the

212

cnurch. Who that is admitted into the priesthood, does not teach that all good is from God, and that a man cannot take any thing of himself which is not given him from heaven; also, that the devil infuses evils into men's thoughts, seduces them, and excites them to do evils? Therefore a priest, who thinks he preaches from holy zeal, prays that the Holy Ghost would teach him, and influence his thoughts and words. Some say they perceive sensibly that they are acted upon; and when their preachings are commended, answer piously, that they did not speak from themselves, but from God. Therefore, also, when they see any one speak and act well, they say he was led by God to do it; and on the other hand, when they see any one speak and act wickedly, they say he was led to it by the devil. That this is the language of the church is well known; but who believes in the truth of it?

292. That all which a man thinks and wills, and consequently says and does, flows from the only Fountain of life, and yet that the only Fountain of life, which is the Lord, is not the cause of a man's thinking what is evil and false, may be illustrated by the following circumstance in the natural world. From its sun proceed heat and light; and these two flow into all the subjects and objects which we see, not only into good subjects and beautiful objects, but also into evil subjects and deformed objects, producing in them various effects; for they flow not only into trees which bear good fruit, but also into such as bear bad fruit, and even into the fruits themselves, causing them to vegetate. In like manner, they flow into good seed, and also into tares; likewise into useful or wholesome shrubs, and into hurtful or poisonous ones. Yet it is the same heat and light, in which there is not any cause of evil; for that exists in the recipient subjects and objects. The heat which hatches eggs containing an owl, a screech-owl, or an asp, is similar to that which hatches eggs containing a dove, a beautiful bird, or a swan. Set both kinds of eggs under a hen, and they will be hatched by her heat, which in itself is harmless. What then has the heat in common with those evil and noxious things? The action of heat, when it flows into marshy grounds, stercoraceous, putrid, and cadaverous substances, is the same as when it flows into vinous, fragrant, vegetating, and living substances. Who but must see that the cause does not exist in the heat, but in the recipient subject? The same light, also, produces in one object beautiful, and in another disagreeable colours; it even brightens itself and shines in white objects, while it becomes opaque and darkness itself in objects verging towards black. It is the same in the spiritual world, where also there are heat and light from the sun thereof, which is the Lord. The heat and light flow from him into their subjects and objects; which subjects and objects there are angels and spirits, speci

213

fically the things appertaining to their voluntary and intellectual faculties; the heat there being the proceeding Divine Love, and the light there the proceeding Divine Wisdom. The cause of their being received differently by one and by another does not exist in the heat and light; for the Lord says, that "He maketh his sun to rise on the evil and on the good, and sendeth rain on the just and on the unjust" (Matt. v. 45). By sun, in the supreme spiritual sense, is meant the Divine Love, and by rain the Divine Wisdom.

293. To this I will add a sentiment of the angels concerning will and intelligence in man: it is this,—that there does not exist in any man one grain of will or prudence that is proper to himself; for they say, if there existed one grain in any man, neither heaven nor hell could hold together, and the whole human race would perish. The reason of this, they say, is, because myriads of myriads of men, as many as have been born since the creation of the world, constitute heaven and hell, in which there is such order and subordination that they respectively make a one,—heaven one beautiful man, and hell one monstrous man; and if any individual person had a single grain of will and intelligence of his own, this one could not possibly exist, but would be distracted, and that divine form would perish; which can no otherwise consist and be permanent, than when the Lord is all in all, and they altogether nothing. Another reason, they say, is, because the divine principle consists essentially in thinking and willing from itself, while the human principle consists essentially in thinking and willing from God; and what is essentially divine cannot be appropriated to any man, for in that case he would be a god. Keep this in remembrance; and if you desire it, it will be confirmed to you by the angels, when you enter into the spiritual world after death.

294. It was observed above, n. 289, that when some were convinced that no one thinks from himself, but from others, and that all those others think, not from themselves, but by influx through heaven from the Lord, they said in astonishment that, this being the case, it would not be their fault if they did evil; also, that thus it would seem that evil is from the Lord; and that they did not comprehend that the Lord alone could cause all to think so diversely. Now as these three suggestions cannot but flow into the thoughts of those who think only of effects from effects, and not of effects from causes, it is necessary that they should be assumed, and explained from their causes. First, *That this being the case, it would not be their fault if they did evil:* for if all that a man thinks flows from others, it seems as if the fault were in those from whom it flows. Yet the fault is in him who receives; for he receives it as his own, and neither knows nor wishes to know any otherwise; because every one desires to be his own, to be guided by himself, and especially

to think and will from himself. This is liberty itself, which appears as the proprium in which every man is: therefore if he knew that whatever he thinks and wills flows from another, he would seem to himself to be in chains and captivity, and no longer master of himself; thus all the delight of his life would perish, and at length his humanity itself. That this is the case I have frequently seen proved. Certain spirits were permitted to perceive and feel that they were led by others, and then their anger was kindled to such a degree that they became as it were beside themselves, saying that they would rather be kept in chains in hell, than not be allowed to think as they will, and will as they think. Not to be allowed to do this, they called being chained with respect to their very lives, which was harder and more intolerable than being chained with respect to their bodies. Not to be allowed to speak and act as they thought and willed, they did not call being chained; because the delight of civil and moral life, which consists in speaking and acting, restrains, and, at the same time, as it were, alleviates the restraint. Now as a man does not desire to know that he is led to think by others, but is desirous to think from himself, and also believes that he does so, it follows that the fault is in himself, and that he cannot free himself from it so long as he continues to think what he does; but if he does not love it, he dissolves his connection with those from whom his thought flows. This is the case when he knows that it is evil, and therefore desires to shun it and desist from it. Then also he is taken away by the Lord from the society which is in that evil, and translated to a society in which it does not exist; but if he knows the evil, and does not shun it, then the fault is imputed to him, and he becomes guilty of that evil. Therefore, whatever a man thinks he does from himself is said to be done from the man, and not from the Lord. SECONDLY, *That thus it would seem that evil is from the Lord.* This may be thought to be a conclusion deducible from what was shown above, n. 288, which is, that influent good from the Lord is turned into evil, and truth into falsity, in hell. But who cannot see that evil and falsity are not from goodness and truth, consequently not from the Lord, but from the recipient subject and object, which is in evil and falsity, and perverts and inverts goodness and truth, as was also fully shown above, n. 292? Whence arise the evil and falsity in a man is repeatedly shown in the preceding pages. An experiment was also made in the spiritual world with those who thought that the Lord could remove evils from the wicked, and introduce good in place thereof, thus could transfer all hell into heaven, and save all; but that this is impossible will be seen at the end of this treatise, where momentaneous salvation and immediate mercy are treated of. THIRDLY, *That they did not comprehend that the Lord alone could cause all to think so diversely.* The divine love of the Lord is infinite, his divine wisdom is infinite; and infinite things of love and of wisdom proceed from the Lord, and flow into all in heaven, thence into all in hell, and from both into all in the world: there cannot, therefore, be wanting to any one something to think and to will, for infinite things are infinitely all. Those infinite things which proceed from the Lord, flow not only universally, but also most particularly; for the divine is universal, existing in things the most particular. It is divine particulars, as was shown above, which compose what is called universal; and the most minute divine particular is also infinite. Hence it may appear that the Lord alone causes every one to think and will according to his quality, and according to the laws of his providence. That all the things which are in the Lord, and proceed from the Lord, are infinite, was shown above, n. 46—69; and also in the treatise ON THE DIVINE LOVE AND THE DIVINE WISDOM, n. 17—22.

295. II. *That the wicked continually lead themselves into evils, but that the Lord continually withdraws them from evils.* It may be more easily comprehended how the Divine Providence operates with the good than how it operates with the evil; and as the latter operation is now treated of, it shall be set forth in the following series. I. That there are things innumerable in every evil. II. That the wicked man from himself continually sinks himself more and more deeply into his evils. III. That the Divine Providence with the wicked is a continual permission of evil, to the end that there may be a continual withdrawal therefrom. IV. That the withdrawal from evil is effected by the Lord by a thousand most secret means.

296. In order then that the Divine Providence with the wicked may be distinctly perceived, and thus comprehended, the above propositions shall be explained in the order in which they are adduced. FIRST, *That there are things innumerable in every evil.* Every evil appears to us as one simple thing. This is the case with hatred and revenge, theft and fraud, adultery and whoredom, pride and high-mindedness, and with every other evil; and it is not known that in every evil there are things innumerable, exceeding in number the fibres and vessels in a man's body; but a wicked man is a hell in its least form, and hell consists of myriads of myriads, every one there being in a human form, although it be a monstrous one, and all the fibres and vessels in it inverted. The spirit itself is evil, appearing to itself as one; but innumerable as are the things which are in it, so innumerable are the concupiscences of its evils; for every man is his own evil or his own good, from the crown of his head to the sole of his foot. Since then a wicked man is such, it is evident that he is one evil, composed of various innumerable ones, which are distinctly evils, and are called con

216

cupiscences of evil. Hence it follows, that all these in their order are to be repaired and converted by the Lord, in order that the man may be reformed; and that this cannot be effected but by the Lord's Divine providence, from the earliest period of the man's life to its termination successively. Every concupiscence of evil appears in hell, when it is represented, like some noxious animal; as for example, like a dragon, a basilisk, a viper, an owl, or a screech-owl, and so forth; and in the same manner do the concupiscences of evil appear about a wicked man, when he is viewed by the angels. All these forms of concupiscences are to be severally changed. The man himself, who with respect to his spirit appears as a monster or a devil, is to be converted, that he may become like a beautiful angel; and each concupiscence of evil is to be converted or changed, that it may appear like a lamb or a sheep, or like a pigeon, or a turtle dove, as the good affections of the angels appear in heaven, when they are represented; and the conversion of a dragon into a lamb, of a basilisk into a sheep, and of an owl into a dove, cannot be effected except progressively, by rooting out evil from its seed, and sowing good seed in its place. But this must be done comparatively like the ingrafting of trees, the roots of which with some of the trunk remain; and yet the ingrafted branch converts the juices extracted from the old root into juices producing good fruit. The branch which is to be ingrafted cannot be taken from any other but from the Lord, who is the tree of life; according also to the Word of the Lord (John xv. 1—7). SECONDLY, *That the wicked man from himself continually sinks himself more deeply into his evils.* It is said, from himself, because all evil is from man; for he converts into evil the good which is from the Lord, as was said above. The true reason why the wicked man immerses himself more deeply in evil, is, because as he wills and does evil, he introduces himself more and more interiorly, and also more and more deeply, into infernal societies. Thence also the delight of evil increases, and so occupies his thoughts, that at last he feels nothing more pleasant; and he that has introduced himself more interiorly and deeply into infernal societies, becomes like one bound in chains. So long as he lives in the world, however, he does not feel his chains; for they are like soft wool, or fine silken threads, which he loves because they are pleasurable; but after death those chains, instead of being soft are hard, and instead of being pleasurable are galling. That the delight of evil is capable of increase is well known from thefts, robberies, depredations, revenges, tyrannies, the desire of lucre, and other evils. · Who does not feel elevations of the delight of these evils, in proportion to his success and the unrestrained practice of them? It is well known that the thief feels such delight in thefts that he cannot desist from them, and what is ·surpris-

217

ing, that he loves one stolen piece of money better than ten that are given him. It would be the same with adulteries, were it not provided that the power of committing that evil decreases with the abuse of it; yet with many there remains a delight in thinking and speaking of it, and if nothing more, a lust of touching. But it is not known what is the reason of this increase of delight, and that it is a consequence of the person's introducing himself into infernal societies more and more interiorly, and more and more deeply, as he commits evils in will and at the same time in thought. If the evils are only in thought, and not in will, he is not yet with evil in an infernal society; but he enters it when they are also in the will. If in this case he also thinks that such evil is contrary to the precepts of the Decalogue, and considers these precepts as divine, he commits it intentionally, and thereby plunges himself more deeply into hell, whence he cannot be drawn out but by actual repentance. It is to be observed, that every man, with respect to his spirit, is in some society of the spiritual world,—a wicked man in some infernal society, and a good man in some celestial society. He also appears there sometimes when he is in deep meditation. Moreover, as sound, together with speech, diffuses itself in the air in the natural world, so does affection, together with thought, diffuse itself among societies in the spiritual world; and there is a correspondence between them,—affection corresponding to sound, and thought to speech. THIRDLY, *That the Divine Providence with the wicked is a continual permission of evil, in order that they may be continually drawn out of it.* The reason why the Divine Providence with wicked men is continual permission, is, because nothing but evil can proceed from their life; for a man, whether he be in good or in evil, cannot be in both at once, nor in either alternately, except he be lukewarm; and evil of life is not introduced by the Lord into the will, and through it into the thought, but it is introduced by man, and this is called permission. Now as all that a wicked man wills and thinks is of permission, it may be asked, How then is the Divine Providence therein, which is said to be in the most minute particulars with every man, the wicked as well as the good? I answer, In this respect, that it continually permits for a certain end, permitting such things as are conducive to that end, and no others; and that it continually examines, separates, and purifies the evils which issue forth by permission, putting off and removing by unknown ways such as are not consistent with the end proposed. These things are done principally in a man's interior will, and from it in his interior thought. The Divine Providence is also continual, in providing that those things which are to be put off and removed shall not be again received by the will; because all things which are received by the will are appropriated to the man;

218

but those which are received in the thought and not in the will are separated and set aside. This is the Lord's continual providence with the wicked, which, as was observed, is a continual permission of evil, to the end that they may be perpetually drawn out of it. Of these operations of Providence a man scarcely knows any thing, because he does not perceive them; the chief reason of which is, that evils are of the concupiscences of his life's love, and those are not perceived as evils, but as delights, to which no one attends; for who attends to the delights of his love? A man's thought swims in them, like a boat carried along in the stream of a river; and they are perceived as a fragrant atmosphere, which is drawn in with full inspiration. He can only perceive something of them in his external thought; but he does not attend to them even there, unless he well knows that they are evils. But of this more will be said in what follows. FOURTHLY, *That the withdrawal from evil is effected by the Lord by a thousand most secret means.* Of these some few only have been discovered to me, and these but of a general nature, which are, that the delights of concupiscences, of which a man knows nothing, are emitted in companies and bundles into his interior thoughts, which are those of his spirit, thence into his exterior thoughts, in which they make their appearance under some sense of pleasure, satisfaction, or cupidity, and are there intermixed with his natural and sensual delights. It is here that the means of separation and purification are, and also the ways of withdrawal and removal. These means are principally the delights of meditation, thought, and reflection for the sake of certain ends, which are of use; and ends which are of use are as many in number as the particulars and singulars of any man's business and function; also, as many in number as there are delights of reflection, in order that he may appear as a civil and moral and also as a spiritual man, besides the undelightful things which interpose. These delights, as they are of his love in the external man, are the means of separation, purification, rejection, and withdrawal of the delights of the concupiscences of evil of the internal man. Take for example an unjust judge, who has in view his own interest and the connections of friendship as the ends or uses of his function. Interiorly he has continually those ends in view, but exteriorly his object is to act as a skilful lawyer and a just man. He is continually in the delight of meditating, thinking, reflecting upon, and intending, to bend what is right, to turn, adapt, and accommodate it, so that it may seem conformable to the laws and consistent with justice. He does not know that his internal delight consists of cunning, fraud, deceit, clandestine thefts, and many other things; and that this delight compounded of so many delights of the concupiscences of evil, rules in the whole and in every particular of his external thought, in which exist the delights of the appearance that he is just and sincere. The internal delights are let down into these external delights, and mixed like food in the stomach, where they are separated, purified, and drawn off; but this is the case only with the more grievous delights of the concupiscences of evil; for in a wicked man there take place no other separation, purification, and removal, than that of the more grievous evils from the less grievous. In a good man, however, there take place a separation, purification, and removal of the less as well as of the more grievous evils; and this is effected by the delights of the affections of good and truth, and of justice and sincerity, into which he enters in proportion as he considers evils as sins, and therefore shuns and holds them in aversion, and still more when he fights against them. These are the means by which the Lord purifies all who are saved. He also purifies them by external means which have respect to fame and honour, and sometimes to interest: yet into these the Lord inserts delights of the affections of good and truth, by which they are so directed and adapted as to become delights of the love of the neighbour. If any one were to see the delights of the concupiscences of evil together, in any form, or were to perceive them distinctly with any sense, he would see and perceive them in such number that they could not be defined; for the whole of hell is no other than the form of all the concupiscences of evil; and no concupiscence of evil there is, or can be to all eternity, exactly like another, or the same with it. Of these innumerable concupiscences a man scarcely knows any thing, much less how they are connected; and yet the Lord, by his Divine Providence, continually permits that they should come forth, to the end that they may be drawn off, which is done in regular order and series; for a wicked man is a hell in its least form, as a good man is a heaven in its least form. That the withdrawal from evils is effected by the Lord by a thousand most secret means, cannot better be seen, and thereby concluded upon, than from the secret operations of the soul in the body. Those with which a man is acquainted are the following: with respect to the food he is to eat, he looks at it, smells it, has an appetite for it, tastes it, chews it with his teeth, turns it about with his tongue, and thus swallows it down into the stomach. But the secret operations of the soul with which he is unacquainted, because he does not perceive them, are the following: the stomach turns about the food it has received, opens and separates its parts by means of its solvent liquor, that is, digests it, and presents such as is properly prepared to the mouths of the vessels opening into the intestines, which drink it up. It also distributes some parts into the blood, some into the lymphatic vessels, some into the lacteal vessels of the mesentery, and conveys some down the intestines.

220

Afterwards, the chyle, which is drawn through the vessels of the mesentery into its receptacle, is conveyed through the thoracic duct into the vena cava, and so into the heart; from the heart into the lungs, thence through the left ventricle of the heart into the aorta, and from the aorta by its different ramifications into the viscera of the whole body, and also into the kidneys; in each of which there is a separation and purification of the blood, and a removal of heterogeneous parts; not to mention how the heart distributes its blood to the brain after it has been purified in the lungs, which is done by the arteries called carotids, and how the brain returns the blood vivified into the above-mentioned vena cava, into which the thoracic duct empties the chyle, and so again to the heart. These, besides innumerable others, are the secret operations of the soul in the body. A man perceives nothing of these, and he that is not skilled in anatomy knows nothing of them. Yet similar things are done in the interiors of a man's mind; for nothing can be done in the body, except from the mind, inasmuch as a man's mind is his spirit, and his spirit is equally a man, with this difference only, that the things which are done in the body are done naturally, and those which are done in the mind are done spiritually: there is a perfect similitude. Hence it is evident that the Divine Providence operates by a thousand hidden ways in every man; that its end is continually to purify him, because its end is to save him; and that nothing more is incumbent upon a man than to remove evils in the external man, the Lord providing the rest, if he be implored.

297. III. *That the Lord cannot entirely lead the wicked out of evils, and into goods, so long as they consider self-derived intelligence to be all, and the Divine Providence nothing.* It appears as if a man could lead himself out of evils, if he would but think that this or that is contrary to the good of the community, contrary to utility, and contrary to the laws of his country and the law of nations; and this a wicked man can do as well as a good man, provided that, by birth, or from the exercise of his faculties, he is able to think within himself analytically and rationally in a distinct manner. He is not able, however, to draw himself out of evil; the reason of which is, that although the faculty of understanding and perceiving things even abstractly is given by the Lord to every one, the wicked as well as the good, as has been shown in many places above, yet still, a man cannot by means of this faculty draw himself out of evil, because evil is of the will, and the understanding does not flow into the will except with light only, illuminating and teaching; and if the heat of the will, that is, the man's life's love, is fervid from the concupiscence of evil, it is frigid as to the affection of good, and therefore does not receive light, but either rejects or extinguishes it, or by some invented false principle converts it

221

into evil. The case herein is as with the light of winter, which is equally as clear as the light of summer, and which flowing into cold trees produces a similar effect. These things however will be seen more fully in the following order. 1. That self-derived intelligence, when the will is in evil, sees nothing but what is false; and that it neither will nor can see any thing else. 2. That if self-derived intelligence then sees truth, it turns itself away, or falsifies it. 3. That the Divine Providence continually causes a man to see truth, and also gives him the affection of perceiving and receiving it. 4. That a man is thereby drawn out of evil, not by himself, but by the Lord.

298. These propositions shall be explained in their proper order to the rational man, whether he be wicked or good, thus whether he be in the light of winter or of summer, for colours appear alike in both. FIRST, *That self-derived intelligence, when the will is in evil, sees nothing but what is false; and that it neither will nor can see any thing else.* This has often been experimentally shown in the spiritual world. Every man, when he becomes a spirit, which he does after death (for he then puts off his material body, and puts on a spiritual one), is alternately let into the two states of his life, the external and the internal. When he is in the external state, he speaks and acts rationally and wisely, just like a rational and wise man in the world; he can also teach others many things which relate to moral and civil life; and if he has been a preacher, he can also teach things relating to spiritual life. But when he is let out of this into his internal state,—when the external is laid asleep, and the internal is awakened,—if he is wicked, the scene is changed; instead of rational, he becomes sensual, and instead of wise, insane; for he thinks then from the evil of his will and its delight, therefore from self-derived intelligence; he sees nothing but what is false, and does nothing but evil, thinking that malice is wisdom, and cunning is prudence; and from self-derived intelligence he fancies himself a god, and imbibes with all his soul the most wicked arts. Such insanity I have often seen: I have also seen spirits let into these alternate states two or three times in an hour; and then it was granted them to see their insanities, and to acknowledge them; yet they would not remain in their rational and moral state, but of their own accord turned themselves to their internal, sensual, and insane state; for this they loved more than the other, because therein consisted the delight of their life's love. Who could suppose that a wicked man is such beneath his outward appearance, and that he undergoes such a metamorphosis when he comes into his interior state? From this experience alone may appear the nature of self-derived intelligence, when it thinks and acts from the evil of its will. The case is different with the good, when they are let into an internal state from an external, they

becoming still more wise and moral than before. SECONDLY, *That if self-derived intelligence then sees truth, it either turns itself away, or falsifies it.* Every man has a voluntary proprium and an intellectual proprium : his voluntary proprium is evil, and his intellectual proprium the falsity thence derived; the latter is meant by the will of man, and the former by the will of the flesh (John i. 13). The voluntary proprium is in its essence self-love, and the intellectual proprium is pride proceeding from that love. These are like two connubial partners, and their marriage is called the marriage of evil and falsity. Every evil spirit is let into this marriage before he is admitted into hell ; and when he is in this state, he does not know what good is ; for he calls his own evil good, because he feels it as his delight. He then also turns himself away from truth, and will not see it ; because the falsity agreeing with his evil is seen by him as beautiful objects are by the eye, and is heard as harmonious sounds by the ear. THIRDLY, *That the Divine Providence continually causes a man to see truth, and also gives him the affection of perceiving and receiving it.* The reason of this is, because the Divine Providence acts from within, and flows thence into the exteriors ; or it acts from the spiritual man upon the things which are in the natural man, and by the light of heaven illuminates his understanding, and by its heat vivifies his will. The light of heaven is in its essence divine wisdom, and the heat of heaven is in its essence divine love : from divine wisdom nothing can flow but truth, and from divine love nothing but good, from which the Lord gives in the understanding the affection of seeing truth, and also of perceiving and receiving it. Thus a man is made a man, not only as to his external face, but also as to his internal. Who does not wish to seem a rational and spiritual man ; and who does not know that he wishes to seem so in order that he may be thought by others to be a true man? If, therefore, he is rational and spiritual in his external form only, and not at the same time in his internal, can he be a man? can he be said to be otherwise than like a player upon the stage, or like an ape whose face nearly resembles a man's? May he not know from thence that he alone is a man who interiorly is such as he desires to be thought by others? He who acknowledges the one, acknowledges the other. Self-derived intelligence can induce the human form only in externals, but the Divine Providence induces it in internals, and through internals in externals ; and when it is induced, a man does not barely appear to be man, but is one. FOURTHLY, *That a man is thereby drawn out of evil, not by himself, but by the Lord.* The reason why a man can be drawn out of evil, when the Divine Providence gives the perception of truth, and at the same time the affection thereof, is, because truth shows and dictates ; and when the will performs what is thus dictated, it

223

joins itself therewith, converting in itself truth into good; for truth then becomes the truth of a man's love, and that which is of the love is good. All reformation is effected by truth, and not without it; for without truth the will is continually in its evil, and if it consults the understanding it is not instructed, but evil is confirmed by falsities. As to what relates to intelligence, it appears to be his own both in a good man and a wicked man; and a good man is also obliged, as well as a wicked man, to act from intelligence seemingly proper to himself; yet he who believes in the Divine Providence is withdrawn from evil, but he who does not is not withdrawn. He believes in it who acknowledges evil to be sin, and desires to be delivered from it; and he does not believe in it who does not acknowledge and desire this. The difference between these two kinds of intelligence is like the difference between that which is thought to exist in itself and that which is thought not to exist in itself, but yet as if in itself; and it is also like the difference between an external without a correspondent internal, and an external with a correspondent internal; consequently, like the difference between the words and gestures of mimics and players, who personate kings, princes, and generals, and those of the kings, princes, and generals themselves; the latter being interiorly as well as exteriorly such, the former only exteriorly, which exterior being put off, they are called comedians, actors, and players.

299. IV. *That the Lord governs hell by opposites, and the wicked who are in the world he governs in hell as to interiors, but not as to exteriors.* He who does not know the nature of heaven and hell, cannot at all know the nature of a man's mind, which is his spirit which lives after death. The reason of this is, because a man's mind or spirit, in all the particulars of its form, is similar to that of heaven or hell: there is no difference, except that one is great and the other small, or that one is an image, and the other its type; therefore a man, as to his mind or spirit, is either a heaven or a hell in its least form. He that is led by the Lord is a heaven, and he that is led by his own proprium is a hell. Now, since I have been made acquainted with the nature both of heaven and hell, and it is important to know what is the nature of man with respect to his mind or spirit, I would briefly give a description of both.

300. All in heaven are no other than affections of good and thence thoughts of truth; and all in hell are no other than concupiscences of evil and thence imaginations of falsity. Both of these are so arranged that the concupiscences of evil and the imaginations of falsity in hell are directly opposite to the affections of good and the thoughts of truth in heaven. Hell, therefore, is under heaven, and diametrically opposite to it; as much so as two men who lie opposite to each other, or stand

opposite as antipodes, consequently inverted, have the soles of
their feet placed against each other, or stand each upon the heels
of the other. Sometimes also hell appears in such a situation,
or thus turned, with respect to heaven. The reason of this is,
because those who are in hell make the concupiscences of evil
their head, and the affections of good their feet; while those
who are in heaven make the affections of good their head, and
the concupiscences of evil the soles of their feet: hence their
mutual opposition. It is said that in heaven there are affections
of good and thence thoughts of truth, and that in hell there are
concupiscences of evil and thence imaginations of falsity: hereby
is meant that there are spirits and angels who are such; for
every one is his own affection or his own concupiscence,—the
angel of heaven his own affection, and the spirit of hell his own
concupiscence.

301. The reason why the angels of heaven are affections of
good and thence thoughts of truth, is, because they are recipients
of divine love and wisdom from the Lord,—all affections of good
being from divine love, and all thoughts of truth from divine
wisdom; and the reason why the spirits of hell are concupiscences of evil and thence imaginations of falsity, is, because they
are in the love of self and in self-derived intelligence,—all concupiscences of evil being from the love of self, and imaginations
of falsity from self-derived intelligence.

302. The arrangement of affections in heaven, and of concupiscences in hell, is wonderful, and known only to the Lord.
They are respectively distinguished into genera and species, and
so conjoined as to act as a one; and as they are distinguished
into genera and species, they are distinguished into greater or
lesser societies; as, also, they are conjoined that they may act
as a one, they are conjoined like all the things which are in a
man. Hence heaven, in its form, is like a beautiful man, whose
soul is the divine love and the divine wisdom, consequently the
Lord; and hell, in its form, is like a monstrous man, whose soul
is self-love and self-derived intelligence, consequently the devil;
for there is no particular devil, who is sole lord there, but self-
love is so called.

303. In order however that the nature of heaven and hell
may be still better understood, instead of the affections of good
suppose the delights of good, and instead of the concupiscences
of evil, the delights of evil; for there exists no affection or concupiscence without its delights, because delights constitute the
life of every one. These delights are distinguished and connected, as was said above respecting the affections of good and
the concupiscences of evil. The delight of his affection fills and
encompasses every angel of heaven; its common delight fills and
encompasses every society of heaven; and the delight of all
together, or that which is most general, fills and encompasses

225

the universal heaven. In like manner, the delight of his concupiscence fills and encompasses every spirit of hell; its common delight every society in hell; and the delight of all, or that which is general, the whole of hell. Since the affections of heaven and the concupiscences of hell are, as was observed above, diametrically opposite to each other, it is evident that the delight of heaven is insupportable in hell; and on the other hand, that the delight of hell is insupportable in heaven: hence proceed their mutual antipathy, aversion, and separation.

304. These delights, as they constitute the life of each individual in particular, and of all in common, are not felt by those who are in them; but their opposites are felt when they approach, especially when they are converted into smells; for every delight corresponds to some smell, and in the spiritual world may be converted into it. Then the delight of heaven in general is felt like the smell of a garden, with a variety according to the fragrances therein from flowers and fruits; and the delight of hell in general is felt like stagnant water, into which have been cast divers kinds of filth, with a variety according to the stench of things putrid and offensive therein. In what manner the delight of each particular affection of good in heaven, and of each particular concupiscence of evil in hell, is felt, has been made known to me; but it would be tedious to explain it here.

305. I have heard many persons recently come from the world complain that they did not know their lot would be according to the affections of their love; saying, that in the world they did not think about them, much less about their delights, because they loved that which was delightful to them; and that they only supposed the lot of every one would be according to his thought arising from intelligence, especially according to thoughts arising from piety, and also from faith: they were however answered, that they might have known, if they would, that an evil life is disagreeable to heaven and displeasing to God, and is pleasing to hell and delightful to the devil; on the other hand, that a good life is grateful to heaven and pleasing to God, and unpleasant to hell and disagreeable to the devil; therefore, that evil is in itself offensive, and good in itself fragrant. Since they might have known this if they would, why did they not shun evils as infernal and diabolical, and why did they favour evils merely because they were delightful? Since also they now knew that the delights of evil have an offensive smell, they might also know that those in whom they abound cannot enter into heaven. After this answer, they betook themselves to those who were in similar delights; for there and there only could they breathe.

306. From the idea now given of heaven and hell it may appear what is the nature of the mind of man (for, as before

said, a man's mind or spirit is a heaven or a hell in its least form), namely, that his interiors are mere affections and thoughts, thence derived, distinguished into genera and species, like greater and lesser societies, and so connected as to act as a one, and that the Lord rules those affections and thoughts, in like manner as he rules heaven or hell. That a man is either a heaven or a hell in its least form, may be seen in the work concerning HEAVEN AND HELL, published in London in the year 1758, n. 51—87.

307. Now to the proposition in question, that the Lord governs hell by opposites, and that the wicked who are in the world he governs in hell as to interiors, but not as to exteriors. As to what relates, FIRST, *To the Lord's governing hell by opposites;* it is shown above, n. 288, 289, that the angels of heaven are not in love and wisdom, or in the affection of good and thence in the thought of truth, from themselves, but from the Lord; and that good and truth flow from heaven into hell: where good is turned into evil and truth into falsity, in consequence of the interiors of their minds being turned in a contrary direction. Now since all things in hell are opposite to all things in heaven, it follows that the Lord governs hell by opposites. SECONDLY, *That the wicked who are in the world are governed in hell by the Lord;* because every man with respect to his spirit is in the spiritual world, and in some society there,—in an infernal society if he is wicked, and in a celestial society if good; for his mind, which in itself is spiritual, cannot be anywhere but among spirits, into whose society it also comes after death. That this is the case has also been said and shown above. But a man is not there like one of the spirits who is registered in the society, for he is continually in a state of reformation; therefore, according to his life and its changes, he is translated by the Lord from one society of hell to another, if he is wicked; and if he suffers himself to be reformed, he is led out of hell and introduced into heaven, and there also translated from one society to another. This is continued until the time of his death, after which he is no longer carried from one society to another, because he is then no longer in any state of reformation, but remains in that state in which the nature of his life has placed him; therefore when a man dies, he is inscribed in his own place. THIRDLY, *That the Lord thus governs the wicked in the world as to their interiors, but differently as to their exteriors.* The Lord governs the interiors of a man's mind in the manner just described, but its exteriors he governs in the world of spirits, which is in the midst between heaven and hell. The reason hereof is, because a man for the most part is different in externals from what he is in internals; for in externals he can put on the semblance of an angel of light, and yet in internals he may be a spirit of darkness. Therefore his external is governed on

227   P

way and his internal another; his external is governed in the
world of spirits, but his internal in heaven or hell, so long as he
is in the world.   Therefore, also, when he dies, he comes first
into the world of spirits, and there into his external, which is
there put off; and this being done, he is transferred to the place
in which he is inscribed.   The nature of the world of spirits
may be seen in the work concerning HEAVEN AND HELL, published in London in the year 1758, n. 421—535.

THAT THE DIVINE PROVIDENCE APPROPRIATES NEITHER EVIL NOR GOOD TO ANY ONE, BUT THAT SELF—DERIVED PRUDENCE APPROPRIATES BOTH.

308. IT is believed by almost every one that a man thinks
and wills from himself, and thence speaks and acts from himself.   Who of himself can suppose otherwise, since the appearance of it is so strong that it differs nothing from his really
thinking, willing, speaking, and acting from himself, which yet
is not possible?   In THE ANGELIC WISDOM CONCERNING THE
DIVINE LOVE AND THE DIVINE WISDOM, it is demonstrated that
there is one only life, and that men are recipients of life; also,
that a man's will is the receptacle of love, and his understanding the receptacle of wisdom, which two constitute that one
only life.   It is likewise demonstrated, that by creation, and
thence continually by the Divine Providence, it is ordained that
that life should appear in a man in such a similitude as if it
were his own, consequently proper to himself; but that this is
an appearance to the end that he may be a receptacle.   Moreover, it is demonstrated above, n. 288—294, that no man thinks
from himself, but from others, and that those others do not
think from themselves, but all from the Lord, the wicked as
well as the good; likewise, that this is known in the Christian
world, especially among those who not only say, but believe,
that all goodness and truth, also all wisdom, and consequently
all faith and charity, are from the Lord; and that every thing
evil and false is from the devil or from hell.   From all these
premises no other conclusion can be deduced than that whatever
a man thinks and wills comes by influx; and that, as all speech
flows from thought as an effect from its cause, and all action in
like manner from the will, therefore whatever a man speaks and
acts comes likewise by influx, although derivately or mediately.
That whatever a man sees, hears, smells, tastes, and feels,
comes by influx, cannot be denied; why not then what he
thinks and wills?   Can there be any difference, except that
such things as are in the natural world flow into or impress the
organs of the external senses, or of the body, while such things

228

as are in the spiritual world flow into or impress the organic substances of the internal senses, or of the mind? Therefore, that as the organs of the external senses, or of the body, are receptacles of natural objects, so the organic substances of the internal senses, or of the mind, are receptacles of spiritual objects. Since this is every man's condition, what then is his proprium? His proprium does not consist in his being such or such a receptacle, because this proprium is nothing but his quality with respect to reception, and is not the proprium of life; for by proprium no one means any thing but that which lives from itself, and thence thinks and wills from itself; but that such a proprium does not exist in any man, yea, that it cannot exist in any one, follows from what has been said above.

309. I will here relate what I have heard from some in the spiritual world. They were such as believed self-derived prudence to be every thing, and the Divine Providence nothing. I said that a man has not any proprium, unless you choose to make his proprium consist in his being such and such a subject, or such and such an organ, or such and such a form; and this is not the proprium which is meant, for it is only his quality: but no man has any proprium in the sense in which proprium is commonly understood. Those who ascribed all things to self-derived prudence, and who may be called *proprietaries*, being the image of such characters, grew so enraged, that a flame appeared issuing from their nostrils, and they said, You utter paradoxes and insanities; would not a man in such case be an empty nothing? He would either be a mere ideal being and fantasy, or he would be an image or statue. To this I could only answer, that it was paradoxical and insane to believe that a man is life from himself, and that wisdom and prudence do not flow from God, but are in the man, consequently also the good which is of charity and the truth which is of faith. For any one to attribute these to himself is called insanity by every wise man, and is therefore also a paradox. Persons so doing are like those who dwell in the house or estate of another, and, being in possession, persuade themselves that they are their own; or like agents and stewards, who think all their master's property their own; and like what the servants would have been to whom the Lord gave the talents to trade with, in case they had rendered no account of them, but kept them as their own, and so acted as thieves. Of such it may very justly be said that they are insane, that they are indeed empty nothings, and that they are idealists, because they have not in themselves from the Lord any good, which is the very essence of life, nor, consequently, have they any truth; therefore such are also called the dead, and likewise nothing, and emptiness, in Isaiah xl. 17, 23; and in other places, makers of images, idols and statues

229

But of these things more below, to be explained in the following order. I. What self-derived prudence is, and what that prudence which is not self-derived. II. That a man from self-derived prudence persuades himself, and confirms himself in the idea, that every good and truth is from himself, and in himself, and in like manner every evil and falsity. III. That every thing of which a man is persuaded, and in which he is confirmed, remains as his proprium. IV. That if a man would believe, as is the truth, that every thing good and true is from the Lord, and every thing evil and false from hell, he would neither appropriate to himself good and account it meritorious, nor would he appropriate evil, and make himself accountable for it.

310. I. *What self-derived prudence is, and what that prudence which is not self-derived.* Those are in self-derived prudence who confirm in themselves appearances, and make them truths, especially this appearance, that self-derived prudence is every thing, and the Divine Providence nothing, except something very general, which nevertheless, as was shown above, cannot exist without particulars of which it must consist. They are also in fallacies, for every appearance confirmed as a truth becomes a fallacy; and in proportion as they confirm themselves from fallacies they become naturalists, in the same proportion believing nothing but what they can at the same time perceive with one of the bodily senses, especially the sight, because this principally acts in union with thought. Such persons at last become sensual; and if they confirm themselves in favour of nature against God, they close the interiors of their mind, and interpose as it were a veil, afterwards thinking what is under the veil, and nothing which is above it. These sensualists were called by the ancients serpents of the tree of knowledge. Of them it is said, in the spiritual world, that as they confirm themselves, they close the interiors of their minds, even at length unto the nose; for the nose signifies perception of truth, and when closed, indicates no perception at all. Their character shall now be described: they are more cunning and crafty than others, and are also ingenious reasoners; and cunning and craftiness they call intelligence and wisdom, nor do they know any other. Those who are not of this description they consider as simple and stupid, especially the worshipers of God and the confessors of the Divine Providence. With respect to the interior principles of their minds, of which they themselves know very little, they are like those called Machiavelists, who make no account of murders, adulteries, thefts, and false testimony, considered in themselves: and if they reason against them, do it only from motives of prudence, that they may not appear to be what they really are. Of the life of a man in this world, they think that it is only like the life of a beast; and of

the life of a man after death, that it is like a vital vapour, which rising from the corpse or grave, relapses again, and so dies. From this madness came the idea that spirits and angels are air, and among those who are enjoined to believe in life everlasting, that the souls of men are the same; that therefore they neither see, hear, nor speak, consequently are blind, deaf, and dumb, and that they only think in their particle of air; for they say, How can the soul be any thing else? Did not the external senses die with the body? and how can they receive them again before the soul is reunited to the body? And because they could have only a sensual and not a spiritual idea of the state of the soul after death, they established this, otherwise the belief of an everlasting life would have perished. More especially they confirm in themselves self-love, calling it the fire of life, and an incitement to various uses in society; and being of this description, they are the idols of themselves; and their thoughts, being fallacies from fallacies, are images of falsity. As they favour the delights of concupiscences, they are satans and devils; those being called satans who confirm in themselves the concupiscences of evil, and those devils who live according to them. The nature of the most cunning sort of sensual men has also been made known to me: they have a deep hell behind, and wish to be invisible; therefore they appear hovering about there as it were spectres, which are their fantasies, and are called genii. Some of them were once sent from that hell, that I might know their quality: they immediately applied themselves to the back part of my neck under the occiput, and thence entered into my affections, not choosing to enter into my thoughts, which they dexterously avoided; they then varied my affections one after another, with a design of bending them insensibly into their opposites, which are concupiscences of evil; and as they did not in the least meddle with my thoughts, they would have infected and inverted my affections, without my knowledge, if the Lord had not prevented. Those persons become of such a quality who in the world do not believe there is a Divine Providence, and search for nothing in others but their cupidities and desires, so leading them till they acquire a perfect ascendency over them; and as they do this so clandestinely and cunningly that the others do not know it, and after death become like themselves, therefore immediately after their arrival in the spiritual world, they are cast into that hell. When seen in the light of heaven they appear without any nose; and, what is wonderful, although they are so cunning, yet they are more sensual than others. As the ancients called the sensual man a serpent, and such a man is a more cunning, crafty, and ingenious reasoner than others, therefore it is said that "the serpent was more subtile than any beast of the field" (Gen. iii. 1); and the Lord says, "Be ye wise as serpents and harmless as doves"

231

(Matt. x. 16). Moreover the dragon, which is also called the old serpent, the devil, and satan, is described as "having seven heads and ten horns, and seven crowns upon his heads" (Rev. xii. 3, 9). By seven heads is signified craftiness, by ten horns the power of persuading by fallacies, and by seven crowns the holy things of the Word and of the church profaned.

311. From this description of self-derived prudence, and of those who are in it, may be seen what is the nature of that prudence which is not-self-derived, and of the persons who are in it, namely, that prudence which is not self-derived is such as is in those who do not confirm in themselves the idea that intelligence and wisdom are from any man, but say, How can a man have wisdom from himself and do good from himself? And when they say this, they see the matter accordingly, for they think interiorly, and also believe that others think in the same manner, especially the learned, because they do not know that any one can think only exteriorly. They are not in fallacies by means of any confirmations of appearances; therefore they know and perceive that murders, adulteries, thefts, and false testimony are sins, and for that reason shun them; also that malice is not wisdom, and that craftiness is not intelligence; and when they hear ingenious reasonings founded in fallacies, they wonder and smile to themselves. The reason hereof is, because in them there is no veil between the interiors and the exteriors, or between the spiritual and the natural things of the mind, as there is in the sensual; therefore they receive influx from heaven, by which they see such things interiorly. They speak with more simplicity and sincerity than others, and place wisdom not in speaking well, but in living well. They are comparatively like lambs and sheep, while those who are in self-derived prudence are like wolves and foxes: they are like those who dwell in a house, and through its windows see the heavens; but those who are in self-derived prudence are like those who dwell in a cellar, and through their windows see nothing but what is under ground: and they are like those who stand upon a mountain, and see such as are in self-derived prudence wandering below in valleys and woods. Hence it may appear that prudence which is not self-derived, is prudence from the Lord, similar to self-derived prudence as to its appearance in externals, but totally different in internals. In internals, prudence which is not self-derived appears in the spiritual world as a man, but self-derived prudence as an image, appearing to have life from this circumstance only, that those who are in it have still rationality and liberty, or a faculty of understanding and willing, and thence of speaking and acting; and that by means of these faculties they can also bear the semblance of men. The reason why they are such images, is, because evils and falses are not alive, but only goods and truths; and

as they know this by means of their rationality (for if they did not know it, they would not put on such appearance), therefore in their semblances of men they possess human vitality. Who does not know that the quality of a man is determined by what he is interiorly; consequently, that he is a real man who is interiorly such as he wishes to seem exteriorly, and that he is a semblance or counterfeit, who is only a man exteriorly and not interiorly. Think as you speak in favour of God, of religion, and of justice and sincerity, and you will be a man; then the Divine Providence will be your prudence, and you will perceive in others that self-derived prudence is insanity.

312. II. *That a man from self-derived prudence persuades himself, and confirms in himself the idea, that every good and truth is in and from himself, and in like manner every evil and falsity.* Institute an argumentation or course of reasoning from analogy between natural good and truth and spiritual good and truth. Inquire what is true and good in the sight of the eye: is not that true therein which is called beautiful, and that good therein which is called delightful? for delight is felt in seeing beautiful objects. Inquire what is true and good in the sense of hearing: is not that true therein which is called harmonious, and that good therein which is called sweet and pleasant? for sweetness or pleasure is felt in hearing harmonious sounds. It is the same with the other senses. Hence it is evident what are natural truth and good. Consider now what are spiritual truth and good. Is spiritual truth any thing but the beauty and harmony of spiritual things and objects? And is spiritual good any thing else but the delight and pleasure arising from a perception of their beauty or harmony? Let us now see whether any thing can be asserted of the one which is not applicable to the other, or of what is natural, and not of what is spiritual. Of that which is natural it is said, that what is beautiful and delightful to the eye flows from external objects, and what is harmonious and sweet to the ear flows from instruments: in what respect is it different with the organic substances of the mind? It is said of the latter, that those things (viz. beauty and delight) are in them, and of the former, that they flow into them, or impress them; but if it be asked, why it is said that they flow in, or enter by influx, no other answer can be given than that there appears to be a distance between the organ of sense and that which impresses or flows into it. If it be asked why, in the other case, it is said of spiritual objects that they are in the mind and its organized substances, no other answer can be given than that there does not appear to be any distance between them. Consequently, it is the appearance of distance which causes a different notion to exist respecting the things which a man thinks and perceives, and those which he sees and hears. This falls to the ground, how-

ever, when it is known that the spiritual principle does not exist in distance as the natural does. Think of the sun and moon, or of Rome and Constantinople : do they not exist in thought without distance, provided such thought be not connected with experience acquired by sight or by hearing? Why then do you persuade yourself, because distance does not appear in thought, that good and truth, also evil and falsity, exist there, and do not enter by influx? To this I will add a fact known by experience, and which is common in the spiritual world. One spirit can infuse his thoughts and affections into another spirit, without the other's knowing but that the same is of his own thought and affection ; this is called in that world thinking from and in another. I have seen it a thousand times, and have also done it a hundred times myself; yet the appearance of distance was considerable ; but as soon as they knew that it was another who infused those thoughts and affections, they were angry, and turned themselves away, acknowledging nevertheless that distance, unless it be discovered, does not appear, in the internal sight or thought, as it does in the external sight or eye, and that hence it is thought to enter into the latter by influx. To this fact I can add my own daily experience : evil spirits having often injected evils and falsities into my thoughts, which appeared to me as if they were in myself, and from myself, or as if I thought them myself ; but as I knew that they were evils and falses, I endeavoured to find out who injected them, when they were detected and driven away, and were at a considerable distance from me. Hence it may appear that all evil with its falsity flows from hell, that all good with its truth flows from the Lord, and that they both appear as if they were in man.

313. The nature and quality of those who are in self-derived prudence, and of those who are in prudence not self-derived, and thence in the Divine Providence, is described in the Word by Adam and his wife Eve in the garden of Eden, where there were two trees, the tree of life and the tree of the knowledge of good and evil ; and by their eating of the latter. That by Adam and his wife Eve, in the internal or spiritual sense, is meant and described the Lord's most ancient church upon this earth, which was more noble and celestial than any that succeeded it, may be seen above, n. 241. By the rest is signified as follows : by the garden of Eden, the wisdom of the men of that church ; by the tree of life, the Lord with respect to his Divine Providence ; and by the tree of knowledge, man with respect to his self-derived prudence ; by the serpent, the sensuality and proprium of man, which in itself is self-love, and the pride of his own intelligence, consequently the devil and satan ; and by eating of the tree of knowledge, the appropriation of good and truth, as if they were not from the Lord and consequently of

the Lord, but from man himself and consequently of man, that is, his own: and as good and truth are things really divine in man, "or by good is meant the whole of love, and by truth the whole of wisdom, therefore if a man claims them to himself as his own, he cannot but think himself like a god. On this account the serpent said, "In the day ye eat thereof, then your eyes shall be opened, and ye shall be as gods, knowing good and evil" (Gen. iii. 5). So also do those think in hell who are in self-love, and thence in the pride of self-derived intelligence. By the condemnation of the serpent is signified the condemnation of man's own proper love and proper intelligence; by the condemnation of Eve, that of the voluntary proprium; and by the condemnation of Adam, that of the intellectual proprium; by thorns and thistles, which the earth shall bring forth, is signified mere falsity and evil; by their being driven out of the garden is signified the deprivation of wisdom; by the guarding of the way to the tree of life, the Lord's provident care to protect from violation the holy things of the Word and of the church; by the fig-leaves with which they covered their nakedness, moral truths, under which were concealed the things appertaining to their love and pride; and by the coats of skins, with which they were afterwards clothed, are signified appearances of truth, in which alone they were principled. This is the spiritual meaning of those things. He that chooses may remain in the literal sense, only he should know that it is so understood in heaven.

314. What sort of persons they are who are infatuated by self-derived intelligence may appear from their imaginations in matters of interior judgment; as, for example, concerning influx, thought, and life. Concerning INFLUX, they think inversely; as that the sight of the eye flows into the internal sight of the mind, which is the understanding, and that the hearing of the ear flows into the internal hearing, which is also the understanding; and they do not perceive that the understanding from the will flows into the eye and the ear, and not only constitutes those senses, but also uses them as its instruments in the natural world. Because this is not according to appearance, they do not perceive it: and if it be affirmed that what is natural does not flow into what is spiritual, but what is spiritual into what is natural, still they think, What is that which is spiritual but something more purely natural? Moreover, does it not appear, that when the eye sees any beautiful object, or the ear hears any harmonious sound, the mind, which is the understanding and will, is delighted, not knowing that the eye does not see from itself, or the tongue taste from itself, or the nose smell from itself, or the skin feel from itself, but that it is the man's mind or spirit which there perceives such things by the sense, and thence is affected according to the quality of the

235

sense? But still the man's mind or spirit does not feel them from itself, but from the Lord; and to think otherwise is to think from appearances, and, if it be confirmed, from fallacies. Concerning THOUGHT, they say, that it is something modified in the air, varied according to its objects, and enlarged in proportion as it is cultivated; therefore, that ideas of thought are images, like meteors appearing in the air; and that the memory is a table upon which they are impressed; not knowing that thoughts exist alike in substances purely organic, as the sight and hearing do in theirs. Let them only look into the brain, and they will see that it is full of such substances. If you injure them you bring on a delirium: destroy them, and you die. But what thought is, and also what memory is, may be seen above, n. 279, towards the end. Concerning LIFE, they know no other than that it is a certain activity of nature, which causes itself to be felt diversely, as the living body moves itself organically. If it be alleged, that in this case nature lives, this they deny, but maintain that nature gives life. If you say, Is not life dissipated when the body dies? they answer, that life remains in a particle of air which is called the soul. If you say, What then is God? is not He life itself? here they are silent, and will not declare what they think: and if you say, Will you not acknowledge that the Divine Love and the Divine Wisdom are life itself? they answer, What is love, and what is wisdom? For in their fallacies they do not see what love and wisdom are, or what God is. These observations are adduced, that it may be seen how a man is infatuated by self-derived prudence, because he draws all his conclusions from appearances, and thence from fallacies.

316. The reason why self-derived prudence persuades and confirms the idea that every good and truth is from man and in man, is, because self-derived prudence is the man's intellectual proprium, flowing from self-love, which is the man's voluntary proprium, and that which is his proprium cannot do otherwise than make all things his own; for it cannot be elevated by him. All who are led by the Divine Providence of the Lord are elevated above their proprium, and then they see that all good and truth are from the Lord: they even see, also, that what is from the Lord in a man is perpetually of the Lord, and never of the man. He that thinks otherwise is like one who, having goods of his master deposited in his hands, lays claim to them or appropriates them to himself as his own, and who is therefore not a steward, but a thief; and as a man's proprium is nothing but evil, therefore he also immerses them into his evil, by which they are consumed, like pearls cast into dung, or dissolved in acids.

317. III. *That every thing, of which a man is persuaded and in which he is confirmed, remains as his proprium.* **It is**

thought by many that no truth can be seen by a man except from things confirmed; but this is false. In things which relate to the civil government and economy of a kingdom or state, what is useful and good cannot be seen unless several of the statutes and ordinances therein be known; or in matters of a judicial nature, unless laws be known; or in natural things, as physics, chemistry, anatomy, mechanics, and the like, unless a man be instructed in sciences; but in things purely of a rational, moral, and spiritual nature, truths appear merely from their own light, provided a man, by means of a good education, be made in some degree rational, moral, and spiritual. The reason is because every man, with respect to his spirit, which is that which thinks, is in the spiritual world, and one among those who live there, consequently he is in spiritual light, which illuminates the interiors of his understanding, and, as it were, dictates; for spiritual light in its essence is the divine truth of the Lord's divine wisdom. Hence a man has power to think analytically, to form conclusions concerning what is just and right in judgments, to see honesty in moral life, and good in spiritual life, and likewise many truths which do not fall into darkness except by the confirmation of falsities: these things a man sees, in the same manner as he sees the mind of another in his face, and perceives his affections from the sound of his voice, without any other knowledge than what is inherent in every one. Why should not a man see by influx, in a certain degree, the interiors of his life, which are spiritual and moral, when there is no animal which does not by influx know the things necessary for it which are natural? Birds know how to make their nests, lay their eggs, hatch their young, and choose their food; besides other wonderful things, which are called instinct.

318. But how a man's state is changed by confirmations and consequent persuasions shall now be shown in the following order. 1. That there is nothing but what may be confirmed, and falsity more easily than truth. 2. That when the falsity is confirmed, truth does not appear; but that from confirmed truth the falsity appears. 3. That to be able to confirm whatever a man pleases is not intelligence, but only ingenuity, which may exist even in the most wicked. 4. That there may be intellectual confirmation, and not at the same time voluntary; but that all voluntary confirmation is also intellectual. 5. That the voluntary and at the same time the intellectual confirmation of evil, causes a man to think that self-derived prudence is all, and the Divine Providence nothing; but not the intellectual confirmation of it alone. 6. That every thing confirmed by the will, and at the same time by the understanding, remains to eternity; but not that which is confirmed by the understanding only. With respect to the FIRST, *That there is nothing but what*

237

may be confirmed, and falsity more easily than truth. What may not be confirmed, when it is confirmed by Atheists that God is not the creator of the universe, but that nature is the creator of herself; that religion is only an external means of restraint, and calculated for the simple and the vulgar; that a man is similar to a beast, and that he dies in like manner? What may not be confirmed, when it is confirmed that adulteries are allowable, also clandestine thefts, frauds, and deceitful arts; that cunning is intelligence, and malice wisdom? Who does not confirm his own heresy? Are there not volumes full of confirmations in favour of the two reigning heresies in the Christian world? If you establish ten heresies of even an abstruse nature, and tell an ingenious person to confirm them, he will confirm them all. If you afterwards view them only from their confirmations, will you not see falsities as if they were truths? As every false principle has a lucid appearance in the natural man, arising from his appearances and fallacies, which is not the case with truth except in the spiritual man, it is evident that falsity can be confirmed more easily than truth. In order that it may be known that every falsity and every evil can be confirmed, in such a manner that the falsity may appear true and the evil good, take the following example: let it be confirmed that light is darkness and darkness light. May it not be said, What is light in itself? Is it any thing but a certain appearance in the eye according to its state? What is light when the eye is shut? Have not bats and owls such eyes that they see light as darkness, and darkness as light? I have heard some persons say that they can see in the same manner, and of the infernals I have heard that although they are in darkness they see one another. Do not men see light at midnight in their dreams? Is not darkness therefore light, and light darkness? But it may be answered, What is this to the purpose? Light is light, as truth is truth; and darkness is darkness, as falsity is falsity. Take another example: and let it be confirmed that a raven is white. May it not be said, that his blackness is only a shade which is not his real colour? His feathers are inwardly white, and so is his body; and these are the substances of which he consists. Since his blackness is only a shade, therefore a raven turns white when he grows old, and some such have been seen. What is black in itself but white? Grind black glass, and you will see that the powder is white. Therefore, when you call a raven black, you speak from the shade and not from the reality. But it may be answered, What is this to the purpose? At this rate it might be said that all birds are white. These cases, although they are contrary to sound reason, are adduced, to the end it may be seen, that falsity diametrically opposite to truth, and evil diametrically opposite to good, may be confirmed. SECONDLY, *That when falsity is confirmed, truth does not appear* ·

but that from confirmed truth, falsity appears. All falsity is in the dark, and all truth in the light; and in the dark nothing appears, nor can it even be known what it is, but by feeling it. Not so in the light. Therefore, also, in the Word, falsities are called darkness, and thence those who are in falsities are said to walk in darkness and in the shadow of death. On the other hand, truths are there called light, and thence those who are in truths are said to walk in the light, and are called the children of light. That when the falsity is confirmed truth does not appear, and that from confirmed truth falsity does appear, is evident from many considerations. For example: who would see any spiritual truth, if the Word did not teach it? Would not there prevail thick darkness, which could not be dispelled but by the light in which the Word is, and with such as should desire to be enlightened? What heretic can see his own falsities except he admit the genuine truth of the church? He does not see them before. I have discoursed with those who have confirmed themselves in faith separated from charity, and asked them whether they did not see so many things in the Word about love and charity, about works and actions, and about keeping the commandments, with the declarations that he is happy and wise who does them, and he is foolish who does them not. They said, that when they read those things they saw no otherwise than that they are faith, and so passed them over as it were with their eyes shut. Those who have confirmed themselves in falsities are like those who see images pictured on a wall, and when in the shade of evening those pictures seem to them in their fantasy like a horse or a man, which visionary image is dispelled by the influent light of day. Who can perceive the spiritual defilement of adultery, unless he is in the spiritual purity of chastity? Who can feel the cruelty of revenge, but he that is in good arising from the love of his neighbour. What adulterer, or revengeful person, does not sneer at those who call their delights infernal, and on the other hand the delights of conjugial and neighbourly love celestial, and so on? THIRDLY, *That to be able to confirm whatever a man pleases is not intelligence, but only ingenuity, which may exist even in the most wicked.* There are some very dextrous confirmers, who know no truth, and yet can confirm both truth and falsity. Some of them say, What is truth? Is there any such thing existing? Is not that truth which I make true? Nevertheless, these are thought intelligent in the world, but they are only plasterers of the wall. None are intelligent but those who perceive truth to be truth, and confirm the same by truths continually perceived. These two kinds of men are not easily distinguished, because it is not easy to distinguish between the light of confirmation and the light of the perception of truth; nor does it appear otherwise than that those who are in the light

230

of confirmation are also in the light of the perception of truth ; when, nevertheless, the difference is as great as between the light of infatuation and genuine light; and the light of infatuation in the spiritual world is of such a nature, that it is turned into darkness when genuine light flows in. Such infatuating light have many in hell, who, when they are admitted into genuine light, see nothing at all. Hence it is evident, that to be able to confirm whatever a man pleases, is only ingenuity, attainable even by the most wicked. FOURTHLY, *That there may be intellectual confirmation, and not at the same time voluntary; but that all voluntary confirmation is also intellectual.* Take these examples by way of illustration. Those who confirm faith separate from charity, and yet live the life of charity, and in general those who confirm the falsity of doctrine, and yet do not live according to it, are those who are in intellectual confirmation, and not at the same time in voluntary confirmation; but those who confirm the falsity of doctrine, and live according to it, are those who are in voluntary and at the same time in intellectual confirmation. The reason hereof is, because the understanding does not flow into the will, but the will into the understanding. Hence, also, it is evident what the falsity of evil is, and what the falsity which is not of evil. The reason why the falsity which is not of evil can be conjoined with good, but not the falsity of evil, is, because the former is the falsity in the understanding and not in the will, while the latter is the falsity in the understanding from evil in the will. FIFTHLY, *That the voluntary and at the same time the intellectual confirmation of evil, causes a man to think that self-derived prudence is all, and the Divine Providence nothing; but not the intellectual confirmation of it alone.* There are many who confirm the efficacy of self-derived prudence in themselves from appearances in the world, but yet do not deny the Divine Providence, and theirs is only intellectual confirmation; while with such as deny at the same time the Divine Providence, the confirmation is also voluntary; but the latter, together with persuasion, takes place principally in those who are worshipers of nature, and at the same time worshipers of themselves. SIXTHLY, *That every thing confirmed by the will, and at the same time by the understanding, remains to eternity; but not that which is confirmed by the understanding only;* for that which is of the understanding only, is not within the man, but without him, since it is only in his thought; and nothing enters into a man, and is appropriated to him, but what is received by the will; for this becomes of his life's love. That this abides to eternity, shall be shown in the next number.

319. The reason why every thing confirmed in the will, and at the same time by the understanding, remains to eternity, is, because every one is his own love, and his love is of his will

also, because every man is his own good or his own evil; for all that is called good which is of the love, and that evil which is opposed to it. As a man is his own love, he is also the form of his own love, and may be called the organ of his life's love. It was said above, n. 279, that the affections of a man's love and the thoughts thence derived, are changes and variations of the state and form of the organic substances of his mind, and it shall now be shown what is the nature and quality of those changes. An idea of them may be had from the heart and lungs, because there are alternate expansions and compressions, or dilatations and contractions, which in the heart are called its systole and diastole; and in the lungs respirations, which are reciprocal extensions and retractions, or distensions and coarctations of its lobes: these are the changes and variations of the state of the heart and lungs. The like takes place in the other viscera of the body, and in the parts thereof, by which the blood and animal juices are received and circulated. There are also similar changes and variations of state in the organic forms of the mind, which, as was shown above, are the subjects of a man's affections and thoughts; with this difference, that the expansions and compressions, or reciprocations, of the latter, are respectively in so much greater perfection, that they cannot be expressed in words of natural language, but only in words of spiritual language, which can only import, that they are vortical ingyrations and egyrations, after the manner of perpetual spiral circumflexions, wonderfully confasciculated into forms receptive of life. But the nature of these purely organic substances and forms in the wicked and in the good shall now be explained. With the good they are spirally convoluted forwards, but with the wicked backwards; and those which are spirally convoluted forwards are turned to the Lord, and receive influx from him; but those which are spirally convoluted backwards are turned towards hell, and receive influx from thence. It is to be observed, that in proportion as they are turned backwards, they are open behind, and closed before; but, on the contrary, in proportion as they are turned forwards, they are open before and closed behind. Hence it may appear what kind of form or what kind of organ a wicked man is, and what kind of form or what kind of organ a good man is, and that they are turned contrariwise; and as an inversion once induced cannot be retwisted, it is evident that such as it is when a man dies it remains to eternity. It is the love of the man's will which makes this turning, or which converts and inverts; for, as was said above, every man is his own love. Hence it is, that every one after death goes in the way of his love,—he who is in good love goes to heaven, and he who is in evil love to hell; nor does he rest till he is in that society where his ruling love is:

241

and, what is wonderful, every one knows the way, as though he smelt it.

320. IV. *That if a man would believe, as is the truth, that every thing good and true is from the Lord, and every thing evil and false from hell, he would neither appropriate to himself good, and make it meritorious, nor would he appropriate to himself evil, and make himself guilty of it.* But as these things are contrary to the belief of those who have confirmed in themselves the appearance that wisdom and prudence are from man, and do not flow in according to the state of the mind's organization, treated of above, n. 319, therefore they shall be demonstrated; and that it may be done distinctly, the following order shall be observed:—1. That he that confirms in himself the appearance that wisdom and prudence are from man, and thence in him as his own, cannot see otherwise than that if this were not the case he would not be a man, but either a beast or a statue; when, nevertheless, the contrary is true. 2. That to believe and think, as is the truth, that every thing good and true is from the Lord, and every thing evil and false from hell, appears to be impossible, when, nevertheless, it is truly human and thence angelic. 3. That so to believe and think is impossible to those who do not acknowledge the Lord's divinity, and who do not acknowledge evils to be sins; but that it is possible to those who acknowledge these two things. 4. That those who are in the acknowledgment of these two things only reflect upon evils in themselves, and, in proportion as they shun and hold them in aversion as sins, cast them out from themselves into hell from whence they come. 5. That thus the Divine Providence neither appropriates evil nor good to any one, but that self-derived prudence appropriates both.

321. But these propositions shall be explained in the order proposed. FIRST, *That he that confirms in himself the appearance that wisdom and prudence are from and in man as his own, cannot see otherwise than that if this were not the case he would not be a man, but either a beast or a statue; when, nevertheless, the contrary is true.* It is a law of the Divine Providence, that a man should think as from himself, and should act prudently as from himself, but yet should acknowledge that he does so from the Lord. Hence it follows, that he that thinks and acts prudently as from himself, and, at the same time, acknowledges that he does so from the Lord, is a man; but not he that confirms in himself an idea that all that he thinks and does is from himself; or he that, because he knows that wisdom and prudence are from God, yet waits for influx; for the latter becomes like a statue, and the former like a beast. That he that waits for influx is like a statue, is evident; for he must stand or sit motionless, with his hands hanging down, and his eyes either

shut or wide open without motion, neither thinking nor breathing; and in such case what life is there in him? That he that believes all he thinks and does to be from himself is not unlike a beast, may also be evident; because he thinks only from the natural mind, which every man has in common with beasts, and not from the rational spiritual mind, which is the mind truly human; for this latter mind acknowledges that God alone thinks from himself, and that a man thinks from God; therefore, also, men who think only from the natural mind know no difference between a man and a beast, except that the former speaks and the latter utters sounds, and they imagine that they both die alike. Of those who wait for influx, it may be further observed that, with the exception of a few who from their hearts desire it, they do not receive any influx. These sometimes receive some answer by lively perception in thought, or by tacit speech therein, but rarely by any manifest speech; and then it is to this effect, that they may think and act as they will or as they can, and that he that acts wisely is a wise man, and he that acts foolishly is a fool. They are never instructed what they ought to believe and to do; and this to the end that human rationality and liberty may not be destroyed, which consists in every one's acting from free-will according to reason, in all appearance as from himself. Those who are instructed by influx what they ought to believe and to do, are not instructed by the Lord, or by any angel of heaven, but by some spirit of an enthusiast, Quaker or Moravian, and are seduced. All influx from the Lord is effected by illumination of the understanding, by the affection of truth, and by the influx of the latter into the former. SECONDLY, *That to believe and think, as is the truth, that every thing good and true is from the Lord, and every thing evil and false from hell, appears to be impossible; when, nevertheless, it is truly human and thence angelic.* To believe and think that every thing good and true is from God appears possible, provided nothing further be said; and the reason is, that it is conformable to theological faith, against which it is not allowable to think; but to believe and think that every thing evil and false is from hell appears impossible, because in this case it would also be believed that a man could not think any thing. Yet every man thinks as from himself, although from hell, because it is the gift of the Lord to every one, that thought, whencesoever it comes, shall appear in him as his own; otherwise a man would not live as a man; nor could he be brought out of hell, and introduced into heaven, that is to say, be reformed, as is abundantly shown above. Therefore, also, the Lord grants to every man to know, and thence to think, that he is in hell if he is in evil, and that he thinks from hell if he thinks from evil; he also grants him to think of the means whereby he may escape out of hell, and not think from thence, but enter into

243

Q

heaven, and there think from the Lord : and he gives him freedom of election; from which considerations it may be seen that a man can think what is evil and false as from himself, and can also think that this or that is evil and false; consequently that it is only an appearance that it is from himself, without which appearance he would not be a man. The essential human principle, and thence the angelic, consists in thinking from the truth; and it is the truth, that a man does not think from himself, but that it is granted him by the Lord to think in all appearance as from himself. THIRDLY, *That so to believe and think is impossible to those who do not acknowledge the Lord's divinity, and who do not acknowledge evils to be sins; but that it is possible to those who acknowledge these two things.* The reason why it is impossible to those who do not acknowledge the Lord's divinity, is, because the Lord alone grants to a man to think and will, and those who do not acknowledge the Lord's divinity, being separated from him, imagine that they think from themselves. The reason why it is also impossible to those who do not acknowledge that evils are sins, is, because they think from hell, and every one there supposes that he thinks from himself. That it is possible, however, to those who acknowledge the Lord's divinity, and that evils are sins, may appear from what has been abundantly adduced above, n. 288—294. FOURTHLY, *That those who are in the acknowledgment of those two things, only reflect upon evils in themselves, and in proportion as they shun and hold them in aversion as sins, cast them out into hell from whence they come.* Who does not or may not know, that evil is from hell, and that good is from heaven? Who may not thence know, that in proportion as a man shuns evil and holds it in aversion, he shuns hell and holds it in aversion? And who may not thence know, that in proportion as any one shuns and holds evil in aversion, he wills good and loves it; therefore, that in the same proportion he is brought out of hell by the Lord, and led to heaven? These things every rational man may see plainly, provided he knows that there is a heaven and a hell, and that evil and good have each their separate origin. Now if a man reflects upon evils in himself, which is the same thing as to examine himself, and shuns them, he then disengages himself from hell, casting it behind him, and introduces himself into heaven, where he sees the Lord face to face. It is said that the man does this; but he only does it seemingly from himself, and therefore from the Lord. When a man acknowledges this truth from a good heart and pious faith, it lies inwardly concealed in every thing that he thinks and does afterwards as from himself; like the prolific principle in seed, which internally accompanies it even until the production of new seed; and like the pleasure of appetite for such food as a man has once found to be salutary: in a word, it is like the heart and soul in every thing that he thinks and does. FIFTHLY; *That thus the Divine Providence neither appropriates evil nor good to any one, but that self-derived prudence appropriates both.* This follows as a consequence of all that has been said. The end of the Divine Providence is good; this it consequently intends in every operation; therefore, it does not appropriate good to any one, for thereby such good would become meritorious; neither does it appropriate evil to any one, for thereby it would make him guilty of evil. Yet a man does both from his proprium, because that is nothing but evil; the proprium of his will being self-love, and the proprium of his understanding the pride of self-derived intelligence, and from the latter proceeds self-derived prudence.

THAT EVERY MAN MAY BE REFORMED, AND THAT THERE IS NO SUCH THING AS PREDESTINATION.

322. SOUND reason dictates that all are predestined to heaven and none to hell; for all are born men, and thence the image of God is in them. The image of God in them consists in their being able to understand truth, and to do good; and to be able to understand truth is from the divine wisdom, and to be able to do good is from the divine love. This power is the image of God, which abides in a man of sound mind, and is not eradicated. Hence it is, that he can be made a civil and moral man; and he that is a civil and moral man can also be made spiritual, for what is civil and moral is the receptacle of what is spiritual. He that knows the laws of the kingdom of which he is a citizen, and lives according to them, is called a civil man, and he that makes those laws his morals and his virtues, and lives conformably to them from reason, is called a moral man. I will now tell you how civil and moral life is a receptacle of spiritual life: live according to those laws, considered not only as civil and moral, but also as divine laws, and you will be a spiritual man. There scarcely exists a nation so barbarous as not to have given the sanction of its laws to the prohibition of committing murder, corrupting the wife of another, stealing, false testimony, and the violation of another's rights. These laws are observed by the civil and moral man, in order that he may be, or seem to be, a good citizen; but if he does not at the same time consider these laws as divine, he is only a civil and moral natural man : if he considers them as divine, he becomes a civil and moral spiritual man. The difference is, that the latter is a good citizen not only of an earthly kingdom, but also of the heavenly kingdom; while the former is a good citizen of an earthly kingdom, but not of the heavenly

245

kingdom. The goods which they do distinguish them: the goods which civil and moral natural men do, are not goods in themselves, for the man and the world are in them; whereas the goods which civil and moral spiritual men do, are in themselves goods, because the Lord and heaven are in them. Hence it is evident that every man, since he is born such that he can be made a civil and moral natural man, is also born such that he can be made a civil and moral spiritual man. It is only to acknowledge God, and not to do evils because they are in opposition to God, but to do good because it is agreeable to him. By this, spirit enters into a man's civil and moral actions, and they receive life; but without it there is no spirit in them, and consequently they have no life; therefore the natural man, however civilly and morally he may act, is called dead, but the spiritual man is called alive. It is of the Lord's Divine Providence, that every nation has some religion, and the foundation of all religion is an acknowledgment that there is a God; otherwise it is not called a religion; and every nation, which lives according to its religion, that is, which refrains from evil because it is against its God, receives something spiritual into its natural principle. What person, when he hears any Gentile say he will not do this or that because it is against his God, does not say within himself, Will not this man be saved? It appears as if it could not be otherwise: this sound reason dictates to him. On the other hand, what person when he hears a Christian say, I make no account of this or that evil; what signifies its being said to be against God? does not say within himself, Can this man be saved? It appears as if he could not: this also sound reason dictates. If he says, I was born a Christian, have been baptized, have known the Lord, have read the Word, and received the sacrament; do these things avail any thing, when he breathes murder, or revenge leading to murder, and does not consider as sins adultery, secret theft, false testimony, or lies, and various violences? Does such a one think any thing of God or of life eternal? Does he think that they have any existence? Does not sound reason dictate that such a one cannot be saved? These things are said of the Christian, because the Gentile thinks more of God from religion in his life than the Christian does. But of this more shall be said below, in the following order. I. That the end of creation is a heaven out of the human race. II. That thence it is of the Divine Providence that every man is capable of being saved, and that those are saved who acknowledge a God and lead a good life. III. That it is a man's own fault if he is not saved. IV. That thus all are predestined to heaven, and none to hell.

323. I. *That the end of creation is a heaven out of the human race.* That heaven consists only of such as were born

man, is shown in the work concerning HEAVEN AND HELL, published at London in the year 1758, and also above; and as heaven does not consist of any others, it follows that the end of creation is a heaven out of the human race. That this was the end of creation was indeed shown above, n. 27—45; but the same will be still more manifestly seen from an explanation of the following points. 1. That every man is created to live to eternity. 2. That every man is created to live to eternity in a state of happiness. 3. That therefore every man is created to go to heaven. 4. That the divine love cannot do otherwise than desire it, and that the divine wisdom cannot do otherwise than provide for it.

324. Since from these considerations it may also be seen that the Divine Providence is no other predestination than to heaven, and that it cannot be changed into any other, it is here to be demonstrated, in the order proposed, that the end of creation is a heaven out of the human race. FIRST, *That every man is created to live to eternity.* In the treatise concerning THE DIVINE LOVE AND THE DIVINE WISDOM, Parts III. and V., it is shown that in every man there are three degrees of life, which are called natural, spiritual, and celestial, and that these three degrees are actually in every one; but that in beasts there is only one degree of life, which is similar to the ultimate degree in a man, called natural. From this it follows, that, by the elevation of his life to the Lord, a man is capable, though beasts are not, of being brought into such a state as to be able to understand those things which are of the divine wisdom, and to will those things which are of the divine love, consequently to receive the divine influence; and he that can receive the Divine influence, so as to see and perceive it in himself, cannot be otherwise than conjoined with the Lord, and from that conjunction cannot but live to eternity. What would the Lord be, with all his creation of the universe, if he had not also created images and likenesses of himself, to whom he might communicate his divine influence? In any other case, would it not be like causing something to be and not to be, or to exist and not to exist, and this for no other purpose but that he might contemplate at a distance a mere shifting of scenes and continual variations as upon a theatre? To what purpose would the divine principle be in men, were it not to the end that they might serve as subjects to receive it more nearly, and to see and feel it? And as the Divine Being is a being of inexhaustible glory, is it likely that he would keep it to himself, or indeed could he? For love wishes to communicate its own to another,—to give, indeed, as much of its own as it can; and what then must the Divine Love do, which is infinite? Can such love give, and then take away again? Would not this be giving what is to perish, which in itself internally is not any

247

thing, because when it perishes it becomes nothing, there not being in it that which really exists? but He gives what really exists, or what does not cease to be, and that is eternal. In order that every man may live to eternity, that which is mortal about him is taken away, namely, his material body, which is taken away by death: thus his immortal part, which is his mind, is stripped naked, and then he becomes a spirit in a human form, his mind being that spirit. That the mind or man cannot die, the sages or wise men of antiquity saw very plainly; for they said, How can the soul or mind die, when it has the faculty of acquiring wisdom? Their interior idea on this subject is known only to few at this day; but it descended into their common perception from heaven, and was this,—that God is wisdom itself, of which man is a partaker, and that God is immortal or eternal. As it has been permitted me to converse with angels, I will also relate something on this subject from experience. I have conversed with some who lived many years ago, with some who lived before the deluge and some after it, with some who lived in the Lord's time, with one of his apostles, and with many who lived in the succeeding ages: they all seemed like men of a middle age, and said that they know not what death is, but only that there is such a thing as damnation. All indeed who have led a good life, when they go to heaven, enter into their juvenile age in the world, and continue in it to eternity, even though they were old and decrepit in the world; and women, although they had been wrinkled and antiquated, return to the flower of their youth and beauty. That every man after death lives to eternity is evident from the Word, where life in heaven is called life everlasting; as in Matthew xix. 29; xxv. 46; Mark x. 17; Luke x. 25; xviii. 30; John iii. 15, 16, 36; v. 24, 25, 39; vi. 27, 40, 68; xii. 50; also, simply, life, Matt. xviii. 8, 9; John v. 40; xx. 31. The Lord said also to his disciples, "Because I live, ye shall live also," John xiv. 19; and concerning the resurrection, that God is the God of the living, and not the God of the dead; also, that they cannot die any more (Luke xx. 36, 38). SECONDLY, *That every man is created to live to eternity in a state of happiness*, follows of course; for he that wills that every man should live to eternity, wills also that he should live in a state of happiness. What would eternal life be without it? All love wills or desires the good of another. The love of parents desires the good of children; the love of the bridegroom and the husband desires the good of the bride and the wife; and the love of friendship desires the good of friends: what then must not the divine love do? And what is good but delight? what divine good but eternal beatitude? All good is called good from its delight or beatitude. All indeed which is given and possessed is called good; but unless it be also delightful, it is sterile good, which is not good in itself. Hence it appears that eternal life is also eternal happiness. This state of man is the end and purpose of creation. That only those who go to heaven are in this state, is not the Lord's fault, but man's. That the fault is in man will be seen in what follows. THIRDLY, *That therefore every man is created to go to heaven.* This is the end of creation; but the reason why all do not go to heaven, is, because they imbibe the delights of hell, which are opposite to the beatitude of heaven; and those who are not in the beatitude of heaven cannot enter into heaven, for they cannot bear it. No one who enters the spiritual world is refused the liberty of ascending into heaven; but he that, when he comes there, is in the delight of hell, has a palpitation at his heart, labours in his breathing, begins to lose all life, is in anguish and torment, and rolls himself about like a serpent laid before the fire: this is the case, because opposites act against each other. Notwithstanding, as they were born men, and thence in the faculty of thinking and willing, consequently in the faculty of speaking and acting, they cannot die; but as they cannot live with any but those who are in a similar delight of life, they are sent to them; those who are in the delights of evil, and those who are in the delights of good, being respectively remanded to those who are like themselves. It is even allowed to every one to be in the delight of his evil, provided he does not infest those who are in the delight of good: but as evil cannot do otherwise than infest good, for in evil there is hatred against good, therefore lest they should do mischief, they are removed, and cast down into their proper places in hell, where their delight is turned to what is undelightful. This however does not prevent a man from being by creation, consequently by birth, of such a quality that he may go to heaven; for every one that dies an infant goes to heaven, is educated and instructed there as a man is in the world, and by the affection of good and truth imbibes wisdom and becomes an angel. The same might be the case with a man that is educated and instructed in the world; for the same capability which is in an infant is in him. Concerning infants in the spiritual world, see the work on HEAVEN AND HELL, published in London in 1758, n. 329—345. The reason why it is not the same with many in the world, is, because they love the first degree of their life, called the natural degree, and will not recede from it and become spiritual; and the natural degree of life, considered in itself, loves nothing but self and the world; for it coheres with the bodily senses, which also communicate with the world: but the spiritual degree of life, considered in itself, loves the Lord and heaven, and also itself and the world; yet God and heaven as superior, principal, and governing, and self and the world as inferior, instrumental,

249

and subservient. FOURTHLY, *That the Divine Love cannot do otherwise than will it, and that the Divine Wisdom cannot do otherwise than provide for it.* That the Divine Essence is divine love and divine wisdom, was fully shown in the treatise concerning THE DIVINE LOVE AND THE DIVINE WISDOM. It is also demonstrated there, n. 358—370, that in every human embryo the Lord forms two receptacles,—one of the divine love, and the other of the divine wisdom,—the receptacle of divine love for the man's future will, and the receptacle of divine wisdom for his future understanding, and that thus he endows every man with a faculty of willing good and of understanding truth. Now as every man has these two faculties given him from his birth by the Lord, and thence the Lord is in them as in his own in the man, it is evident that his divine love cannot will otherwise than that every man should go to heaven and there enjoy eternal beatitude, and also that his divine wisdom cannot do otherwise than provide for it. As, however, it is of his divine love that a man should feel heavenly beatitude in himself as his own, and this cannot be done unless he is kept perfectly in the appearance that he thinks, wills, speaks, and acts from himself, therefore the Lord cannot lead him any otherwise than according to the laws of his Divine Providence.

325. II. *That thence it is of the Divine Providence that every man is capable of being saved, and that those are saved who acknowledge a God and lead a good life.* That every one is capable of being saved is evident from what has been demonstrated above. Some are of opinion that the church of the Lord is only in the Christian world, because the Lord is known there only, and the Word is there only; yet there are many who believe that the church of God is common, or extended and spread over the whole earth, consequently among those likewise who are ignorant of the Lord, and have not the Word; urging, that this is not their fault, that there is no help for their ignorance, and that it is not consistent with the love and mercy of the Lord that any one should be born for hell, when they are nevertheless all equally men. Now as there is a belief among Christians,— among many at least, if not among all,—that the church is common, and it is also called a communion, it follows that there are some very common or general essentials of the church, which are the constituents of all religions, and form such communion. That these most common or general essentials are the acknowledgment of a God, and the good of life, will be seen in the following order. 1. That the acknowledgment of a God effects a conjunction of God with man, and of man with God, and that the denial of a God produces a disjunction. 2. That every one acknowledges God, and is joined to him, according to the good of his life. 3 That the good of life, or to live well, is to shun

evils because they are contrary to religion, therefore against God. 4. That these are the common essentials of all religions, by which every one may be saved.

326. But these propositions are to be viewed and demonstrated separately. I. *That the acknowledgment of a God effects a conjunction of God with man, and of man with God, and that the denial of a God produces a disjunction.* Some may think that those who do not acknowledge a God can be saved as well as those who do, provided they lead a moral life; saying, What does acknowledgment signify? Does it not consist in thought only? Cannot I easily acknowledge, when I know for certain, that there is a God? I have heard of him, but I never saw him: let me see him, and I will believe. Such is the language of many who deny God, when it is permitted them to reason freely with one who acknowledges God. But that the acknowledgment of a God conjoins, and the denial of a God separates, shall be illustrated by some particulars known to me in the spiritual world. In that world, when any one thinks of another and desires to speak with him, the other is immediately present. This is common in the spiritual world, and never fails; the reason of which is, that in that world there is no distance, as in the natural world, but only an appearance of it. Another particular is, that as thought from some knowledge of another causes his presence, so love from some affection for another, causes conjunction with him, by which it comes to pass that they go together, converse in a friendly manner, dwell in one house or in one society, often meet, and do mutual good offices to each other. The reverse also takes place; for he that does not love another, more especially he that hates another, does not see or meet him, and the distance between them is in proportion to the degree in which there is a want of love, or in which hatred prevails. Even if he is present, and then remembers his hatred, he becomes invisible. From these particulars it may appear what is the cause of presence and of conjunction in the spiritual world, namely, that presence proceeds from the remembrance of another with a desire to see him, and conjunction proceeds from the affection which is of love. It is the same with all things which are in the human mind: therein are things innumerable, and all the particulars there are consociated or conjoined according to affections, or as one thing loves another. This is spiritual conjunction, which is like itself both in things general and in things particular. This spiritual conjunction derives its origin from the conjunction of the Lord with the spiritual world and the natural world, in general and in particular. From this consideration it is evident, that in proportion as any one acknowledges the Lord, and thinks of him from knowledge, the Lord is present; and in proportion as any one acknowledges him from the affection of love, the Lord

251

is conjoined with him: on the contrary, that in proportion as any one does not acknowledge the Lord, the Lord is absent; and in proportion as any one denies him, he is separated from him. Conjunction causes the Lord to turn the face of a man to himself, and then to lead him; and disjunction causes hell to turn the face of a man to itself, and to lead him: all the angels of heaven, therefore, turn their faces to the Lord as the sun, and all the spirits of hell turn away their faces from the Lord. Hence is evident what is the effect produced by the acknowledgment of a God, and what by the denial of a God. Those also who deny God in the world, deny him after death, becoming organized according to the description above, n. 319; and the organization induced in the world remains to eternity. SECONDLY, *That every one acknowledges God, and is conjoined with him, according to the good of his life.* All who know any thing of religion may know God. They can also speak of God from science or the memory, and some even think of God from the understanding; but this, unless a man leads a good life, produces nothing but presence; for he can turn himself from God notwithstanding, and turn himself to hell, which is the case if he leads a bad life. None can acknowledge God in their hearts except those who lead a good life; and these, according to the good of their life, the Lord turns away from hell, and turns to himself. The reason is, because these alone love God; for they love divine things, which are from him, by doing them. The divine things, which are from God, are the precepts of his law; and these are God, because he is his own proceeding divine. As this is to love God, therefore the Lord says, "He that keepeth my commandments, he it is that loveth me; and he that loveth me not keepeth not my sayings" (John xiv. 21—24). This is the reason why there are two tables of the Decalogue,—one for God and the other for man. God continually operates, that a man may receive the things which are in his table; but if he does not the things which are in his table, he does not receive with acknowledgment of heart the things which are in God's table; and if he does not receive them, he is not conjoined. Therefore those two tables were joined together, that they might be one, and were called the tables of the covenant; and covenant signifies conjunction. The reason why every one acknowledges God, and is conjoined with him according to the good of his life, is, because good of life is similar to the good which is in the Lord, and which therefore is from the Lord; consequently, when a man is in the good of life, conjunction is effected. It is the contrary with evil of life; for this rejects the Lord. THIRDLY, *That the good of life, or to live well, is to shun evils because they are contrary to religion, therefore against God.* That this is the good of life, or to live well, is fully shown in THE DOCTRINE OF LIFE FOR THE NEW JERU

252

SALEM, from beginning to end. To which I will only add, that if you do good in all abundance; if, for example, you build churches, adorn and fill them with donations, lay out money in hospitals and charities, give alms daily, help widows and orphans, regularly perform the ceremonies of divine worship, if even you think, speak, and preach things holy as from the heart, and yet do not shun evils as sins against God, all those goods are not goods, but are either hypocritical or meritorious; for there is inwardly evil in them notwithstanding, since the life of every one is in all and every thing that he does. Goods are no otherwise made goods than by the removal of evil from them. Hence it is evident, that to shun evils because they are contrary to religion, and therefore against God, is to live well. FOURTHLY, *That these are the common essentials of all religions, by which every one may be saved.* To acknowledge a God, and not to do evil because it is against God, are the two things by virtue of which religion is religion. If one of them is wanting, it cannot be called religion; for to acknowledge a God and to do evil is contradictory, as well as to do good and not to acknowledge a God: one does not take place without the other. It is provided by the Lord that there is some religion almost everywhere, and that in every religion there are these two essentials. It is provided by the Lord that every one who acknowledges a God, and abstains from evil because it is against God, has a place in heaven; for heaven in the complex resembles one man, whose life or soul is the Lord. In that celestial man·there are all things which are in a natural man; with that difference which exists between things celestial and natural. It is well known that in a man there are not only organized forms, consisting of blood-vessels and nervous fibres, which are called viscera, but also skins, membranes, tendons, cartilages, bones, nails, and teeth, which have life in a less degree than the organized forms themselves, to which they serve as ligaments, teguments, and supports. That celestial man, which is heaven, in order that there may be all these parts in him, cannot be composed of men all of one religion, but of men of different religions; and hence, all who apply to their lives those two universals of the church have a place in that celestial man, that is, in heaven, and there enjoy felicity, each in his degree; but on this subject·see more above, n. 254. That these two essentials are primary in every religion may appear from their being the two essentials which the Decalogue teaches; and the Decalogue was primary in the Word, being promulgated from Mount Sinai by Jehovah *viva voce*, and written upon two tables of stone by the finger of God; then, being deposited in the ark, it was called Jehovah, and constituted the holy of holies in the tabernacle and the most sacred place in the temple at Jerusalem; and all things there derived their sanctity from it alone. Con-

253

cerning the Decalogue in the ark, more may be seen from the Word in THE DOCTRINE OF LIFE FOR THE NEW JERUSALEM, n. 53—61; to which I will add as follows: it is known from the Word that the ark, in which were the two tables whereupon the Decalogue was written, was taken by the Philistines, and placed in the temple of Dagon, in Ashdod; that Dagon fell down before it to the earth; that afterwards his head and the palms of his hands were separated from his body, and lay upon the threshold of the temple; that the Ashdodites and Ekronites, by reason of the ark, were smitten with emerods to the number of several thousands, and that their country was wasted by mice; also, that the Philistines, by the advice of the chiefs of their nation, made five emerods, five golden mice, and a new cart, upon which they set the ark, with the emerods and golden mice beside it, and sent back the ark, by two kine, which lowed in the way before it, to the children of Israel, by whom the kine and the cart were sacrificed. See 4 Sam. chaps. v. and vi. It shall now be shown what all these particulars signified. The Philistines signified those who are in faith separate from charity: Dagon represented their religion; the emerods, whereby they were smitten, signified natural loves, which when separated from spiritual love are unclean; the mice signified the devastation of the church by falsifications of truth; the new cart upon which they sent back the ark, signified new, but natural, doctrine, for chariot in the Word signifies doctrine grounded in spiritual truths; the kine signified good natural affections; the golden emerods signified natural loves purified and made good; the golden mice signified the vastation of the church removed by good, for gold in the Word signifies good; the lowing of the kine in the way signified the difficult conversion of the concupiscences of evil in the natural man into good affections; and the offering the kine with the cart, as a burnt-offering, signified that thus atonement would be made to the Lord. These are the things which are spiritually meant by those historical facts: connect them into one sense, and make the application. That by the Philistines are represented those who are in faith separate from charity may be seen in THE DOCTRINE OF THE NEW JERUSALEM CONCERNING FAITH, n. 49—54; and that the ark, by reason of the Decalogue therein contained, was the most holy thing of the church, see the DOCTRINE OF LIFE FOR THE NEW JERUSALEM, n. 53—61.

327. III. *That it is a man's own fault if he is not saved.* This truth is acknowledged by every rational man as soon as it is heard, viz. that evil cannot flow from good, or good from evil, because they are opposites; consequently, that from good nothing but good can flow, and from evil nothing but evil. When this truth is acknowledged, the following is acknowledged also, viz. that good can be turned into evil, not by a good but by an

evil recipient; for every form turns what is influent into its own quality. See above, n. 292. Now as the Lord is good in its very essence, or good itself, it is evident that evil cannot flow from him, or be produced by him; but that it can be turned into evil by a recipient subject, whose form is a form of evil. Such a subject is every man with respect to his proprium, which continually receives good from the Lord, and continually turns it into the quality of its form, which is a form of evil. Hence it follows that it is a man's own fault if he is not saved. Evil is indeed from hell; yet as a man receives it thence as his own, and thereby appropriates it to himself, it makes no difference whether you say that evil is from man or from hell. But whence there is an appropriation of evil in such a degree that religion perishes, shall be shown in the following series. 1. That every religion, in process of time, decreases, and is consummated. 2. That every religion decreases and is consummated by an inversion of the image of God in man. 3. That this takes place from a continual accumulation of hereditary evil in successive generations. 4. That it is nevertheless provided by the Lord, that every one is capable of being saved. 5. That it is also provided that a new church should succeed in place of the former vastated church.

328. These propositions are to be demonstrated in their series. FIRST, *That every religion in process of time decreases and is consummated.* Upon this earth there have been several churches, one after another; since, wherever the human race exists, there a church exists; for, as was demonstrated above, heaven, which is the end of creation, consists of the human race; and no one can enter heaven unless he be in the two universals of the church, which, as is shown above, n. 326, are the acknowledgment of a God, and the leading of a good life; hence it follows that there have been churches upon this earth from the most ancient times down to the present. These churches are described in the Word, but not historically, with the exception of the Israelitish and Jewish church, before which, nevertheless, there existed several that are only described in the Word under the names of nations and persons, and certain particulars concerning them. The most ancient church, which was the first, is described by Adam and his wife Eve. The succeeding church, which is to be called the ancient church, is described by Noah and his three sons, and their posterity. This was extensive and spread over many kingdoms of Asia, namely, the land of Canaan on both sides Jordan, Syria, Assyria and Chaldea, Mesopotamia, Egypt, Arabia, Tyre and Sidon; and among these was the ancient Word, mentioned in THE DOCTRINE OF THE NEW JERUSALEM CONCERNING THE SACRED SCRIPTURE, n. 101—103. That such church existed in those kingdoms is evident from various particulars recorded concerning

them in the prophetic parts of the Word. That church, however, was remarkably changed by Eber, from whom the Hebrew church had its origin; in which latter sacrificial worship was first instituted. From the Hebrew church sprang the Israelitish and Jewish church, established with much solemnity for the sake of the Word which was therein to be written. These four churches are meant by the image seen by Nebuchadnezzar in a dream, whose head was of pure gold, the breast and arms of silver, the belly and thighs of brass, and the legs and feet of iron and clay (Dan. ii. 32, 33). The same is meant by the golden, silver, copper, and iron ages mentioned by ancient writers. That the Christian church succeeded the Jewish church is well known; and it may be seen from the Word that all these churches respectively declined in process of time, till there was an end of them, which is called the consummation. The consummation of the most ancient church, which was occasioned by eating of the tree of knowledge, whereby is signified the pride of self-derived intelligence, is described by the deluge. The consummation of the ancient church is described by various devastations of the nations treated of in the historical as well as in the prophetical parts of the Word, especially by the casting out of the nations from the land of Canaan by the children of Israel. The consummation of the Israelitish and Jewish church is understood by the destruction of the temple at Jerusalem; by the carrying away of the Israelitish people into perpetual captivity, and of the Jewish nation to Babylon; and, lastly, by the second destruction of the temple, also of Jerusalem at the same time, and the dispersion of that nation; which consummation is foretold in many places in the prophets, and in Daniel ix. 24—27. The successive vastation of the Christian church, to its final period, is described by the Lord, in Matthew xxiv., Mark xiii., and Luke xxi.; and the consummation itself in the Apocalypse. Hence it may appear that in process of time the church decreases and is consummated; and that it is the same with religion. SECONDLY, *That every religion decreases and is consummated by an inversion of the image of God in man.* It is well known that man was created in the image of God according to the likeness of God (Genesis i. 26): it shall now be explained what an image of God is, and what a likeness of God. God alone is love and wisdom; and man was created that he might be a receptacle of both,—that his will might be a receptacle of divine love, and his understanding a receptacle of divine wisdom. That these two principles are in man from creation, that they constitute the man, and that they are also formed in every one in the womb, was shown above. Man, then, is an image of God by his being a recipient of divine wisdom, and a likeness of God by his being a recipient of divine love; therefore the receptacle which is called the understanding is an image of God, and the receptacle which is called the will is a likeness of God; and since man was created and formed to be a receptacle, it follows that he was created and formed that his will might receive love from God, and his understanding wisdom from God. These a man receives, when he acknowledges God, and lives according to his commandments; but in a greater or less degree in proportion as by religion he knows God and his commandments, consequently, in proportion as he knows truths; for truths teach what God is and how he is to be acknowledged, also what his commandments are, and how a man is to live according to them. The image and likeness of God, although seemingly, are not actually destroyed in man; for they remain inherent in his two faculties called liberty and rationality, which have been abundantly treated of above. They became seemingly destroyed, when he made the receptacle of the divine love, which is his will, a receptacle of self-love, and the receptacle of the divine wisdom, which is his understanding, a receptacle of self-derived intelligence. He thereby inverted the image and likeness of God; for he turned those receptacles away from God, and turned them to himself. Hence it is, that they are closed above and opened below, or closed before and opened behind, when nevertheless by creation they were open before and closed behind; and when they are thus inversely opened and closed, the receptacle of love, or the will, receives influx from hell or from its proprium, and so also does the receptacle of wisdom, or the understanding. Hence arose in the churches the worship of men instead of the worship of God, and worship grounded in doctrines of falsity instead of that grounded in doctrines of truth,—the latter from self-derived intelligence, the former from self-love. From these considerations it is evident, that religion in process of time decreases and is consummated by an inversion of the image of God in man. THIRDLY, *That this takes place from a continual accumulation of hereditary evil in successive generations.* It was stated and shown above, that hereditary evil is not from Adam and his wife Eve in consequence of their eating of the tree of knowledge, but that it is successively derived from parents and transplanted into their offspring, thus by continual additions is augmented from generation to generation. When evil is thereby accumulated among many, it spreads and extends itself to others; for in all evil there is a lust of seducing, which in some is ardent in consequence of their rage against what is good; and thence proceeds the contagion of evil. When this has invaded the dignitaries, rulers, and leading men in the church, religion is perverted, and the means of cure, which are truths, are corrupted by falsifications; hence in such case proceed the successive vastation of good and desolation of truth in the church, until the consummation is complete. FOURTHLY, *That nevertheless it is provided by the Lord, that every one is*

257

capable of being saved. It is provided by the Lord that there should be a religion everywhere, and that in every religion there should be the two essentials of salvation, which consist in acknowledging a God, and in not doing evil because it is against God. Other things appertaining to the understanding and thence to the thought, which are called matters of faith, are provided for every one according to his life, for they are accessories to life; and if they precede, still they do not receive life before. It is also provided that all who have lived well and acknowledged a God should be instructed after death by the angels; and then those who have been in these two essentials of religion in this world accept the truths of the church, such as they are in the Word, and acknowledge the Lord as the God of heaven and the church; which doctrine they receive more readily than Christians who have carried out of the world with them an idea of the Lord's humanity separate from his divinity. It is moreover provided by the Lord, that all who die in their infancy, wherever they may be born, should be saved. There is also given to every man after death an opportunity of amending his life, if possible. All are instructed and led of the Lord by angels; and as they then know that they are living after death, and that there are such places as heaven and hell, they at first receive truths; but those who have not acknowledged a God, and shunned evils as sins in this world, are in a short time after disgusted with truths, and recede: those who have acknowledged them with their mouths, and not in their hearts, being like the foolish virgins, who had lamps, but no oil, and sought oil of others, and also went and bought it, yet were not admitted to the marriage. Lamps signify the truths of faith, and oil signifies the good of charity. Hence it may appear, that by the Divine Providence every one is capable of being saved, and that it is a man's own fault if he is not saved. FIFTHLY, *That it is also provided that a New Church should succeed in place of the former vastated church.* This has been the case from the most ancient times, namely, that when a former church was vastated, a new one succeeded. After the most ancient church the ancient church succeeded; after the ancient, the Israelitish or Jewish; after that, the Christian church; and that after this last, a New Church will succeed is foretold in the Apocalypse, in which such church is signified by the New Jerusalem descending from heaven. The reason why a New Church is provided by the Lord to succeed the former vastated church, may be seen in THE DOCTRINE OF THE NEW JERUSALEM CONCERNING THE SACRED SCRIPTURE, n. 104—113.

329. IV. *That thus all are predestined to heaven, and none to hell.* That the Lord casts none into hell, but that the spirit casts himself thither, is shown in the work concerning HEAVEN AND HELL, published in London in the year 1758, n. 545—550

This is the case with every wicked and impious person after death, and it is the same with the wicked and impious in this world; with this difference, that in this world they may be reformed and embrace and imbibe the means of salvation, but not so after their departure out of the world. The means of salvation relate to these two things,—the shunning of evils because they are contrary to the divine laws in the Decalogue, and the acknowledgment that there is a God. This every one may do, provided he does not love evils; for the Lord flows continually with power into the will that he may be able to shun evils, and with power into the understanding that he may be able to think that there is a God; yet no person can do the one without at the same time doing the other: these two things are joined together like the two tables of the Decalogue: of which one is for the Lord, and the other for man. The Lord from his table illuminates every one, and gives power; but in proportion as a man does the things which are in his own table, he receives power and illumination: before this the two appear as if they were laid upon one another and sealed up; but as a man does the things which are in his table, they are disclosed and opened. What is the Decalogue at this day but as a book that is shut, or open only in the hands of infants and children? Tell any one who is of an advanced age, You must not do such a thing, because it is contrary to the Decalogue,—and who attends to you? but if you say, Do not such a thing, because it is contrary to the divine laws, this he can attend to; and yet the precepts of the Decalogue are the very essential divine laws. An experiment was made with several in the spiritual world, who, when the Decalogue or catechism was repeated, rejected it with contempt; the reason of which is, that the Decalogue in its second table, which is man's table, teaches that evils are to be shunned; and he that does not shun them, whether from impiety or from a religious notion that works are of no avail, but faith only, when the Decalogue or catechism is repeated, hears it with some contempt, as though he heard mention made of some child's book, which is no longer of any use to him. These particulars are stated in order that it may be known, that there is not wanting to any man a knowledge of the means by which he may be saved, or the power of being saved if he will; from which it follows, that all are predestined for heaven, and none for hell. As however there prevails among some a belief in predestination to no salvation, which is damnation, and as such a belief is hurtful, and cannot be dispelled unless reason also sees the madness and cruelty of it, therefore it shall be treated of in the following series. 1. That any other predestination than predestination to heaven, is contrary to the divine love and its infinity. 2. That any other predestination than predestination to heaven is contrary to the divine wisdom and its infinity. 3. That it is an insane heresy to suppose that those only are saved who are born within the church. 4. That it is a cruel heresy to suppose that any of the human race are predestined to be damned.

330. That it may appear how hurtful is a faith in predestination, as commonly understood, these four propositions shall be resumed and confirmed. FIRST, *That any other predestination than predestination to heaven, is contrary to the divine love, which is infinite.* That Jehovah, or the Lord, is divine love, and that the divine love is infinite, and the *esse* of all life; also, that man was created in the image of God according to the likeness of God, is demonstrated in the treatise concerning THE DIVINE LOVE AND THE DIVINE WISDOM. Since also every man is formed in the womb in that image according to that likeness by the Lord, as is also demonstrated, it follows, that the Lord is the heavenly Father of all men, and that men are his spiritual children. So is Jehovah or the Lord called in the Word, and so are men called therein; therefore he says, "Call no man your Father upon the earth; for one is your Father, which is in heaven" (Matt. xxiii. 9); by which is meant that He alone is the Father as to life, and that an earthly father is only such as to the covering of life, which is the body. In heaven, therefore, no other Father is made mention of than the Lord. That men, who do not invert that life, are called his sons, and said to be born of him, is also evident from many passages in the Word. Hence it may appear, that the Divine Love is in every man, the wicked as well as the good; consequently, that the Lord who is divine love, cannot act any otherwise with them than as a father upon earth does with his children, only with infinitely more tenderness, because the divine love is infinite; also, that he cannot recede from any one, because the life of every one is from him. It appears as if he receded from the wicked, whereas it is the wicked themselves who recede; but still out of love he leads them: therefore the Lord says, "Ask, and it shall be given you; seek, and ye shall find; knock, and it shall be opened unto you. What man is there of you, who if his son ask bread, will give him a stone? If ye then, being evil, know how to give good gifts unto your children, how much more will your Father who is in the heavens give good things to them that ask him?" (Matt vii. 7—11); and in another place, that "he maketh his sun to rise on the evil and on the good, and sendeth rain on the just and on the unjust" (Matt. v. 45). Moreover, it is well known in the church that the Lord desires the salvation of all, and not the death of any. Hence it may be seen that any other predestination than predestination to heaven is contrary to the divine love. SECONDLY. *That any other predestination than predestination to heaven, is contrary to the divine wisdom, which is infinite.* The divine love through its divine wisdom

provides means by which every man may be saved; therefore to say that there is any other predestination than predestination to heaven, is to say that it cannot provide means by which salvation may be effected, when, nevertheless, as was shown above, all are possessed of the means, and these are from the Divine Providence, which is infinite. The reason why there are some who are not saved, is, because the divine love desires that a man should feel in himself the felicity and bliss of heaven, for otherwise it would be no heaven to him; and this cannot be effected unless it appear to him that he thinks and wills from himself; for without that appearance nothing could be appropriated to him, nor would he be a man. For this reason there is a Divine Providence, which is of the divine wisdom from the divine love. By this, however, is not taken away the truth that all are predestined for heaven, and none for hell; yet it would be taken away if the means of salvation were wanting. But it was shown above, that the means of salvation are provided for every one, and that heaven is of such a nature that all who live well, of whatever religion they be, may have a place there. A man is like the earth, which produces all kinds of fruits, and by virtue of which faculty earth is earth; but its producing evil fruit does not take away its power of producing good fruit also, which would be taken away, however, if it could only produce evil fruit. A man may also be compared to an object which variegates the rays of light in itself: if this presents to the eye disagreeable colors only, it is not the fault of the light; for its rays may also be variegated to produce pleasing colors. THIRDLY, *That to suppose that those only are saved who are born within the church is an insane heresy.* Those who are born without the church are men as well as those who are within it; they are of the same heavenly origin, and are equally living and immortal souls; they have a religion by which they acknowledge that there is a God, and that they ought to live well; and, as was shown above, he that acknowledges a God and lives well, becomes spiritual in his degree, and is saved. It is alleged that they are not baptized; but baptism does not save any except those who are spiritually washed, that is, regenerated; for baptism is a sign and memorial thereof. It is alleged also that the Lord is not known to them, and that without the Lord there is no salvation; yet no one has salvation merely by the Lord's being known to him, but by living according to his precepts; and the Lord is known to every one who acknowledges a God, for he is the God of heaven and earth, as he himself teaches in Matt. xxviii. 18; and other places. Besides, those who are without the church have an idea of God as a man more than the Christians; and those who have this idea, and live well, are accepted by the Lord, for they acknowledge God to be one in person and in essence, which Christians do not.

They also think of God in their life; for they consider evils as sins against God, and those who do this think of God in their life.   Christians have the precepts of their religion from the Word; but there are few who draw any precepts of life from it. The Papists do not read it; and those of the Reformed Church who are in faith separate from charity do not attend to those things in it which relate to life, but only to those which relate to faith, and yet the whole Word is nothing else but the doctrine of life.   Christianity prevails only in Europe; the religion of the Mahometans and Gentiles in Asia, the Indies, Africa, and America; and the human race in the last-mentioned parts of the world is ten times more numerous than in the Christian countries, yet in the latter there are but few who place religion in a good life: what then can be greater madness than to think that the latter only are saved, and the former condemned, or that a man possesses heaven by his birth, and not by his life? Therefore the Lord says, "I say unto you, that many shall come from the east and west, and shall sit down with Abraham, Isaac, and Jacob in the kingdom of heaven; but the children of the kingdom shall be cast out" (Matt. viii. 11, 12). FOURTHLY, *That to suppose any of the human race are predestined to be damned is a cruel heresy.*   For it is cruel to think that the Lord, who is love itself and mercy itself, would suffer so vast a multitude of men to be born for hell, or that so many myriads of myriads should be born condemned and devoted, that is, born devils and satans; and that he would not out of his divine wisdom provide that those who live well and acknowledge a God should not be cast into everlasting fire and torment. The Lord is the Creator and Saviour of all; He alone leads all, and wills not the death of any one: therefore it is cruel to think and believe that so great a multitude of nations and people under his auspices and inspection should be predestined to be delivered as a prey to the devil.

THAT THE LORD CANNOT ACT AGAINST THE LAWS OF THE DIVINE PROVIDENCE, BECAUSE TO ACT AGAINST THEM WOULD BE TO ACT AGAINST HIS DIVINE LOVE AND HIS DIVINE WISDOM, CONSEQUENTLY AGAINST HIMSELF.

331. IN THE ANGELIC WISDOM CONCERNING THE DIVINE LOVE AND THE DIVINE WISDOM, it is shown that the Lord is divine love and divine wisdom, and that these two principles are the very *esse* and life from which every thing is and lives. It is shown, also, that the same proceed from him, and that this proceeding divine is Himself.   Among the things which proceed from him the Divine Providence is primary; for this is

continually in the end for which the universe was created. The operation and progression of the end by its means is what is called the Divine Providence. Now as the proceeding divine is himself, and the Divine Providence is the primary thing that proceeds, it follows, that to act against the laws of his Divine Providence is to act against himself. It may also be said that the Lord is Providence, as it is said that God is order; for the Divine Providence is the divine order primarily respecting the salvation of men; and as there is no order without laws, for laws constitute it, and every law derives this from order that it also is order, it follows, that as God is order, he is also the law of his own order. The same may be said of the Divine Providence, that as the Lord is his own providence, he is also the law of his own providence. Hence it is evident that the Lord cannot act against the laws of his Divine Providence, because to act against them would be to act against himself. Now there can be no operation but upon a subject, and by means operating upon that subject; operation, except upon a subject, and upon that by certain means, is impossible; and the subject of the Divine Providence is man; the means are divine truths whereby he has wisdom, and divine goods whereby he has love; and the Divine Providence by these means operates its end, which is man's salvation; for he that wills an end, also wills means. Therefore when he effects the end, he effects it by means. These particulars, however, will be made more evident when they are reviewed in the following order. I. That the operation of the Divine Providence in saving a man begins at his birth, continues to the end of his life, and afterwards to eternity. II. That the operation of the Divine Providence is continually effected by means out of pure mercy. III. That momentaneous salvation from immediate mercy is impossible. IV. That momentaneous salvation from immediate mercy is the fiery flying serpent in the church.

332. I. *That the operation of the Divine Providence in saving a man begins at his birth, continues to the end of his life, and afterwards to eternity.* It was shown above that a heaven out of the human race is the very end of the creation of the universe; that this end in its operation and progression is the Divine Providence for the salvation of men; and that all things which are without man and serve for his use are secondary ends of creation, which in the aggregate have relation to all things that exist in the three kingdoms—the animal, vegetable, and mineral. When these things constantly proceed according to the laws of divine order established at their first creation, how can the primary end, which is the salvation of the human race, proceed otherwise than constantly according to the laws of its order, which are the laws of the Divine Providence? Only observe a fruit tree; does it not first spring from a small seed as a

263

tender germ, afterwards grow successively into a stalk, spread forth its branches, which are then covered with leaves, and afterwards put forth flowers and bear fruit, wherein it deposits new seeds, by which it provides for its perpetuity? It is the same with every shrub and herb of the field. Do not all and singular things therein constantly and wonderfully proceed according to the laws of their order from end to end? Why then should not the primary end, which is a heaven out of the human race, do the same? Can any thing possibly take place in its progression which does not most constantly proceed according to the laws of the Divine Providence? As there is a correspondence between the life of a man and the vegetation of a tree, draw a parallel or comparison. A man's infancy may be compared to the tender germ of a tree springing out of the earth from the seed; his childhood and youth, to that germ increasing to a stem and branches; natural truths, which every man first imbibes, to the leaves with which its branches are covered, leaves having no other signification in the Word; a man's initiation into the marriage of good and truth, or the spiritual marriage, to the flowers which that tree produces in the spring-time, spiritual truths being the small leaves of those flowers; the first-fruits of the spiritual marriage, to the beginnings of the fruit; spiritual goods, which are the goods of charity, to the fruit, being also signified by fruit in the Word; the procreations of wisdom from love, to the seeds, by means of which procreations a man becomes like a garden and a paradise. A man is also described in the Word by a tree, and his wisdom from love by a garden. Nothing else is signified by the garden of Eden. A man indeed is an evil tree from the seed; but yet there is provided an ingrafting or inoculation of branches taken from the tree of life, by which the juices drawn from the old root are converted into such as produce good fruit. This comparison is made, in order that it may be known that when there is so constant a progression of the Divine Providence in the vegetation and regeneration of trees, it must by all means be constant in the reformation and regeneration of men, who are of much more value than trees, according to these words of the Lord: "Are not five sparrows sold for two farthings, and not one of them is forgotten before God? but even the very hairs of your head are all numbered. Fear not therefore: ye are of more value than many sparrows. And which of you with taking thought can add to his stature one cubit? If ye then be not able to do that thing which is least, why take ye thought for the rest? Consider the lilies how they grow. If God so clothe the grass, which is to-day in the field, and to-morrow is cast into the oven, how much more will he clothe you, O ye of little faith?" (Luke xii. 6, 7, 25—28.)

333. It was said above that the operation of the Divine Pro

vidence in saving a man begins at his birth, and continues to the end of his life. That this may be understood, it is to be observed, that the Lord sees what a man is, and foresees what he desires to be, consequently what he will be ; and in order that he may be a man, and thereby immortal, the freedom of his will cannot be taken away, as has been abundantly shown above; therefore the Lord foresees his state after death, and provides for it from his birth to the end of his life ; with the wicked he provides by permitting and continually withdrawing them from evils ; with the good he provides by leading them to good. Thus the Divine Providence is continually in the operation of saving men ; but more cannot be saved than desire to be saved. Those who acknowledge God, and are led by him, desire to be saved ; and those who do not acknowledge God, but guide themselves, do not desire to be saved : for the latter do not think of eternal life and salvation, but the former do. This the Lord sees, but still he leads them, and leads them according to the laws of his Divine Providence, against which he cannot act, because to act against them would be to act against his divine love and divine wisdom, that is, to act against himself. Now as he foresees the state of all after death, and also foresees the places of those who are not willing to be saved, in hell, and the places of those who are willing to be saved, in heaven, it follows, as before said, that he provides for the wicked their places by permitting and withdrawing, and for the good their places by leading them ; and unless this were done continually from the birth of every one to his life's end, neither heaven nor hell could subsist ; for without such foresight and at the same time providence, both heaven and hell would be nothing but confusion. That every one has his place provided for him by means of the Lord's foreknowledge, may be seen above, n. 202, 203. This may be illustrated by the following comparison : Supposing an archer or marksman were to shoot at a mark, and a right line were drawn from the mark to the distance of a mile beyond it,—if in shooting, the arrow or ball were to miss the mark a nail's breadth only, it would, at the end of the mile, diverge immensely from the line drawn beyond the mark. Such would be the case if the Lord did not every moment, even the most minute point of time, have respect to eternity in foreseeing and providing every one his place after death : this, however, is done by the Lord, because all the future is present to him, and all the present is to him eternal. That the Divine Providence, in all it does, has respect to infinity and eternity, may be seen above, n. 46—69, 214, and the subsequent numbers.

334. It was said that the operation of the Divine Providence continues to eternity, because every angel is perfected *in wisdom* to eternity ; but every one according to the *degree of affection* for goodness and truth he was in when he departed out

of the world. It is this degree which is perfected to eternity. What is beyond this degree is without the angel, and not within him; and that which is without him cannot be perfected within him. This is meant by the good measure, pressed down, shaken, and running over, which shall be given into the bosom of those who give and forgive others (Luke vii., 37, 38), that is, who are in the good of charity.

335. II. *That the operation of the Divine Providence is continually effected by means which are out of pure mercy.* There are means and modes of the Divine Providence: means are all those things by virtue of which a man is made a man, and perfected with respect to his understanding and his will; modes are those things by which such means are effected. The means by virtue of which a man is made a man, and perfected with respect to his understanding, are included under the general appellation of truths, which become ideas in the thought, are called things in the memory, and are in themselves knowledges from which sciences are derived. All these means considered in themselves are spiritual; but as they exist in things natural, they appear from their clothing or covering as natural things, and some as material. They are infinite in number and variety, and are more or less simple and compound, and more or less perfect or imperfect. There are means for forming and perfecting civil natural life; also for forming and perfecting moral rational life; and for forming and perfecting spiritual celestial life. These means succeed, one kind after another, from infancy to a man's latest age, and after that to eternity; and as they succeed, by increasing, those which were prior become means of those which are posterior, since they enter into every thing that has a form as mediate causes; for from these every effect or conclusion is efficient, and thence becomes a cause. Thus posteriors successively become means; and as this goes on to eternity, there is no postreme or ultimate that closes the whole; for as eternity is without end, so wisdom, which increases to eternity, is also without end. If there were any end to wisdom in a wise man, the delight of his wisdom, which consists in its perpetual multiplication and fructification, would perish; so would also the delight of his life; and in place of it would succeed the delight of glory, in which alone there is no celestial life. In such case a man no longer becomes wise like a young man, but like an old man, and at length like a decrepit man. Although the wisdom of a wise man in heaven increases to eternity, yet there is no such approximation of angelic wisdom to the divine wisdom as to reach it. It may be illustrated by what is said of a right line drawn about an hyperbola, continually approaching, but never touching it; and by what is said of squaring the circle. Hence may appear what is meant by means by which the Divine Providence operates, that a man

may be a man, and be perfected in regard to his understanding, and that these means are included under the general appellation of truths. There is also a similar number of means, by which a man is formed and perfected in regard to his will ; but these are comprehended under the general appellation of goods. From the latter a man derives love, and from the former wisdom. The conjunction of them makes the man ; for such as is the conjunction such is the man. It is this conjunction which is called the marriage of goodness and truth.

336. The modes also by which the Divine Providence operates upon means and by means, in forming a man and perfecting him, are also infinite in number and variety. They are as numerous as the operations of the divine wisdom from the divine love for the salvation of man, consequently as numerous as the operations of the Divine Providence according to its laws above described. That these modes are of a very hidden nature was illustrated above by the operations of the soul upon the body, concerning which men know so little that it can scarcely be called any thing ; as, how the eye, the ear, the nose, the tongue, and the skin feel, how the stomach digests, the mesentery prepares the chyle, the liver elaborates the blood, the pancreas and spleen purify it, the kidneys separate impure humours from it, the heart collects and distributes it, the lungs decant it, and how the brain sublimates the blood and vivifies it anew, besides innumerable other things, all of which are arcana into which scarce any science can enter. It is therefore evident, that still less can the secret operations of the Divine Providence be entered into ; it is sufficient that its laws are known.

337. The reason why the Divine Providence effects all things out of pure mercy, is, because the divine essence itself is pure love : it is that which operates by the divine wisdom ; and that operation is what is called the Divine Providence. The reason why that pure love is pure mercy, is, 1. That it operates with all who are in the world, who are such that they can do nothing from themselves. 2. That it operates with the evil and unjust, as well as with the good and just. 3. That it leads the former in hell, and snatches them out of it. 4. That it continually strives with them there, and fights for them against the devil, that is, against the evils of hell. 5. That for this purpose it came into the world, and underwent temptations even to the last of them, which was the passion of the cross. 6. That it acts continually with the unclean that it may cleanse them, and with the insane that it may heal them ; consequently, it labours continually out of pure mercy.

338. III. *That momentaneous salvation from immediate mercy is impossible.* In the foregoing pages it is shown that the operation of the Divine Providence for the salvation of man begins at his birth, continues to the end of his life, and after-

wards to eternity; also, that this operation is continually carried on by means out of pure mercy: hence it follows, that there is no such thing as momentaneous salvation or immediate mercy. But as many, who do not think at all from the understanding concerning matters of the church or of religion, believe that they are saved from immediate mercy, consequently that salvation is momentaneous, and yet this is contrary to the truth, and is besides a hurtful belief, it is requisite that it should be considered in its proper order. 1. That a belief in momentaneous salvation from immediate mercy is taken from the natural state of man. 2. That such a belief proceeds from ignorance of his spiritual state, which is totally different from his natural state. 3. That the doctrines of all the churches in the Christian world considered interiorly are against momentaneous salvation from immediate mercy; but yet that it is established by men of the external church. FIRST, *That a belief in momentaneous salvation from immediate mercy is taken from the natural state of man.* The natural man from his own state knows no otherwise than that heavenly joy is like worldly joy, and enters by influx and is received in the same manner; for example, that it is like a man who had been poor becoming rich, and so being removed from a sorrowful state of poverty to a happy state of opulence; or like a man who had before been of no estimation, being honoured, and so being removed from a state of contempt to a state of glory; or like going out of the house of mourning to nuptial joys. Since these states can be changed within a day, and no other idea is entertained of the state of man after death, it is evident whence it arises that there is a belief in momentaneous salvation from immediate mercy. In the world, also, it is possible for many persons to be in one company, in one civil society, and to be merry together, yet all of them to differ in their minds. This is the case in a natural state; and the reason is, that the external of one man may be accommodated to the external of another, although their internals be dissimilar. From this natural state it is concluded, that salvation consists only in admission to the angels in heaven, and the admission is from immediate mercy; therefore it is also believed that heaven can be given to the wicked as well as the good, and that then there is a consociation similar to what takes place in the world, with this difference only, that it is full of joy. SECONDLY, *But that this faith proceeds from ignorance of a spiritual state, which is totally different from a natural state.* The spiritual state, which is the state of man after death, is treated of in many places above, where it is shown that every one is his own love, that no one can live with any others but such as are in a similar love, and that if he comes to others, he cannot respire his own life. Hence it is that every one after death enters into a society similar to himself, composed of such as are in a similar

268

love; that he acknowledges them as his relatives and friends; and, what is wonderful, that when he meets with them and sees them, it is as though he had known them from his infancy. This circumstance has its ground in the nature of spiritual affinity and friendship. Yea more, no one in a society can dwell in any other house than his own; every one having his own house, which he finds prepared for him as soon as he comes into the society. He may be in company with others out of his house, but yet he cannot dwell anywhere but in it; and what is still more, no one can sit in an apartment in another's house in any place but his own: if he sits in any other place, he becomes impotent of mind and silent; and, what is wonderful, every one when he enters a room knows his own place. It is the same in temples, and also in assemblies when they are met together. From these circumstances it is evident that a spiritual state is totally different from a natural state, and such indeed that no one can be anywhere but where his reigning love is; for there is the delight of his life, and every one desires to be in the delight of his life. A man's spirit cannot be anywhere else, because that constitutes his life, even his very respiration, as also the pulsation of his heart. It is otherwise in the natural world, where the external man is taught from his infancy to feign, in his countenance, speech, and gesture, delights different from those of his internal. Therefore, from the state of a man in the natural world, a conclusion cannot be formed concerning his state after death; for the state of every one after death is spiritual, and is such that he cannot be anywhere but in the delight of his love, which he acquired to himself by his life in the natural world. Hence it may plainly appear, that no one who is in the delight of hell can be let into the delight of heaven, which in general is called heavenly joy; or, what amounts to the same, he that is already in the delight of evil cannot be let into the delight of good. It may be still more clearly concluded from this circumstance that the liberty of ascending into heaven is not refused any one after death: the way is shown him, leave is given, and he is introduced; but when he comes into heaven, and by breathing draws in its delight, if he be in evil, he begins to feel anguish in his breast, to be tormented at heart, to experience a-swoon, in which he writhes himself like a snake placed before the fire, and with his face averted from heaven and turned toward hell, escapes headlong; and he cannot rest except in a society of his own prevailing love. Hence it may appear that to go to heaven is not allowed to any one from immediate mercy, consequently, that it does not consist of admission merely, as many in this world imagine; and that salvation is not momentaneous, for this supposes immediate mercy. There were some, who in the world believed in momentaneous salvation from immediate mercy, and when they became spirits were desirous that their infer-

269

nal delight or the delight of evil might, by means of the divine omnipotence and the divine mercy together, be changed into heavenly delight, or the delight of good; and as this was their desire, it was permitted that it should be done by angels, who instantly removed their infernal delight: but then, because it was the delight of their life's love, consequently their life itself, they lay as if they were dead, deprived of all sense and motion; and it was impossible to infuse into them any other life than their own, because all things of their minds and bodies were in a state of retroversion, and could not be contrariwise retorted or wrested. They were therefore revived by the intromission of the delight of their life's love; and they afterwards said, that in that state they felt interiorly something direful and horrible, which they would not make known. Hence it is said in heaven, that it is easier to convert an owl into a dove, or a serpent into a lamb, than an infernal spirit into an angel of heaven. THIRDLY, *That the doctrines of the churches in the Christian world interiorly considered are against momentaneous salvation from immediate mercy, but yet that it is established by men of the external church.* The doctrines of all churches, viewed interiorly, teach life. Where is there any church whose doctrine does not teach that a man ought to examine himself; to see and acknowledge his sins; to confess them, repent, and then lead a new life? Who is admitted to the holy communion without this admonition and command? Inquire, and you will be confirmed. What church is there whose doctrine is not founded upon the precepts of the Decalogue? and the precepts of the Decalogue are precepts of life. What man is there of the church, in whom there is any thing of the church, that does not acknowledge, as soon as he hears it, that he that lives well is saved, and that he that lives wickedly is condemned? Therefore in the Athanasian Creed, which is also the doctrine received in the whole Christian world, it is said, that the Lord will "come to judge the quick and the dead; and those that have done good shall go into life everlasting, and those that have done evil into everlasting fire." From which it is evident that the doctrines of all churches, viewed interiorly, teach life. As they teach life, they teach that salvation is according to life; and a man's life is not inspired in a moment, but formed successively, and reformed as a man shuns evils as sins, consequently, as he knows what sin is and sees and acknowledges it, as he does not will it and therefore desists from it, and as he also knows the means which relate to the knowledge of God. By these, which cannot be infused in a moment, a man's life is formed and reformed; for hereditary evil, which in itself is infernal, is to be removed, and in place of it, good, which in itself is celestial, is to be implanted. A man, from his hereditary evil, may be compared to an owl as to understanding, a d a serpent as to will; and a reformed man may be compared to a dove as to understanding, and a lamb as to will; therefore momentaneous reformation and thence salvation may be compared to the momentaneous conversion of an owl into a dove and a serpent into a lamb. Who that knows any thing of the life of man does not see that this cannot be effected, except the nature of the owl and serpent be taken away, and the nature of the dove and lamb be implanted? Besides, it is well known that every intelligent man may become more intelligent, and every wise man more wise; that intelligence and wisdom in a man may increase, and in some do increase, from infancy to their life's end; and that thus the man is continually perfected. Why should not this be more eminently the case with spiritual intelligence and wisdom, which ascends by two degrees above natural intelligence and wisdom? When it ascends, it becomes angelic, which is unutterable: that this in the angels increases to eternity was stated above. Who may not comprehend, if he will, that what is perfected to eternity cannot possibly be perfect in an instant?

339. Hence then it is evident, that all who think from life concerning salvation, do not think of any momentaneous salvation from immediate mercy, but of the means of salvation, on and by which the Lord operates according to the laws of his Divine Providence, and by which therefore every man is led out of pure mercy by the Lord. But those who do not think from life concerning salvation, imagine there is something momentaneous in salvation, and something immediate in mercy; as also do those who separate faith from charity. Charity is life, and they suppose there is something momentaneous in faith at the hour of death, if not before. Those also do the same who believe remission of sins without repentance to be absolution from sins, consequently salvation, and who with this idea receive the Lord's Supper; likewise those who have faith in the indulgences of monks, in their prayers for the dead, and in their dispensations grounded in the power they claim over the souls of men.

340. IV. *That momentaneous salvation from immediate mercy is the fiery flying serpent in the church.* By a fiery flying serpent is meant evil shining from infernal fire: the same as is meant by the fiery flying serpent in Isaiah, "Rejoice not thou, whole Palestina, because the rod of him that smote thee is broken: for out of the serpent's root shall come forth a cockatrice, and his fruit shall be a fiery flying serpent" (xiv. 29). Such an evil flies in the church when there is faith in momentaneous salvation from immediate mercy; for thereby, 1. Religion is abolished; 2. Security is induced; and 3. Damnation is imputed to the Lord. As to what concerns the FIRST, *That thereby religion is abolished;* there are two essentials and at the same time universals of religion, an acknowledgment of a God and repentance.

271

These two essentials are useless to those who think to be saved barely from mercy, without regard to their lives; for what need have they of any thing more than to say, God have mercy upon me? As to every thing else appertaining to religion, they are in the dark, indeed they love darkness. Of the first essential of the church, which is an acknowledgment of God, they only think, What is God? Who ever saw him? If it is affirmed that there is a God, and that he is one, they assent that he is one; if it is affirmed that there are three, they also say that there are three, but that these three are to be called one. This is their acknowledgment of God. Of the other essential of the church, which is repentance, they think nothing at all, and consequently nothing of sin, and at length do not know that there is such a thing as sin. They then hear, and imbibe it with pleasure, that the law does not condemn, because a Christian is not under its yoke. If you only say, God have mercy upon me for thy Son's sake, you will be saved. This is repentance of life with them. But remove repentance, or, what amounts to the same, separate life from religion, and what remains but the words, Have mercy upon me? Hence it is, that they cannot conceive otherwise but that salvation is effected in a moment by means of those words, if not before, yet at the hour of death. In such case, what is the Word to them but like an obscure and enigmatical voice uttered from a tripod in a cave? or like an unintelligible response from the oracle of an idol? In a word, if you remove repentance, that is, separate life from religion, what else is a man but evil shining from infernal fire, or a fiery flying serpent in the church? for without repentance a man is in evil, and evil is hell. SECONDLY, *That by faith in momentaneous salvation from pure mercy alone, security of life is induced.* Security of life arises either from the belief of the impious that there is no life after death, or from the belief of those who separate life from salvation. A person of the latter description, although he believe in eternal life, still thinks, Whether I live well, or live ill, I can be saved, because salvation is pure mercy, and the mercy of God is universal, as he wills not the death of any one. If haply a thought occurs that mercy is to be implored by a form of words agreeable to the commonly received faith, he may think that this, if not before, can be done at the hour of death. Every man that is in such a state of security makes light of adulteries, frauds, injustice, violence, blasphemies, and revenge; and gives a loose to his flesh and his spirit in the commission of all these evils. Nor does he know what spiritual evil is, and its concupiscences. If he hears any thing thereof out of the Word, it may be compared to something falling upon ebony and rebounding, or to something which falls into a ditch and is swallowed up. THIRDLY, *That by such a faith damnation is imputed to the Lord.* Who but must conclude that, if he is not saved, it is not the man's fault, but the Lord's, when every one can be saved from pure mercy? If it be affirmed that faith is the means of salvation, he will urge, What man is there to whom such faith may not be given, as it only consists in thought, which can be infused in every state of the spirit abstracted from worldly things, even with confidence? He may further urge, I cannot take it of myself; if therefore it is not given, and a man is damned, what else can the damned think than that it is the Lord's fault, who could save him and would not? And would not this be to call the Lord unmerciful? Besides, in the warmth of his faith, he may ask, Why can the Lord see so many damned in hell, when he is nevertheless able to save all in a moment from a principle of pure mercy? Not to mention other suggestions of a similar nature, which can be called nothing but impious impeachments of the Divinity. Hence then it may appear, that faith in momentaneous salvation from pure mercy is the fiery flying serpent in the church.

* * * * * * *

Excuse my adding this relation to fill up the superfluous paper. Certain spirits by permission ascended from hell, and said to me, You have written a great deal from the Lord, write something also from us. I replied, What shall I write? They said, Write, that every spirit, whether he be good or evil, is in his own delight,—the good in the delight of his good, and the evil in the delight of his evil. I asked them, What may your delight be? They said that it was the delight of committing adultery, stealing, defrauding, and lying. Again I asked, What is the nature of those delights? They replied, that they were perceived by others as stenches from excrement, putrid smells from dead bodies, and the effluvia of stagnated urine. I said, Are those things delightful to you? They replied, Most delightful. I said, Then you are like the unclean beasts which live in such filth. They answered, If we are, we are; but such things are the delights of our nostrils. I asked, What more shall I write from you? They said, Write this, that it is permitted every one to be in his own delight, even the most unclean as it is called, provided it does not infest good spirits and angels; but as we could not do otherwise than infest them, we were driven out, and cast into hell, where we experience direful sufferings. I asked, Why did you infest the good? They replied, that they could not do otherwise. It is as if a certain fury invaded us, when we see any angel, and feel the divine sphere about him. I said, Then you are even like wild beasts.

273

On hearing this, rage came upon them, which appeared like the fire of hatred ; and to prevent their doing any mischief, they were remanded to hell.   Concerning delights perceived as odors and stenches in the spiritual world, see above, n. 303. 304, 305, 324.

274

INDEX

TO

THE DIVINE PROVIDENCE.

The Numbers refer to the Paragraphs, and not to the Pages.

Darkness of ignorance, **276**. Every man, hereditarily from his parents, is born into the love of self and the love of the world, and into evils of every description from these two kinds of loves as fountains, 83. If a man were born in the love in which he was created, he would not be in any evil, nor indeed would he know what evil is, 275.

BRAIN.—Its organization, 279. The brain sublimates the blood, and vivifies it anew, 336.

BRIDE.—Why heaven and the church are called the Bride in the Word, 8.

BRIDEGROOM. Why the Lord in the Word is called the Bridegroom, 8.

CAIN signifies wisdom or faith specifically, wisdom separate from love, or faith separate from charity. Cain, who slew Abel, is this faith which annihilates love and charity, 242. See *Abel*. What is meant by the mark set upon Cain, 242.

CALF OF GOLD.—Why the worship of it was permitted, 243.

CALVIN, 50.

CANCER.—The evils which remain shut up, and do not appear, are compared to a cancer, 251.

CAPTIVITY of the Jewish people in Babylon represents the vastation of the church, 246.

CAROTID ARTERIES, 296.

CART, the new, 1 Sam. vi., signified new, but natural doctrine, 326.

CARTILAGES, the, of the Grand Man, or of heaven, are constituted of those to whom the Gospel cannot reach, but only some religion, 254, 326.

CATECHISM or Decalogue, regarded as a child's book, which is no longer of any use, 329.

CATHOLICISM, Roman.—Its dominion, 215. Why it has been permitted, 257. Why it is of the Divine Providence of the Lord, that they should divide the Holy Supper, giving the bread alone to the people, also that they should make it corporeal and material, and account this doctrine to be a primary tenet of religion, 257.

CATHOLICS, Roman, in general suffer themselves to be forced to religion, but it is the case with those in whose worship there is nothing internal, but all is external, 136.

CAUSE.—Whatever is done from any cause is done from the Divine Providence of the Lord, according to some of its laws, 246. Nothing can be and exist without a cause, 212. The causes of permissions are laws of Divine Providence, 249. If the cause is taken away from the effect, the effect perishes, 8. The cause is called the middle end, 108.

CAUSE, to be the.—The Lord is not the cause of a man's thinking what is evil and false, 292. Those who are not saved, are themselves the cause of it, 330.

CENTRE.—From the centre to the circumference, 79. The things which are of the centre diffuse themselves towards the cir-

cumference, 86. Evils with falses are with the wicked as it were in the centre, and good principles with truths in the circumference; but good principles with truths are in the centre with the good, and evils with falsities in the circumference, 86. Thus good, in the circumference with the wicked, is defiled by the evils of the centre, and evils in the circumference with the good are rendered mild by the good principles of the centre, 86. Whatever is in the centre is directly under inspection, and is seen and perceived, 283.

CHALDEA signifies the profanation of truth in those who attribute to themselves things divine, 281. Also, the profanation of what is holy, 251. Chaldea was one of those countries in which the ancient church existed, and where the ancient Word was known, 328.

CHANGES and variations of state and form in the organic substances of the mind, 195, 279. 319. What is the nature and quality of these changes, 319. Changes and variations of state in organic substances are of such a nature, that when once they become habitual, they are permanent, 279.

CHARIOT, in the Word, signifies doctrine grounded on spiritual truths, 326.

CHARM, the, resulting from speaking with the dead is an internal restraint; but this restraint is dissolved, and the inclosed evils break out with blasphemy and profanation, 134.*

CHRIST.—No one can even name the Lord, or utter His names, Jesus and Christ, but from Him, 58.

CHRISTIANS, the, of the ancient church could not comprehend that God, the Creator of the universe, himself came into the world, and took upon Him the human nature; they, therefore, in thought, separated His divinity from His humanity, 255. Those who deny the sanctity of the Word, are not reputed as Christians, 256.

CHRISTIAN RELIGION.—Why it is established only in the smallest quarter of the habitable globe, and why it is divided there, 256. Why, in many kingdoms in which it has been received, there are some who claim to themselves divine power, and wish to be adored as gods; and why they invoke dead men, 257. Why, among those who profess the Christian religion, there are some who place salvation in certain words, which they think and speak, and not in any good they do, 258. See *Christian World*. Why heretofore it was not known that the very essence of the Christian religion is to shun evils as sins, 265.

CHRISTIAN WORLD. — Why the whole Christian world worship God under three Persons, which is three Gods, and why hitherto they have not known that God is one in person and in essence, in whom there is a Trinity, and that that God is the Lord, 262. Why there have been and still are so many heresies in the Christian world, 259. See *Heresies*.

CHURCH, the, is a communion of all those

CONFIRM, to.—Every thing of which a man is persuaded, and in which he is confirmed, remains as his proprium, 317. There is nothing but what may be confirmed, and falsity more easily than truth, 818. It may be confirmed in such a degree that it appears as truth, 286, 818. When falsity is confirmed, truth does not appear, but from confirmed truth falsity does appear, 818. To be able to confirm whatever a man pleases is not intelligence, but only ingenuity, which may exist even amongst the most wicked, 318. Every thing confirmed by the will, and at the same time by the understanding, remains to eternity, but not that which is confirmed by the understanding only, 818. He who confirms evil loves, offers violence to divine goods, and he who confirms false principles, offers violence to divine truths, 231.

CONFIRMATION, the, of what is false is a negation of the truth, and the confirmation of evil is a rejection of good, 231. There may be intellectual confirmation and not at the same time voluntary; but all voluntary confirmation is also intellectual, 818. The voluntary, and at the same time the intellectual confirmation of evil, causes a man to think that self-derived prudence is all, and the Divine Providence nothing, but not the intellectual confirmation of it alone, 818.

CONFIRMERS.—There are some very dexterous confirmers, who know no truth, and yet can confirm both truth and falsity, 818.

CONFLICT and COMBAT between good and evil in man when he is reformed, 284.

CONFUSED.—All imperfection of form results from what is confused or indistinct, 4.

CONJOIN, to.—How a man is more and more nearly conjoined to the Lord, 33. Every one acknowledges God, and is conjoined with Him according to the good of his life, 326. The Lord is so conjoined to a man, spirit, and angel, that all which has relation to the divine is not from them, but from the Lord, 326. A man becomes wiser in proportion as he is more nearly conjoined to the Lord, 34; also happier, 87; he also appears to himself to be more distinctly at his own disposal, and perceives more evidently that he is the Lord's, 42. The Lord joins a man to himself by appearances and by correspondences, 219. The Lord, by his Divine Providence, joins himself to things natural by things spiritual, and to things temporary by things eternal, according to uses, 220. The Lord joins himself to uses by correspondences, and so by appearances, according to confirmations, by a man, 220. The understanding does not join itself with the will, nor the thought of the understanding with the affection of the will, but the will and its affection join themselves with the understanding and its thought, 80.

CONJUGIAL love is celestial spiritual love itself, which is an image of the love of the Lord and of the church, 144.

CONJUNCTION with the Lord is the reception of love and wisdom from him, 164. Conjunction with the Lord and regeneration make one, 92. There is a conjunction nearer and nearer, and also one more and more remote, 28, 32. How a man is more and more nearly conjoined to the Lord, 33. In what manner the conjunction of the Lord with the angels, and of the angels with the Lord, is effected, 28. The conjunction of the Lord with a man, and the reciprocal conjunction of a man with the Lord, is effected by the two faculties of liberty and rationality, 92. They are effected by his loving his neighbor as himself, and loving the Lord above all things, 94. There is a conjunction of the Lord with every man, as well the wicked as the good; it is thence that a man has immortality: but he alone has eternal life—that is, the life of heaven—in whom there is a reciprocal conjunction from inmost parts to ultimates, 96. The acknowledgment of God effects a conjunction of God with man, 326. Upon the conjunction of the Creator with man, the connection of all things depends, 8. Conjunction, in the spiritual world, proceeds from the affection which is of love, 326. All conjunction in the spiritual world is effected by inspection, 29; examples, 326. Spiritual conjunction is like itself, both in things general and in things particular; it derives its origin from the conjunction of the Lord with the spiritual world and with the natural world in general and in particular, 326. Conjunction of the will with the understanding, 165. Conjunction of all things of the will and understanding, or of the mind of a man, with his life's love, 108.

CONNECTION, the, of all things depends on the conjunction of the Creator with man, 8.

CONSENT is equivalent to act, 111.

CONSTANT or fixed things were created, in order that things inconstant or unfixed might exist, 190. Enumeration of certain constant things, 190.

CONSUMMATION.—The end of a church is called its consummation, 328. The manner in which the consummations of the most ancient church, the ancient church, the Israelitish and Jewish church, and the Christian church, are described in the Word, and the mode in which they successively took place, 328.

CONTAGION of evil, whence it arises, 328.

CONTIGUITY.—What is living in man or an angel is from the proceeding divine, which is joined to him by contiguity, and appears to him as his own, 57.

CORRESPONDENCES.—All things of the mind correspond to all things of the body 181. The Lord conjoins himself to uses by means of correspondences, 220. All things in the Word are mere correspondences of things spiritual and celestial; and because they are correspondences, they are also appearances, 220. The science of correspondences, which is the science of representations, was, amongst the ancients, the peculiar science of their wise men, and was cultivated particularly in Egypt, 255.

COVENANT.—Why the two tables of the law are called the covenant, 326.

COVERINGS.—After death a man is equally a man as in the world; with this difference only, that he has put off that covering which constituted his body in the world, 124.

Cows signify good natural affections, 326.

CREATE, to.—All things were created from the divine love by the divine wisdom, 3. The divine love and divine wisdom are in a certain image in every created thing, 5. In every created thing there is something which may be referred to the marriage of good and truth, 74. No angel or spirit was immediately created such, but all were first born men, 220. Every man is created to live to eternity in a state of happiness, 324. Man was created that he might be a receptacle of the love and wisdom of God, 328. The difference between creating and proceeding from, 219.

CREATION.—The end of creation is a heaven out of the human race, 323. All things which are without man, and serve for his use, are secondary ends of creation, 332. The Lord created the universe to the end that an infinite and eternal creation might exist therein from himself, 202, 203. By the creation of heaven and earth, in the first chapter of Genesis, is signified the new creation or regeneration of the men of the most ancient church, 241.

CREATION, the first, 332.

Obs.—By this expression, which we meet with occasionally in the writings, the author does not mean that there has been a first and second creation; but as preservation is perpetual creation, and as in preserving God continually creates, this expression points out more particularly the creation of the universe.

CROWNS.—The seven crowns upon the head of the dragon, Apoc. xii. 8, signifies the holy things of the Word and of the church profaned, 310.

CRUCIFY.—Why the Jewish nation was permitted to crucify the Lord, 247.

CRUELTIES.—Their origin, 276.

CUNNING.—The perceptions of concupiscences are all sorts of craft and cunning, 206.

CUNNING, the.—Their fate in the other life, 310.

CUP of cold water, Matt. x. 42, signifies something of truth, 230.

CURE, to.—The evils of a man's life's love are cured by spiritual means, as diseases are by natural means, 281. How the Lord cures man, 281, 282. The healing of the understanding alone would be like a palliative—it is the will itself which must be cured, 282. In what way the Lord heals the love of a man's will, 283.

CURSE, the, of Cain involves the spiritual state into which those who separate faith from charity, or wisdom from love, come after death, 242. What are real curses, 217, 250.

DAGON represented the religious principle of those who are in faith separated from charity, 326.

DAMNATION is non-salvation, 329. The first state of man is a state of damnation, 88. By a belief in momentaneous salvation, through immediate mercy, damnation is imputed to the Lord, 340.

DAMNED, to be.—To suppose any of the human race are predestined to be damned, is a cruel heresy, 330.

DANES.—What is taught them in the prayer at the holy communion, 114.

DARKNESS.—In the Word, falsities are called darkness; and thence those who are in falsities are said to walk in darkness, 818. Outer darkness, 231.

DARKNESS.—When an angel of heaven looks into hell, he sees nothing there but profound darkness; and when a spirit of hell looks into heaven, he sees nothing there but darkness, 167.

DAVID, by, in several passages of the Word is represented the Lord, who was about to come into the World, 245.

DEATH is a continuation of life, 277*. By death a man puts off the grosser substances of nature, of which his body consists, and retains the purer substances of nature, which are next to what is spiritual, and which then are his continents, 220. Thus the death of the body is the rejection of temporary and natural ultimates, 220. In the spiritual world it is not asked after death, what has your faith been, or what your doctrine? but, what has your life been? 101. Why the natural man, however civilly and morally he may act, is called dead, 222.

DECALOGUE, the, was primary in the Word, being deposited in the ark; it was called Jehovah, and constituted the holy of holies in the tabernacle, and the most sacred place in the temple at Jerusalem, 326. There are two tables of the Decalogue, one for God, and the other for man, 326. The Decalogue taught to children, 258, 265. The Decalogue, at this day, is as a book that is shut, or open only in the hands of infants and children, 329.

DEGREES.—There are two kinds of degrees—discrete degrees, or those of altitude; and continuous degrees, or those of latitude, 32. Every man by creation, and thence by birth, has three discrete degrees, or degrees of altitude; the first is the natural degree, the second the spiritual degree, and the third the celestial degree, 32, 324. These degrees are actually in every one; but in beasts there is only one degree of life, which is similar to the ultimate degree in a man, called natural, 324. These degrees are actually opened in man by the Lord according to his life in the world, but not perceptibly and sensibly till after his departure out of the world, 32. There are

EQUILIBRIUM between heaven and hell, 28. Every man is kept in this equilibrium as long as he lives in the world, and is thus in the liberty of thinking, willing, speaking, and acting, in which he may be reformed, 28.

ERROR of the age as to the remission of sins, 279. As to immediate mercy, and momentaneous salvation, 280.

ESSE, an, without *existere* is not any thing, 11. See *Existere*.

ESSENCE.—There is one only essence, from which are all the essences that are created, 157. The very divine essence is pure love, 337.

ESSENTIALS, there are three, of the church, what they are, 259. There are two essentials, and the same time two universals of religion, 340.

ETERNAL, 46–69. The eternal is no other than the divine existere, 48. See *Infinite, Image*.

ETHER, 190.

EVE.—The condemnation of Eve signifies the condemnation of the voluntary proprium, 313. See *Adam*.

EVIL, hereditary. See *Hereditary*.

EVIL and its attendant falsity serve for the conjunction of good and truth in others, by equilibrium, 21, 28.

EVIL is the delight of the concupiscence of acting and thinking contrary to divine order, 279. There are myriads of concupiscences which enter into and compose every evil, 279, 296. Every evil springs from the love of self and the love of the world, 83. Evil and the devil are one, 33. Every evil is followed by its punishment, 249. Evils are permitted to the end that salvation may be effected, 249, 281. In every evil lies inwardly concealed an acknowledgment of nature and human prudence alone, 205. There is inherent in every evil a hatred against good, 233. Evil cannot be taken away from any one unless it appear, be seen, and acknowledged, 183, 278. So long as evils remain in the concupiscences, and thence in the delights of the love of them, there is neither any faith, charity, piety, or worship, except only in externals, 83. The evils of concupiscences of his life's love are perceived by man not as evils, but as delights, to which he does not pay any attention, 296. In proportion as evils are removed, they are remitted, 279. See *Evil and False, Hereditary*.

EVIL and FALSE.—Every thing evil and false is from hell, 321. Evil cannot exist without its falsity, 233. Evil from its delight, and falsity from its pleasantness, may be called and thought good and true, 195. To every one, that is evil which destroys the pleasure of his affection, and that false which destroys the pleasantness of his thought thence derived, 195. Evil and its attendant falsity serve for equilibrium, relation, and purification, and thereby for the conjunction of good and truth in others, 21.

EXAMINATION, self.—What it is, 278. It ought to be not only external, but internal also, 152. What internal examination is. It is by an examination of the internal man that the external is essentially explored, 152.

EXISTERE, the, without the Esse is not any thing, 11. See *Esse*.

EXPULSION, the, of Adam and Eve from the Garden of Eden, signifies the total deprivation of wisdom, 313.

EXTERNAL, the, has its essence from the internal, 224. The external is able to appear otherwise than according to its essence from the internal, as is the case with hypocrites, 224. The external of a man's thought is in itself such as it is in its internal, 106. External things have such a connection with internal things, that in every operation they make one, 180.

EYE, the, in the Word signifies the understanding, 264. The eye is the form of the sight, 279. The eye of every one is formed for the reception of the light in which he is, 167. The eye does not see from itself, but it is man's mind or spirit which there perceives such things by the sense, and thence is affected according to the quality of the sense, 314. Men know little of the mode in which the eye sees, 386. The understanding from the will flows into the eye, and not only constitutes that sense, but also uses it as its instrument in the natural world, 314.

EYES, the, correspond to wisdom and its perceptions, 29.

FACE, the, is the type of the mind, 277. The external face is the appearance, and the internal face is the essence, 220, 224. The internal lies interiorly concealed in the face of the external, 224. In the spiritual world each one, as to the face, appears such as he is, 224. To see the Divine Providence on the back and not in the face, is to see it after, and not before, 187.

FACULTY, the, of willing, which is called liberty, and the faculty of understanding, which is called rationality, are as it were inherent in a man, 98. These two faculties are from the Lord in man, 78. Without these two faculties a man would not have will and understanding, and therefore would not be a man, 96. He could not be conjoined to the Lord, and consequently be reformed and regenerated, 96, 85; he would not have immortality and eternal life, 96. These two faculties are equally with the wicked as with the good, 15, 96, 99, 285. The Lord preserves these two faculties inviolable and as sacred, in every proceeding of his Divine Providence, 96. See *Liberty, Rationality*.

FAITH separate from charity, 264, 265. Blindness of those who are in this faith, 115. The danger of persuasive faith, 131.

FALLACIES blind the understanding, 175. Every appearance confirmed as a truth becomes a fallacy, 310, 220.

FALSIFICATION, the, of truth consists in doing violence to Divine truths, by confirming false principles, 231. In the Word,

FOREHEAD, the, corresponds to love and its affections, 29.

FOREKNOWLEDGE, a, of the future takes away the essential human principle, which consists in acting from liberty according to reason, 178, 179. See *Future.*

FORM.—There is one only form from which are all the forms that are created, 157. Every form turns what is influent into its own quality, 527. In every form what is common and what is particular, or what is universal and what is singular, by a wonderful conjunction act as one, 150. Whatsoever exists derives from its form that which is understood by quality, predicate, change of state, relation, and the like, 4. The form makes a one so much the more perfectly in proportion as the things which enter into it are distinct from each other, and nevertheless united, 4. Form of heaven, 62, 63. This form is made more and more perfect to eternity, according to the increase of members, the union becoming more perfect in proportion as more enter the form of Divine love, which is the form of forms, 62. Organic form of the mind, 279, 319. Forms of government of the life's love, 107. See *Substance.*

FORM, to.—All of the understanding and will must be formed by the external before it is formed by the internal, 136. All of the understanding and will being formed first by the things which enter through the senses of the body, especially the sight and hearing, 136.

FORESIGHT, the, of the Lord, is like His Providence, continual; one does not exist without the other, 67, 333. Without the foresight of the Lord, and at the same time His Providence, neither heaven nor hell could subsist, 333.

FORTUNE.—What is called fortune is nothing else but Divine Providence in ultimates, where, by constant and inconstant things, it deals wonderfully with human prudence, and at the same time conceals itself, 212. The Divine Providence, which is called fortune, is in the smallest particulars of matters, even those which are trifling, 251, 212. That which is called the fortune of war, is the Divine Providence operating especially in the counsels and designs meditated by the general, although he at the time, and afterwards, may ascribe the whole to his own prudence, 251. See *Accidents.*

FOUNTAIN, the only, of life is the Lord, 292.

FOUNTAINS.—Why the ancients consecrated fountains, 255.

FOXES.—Those who are in self-derived prudence are like foxes, 311.

FRAUDS.—Their origin, 276.

FREELY.—To will freely as of himself, is from the faculty given to man, called liberty, 96. So long as the delight of the love of evil reigns, a man cannot freely will what is good and true, 86. Every man may freely think whatever he will, as well against God as in favor of God; and he who thinks against God is rarely punished in the natural world, because there he is always in a state capable of reformation, but he is punished in the spiritual world after death, for then he can no longer be reformed, 249, 278.

FRENCH.—The French nation, why it is called a noble nation, 257.

FRIENDSHIP, spiritual, 338.

FRUCTIFICATIONS and multiplications have not failed in the natural world from the beginning of creation, and will not fail to eternity, 56. So with men, affections can be fructified, and perceptions multiplied without end, 57. This faculty of fructification and multiplication without end, or to infinity and eternity, exists in things natural with men, in things spiritual with spiritual angels, and in things celestial with celestial angels, 57.

FRUITS in the Word, signify spiritual goods, 332. The first fruits of the spiritual marriage are like the beginnings of the fruits, 332.

FUTURE, all the, is present to the Lord, and all the present is to Him eternal, 333. It is not granted to any one to know the future, but every one is allowed to conclude concerning things to come from reason, 179. The desire of foreknowing the future is connate with most people, but it derives its origin from the love of evil, it is therefore taken away from those who believe in Divine Providence, 179.

GARDEN, 241, 313. See *Eden.*

GARMENTS, white, signifies a state of purification from evils, 279.

GENESIS.—The learned have in vain endeavored to explain what is contained in the first chapter, 241. This chapter treats of the new creation or regeneration of the man of the most ancient church, 241.

GENII.—The most cunning sort of sensual men are called genii; they have a deep hell behind and wish to be invisible, therefore they appear hovering about there like spectres, which are their fantasies, 310.

GENTILES, the, and Mahometans, are ten times more numerous than Christians, yet among the latter there are but few who place religion in a good life: what then can be greater madness than to think that the former are condemned, or that a man possesses heaven by his birth and not by his life, 330. The Gentiles who have lived well in the world are instructed after death, and come into heaven more easily than Christians, 328, 330. The Gentile thinks more of God from religion in his life than the Christian does, 322.

GERMANS.—Instruction given to them in the prayer at the holy communion, 114.

GLORIES.—Its functions, 279.

GOATS signify those who separate faith from charity, 255. By the goats in Matt. xxv. 41-46, are meant those who omit to think of evil, and who consequently are continually in it, 101.

GOD is one in person and in essence, 262, 263. This one God is the Lord Jesus

derstanding, 166, 817. Natural light is from the sun of this world, and thence in itself void of life ; but spiritual light is from the sun of the spiritual world, and thence in itself living, 166. There are three degrees of light in the spiritual world—celestial light, spiritual light, and spiritual-natural light; celestial light, or that of the third heaven, is a ruddy, flaming light; spiritual light, with those of the middle heaven, is a white, shining light; and spiritual-natural light, is such as is the light of day in our world, and is with those who are in the lowest heaven, and in the world of spirits, 166. The light in hell is also of three degrees, the light in the lowest hell being like the light of burning coals ; the light in the middle hell like that from the flame of a wood fire; and the light in the highest hell like the light of candles, and to some like the light of the moon by night, 167. All the light of the spiritual world has nothing in common with that of the natural world, they being as different as life and death, 166, 169. It is not easy to distinguish between the light of confirmation and the light of the perception of truth, 818. Nevertheless the difference is as great as between the light of infatuation and genuine light, 818. The light of infatuation in the spiritual world is such, that it is changed into darkness when genuine light flows in, 818. In the Word, those who are in truths, are said to walk in the light, and are called the children of light, 818. Who those are who are meant by the devils, who pretend to be angels of light, 223.

LIKENESS.—See *Image*.

LIPS.—Their functions, 279.

LIVE, to.—Man lives from the Lord alone, and not from himself, 156, 157. Without the appearance that a man lives from himself he would not be a man, 156. Man lives as a man after death, 274. To live well, or the good of life, is to shun evils because they are contrary to religion, therefore against God, 825, 326.

LIVER.—Its organization, 180, 279. It elaborates the blood, 836.

LOBES of the lung, 819.

LOOK at, to.—The Lord looks at the angels in the forehead, and the angels direct their eyes towards the Lord, 29. The more interiorly any object is inspected, the more wonderful, perfect, and beautiful are the things seen in it, 6.

LORD, the, is the only God of heaven and earth, 330. The Lord is perfect man, 65. How the Lord is the Divine Truth of the Divine Good, 172. The Lord is the Word, because it is from Him and concerning Him, 172. That the Lord alone is heaven, 29. The Lord is not in heaven among the angels, or with them as a king in His kingdom ; as to appearance in the sun there, He is above them, but as to the life of their love and wisdom, He is in them, 81. The Lord, for the sake of reception and conjunction, wills that whatsoever a man does

freely according to reason, may appear to him as his own, 77. The Lord alone causes every one to think and will according to his quality, and according to the laws of His Providence, 294. A man is led of the Lord by influx, and taught by illumination, 165, 166. When a man is taught from the Word, he is taught from the Lord, 172.

Obs.—In all the writings of our author, by the *Lord* is meant Jesus Christ, the Saviour of the world, who is the one and only Lord.

LOT.—Why a man does not know what will be his lot after death, 179. Those who believe in Divine Providence have confidence that the Lord will appoint their lot, hence they do not desire to foreknow it, 179. The life of every one continues with him, and thence is his lot, because the lot is of the life, 179.

LOVE, the, is the life of man, 18. Love is as the fire of life. from which is the light of life, 167. The life's love of no one can exist without derivations which are called affections, 106. The life's love produces from itself subordinate loves, which are called affections, 194. The life's love, which is also the governing love, remains with every one after death and cannot be removed, 281. The life's love of every one makes to itself an understanding and so also a light, 167. Love pertains to the will, 136. The love of the will flows into the understanding, there causing its light to be felt; hence it comes into the thoughts and also into the intentions, 281. The love of the will infuses into the understanding whatever it chooses, but not *vice versa*, 297. The love of the will forms faith to itself, 186. Love dwells in its affections as a master in his domain, or as a king in his kingdom, 106. Love wishes to communicate its own to another, 324. Pure love is the Divine Essence which operates by the Divine Wisdom, 337. Celestial love and infernal love. Celestial love is love to the Lord and towards the neighbor, and infernal love is the love of self and of the world, 106, 107, 199. Love of self, what it is, 206, 215. Self-love, which is the head of all evils, is more ingenious than other loves in adulterating goods and falsifying truths, 233. The man who subdues this love subdues easily all other loves, 146. Spiritual love is such that it wishes to give what it has to another, and in proportion as it can do this, it is in its *esse*, in its peace, and in its blessedness, 27. The love in which man was created is the love of his neighbor, that he may wish him as well as he wishes himself, and even better, and that he may be in the delight of that love, when he does good to him, 275. This love is truly human, 275. When the love of the neighbor was turned into the love of self, and this latter increased, then human love was turned into animal love, 276. Love of means, 109, 110. What is the nature of the love of dignities and riches for their own sake, and what the nature of the love of them for the sake of use, 215. These two loves are as distinct from each other as heaven and hell, 215. Conjugial love is spiritual celestial love itself, 144. Love and liberty are one, 73. To act from love is to act from liberty, 48. See *Liberty*.

Love, to, God is to obey the precepts of His law, 326. What it is to love the Lord above all things, and our neighbor as ourselves, 94.

Love and Wisdom.—Love is the esse of wisdom, and wisdom is the quality of love, 13. Love in its form is wisdom, 13. Love without wisdom cannot do anything, nor wisdom without love, 3, 4. Love calls all which appertains to it good, and wisdom calls all which appertains to it truth, 5. Love pertains to the will, and wisdom to the understanding, 136. Love and wisdom enter into a man by his face, and not by the hinder part of the head, 95. Love and wisdom are neither in space nor time, 49. How love is conjoined to wisdom, 28.

Lowing, the, of the kine in the way, 1 Sam. vi., signifies the difficult conversion of the concupiscences of evil in the natural man into good affections, 326.

Lucifer, by, Isaiah xiv., is meant Babel; that is, the profanation of good by those who attribute to themselves things divine, 231, 257.

Lukewarm, the, Rev. iii. 14, 15, signifies profaners, 231, 298.

Luminous.—In the spiritual world there appears sometimes something luminous about the head, or about the mouth, and above the chin, 169.

Lungs, the, correspond to the understanding, 193. The lungs decant the blood, 336, 296. Changes and variations of state of the lungs, in speaking and singing, 279. Disease of the lungs, whence it arises, 180. See *Heart*.

Luther confessed that when he established Solifidianism, he was warned by an angel of the Lord not to do it: the reason why he did not obey the injunction, 258.

Machiavelists, 310.

Mahometan Religion, the, was raised up by the Divine Providence of the Lord, 255. Why this religion has been received by so many empires and kingdoms, 255.

Mahometans, all the, who acknowledge the Lord, and at the same time live according to the commandments of the Decalogue, which they also possess, by shunning evils as sins, are received into that heaven which is called the Mahometan heaven, 255.

Mammon, by the, of unrighteousness Luke xvi. 8, 9, are meant the knowledges of things good and true which the wicked possess, and which they use solely for the purpose of acquiring to themselves dignities and riches, 250.

Man is the form of his own love, 319. Man by creation is a heaven in its least form, and thence an image of the Lord, 57; but by birth a man is like a little hell,

251, 296. If a man were born in the love in which he was created, he would not be in any evil, nor indeed would he know what evil is: he would be born, not in the darkness of ignorance, but in a certain light of knowledge, and thence also of intelligence, 275. He alone is man who is interiorly such as he desires to be thought by others, 296. A wicked man is a hell in its least form, as a good man is a heaven in its least form, 296, 299, 306. Every man with respect to his spirit is in some society of the spiritual world,—a wicked man in some infernal society, and a good man in some celestial society; he also appears there sometimes when he is in deep meditation, 296. In the celestial or grand man, of which the Lord is the life or soul, there are all things which are in a natural man, with that difference which exists between things celestial and natural, 326. Every man is both in evil and in good; for he is in evil from himself, and in good from the Lord, and he cannot live unless he is in both; the reason why, 227. Every man lives as a man after death, 274. Every man whilst he lives in this world is kept in equilibrium between heaven and hell, and thus in the liberty of thinking, willing, speaking, and acting, in which liberty he may be reformed, 23. Man ought to do good and think truth as from himself, but still to acknowledge that they are from the Lord, 116. Man knows his thoughts, and thence his intentions, because he sees them in himself, 197. If a man believed, as is the truth, that every thing good and true is from the Lord, and every thing evil and false from hell, he would neither appropriate to himself good, and make it meritorious, nor would he appropriate to himself evil, and make himself guilty of it, 320. If a man manifestly saw the Divine Providence, he would interfere with the order and tenor of its progress, and pervert and destroy it, 180. A man is not admitted interiorly into the truths of wisdom and goods of charity, except so far as he can be kept in them to the end of life, 221. Why it was not known heretofore that man lives as a man after death, and why this was not discovered till now, 274. Correspondence of the life of man with the vegetation of a tree; parallel or comparison drawn, 332. By the will of man, John i. 13, is meant the intellectual proprium, which is the false of evil, 298.

Man's Own.—What does not appear as man's own cannot be made of his love, and so appropriated as his own, 48.

Marriage, the, of good and truth is the same thing as the union of love and wisdom, 7. The marriage of good and truth is from the marriage of the Lord with the church, and the latter from the marriage of love and wisdom in the Lord, 21, 8. Since the marriage of good and truth existed by creation in every created thing, and since this was afterwards separated, the Lord must operate continually that it may be restored, 9. This marriage has been broken by the separation of faith from charity, 22. In the Word, and in all and every thing of the Word, there is a marriage of good and truth, 21. The conjunction of the Lord with the church and of the church with the Lord is called the celestial and spiritual marriage, 28, 83. There exists a marriage of good and truth in the cause, and there exists a marriage of good and truth from the cause in the effect, 12. Marriage of evil and of the false, 298.

MASSES.—The Divine Providence has permitted that the Roman Catholic should place the sanctity of worship in masses not understood by the vulgar; the reason why, 257.

MEANS, the, of Divine Providence are all those things by virtue of which a man is made man, and perfected with respect to his understanding and will, 335. These means are infinite in number and variety, 335. The means by which man is led to the Lord, 221, 249. Means of separation, of purification, of withdrawal and expulsion of evil, 296. Means of salvation, 329.

MEDIATELY.—What is effected mediately by preaching does not take away the immediate teaching of the Lord, 172.

MEDITATION.—When man is in profound meditation, he sometimes appears as to his spirit in a society in the spiritual world, 296.

MELANCTHON, 50.

MEMBRANES, the, of the grand man or of heaven are constituted of those to whom the gospel cannot reach, but only some religion, 254.

MEMORY is the permanent state of the changes of state and of form in the purely organic substances of the mind, 279. When truths are only in the understanding and thence in the memory, they are not within the man but without him, 233; the memory of a man compared to the ruminatory stomach in which certain animals deposit their food, 233. So long as the food is there it is not within their body, but without it, but as soon as they bring it up thence and swallow it, it enters into the life and nourishes the body, 233. In man's memory, there is not only materials but spiritual food, namely truths, and this food in itself consists of knowledges, 233; in proportion as the man by the exercise of his thinking principle takes in thence, his spiritual mind is nourished, 233. Man has an external or natural, and an internal or spiritual memory, 227. This memory is the book of his life, which after death is opened, and according to which he is judged, 227.

MERCY, pure, is pure love, 337. It is consequently the Lord, 337. Immediate mercy is not possible, because man's salvation is effected by means according to which the Lord leads him, 221. From being wicked, man cannot be made good by the immediate mercy of the Lord, 279, 338. See *Salvation.*

MERITORIOUS.—The good in which a man is, if it is done for the sake of salvation, is a meritorious good, 90.

MESENTERY, 164, 180, 296, 338.

MESOPOTAMIA was one of those countries in which the ancient church existed, and where the ancient Word was known, 328.

MICE, the, by which the country of the Philistines was wasted, 1 Sam. vi., signify the devastation of the church by the falsifications of truth, 326; and the golden mice made by the Philistines signify the vastation of the church removed by good, 326.

MIND, the, (*animus*), is composed of affections, perceptions, and thoughts, 56. Disease of the mind takes away rationality, and thereby the liberty of acting according to reason, 141. See *Mind (Mens), Liberty.*

Obs.—The *animus* is a sort of external mind, formed by external affections and inclinations, resulting principally from education, society, and custom. See *C. L., No.* 248; see also *Mind (Mens), Obs.*

MIND (*Mens*).—The mind of man in all the particulars of its form, is similar to that of heaven or hell, there is no difference, except that one is great and the other small, 299. The human mind consists of three degrees, 75. There is in man a natural, spiritual, and celestial mind, 147. So long as man is in the concupiscences of evil and their delights, he is in the natural mind only, and so long as the spiritual mind is shut, 147. The natural mind, man has in common with beasts; the rational spiritual mind is the truly human mind, 321. The mind of man which in itself is spiritual, cannot be anywhere but among spirits, into whose society it also comes after death, 307. Such as is the mind, such is the body, consequently the entire man, 112. The human mind is continually in these three principles, end, cause, and effect; if one of these is wanting, the mind is not in its life, 178. How the Lord governs the interiors and exteriors of man's mind, 307.

Obs.—The Mind (*Mens*) is composed of two faculties which make man truly man, namely, the will and understanding. The mind composed of the spiritual will and understanding is the internal man; it incloses the inmost man or soul (*anima*), and it is enveloped by the natural mind or external man, composed of the natural will and understanding; this natural mind, with a mind still more exterior or external called the *animus*, which is formed by external affections and inclinations, resulting principally from education, society, and custom, is the exterior man. The whole organized into a perfect human form, is called the spirit (*spiritus*). The spirit, in our world,

ONE.—The Divine Love and Wisdom proceed from the Lord as a One, 4. A one does not exist without a form, but the form itself makes a one, 4. The form makes a one so much the more perfectly as the things which enter into it are distinct from one another, and nevertheless united, 4. How things perfectly distinct are united, and thus make a one, 4.

OPERATION, the, and progression of the end by its means, is what is called Divine Providence, 331. There can be no operation but upon a subject, and by means operating upon that subject, 331. The continual operation of Divine Providence with every one, has nothing for its end but their reformation, and thereby salvation, 257. Man does not perceive or know any thing of the operation of Divine Providence, 175. If a man perceived and felt the operation of Divine Providence, he would not act from liberty according to reason, and nothing would appear to him as his own, 176. Every operation of the Lord is from primary and ultimate things at once, consequently in full, 220. The operations of the Lord in man's internals are not apparent to him, 174. The operations of the organic substances of the body are natural, and those of the organic substances of the mind are spiritual, but both act together as a one by correspondences, 279. Secret operations of the soul in the body, 296, 386.

OPPOSITES combat each other, until one destroys the other, 18. Two opposites cannot exist together in one substance or form, without its being distracted and perishing, 233. Every thing is known from its opposite, 88.

OPPOSITION, mutual, of heaven and hell, 300. Good is known as to its quality, by relation to what is less good, and by opposition to evil, 24.

OPULENCE is a thing which is only something imaginary, 250. When and with whom opulence is replaced by poverty in the other life, 220.

ORDER.—God is order, 331. He is also the law of His own order, for there is no order without laws, 331.

ORGANIZATION, the, induced in the world remains to eternity, 326.

ORGANIZE, to.—Every part of the brain is organized, 279.

ORGANS.—The things which are in the natural world flow into the organs of the external senses of the body, and such things as are in the spiritual world flow into the organic substances of the internal senses or of the mind, 308. Therefore, as the organs of the external senses or of the body are receptacles of natural objects, so the organic substances of the internal senses or of the mind are receptacles of spiritual objects, 308.

ORIGIN of kingdoms and empires, 215. Origin of the love of possessing wealth beyond the necessaries of life, 215.

OUTMOST.—There is a perpetual connection of the outmost with the inmost, 19.). As the outmost acts or is acted upon, so also the interiors from the inmost act or are acted upon, 180.

> *Obs.*—By the outmost is signified that which is the most external. in opposition to the inmost, which is the most internal.

OWLS.—Why owls see objects by night as clearly as other birds see them by day, 167.

PALACE OF WISDOM.—The twelve steps to the palace of wisdom signify principles of good conjoined to those of truth, and principles of truth conjoined to those of good, 86.

PANCREAS.—Its organization, 180, 279. It purifies the blood, 386.

PARABLES.—Why the Lord spoke in parables, 231.

PARTICULAR.—In every form what is common and what is particular, by a wonderful conjunction, act as one, 180. That which exists from particulars is called common, 201.

PAUL.—Saying of Paul (Rom. iii. 28) explained, 115.

PEOPLE.—The Israelitish and Jewish people represented the church, 245.

PERCEIVE.—If a man perceived and felt the operation of Divine Providence, he would not act from liberty according to reason, nor would any thing appear to him as his own, 176.

PERCEPTION, every, of a thing arises from the relation or opposition of that thing to some other, 24. The perceptions and thoughts are derivations from spiritual light, 178. The Divine Good and the Divine Truth are given to the evil and to the good ; if they were not, no one would have perception and thought, 178. Perception and thought are of life, therefore from the same fountain from which is life, 178. See *Life.*

> *Obs.*—Perception is a sensation derived from the Lord alone, relative to the good and the true, *A. C.*, 104. Perception consists in seeing that a truth is truth, and that a good is good ; also, in seeing that an evil is evil, and a false is false, *A. C.*, 7680.

PERFECT, to be.—What is perfected to eternity cannot possibly be perfect in an instant, 388. Each degree of wisdom may be perfected to its height, but yet cannot enter into a superior degree, 84.

PERFECTIONS increase and ascend with degrees and according to them, 279.

PERIPHERY.—See *Centre.*

PERISH, to.—A man would totally perish if he had not full liberty to think and to will, 281.

PERITONEUM.—Its organization, 180.

PERMISSION.—The laws of permission are also the laws of Divine Providence, 234. The Divine Providence with the wicked is a continual permission of evil, in order that they may be continually drawn out o.

296

eral, all impiety, 229. There are several kinds of profanation of what is holy, 226, 229, and following: in general seven kinds, 231. The worst kind of profanation, 229. See *To Profane.*

PROFANATION, the, of good, consists in doing violence to divine goods, in order to confirm evil loves, 231. In the Word, adulterations of good are described by adulteries, falsifications of truth by whoredoms, 233. These adulterations and falsifications are effected by reasonings from the natural man, which is in evil, 233.

PROFANE, to, is to mix things holy with profane, 228, 258. To profane in the worst manner is to receive and acknowledge things holy, and afterwards to depart from and deny them, 228. What is meant by profaning the name of God, 230.

PROFANE, the, are those who profess to believe in God, maintain the sanctity of the Word, acknowledge the spiritual things of the church, and yet with the mouth only, 229. These profane what is holy in and with them; but the impious, who deny the Divine Being, and all things divine, have nothing holy in them to profane, 229. See *Profaners.*

PROFANERS, by, are meant all impious persons who in their hearts deny God, the sanctity of the Word, and consequently the spiritual things of the church, which are sanctity itself, and concerning which they speak impiously, 229. Difference between those profaners and those who are called profane, 229.

PROGRESSION.—In every created thing there is a constant and wonderful progression according to the laws of its order, 332. In the progression of every created thing, the First from which it is derived exists intimately, 56.

PROPHET.—By the name and reward of a prophet, Matt. x. 41, is meant the state and felicity of those who are in divine truths, 230.

PROPRIUM, the, of man is the love of self, and thence the love of the world, or the loves of the world, and thence the love of self, 206. There is with man a voluntary and an intellectual proprium, 298. The voluntary proprium is in its essence self-love, or evil, and the intellectual proprium is pride proceeding from that love, or the false of evils, 298. The proprium of man as to the affections which are natural, is not unlike the life of a beast, 233. There does not exist in any man one grain of will or of prudence that is proper to himself, 293. No man has any proprium, in the sense in which proprium is commonly understood, 309. Things proper to nature are especially spaces and times, both subject to limit and termination, 219; the things which are proper to a man, are those of his proper will and proper understanding, 219. Things proper to the Lord are all infinite and eternal, consequently without limit and without end; the things which are thence, as it were, proper to a man, are of the Lord alone in him, 219.

298

PROVIDE, to.—It is provided by the Lord that every one is capable of being saved, 328. It is also provided that a new church should succeed in place of the former vastated church, 328.

PROVIDENCE, the Divine, is the government of the Divine Love and Divine Wisdom of the Lord, 1 and following, 331, 337. The restoration of the marriage of good and truth, and the conjunction thereby of the created universe with the Lord through man, is of the Divine Providence, 9. The Divine Providence of the Lord has for its end a heaven out of the human race, 27, 202. In all that it does it regards what is infinite and eternal, 46. It regards what is infinite and eternal from itself in finites, 52, 58. In all its proceedings with a man, it has respect to his eternal state, 59. The laws of Divine Providence, hitherto hid in wisdom among the angels, are now revealed, 70. It is a law of Divine Providence that man should act from freedom according to reason, 71, 97. It is a law of Divine Providence that man, as from himself, should remove evils as sins in the external man, 100. It is a law of Divine Providence that man should not be forced by external means to think and will, and so to believe and love the things which are of religion, but that a man should lead, and sometimes force, himself to it, 129. It is a law of Divine Providence that a man should be led and taught from the Lord out of heaven by the Word, and by doctrine and preaching from the Word; and this, in all appearance, as from himself, 154. It is a law of Divine Providence that a man should not perceive and feel any thing of the operation of the Divine Providence, but yet should know and acknowledge it, 175. If a man perceived and felt the operation of Divine Providence, he would not act from liberty according to reason, nor would any thing appear to him as his own, 176. If a man plainly saw the Divine Providence, he would interfere with the order and tenor of his progress, and would prevent and destroy it, 180. If a man manifestly saw the Divine Providence, he would either deny God, or make himself a god, 182. The Divine Providence never acts in unity with the love of a man's will, but continually against it, 183, 234. The Lord tacitly leads a man by his Divine Providence, as an imperceptible tide or prosperous current does a ship, 186. It is granted a man to see the Divine Providence on the back, and not in the face, also in a spiritual state, and not in a natural state, 187. To see the Divine Providence on the back and not in the face, is to see it after and not before; and to see it from a spiritual state, and not from a natural state, is to see it from heaven, and not from the world, 187. The Divine Providence operates through means, and means are effected through man or through the world, 187. The man who is made spiritual by the acknowledgment of God, and wise by the rejection of his pre-

heart, to renounce them and lead a new life according to the precepts of faith, *A. C.*, 8389.

REPRESENTATIVE.—A wicked man as well as a good man may be the representative of the internal principles of a church, by the external things of worship, 182.

RESIDE, to.—The Lord resides in liberty and rationality in every man, in the wicked as well as in the good, and by them he joins himself to every man, 96.

RESPECT, to have, to God in the life is nothing else but to think this or that evil a sin against God, and therefore not to do it, 20; it is to shun evils as sins, 98.

RESTORATION, the, of the marriage of good and truth, and the conjunction thereby of the created universe with the Lord, is of the Divine Providence, 9.

RESURRECTION.—All who have any religion have in them an inherent knowledge that men live after death, 274. See *Inherent.*

REVENGE.—Its origin, 276.

REWARD, the, Matt. x. 41, signifies felicity; the reward of a prophet, the felicity of those who are in divine truths; and the reward of a righteous man, the felicity of those who are in divine goods, 230.

RICH.—What is the state after death of those who in riches had respect to themselves alone, 185.

RICHES are blessings and they are curses, 216, 217. They are blessings with those who do not place their hearts in them, and they are curses with those who do place their hearts in them, 217. Riches are natural and temporary with those who have respect to them alone, and to themselves in them; but they are spiritual and eternal with those who have respect to good uses in them, 220. What is the nature of the love of dignities and riches for their own sake, and what the nature of the love of them for the sake of use, 215. How the love of riches arose, 215. The Lord never withholds a man from acquiring wealth, but from the cupidity of acquiring wealth for the sake of opulence only, 183. See *Dignities.*

RIGHTEOUS.—By the name and reward of a righteous man, Matt. x. 41, is signified the state of felicity of those who are in divine goods, 230.

SABBATH, the, in the Israelitish church was the most holy worship; it signified the union of truth with good, and of good with truth, 21.

SACRIFICES.—Worship by sacrifices existed neither in the most ancient church, nor yet in the ancient church, but was first instituted in the Hebrew church, which had its origin from Eber, 328.

SAGES, or wise men of antiquity; what their idea was in regard to the immortality of the soul, 324.

SAINTS.—Why Divine Providence has permitted that among the Roman Catholics they should invoke dead men, called saints, 357.

SALVATION.—The Lord wills the salvation of all, 221. Without the Lord there is no salvation, yet no man has salvation merely by the Lord's being known to him, but by living according to His precepts, 330. See *To Save.* Salvation is the only end of Divine Providence, 257. Salvation cannot be effected except by an acknowledgment of the Lord's divinity, and confidence that it is wrought by him, when a man lives according to His commandments, 257. Momentaneous salvation from immediate mercy is impossible, 338 to 340. This salvation is the fiery flying serpent in the church, 340.

SATAN and the false of evil are one, 83. They are called satans who confirm in themselves the concupiscences of evil, 310. See *Devil*, and *Hell.*

Obs.—In the spiritual world those who are wicked as to the understanding inhabit the anterior part, and are called satans; and those who are wicked as to the will inhabit the posterior part, and are called devils, *C. J.*, 492. In the Word, by devil is understood that hell which is behind, and where are the most wicked, called evil genii: and by satan, that hell in which are those who are not so wicked, and who are denominated evil spirits, *H. and H.*, 544.

SAVE, to.—It is of the Divine Providence that every man is capable of being saved, and that those are saved who acknowledge a God and lead a good life, 325. The operation of Divine Providence in saving a man begins at his birth, and continues to the end of his life, 332 to 334. More can not be saved than desire to be saved, 333. Who those are who desire to be saved, and who do not desire to be saved, 333. No mortal could have been saved except the Lord had come into the world, 124. Every one, in whatever heresy he may be with respect to his understanding, may still be reformed and saved, 259. To suppose that those only are saved who are born within the church, is an insane heresy, 330.

SCIENCES, the, can never be exhausted, 57.

SECURITY of life arises either from the belief of the impious, that there is no life after death, or from the belief of those who separate life from salvation, 840.

SEE, to, in himself, is in his internal man; to understand by reasons, is in his external man, 150.

SEED, the, is the primitive form of the love in which the father is—the form of his ruling love, with its proximate derivations, which are the inmost affections of that love, 277. The seed, by which impregnation is effected, is clothed with a body from the mother, 277.

SELF-SUBSISTING, the, principle is omnipresent, omniscient, and omnipotent, 157 This self-subsisting principle is the Lord from eternity, or Jehovah, 157.

SENSE, why the spiritual, of the Word

heretofore unknown, was not revealed sooner, 264. The natural senses of the body, and the spiritual senses of the mind, 814.

Obs.—By the *spiritual sense* of the Word is understood both the celestial and spiritual, when no distinction is made between the spiritual sense, properly so called, and the celestial.

SENSITIVE, all the, principles are derived from relation and from opposition, 24.

SERPENT, the, which seduced our first parents is the sensuality and proprium of man, which in itself is the love of self, and the pride of self-derived intelligence, 211, 818. The head of the serpent, Gen. iii. 15, is self-love, 211, 241. The fiery flying serpent, Isa. xiv. 29, signifies evil shining from infernal fire, 840.

SERVITUDE is the opposite of liberty, 43. Every man wishes to remove slavery from himself, 148. Man in general does not know what spiritual liberty and what spiritual servitude are; he believes spiritual servitude to be liberty, and spiritual liberty to be servitude, 149. To be led by evil is servitude, and to be led by good, or by the Lord, is liberty, 43. Why man does not desire to come out of spiritual servitude into spiritual liberty, 149.

SHEEP.—To call his sheep by name, John x. 8, is to teach and lead every one who is in the good of charity, according to the state of his love and wisdom, 230.

SHEPHERD, the, of the sheep, is he who approaches the Lord, 230.

SICKNESS.—When man is in sickness and thinks of death, and of the state of his soul after death, he is not then in the world, but is abstracted in spirit, in which state alone man can be reformed, 142. No one is reformed in a state of mental sickness or disorder; for when the body is sick, the mind also is sick, 141, 142. What are the disorders of the mind, 141. It is vain to think a person can repent or receive any faith under sickness, for there is nothing of action in such repentance, and nothing of charity in such faith, 142. If such persons are not reformed before sickness, they become after it, if they die, such as they were before it, 142.

SIDON was one of those countries in which the ancient church existed, and where the ancient word was known, 328.

SIGHT.—Man has an internal and external sight, 166. The understanding, which is a man's internal sight, is no otherwise illuminated by spiritual light than as a man's eye or external sight is by natural light, 166. The eye of every one is formed for the reception of the light in which it is, 167.

SIGN, the, that any one is led by the Lord, is that he loves his neighbor, 208.

SIGNS.—No one is reformed by miracles and signs, because they force, 129, 130. What is meant by the sign set on Cain lest he should be slain, 242.

SIMPLE.—In proportion as a thing is

more simple and more pure, it is more full and complete, 6.

SIMULTANEOUS.—In the ultimate principle there is the simultaneous, derived from the first of all principles, 124.

SINGULAR.—In every form, what is universal and what is singular, by a wonderful conjunction, act as one, 180. That is called universal which is formed from singulars connected together, 201. The Divine Providence exists in the most minute particulars in nature, and in the most minute particulars in human prudence, and by governing these particulars, governs universally, 201. The Divine Providence of the Lord is universal, because it is in particulars, and it is particular because it is universal, 124.

SINS, when, are removed they are also remitted, but not *vice versa*, 280. Sins are not removed by repentance, 180. See *Repentance*. To confess ourselves guilty of all sins, and not to seek them out in ourselves, is to imagine we have religion when yet we have it not, 278, 279.

Obs.—Sin is evil against God, and also consequently against our neighbor, *T. C. R.*, 525.

SKELETONS.—Profaners appear, in the spiritual world, like skeletons, 226.

SKIN, the, does not feel from itself, but it is in the man's mind or spirit, which there perceives such things by the sense, and thence is affected according to the quality of the sense, 814. Man knows little of the manner in which the skin feels, 336. The skin of the grand man, or of heaven, is constituted of those to whom the gospel cannot reach, but only some religion, 254, 326.

SMELL.—Every delight corresponds to some smell in the spiritual world, and these may be converted into it, 304.

SMELL, to.—Whatever a man smells comes by influx, 308.

SMOKE.—Those who are in the love of self are encompassed by the smoke, as it were, of a conflagration, which no spiritual truth in its light can pervade, 250.

SOCIETY.—The universal heaven is arranged into societies according to the affections of good, opposite to the concupiscences of evil, 278*. Every man, with respect to his spirit, is in some society in the spiritual world, in a celestial society if he is in the affection of good, and in an infernal society if he is in the concupiscence of evil, 278*, 296, 307. He also appears there sometimes when he is in profound meditation, 296. Every society in heaven is before the Lord as one man, 64.

SOCINIANISM.—Its origin, 262. It reigns in the hearts of more people than is imagined, 262.

SOCINIANS.—Their fate in another life, 281.

SOLE SUBSISTING PRINCIPLE, the, is omnipresent, omniscient, and omnipotent, and this sole subsisting principle is the Lord from eternity, or Jehovah, 157.

and variations of will are thoughts, which are of the understanding, 279. 319.

SUN, the.—The Lord produced from Himself the sun of the spiritual world, and by that sun, all things in the universe, 5. This sun is not only the first, but the one only substance from which all things are, 5. This sun, in which is the Lord, and which is not in space, is in all things, 6. The Lord appears as a sun above the heavens, 162. In the Word, the sun signifies the divine good of the divine love, 173, 292.

SUPPER, the Holy, instituted by the Lord, confirms the remission of sins to those who repent, 122. See *Remission, Repentance.*

SUPPORT is perpetual creation, 3.

SWEDENBORG declares that he has conversed with many persons after death, as well with those in Europe as with those in Asia and Africa, and that they were near him, 50; that he has had conversations with some who lived many years ago, with some who lived before the deluge, and some after it, with some who lived in the Lord's time, with one of His apostles, and with many who lived in the succeeding ages; and that they all appeared to him as men of a middle age; and that they said they did not know what death is, but only that there is such a thing as damnation, 324. That the Lord was revealed to him, and afterwards continually appeared before his eyes as the sun in which He is; that for several years, during which he had discoursed with spirits and angels, no spirit has dared, nor has any angel wished to say any thing to him, much less to instruct him about any thing in the Word, or any doctrinal from the Word; but the Lord alone has taught and illuminated him, 185. That when it was granted him by the Lord to speak with spirits and angels, it was revealed to him that man does not think or will from himself, but from the Lord, if he is good, and if evil, from hell; that this was demonstrated to him by his own experience; that he opened afterwards this arcanum to some novitiate spirits, telling them that he thought more interiorly, and perceived what flowed into his exterior thought, whether it were from heaven or from hell; that he rejected the latter and received the former, but still it appeared to himself, as to them, that he thought and willed from himself, 290.

SWEDES, the.—Instruction which is given to them in the prayer for the holy communion, 114, 258.

SWORD, to be devoured by the, signifies to perish by the falsity of evil, 278.

SYRIA was one of those countries in which the ancient church existed, and where the ancient Word was known, 328.

SYRIANS, the, in the Word, signify a species of evil, 251.

SYSTOLE.—What it is, 319.

TABLES OF THE LAW, there are two, one for the Lord, and the other for man, 95, 326. In proportion as a man, as from himself, obeys the laws of his own table, in the same proportion the Lord enables him to obey the laws of His table, 95. The laws of man's table relate to the love of his neighbor, and those of the Lord's table to the love of the Lord, 95. See *Decalogue.*

TACITLY.—The Divine Providence acts tacitly in regard to man, 183.

TALENT, the, given to the servants to traffic with, Luke xix., Mark xxv., signifies the prudence which we are to use, 210.

TASTE cannot exist without its form, which is the tongue, 279.

TASTE, to.—All that man tastes comes by influx, 308.

TEACH, to.—The Lord alone teaches man, though mediately, through the Word in illumination, 135. To be taught from the Word is to be taught by the Lord, 172. How man is taught by the Lord, 154–174. Every one is taught according to the understanding of his love, and what is over and above does not remain, 172.

TEETH, the, of the grand man, which is heaven, are constituted of those to whom the gospel could not reach, but only some religion, 826, 254.

TEMPLE, the, built by Solomon, signifies the divine humanity of the Lord, and also the church, 245. The destruction of the temple signifies the vastation of the church itself, 246.

TEMPORARY things which are proper to man in the natural world relate, in general, to dignities and riches, and in particular to the necessities of each man, which are food, clothing, and habitation, 214, 215, 220. These a man puts off by death, and puts on things spiritual and eternal corresponding to them, 220. Nothing can proceed from man but what is temporary, and nothing from the Lord but what is eternal, 219. Things temporary and eternal are separated by man, but are joined by the Lord, 218.

TEMPTATIONS, spiritual, are no other than combats against evils and falsities, 25. Genuine temptations, 141.

TENDONS, the, of the grand man, or of heaven, are composed of those whom the gospel has not reached, but who have only some religion, 826, 254.

THEFTS.—Their origin, 276.

THIEF and ROBBER, the, John x. 1, is he who does not approach the Lord, 230.

THINK, to.—No one thinks from himself, but thought flows in, 288. Every one thinks from others, and these also not from themselves, but still from others, 289, 294. All think from the Lord, the wicked as well as the good, 308. He whose thoughts are not elevated above the sensual is involved in darkness with respect to the state of his life, 274. What it is, while thinking from the present, to think, at the same time, from what is eternal, 59. It is a law of Divine Providence that man should think as from himself, but yet should acknowledge that he does so from the Lord, 321. No one thinks from space and time when he thinks of those who are in the spiritual world, 50.

THINK and WILL, to.—The divine principle consists essentially in thinking and willing from itself, while the human principle consists essentially in thinking and willing from God, 293. To think and to will is spiritual, but to speak and to act is natural, 71.

THISTLES signify evil, 313.

THORNS signify falsity, 313.

THOUGHT is nothing else than the form of affection, 198. No thought of man can exist except from some affection of his life's love, 198. All a man's thoughts are from the affections of his life's love, and there do not and cannot exist any thoughts at all without these affections, 198. The thoughts which are of the understanding are mere changes and variations of the state of the purely organic substance of the mind, 279. Every man has an internal and an external of thought, 103, 106–110, 120, 139, 145, 150. By the external and internal of thought is understood the same thing as by the external and internal man, 103. The internal and external of thought are distinct as prior and posterior, or as superior and inferior, 145. Man knows nothing of the internal of his thoughts before he comes into the spiritual world, and its light, which is the case after death, 233. The internal of thought coheres with the external of thought, in so close a connection, that they cannot be separated, 233. Exterior and interior thought is given to a man, and from his interior thought he can see his exterior thought, and also reflect upon it and judge of it, whether it be evil or not evil, 104. Thought, by virtue of exterior illumination from the Lord, sees a thing on both sides, on one side seeing the reasons which confirm it, and on the other the appearances which invalidate it; the latter it dispels, and the former it collects, 168. By virtue of thought, abstracted from time and space, are comprehended the divine omnipresence and the divine omnipotence, and likewise the divine from eternity, 51. Speech ceases if it is deprived of thought, 8. See *Affection and Thought, Perception, Illumination.*

THREATS.—No one is reformed by threats, because they force, 129, 186. See *To Force.*

TIME is only an appearance according to the state of affection from which thought is derived, 49. See *Space and Time.*

TONGUE, the, 180, 279, 386. The tongue is the form of taste, 279. The tongue does not taste from itself, but it is the mind or spirit which perceives the taste by the sense, and thence is affected according to the quality of the sense, 314. Man knows little in what way the tongue feels, 386. Spirits speak with a man in his mother tongue, but only a few words, 185.

TORMENTS.—Dreadful torments which evil spirits experience when they approach heaven, 324, 338.

TRACHEA, or windpipe, its functions, 279, 180.

TREE.—Correspondence of the life of man with the growth of a fruit-tree, 332. Man in the Word is described by a tree, 332. Where the tree falls there it lies, so also it is with a man's life—as it was at his death, such it remains, 277. Celestial love, with the affections of good and truth, and the perceptions thence derived, may be compared to a beautiful tree with branches, leaves, and fruits, 107. The tree of life signifies the Lord with respect to His Divine Providence, and the tree of knowledge man with respect to his self-derived prudence, 313, 241.

TRINE, the, in one exists in the Lord only, 123.

TRINITY, the Divine, is in the Lord, 262, 263.

TRUTH, by, is understood that which universally comprehends and involves all things of wisdom, 11. All things appertaining to wisdom are called truths, 11. Genuine truths, of which the spiritual sense of the Word consists, were not revealed by the Lord till after the last judgment was accomplished, and the New Church, which is meant by the holy Jerusalem, was about to be established by the Lord, 264.

TYRE was one of those countries in which the ancient church existed, and where the ancient Word was known, 328.

ULTIMATES, the, in man are the things which are in the external of his thought, 125. The Lord acts from inmost principles, and from ultimates or lowest principles, at the same time, 124, 220. Inmost and intermediate principles exist together in ultimates, 124. The ultimates of life which a man carries with him after death, are quiescent, and conspire, that is, act as one, with his interiors, 277. Ultimates are reformed in this world, conformably to primaries, 227.

UNDERSTAND, to.—Difference between a man's understanding a thing by reasons, and seeing it in himself, 150. To understand is the companion of volition; in the same proportion as you will, in the same proportion you can understand, 96.

UNDERSTANDING, the, is a man's internal sight, 166. The understanding, which is a man's internal sight, is no otherwise illuminated by spiritual light, than as a man's eye, or external sight, is by natural light, 166. There is an internal understanding and an external understanding, 111. Understanding is given to man that he may explore himself, 278. See *Understanding and Will.*

UNDERSTANDING and WILL.—In every man there are two faculties, one of which constitutes the understanding and the other the will, 285. The faculty which constitutes the understanding consists in his being able to understand and think, and that which constitutes the will consists in his being able freely to think and thence also to speak and act, provided it be not contrary to reason, 285. Man without liberty and rationality would have neither will nor understanding, and therefore would not be a man, 96. The understanding has been separated from the will in order that a man may see what his will is, 278, 283, 318. The love of the will infuses into the understanding whatever it chooses, and not *vice versa;* obliterating indeed every thing in the understanding which is not from itself, 209. The understanding without the will cannot do any thing, 8. The will of man's life is led, and the understanding of his life is taught, 156.

UNION, the, of truth with good, and of good with truth in man, is the church and heaven, 21. This union is called the marriage of good and truth, 8. In proportion as men enter into the form of the divine love, which is the form of forms, the more perfect this union which makes heaven becomes, 62. Union of charity and faith, of the will and understanding, 82.

UNITE, to.—No one can unite all the affections of the love of good into the form of the divine love, but He who is Love itself, and at the same time Wisdom itself, and at once infinite and eternal, 63. It is the perpetual object of the Divine Providence to unite in man good to truth and truth to good, 21.

UNIVERSE, the, with all and every thing appertaining to it, was created from the Divine Love by the Divine Wisdom, 3. The Lord did not create the universe for His own sake, but for the sake of those with whom He will dwell in heaven, 27. He created the universe from Himself, and not from nothing, 46.

UNIVERSAL, what is, and what is particular, by a wonderful conjunction, act as one, 180. That is called universal which is formed of singulars connected together, 201. A universal without a singular is nothing, 278. The divine is universal, existing in things the most singular; it is divine particulars which compose what is called universal, 294. The Divine Providence is universal, because it is in things the most singular, 201, 202. See *Singular.*

UNIVERSALS, the two, of the church are the acknowledgment of a God and the leading of a good life, 326, 328.

USE is good, and derives its quality from truth, 11. Uses are goods, which are called goods of charity, 220, 215. By uses are meant not only the necessaries of life which relate to food, clothing, and habitation for a man and his family, but also the good of his country, of society, and of his fellow-citizens, 220. By doing uses or good, is meant serving others, and ministering to them, 215. To perform uses for the sake of fame or interest, is to do them for the sake of self; to perform uses for the sake of uses, is to perform them from the Lord, 215. He who performs uses for the sake of uses, is led by the Lord, and he who performs uses for the sake of self and the world is led by the

devil, 215, 217. All those who shun evils as sins perform uses from the Lord, while all those who do not shun evils as sins perform uses from the devil, 215. The kingdom of the Lord is a kingdom of uses, 26, 250. The Lord by his Divine Providence joins himself to things natural by things spiritual, and to things temporal by things eternal, according to uses, 220. The Lord joins himself to uses by correspondences, and so by appearances according to confirmations by a man, 220. How the lust of doing uses for the sake of self-glory is kindled, 250. Man ought to be in the love of uses, and thence of himself, and not first in the love of himself and thence of uses, 188.

VARIATIONS of state in the forms of the mind, 195, 279, 319. See *Changes.*

VARIETY, there is a, in all things, so that there does not exist, nor can exist to eternity, any one thing the same with another, 56. Thus the variety is infinite and eternal, 56, 57. There is a variety in every thing, from its greatest to its least, 24. Variety cannot exist except in things constant, stated, and certain; examples, 190. There is an infinite number of varieties; enumeration of certain of them, 190.

VASTATION, successive, of good, and successive desolation of truth, 328. Vastation of good in the church even to its consummation, 328.

VEIL between the interiors and the exteriors, or between the spiritual and natural of the mind, 311. To think beneath the veil, 310.

VENA CAVA, 296.

VENTRICLE, left, 296. The memory of man compared to the ruminating ventricle or stomach of certain animals, 233.

VESSELS, lymphatic and lacteal, 296.

VICTORY.—Why it seems as if victory declared on the side of prudence, and sometimes not on the side of justice, 252, 251.

VIRGINS, the foolish, who had lamps but no oil, and were therefore not admitted to the marriage, represent those who have acknowledged truths with their mouths, but not in their hearts, 328.

VISCERA, 279, 296, 180.

VISIONARIES and enthusiastic spirits, who from the delirium they were in called themselves the Holy Ghost, 134.

VISIONS are of two kinds, divine and diabolical; divine visions are effected by representatives in heaven, and diabolical visions are effected by magic in hell, 184. There are also fantastical visions, which are mere illusions of an abstracted mind, 134. Divine visions are such as the prophets had, who, when they were in them, were not in the body, but in the spirit, 184. Such visions do not exist at this day; for if they did they would not be understood, because they are effected by representatives, the particulars of which signify internal things of the church and arcana of heaven, 184. Diabolical visions some-

itual things which are done in the spiritual world, 251. In the spiritual world all are spiritual, even as to their bodies, 167. The world of spirits is in the midst between heaven and hell, 307. When a man dies he comes first into the world of spirits, and there into his external, which is there put off; and this being done, he is transferred to the place in which he is inscribed, whether it be heaven or hell, 307.

WORLD, Christian.—Why in the Christian world they worship God under three persons, which is three Gods, and why hitherto they have not known that God is one in person and in essence, in whom there is a trinity, and that that God is the Lord, 262. Why there have been and still are in the Christian world so many heresies, 259. See *Heresies*.

WORSHIP.—It is dangerous to force men to divine worship, 136. Constrained worship shuts in evils, which then lie concealed like fire in wood, under the ashes, which continues to kindle and spread till it breaks out into a flame, 136. On the contrary, worship which is not constrained but spontaneous, does not shut in evils, which, therefore, are like fires that immediately burn out and are dispersed, 136. With those who are in internal worship alone, without external worship, the internal is constrained, 186. Constrained worship is corporeal, inanimate, obscure, and gloomy, 187. Unconstrained worship, when it is genuine, is spiritual, living, lucid and joyful, 187. Worship before the coming of the Lord was a representative worship, 255.

WORSHIP, to, other gods, 154. Why there are some men who worship the sun and moon, and others who worship idols and graven images, 254.

WORSHIPPER, every, of self and of nature confirms himself against the Divine Providence, 249; under what circumstances, 249–252. Worshippers of themselves and of the world, worshippers of men and of images, worshippers of the Lord, 154.

YOKE.—Concerning those who believe they are not under the yoke of the law, 43, 101.

ZEAL.—A man may burn as it were with zeal for the salvation of souls, and this, nevertheless, from infernal fire, 139.

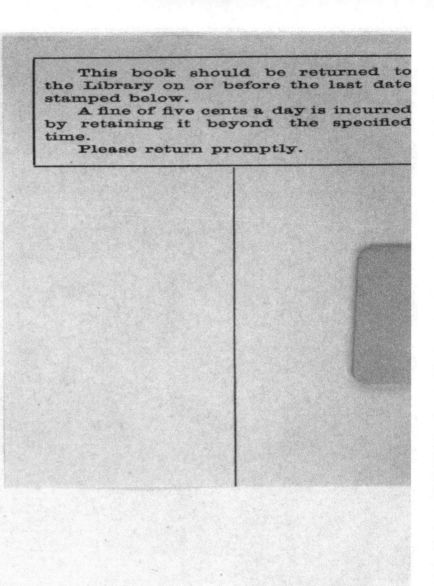